FROMMER'S
EasyGuide
TO
PUERTO RICO

By
John Ma[...]

Easy Guides are ✦ Quick To Read ✦ Light To Carry
✦ For Expert Advice ✦ In All Price Ranges

FrommerMedia LLC

Published by
FROMMER MEDIA LLC

Copyright © 2015 by Frommer Media LLC. All rights reserved. No part of this publication may be repro-
duced, stored in a retrieval system, or transmitted in any form or by any means, electronic, mechanical,
photocopying, recording, scanning or otherwise, except as permitted under Sections 107 or 108 of the
1976 United States Copyright Act, without the prior written permission of the Publisher. Requests to the
Publisher for permission should be addressed to support@frommermedia.com.

Frommer's is a registered trademark of Arthur Frommer. Frommer Media LLC is not associated with any
product or vendor mentioned in this book.

ISBN 978-1-62887-156-2 (paper), 978-1-62887-157-9 (e-book)

Editorial Director: Pauline Frommer
Editor: Melissa Klurman
Production Editor: Heather Wilcox
Cartographer: Elizabeth Puhl
Cover Design: Howard Grossman

For information on our other products or services, see www.frommers.com.

Frommer Media LLC also publishes its books in a variety of electronic formats. Some content that
appears in print may not be available in electronic formats.

Manufactured in the United States of America

5 4 3 2 1

AN IMPORTANT NOTE

The world is a dynamic place. Hotels change ownership, restaurants hike their prices, museums
alter their opening hours, and busses and trains change their routings. And all of this can occur
in the several months after our authors have visited, inspected, and written about, these hotels,
restaurants, museums and transportation services. Though we have made valiant efforts to keep
all our information fresh and up-to-date, some few changes can inevitably occur in the periods
before a revised edition of this guidebook is published. So please bear with us if a tiny number
of the details in this book have changed. Please also note that we have no responsibility or liabil-
ity for any inaccuracy or errors or omissions, or for inconvenience, loss, damage, or expenses suffered by anyone as a result of assertions in this guide.

CONTENTS

ABOUT THE AUTHOR

John Marino has written extensively about Puerto Rico and the Caribbean for Reuters, "The Washington Post," "The New York Times," and other publications. He lives in San Juan, Puerto Rico, with his wife, Jova, and son, Juan Antonio, who both provided valuable insight for this book.

ABOUT THE FROMMER'S TRAVEL GUIDES

For most of the past 50 years, Frommer's has been the leading series of travel guides in North America, accounting for as many as 24 percent of all guidebooks sold. I think I know why.

Although we hope our books are entertaining, we nevertheless deal with travel in a serious fashion. Our guidebooks have never looked on such journeys as a mere recreation, but as a far more important human function, a time of learning and introspection, an essential part of a civilized life. We stress the culture, lifestyle, history, and beliefs of the destinations we cover and urge our readers to seek out people and new ideas as the chief rewards of travel.

We have never shied from controversy. We have, from the beginning, encouraged our authors to be intensely judgmental, critical—both pro and con—in their comments, and wholly independent. Our only clients are our readers, and we have triggered the ire of countless prominent sorts, from a tourist newspaper we called "practically worthless" (it unsuccessfully sued us) to the many rip-offs we've condemned.

And because we believe that travel should be available to everyone regardless of their incomes, we have always been cost-conscious at every level of expenditure. Although we have broadened our recommendations beyond the budget category, we insist that every lodging we include be sensibly priced. We use every form of media to assist our readers and are particularly proud of our feisty daily website, the award-winning Frommers.com.

I have high hopes for the future of Frommer's. May these guidebooks, in all the years ahead, continue to reflect the joy of travel and the freedom that travel represents. May they always pursue a cost-conscious path, so that people of all incomes can enjoy the rewards of travel. And may they create, for both the traveler and the persons among whom we travel, a community of friends, where all human beings live in harmony and peace.

Arthur Frommer

THE BEST OF PUERTO RICO

It's only the size of Connecticut, but Puerto Rico pulsates with more life than any other island in the Caribbean. Whether it's the beat of *bomba y plena*, salsa, or reggaeton, there's a party going on here 24/7. The 3.8 million people who live here have perfected the art of having fun on their dazzling island, and visitors are free to join right in. Puerto Ricans love their island and take pride in showing off its charms, which makes them among the world's great hosts. Especially on weekends, there seems to be something going on just about everywhere—whether it's an art fair in Old San Juan, a pig roast in the rural mountain area outside town, or a volleyball competition or free concert on the beach in Isla Verde. More so than on any other island, visitors are more likely to rub elbows with locals in Puerto Rico because so many of them are out enjoying themselves. For island hotels and restaurants, local residents are an important and loyal part of their clientele.

Puerto Rico is blessed with towering mountains, rainforests, white sandy beaches along Caribbean shores, and a vibrant culture forged from a mix of Caribbean, Hispanic, African, and U.S. influences. Culture vultures will find a wealth of historic buildings and monuments, many of them dating back some 500 years to the Spanish conquistadors. There are three world-class museums and a thriving gallery scene in San Juan. The city is more intimate but just as exciting as Miami or Las Vegas, and the sophisticated fashion sense of the city and its inhabitants will genuinely impress visitors. San Juan's nightlife, dining scene, casinos, and live-performance calendar are just as noteworthy. Add some of the best golf and tennis in the West Indies, posh beach resorts, tranquil and offbeat inns and guesthouses, and you've got a formidable attraction.

Good service, once notoriously lacking in Puerto Rico, has been improving for several years now. You'll still find both not-so-benign neglect and outright gruff service, but the majority of hotel and restaurant employees are absolutely delightful these days.

Puerto Rico is a crowded island, which makes for some traffic congestion, especially during the morning and afternoon rush hours, but visitors won't really notice except during holiday weekends. There are country and coastal retreats where visitors can escape the masses, but you are never too far away from anybody in Puerto Rico.

Tourists are generally safe, and crime in a tourist district is rare. But homeless drug addicts and mentally ill beggars are a common sight in San

Juan. There are some unfortunate problems with littering and treatment of animals—but great strides in these areas are being made. Most of Puerto Rico's crime and social problems remain largely invisible to tourists.

A clue to the Puerto Rican soul is reflected in the national anthem, "La Borinqueña," which describes the island as a "flowering garden of exquisite magic . . . the daughter of the sea and the sun." Get to know this garden and the people who call it home.

THE most authentic PUERTO RICO EXPERIENCES

o **Exploring Old San Juan:** The city's restored historic district is one of the best living examples of Spanish colonial architecture in the Americas, and the area is chock-full of oceanfront fortresses, Gothic cathedrals, turn-of-the-century residences, and smart Art Deco commercial buildings. Several plazas feature gorgeous statues and streaming fountains, and there are gorgeous oceanfront and bayside promenades. Yet, Old San Juan is very contemporary, with avant-garde cuisine, art, and performances emanating from its restaurants, galleries, and clubs.

o **Hanging Out in Santurce:** San Juan's "downtown," the place to shop and bop, had its heyday in the 1950s, but has been on a steady rise in the last several years. The area is home to important cultural institutions, like the Luis A. Ferré Performing Arts Center and the Puerto Rico Art Museum, and a growing number of new restaurants, cafes, and shops has brought renewed energy. To immerse yourself in the scene, visit the museum, then have a cheap and tasty lunch at one of the *fondas* along Avenida Ponce de León and its side streets. Another option is to head to Plaza del Mercado, with a festive tropical fruit and merchandise market, and then spend time at the restaurants and bars surrounding it. You'll meet more locals than visitors.

o **Joining in a Local Festival:** Regardless of when you're visiting Puerto Rico, chances are there's a **Fiestas Patronales** taking place in one of the island's 78 towns. Each town's government throws an annual weeklong celebration of food, music, fun, and games that rage on for several nights; town halls have been won and lost over the quality of the annual parties. Long ripped from their religious origins, the annual festivals may be named after their town's patron saint, but the main features are free live-music performances by top salsa and local performers, rides and games for the kids, and food and drink kiosks for the entire family. There are other festivals, like the annual **Flower Festival** in Aibonito and the annual **Coffee Festival** in Maricao. A requisite at all big festivals is an area for island artisans, with the finest in Puerto Rico traveling across the island to show their wares.

o **Taking a Sunday Drive:** Wherever you go in Puerto Rico, you'll find people driving around for fun on Sunday afternoons, from the oceanside boulevard of Old San Juan to the bayside drive in the western city of Mayaguez. It could be along the coastal Piñones road, lined by wooden shacks selling fresh coconut milk, fried codfish fritters, and fish kcbabs, to the El Yunque rainforest, or south from San Juan to the mountain *lechoneras* of Cayey serving roast pork, blood sausage, and other hearty *jibaro* fare, or the wooden seafood restaurants fronting the water in the south coast town of Santa Isabel. If you have the right attitude, you will have a glorious afternoon. You won't get anywhere quickly, but there's no reason at all that you should want to.

- **Getting Friendly with Locals: Viernes Social** (Social Fridays) is an island-wide tradition of schmoozing, drinking, dancing, and eating after work on Friday that is faithfully adhered to by workers across the social strata and from Mayaguez to Humacao, and San Juan to Ponce. Regardless of where you are, a neighborhood gas station or an open air *comida criolla* cafe, chances are it will have turned into a lively mix of laughter and story telling, dancing and flirting if it's anytime after 4pm on Friday afternoon. Make sure you go out for sundown cocktails on Fridays if you want to mix it up with the locals, which is always a good idea in Puerto Rico.

- **Sipping a Piña Colada:** After a day on the beach, make sure you spend at least one afternoon enjoying a piña colada or two. A refreshingly sweet mix of coconut, pineapple, and rum, thought to have been invented at San Juan's Caribe Hilton, a piña colada is one of the finest libations you will likely try anywhere, especially after lots of fun and sun on the beach.

THE best OF THE OUTDOORS

- **Hiking & Bird-Watching at El Yunque:** Thirty minutes by road east of San Juan in the Luquillo Mountains and protected by the U.S. Forest Service, El Yunque is Puerto Rico's greatest natural attraction. It sprawls across 28,000 acres (1,133 hectares) of the rugged Sierra de Luquillo mountain range, and contains some 240 species (26 endemic) of trees and plants and 50 bird species, including the rare Puerto Rican parrot (scientific name: *Amazonavitatta*). Visitors can walk one of the dozens of trails that wind past waterfalls, while the island's colorful parrots fly overhead the song of Puerto Rico's *coquí,* a small tree frog, fills the air. See "El Yunque," in chapter 6.

- **Descending into the Río Camuy Caves:** Some 2½ hours west of San Juan, visitors board a tram to descend into this forest-filled sinkhole at the mouth of the Clara Cave. They walk the footpaths of a 170-foot-high (52m) cave to a deeper sinkhole. Once they're inside, a 45-minute tour helps everyone, including kids, learn to differentiate stalactites from stalagmites. At the Pueblos sinkhole, a platform overlooks the Camuy River, passing through a network of cave tunnels. See "Arecibo & Camuy," in chapter 6.

- **Take in the View at Las Cabezas de San Juan Nature Reserve:** This 316-acre (128-hectare) nature reserve about 45 minutes from San Juan encompasses seven different ecological systems, including forestland, mangroves, lagoons, beaches, cliffs, and offshore coral reefs. Tours led by park staff end with a climb to the top of the still-working 19th-century lighthouse for views over Puerto Rico's eastern coast and nearby Caribbean islands. One of the finest phosphorescent bays in the world is located here; take a nighttime boat tour to experience the glow firsthand. See the box, "To the Lighthouse: Exploring Las Cabezas de San Juan Nature Reserve," in chapter 9.

- **Guánica State Forest:** At the opposite extreme of El Yunque's lush and wet rainforest, Guánica State Forest's climate is dry and arid, the Arizona-like landscape riddled with cacti. The area, cut off from the Cordillera Central mountain range, gets little rainfall. Yet it's home to some 50 percent of all the island's terrestrial bird species, including the rare Puerto Rican nightjar, once thought to be extinct. The forest has 36 miles (58km) of trails winding through four forest types, all available for hiker's to explore. See chapter 7.

○ **Mona Island:** Off the western coast of Puerto Rico, the "Galápagos of Puerto Rico" is home to unique wildlife such as giant iguanas and three species of endangered sea turtles. Some 20 endangered animals also have been spotted here. Eco-tourists like to hike among Mona's mangrove forests, cliffs, and complex honeycomb of caves; hikers can camp at Mona for a modest fee, but they will also have to hire transportation to and from the island. See the box, "Mona Island: The Galápagos of Puerto Rico," in chapter 8.

THE best BEACHES

White sandy beaches and idyllic offshore islands are what put Puerto Rico on tourist maps in the first place. The best beaches are labeled on the "Eastern Puerto Rico" map, on p. 192.

○ **Best for Singles (Straight & Gay):** Sandwiched between Condado and Isla Verde along San Juan's coast, **Ocean Park** is a wide beach fronting a residential neighborhood of beautiful homes. A top spot for swimming and kite surfing, the beach is also a favorite for young and beautiful *sanjuaneros* to congregate, especially on weekends. Knowledgeable tourists also seek out Ocean Park's guesthouses that cater to young urban professionals from the East Coast, both gay and straight. There definitely is a South Beach/Río vibe here, but it's decidedly more low-key and Caribbean. See "Diving, Fishing, Tennis & Other Outdoor Pursuits," in chapter 5.

○ **Best Beach for Families: Luquillo Beach,** 30 miles (48km) east of San Juan, has better sands and clearer waters than most in San Juan. The vast sandy beach opens onto a crescent-shaped bay edged by a coconut grove. Coral reefs protect the crystal-clear lagoon from the often rough Atlantic waters that can buffet the northern coast, making Luquillo a good place for young children to swim. Much photographed because of its white sands, Luquillo also has picnic areas with changing rooms, lockers, and showers. See "Luquillo Beach," in chapter 6.

○ **Best for Swimming: Pine Grove Beach,** which stretches between the Ritz-Carlton and the Marriott Courtyard at the end of Isla Verde near the airport, is a crescent, white-sand beach, whose tranquil, blue waters are protected by an offshore reef from the often rough Atlantic current. By the Ritz-Carlton and the Casa Cuba social club to the west, the water is completely sheltered, and a long sandbar means shallow water stretches a long way offshore. Here the waves are well formed but never too big, which makes it a perfect spot to swim and learn to surf. See p. 101.

○ **Best for Scenery:** In the southwestern corner of Puerto Rico, **Boquerón Beach** and its surrounding neighborhoods bring to mind a tropical Cape Cod. The beach town of Boquerón itself, stands along the coast just beside the beach running along a 3-mile (4.8km) bay, with palm-fringed white sand curving away on both sides. The water is always tranquil, making it perfect for families and swimming. There's fine snorkeling, sailing, and fishing as well. See "The Southwest Coast," in chapter 7.

○ **Best for Surfing:** Puerto Rico's northwest coast is generally regarded as one of the best surf spots across the globe and it draws surfers from around the world. **Rincón** is the center of the island surf scene, which also extends to neighboring **Isabela** and **Aguadilla.** Dubbed the "Caribbean Pipeline," winter waves here can approach 20 feet (6.1m) in height, equaling the force of the surf on Oahu's north shore. See "Rincón," in chapter 8.

o **Best for Windsurfing:** Puerto Rico is filled with great places for windsurfing and, increasingly, kite surfing. San Juan itself is a windsurfer's haven, and you'll see them off the coast from **Pine Grove** beach near the airport all the way west to where **Ocean Park** runs into **Condado** at **Parquedel Indio. Punta Las Marías,** between Ocean Park and **Isla Verde,** is another center of activity. See chapter 5.

o **Best for Snorkeling:** The islands of **Vieques** and **Culebra** have great snorkeling. Culebra's most popular beach, **Flamenco,** is picture perfect and has very good snorkeling, and just a 20-minute hike from its parking lot leads to the **Playa Tamarindo** and **Playa Carlos Rosario,** beaches enveloped by a barrier reef; a quarter-mile (.4km) to the south is a spot called **"The Wall,"** which has 40-foot (12m) drop-offs and rainbow-hued fish. See p. 221.

THE best HOTELS

o **Old San Juan:** At **Hotel El Convento** (San Juan; ℂ 787/723-9202), you can spend the afternoon wandering the Old City or lolling around the rooftop splash pool, with its sweeping vistas of San Juan Bay and the bluff overlooking the Atlantic Ocean. There are bougainvillea and tropical flowers hanging from seemingly every window and terrace, as well as colorful, restored Spanish colonial architecture everywhere you turn. You'll feel spoiled by your room's marble bathroom and elegant bed. **Gallery Inn at Galería San Juan** (San Juan; ℂ 787/722-1808) is a legendary bohemian property overlooking an oceanfront bluff adjacent to the centuries-old San Cristobal. An art studio and gallery, this charming colonial inn has sculpture gardens and flowery courtyards and plush accommodations.

o **Near San Juan:** Two of the Caribbean's new ultra luxury resorts, which offer a Garden of Eden experience for well-heeled travelers, are within easy reach of San Juan and its international airport. Both the **St. Regis Bahía Beach Resort** (Río Grande; ℂ 787/809-8000) and the **Dorado Beach, a Ritz Reserve** (Dorado; ℂ 787/626-1100) offer world-class spas, golf, beach and nature facilities for guests who expect the highest level of comfort and service.

o **Southwest:** The comfortable and tropically elegant **Copamarina Beach Resort** (Caña Gorda; ℂ 787/821-0505), a low-flung property that stretches between the strangely beautifully Guánica Dry Forest and glistening coastline with emerald blue waters and lush coastal mangrove forest, is a low maintenance, great value paradise.

o **Northwest:** In land of big surf and natural beauty the **Horned Dorset Primavera** (Rincón; ℂ 787/823-3040) stands tall above the rest. With private plunge pools and oceanfront terraces, this small, tranquil estate in western Puerto Rico is a pocket of posh with luxurious accommodations, beautiful natural surroundings, and wonderful gourmet food and libations.

o **Vieques:** The **Inn on the Blue Horizon** (Vieques; ℂ 787/741-3318) is a tropical vision on an oceanfront bluff overlooking the idyllic south coast of Vieques and the neighboring village of Esperanza. Relax with the sea breeze in the sumptuous furnishings of the main building's open-air atrium, or watch the sunset at the circular Blue Moon Bar, which overlooks the striking coastline. If you want to really turn off the world and relax, the simple beauty of **Hix Island House** (Vieques; ℂ 787/741-2302) is unsurpassable. Nestled in the island town's central lush hills, the resort unfolds as if part of the landscape offering visitors extraordinary views and making the natural surroundings an intimate part of a guest's stay.

THE best RESTAURANTS

San Juan

o **Best for a Splurge:** Go French at the charming **Bistro de Paris** (p. 65), which brings the sophistication and good taste of the city of lights to San Juan, or sample what one of the best of chefs in Puerto Rico is cooking up at the hip and chic **Santaella** (p. 67).

o **Best for Romance: El Picoteo,** at Hotel El Convento (p. 56), wraps around the gorgeous interior courtyard of Old San Juan's most stunning historic property. With dozens of delectable tapas on the menu, and tropical foliage blooming against the Spanish colonial facades, this is a great spot to linger. At the luminous, seashell-shaped **Perla Restaurant** (p. 60), on the beach of Hotel La Concha, a meal is always an elegant event.

o **Best Bang for Your Buck: Café del Angel** (p. 63) in Condado and **Mi Casita** (p. 70) in Isla Verde both serve tasty Puerto Rican food as well as U.S. standards at bargain rates.

o **Best for a Taste of the Island: Parrot Club** (p. 54) is known for its Nuevo Latino cuisine, reinvigorating Puerto Rican and Cuban standards with fresh ingredients and new riffs, AND it has the best service in town. For *comida criolla* just like *abuela* makes, try **El Jibarito** (p. 59), a popular spots with local, or **Raíces** (p. 57), which not only offers authentic island cuisine, but a full immersion into Puerto Rican culture.

o **Best for Families: Ciao Mediterranean Café** (p. 70) on the beach at Isla Verde and **The Place** (p. 64) in Condado have friendly atmospheres and menus that are equally appealing to kids and parents.

o **Best for After Hours:** With the most extensive after-hours menu in town, **The Greenhouse** (p. 63) is the place to go when midnight munchies strike, no matter what you're craving.

o **Best for Meat Eaters:** Like all great restaurant towns, San Juan is filled with fantastic steakhouses. **BLT Steak** (p. 69), French chef Laurent Tourondel's extravagant reinvention of the American steakhouse, gets our vote for top steak palace.

o **Best for Seafood Lovers:** For the best of what's fresh from the sea, head to vibrant and cool **Aguaviva** (p. 53) in Isla Verde or **Tasca del Pescador,** a family-run spot serving delicious Puerto Rican seafood at great prices the heart of Santurce (p. 68).

o **Best for Burgers and Pizza:** Local veteran **El Hamburger** (p. 60) cooks up delicious burgers, dogs, fries, and onion rings. New kid of the block **Melanzana Bistro & Pizzeria** (p. 65) has the voluptuous feel of a Fellini film and authentic Neapolitan pizza and other fine Italian fare.

THE best FAMILY EXPERIENCES

Puerto Rico has a bounty of attractions, natural wonders, and resorts that welcome families who choose to play together. Here are some of the best.

o **Stay at a Kid-Friendly Resort:** Near Old San Juan, the **Caribe Hilton** (© **787/721-0303**) has lots of kids' activities, and its private beach and huge infinity pool will give parents piece of mind, whether your child is 4 or 14. Kids will keep busy with a video arcade, bicycle rentals, a kids club, tennis courts, and watersports equipment rentals. In Condado, try **San Juan Marriott Resort & Stellaris Casino** (② 787/722-7000), with a water slide, kids camp and activities, and some super friendly staff members that love to cater to the kids. See p. 79. On the west coast in Aguadilla, the whole family will love the **Marriott Courtyard Aguadilla** (② 787/658-8000), with its pool, aquatics playground, and spacious guest rooms. It's near some of the prettiest beaches on the island, too, and near attractions such as the Camuy Caves, Arecibo Observatory, a local water park, and an ice skating rink. See p. 187. **El Conquistador Resort & Golden Door Spa** (② 800/468-5228 or 787/863-1000), in Las Croabas, offers the gold standard in family resorts with an extensive kids club, Camp Coquí, along with Coquí Waterpark which has pools, water slides, a rope bridge, and a lazy river attraction. The resort has some of the best facilities and restaurants in Puerto Rico, including a private beach island. See p. 195.

o **Having Adventures in Old San Juan:** Your kids will love Old San Juan, as long as you take them to the places they will want to go. For toddlers and the under 10-set, the **Museo del Niño** (Children's Museum; p. 99) offers lots of fun, from the rooftop nature exhibits to the padded play area with dress-up costumes. Exploring the Old City's two fortresses—**El Morro** and **San Cristobal**—feels like you're visiting a true-life "Pirates of the Caribbean," and the grassy grounds of **El Morro** is perfect for flying kites. The **Bahia Urbana Park** at the entrance to Old San Juan on San Juan Bay has a Trapeze School and replicas of old sailing ships and activities for the kids. See chapter 5.

o **Hitting the North Coast's Attractions:** An hour west of San Juan, the **Arecibo Observatory** is the world's largest radar/radio-telescope; with its huge dish and suspended cable bridges springing from the lush, mountainous terrain, the structure itself is just as fascinating as the work inside. Further west is the **Río Camuy Cave Park,** a world of subterranean marvels, with surging underground rivers and intricate cavern networks. The kids will also enjoy the **Arecibo Lighthouse & Historic Park** (Hwy. 655, El Muelle, Barrio Islote, Arecibo; ② 787/880-7540; www.arecibo lighthouse.com). The park is housed in a 114-year-old lighthouse and offers visitors replicas of slave quarters, a pirate ship, cave, and other exhibits. See chapter 6.

THE best HISTORIC SITES

o **The Historic District of Old San Juan:** There's nothing like it in the Caribbean. Partially enclosed by old walls dating from the 17th century, Old San Juan was designated a U.S. National Historic Zone in 1950. Some 400 massively restored buildings fill this district, which is chockablock with tree-shaded squares, monuments, and open-air cafes as well as shops, restaurants, and bars. If you're interested in history, there is no better stroll in the Caribbean. It continues to be a vibrant cultural center and enclave of the arts and entertainment, as well as one of the region's culinary capitals. See "Seeing the Sights," in chapter 5.

o **Castillo de San Felipe del Morro** (Old San Juan): In Old San Juan and nicknamed El Morro, this fort was originally built in 1540. It guards the bay from a rocky promontory on the northwestern tip of the old city. Rich in history and legend, the site covers enough territory to accommodate a 9-hole golf course. See p. 86.

o **The Historic District of Ponce:** Second only to Old San Juan in terms of historical significance, the central district of Ponce is a blend of Ponce Creole and Art Deco building styles, dating mainly from the 1890s to the 1930s. One street, Calle Isabel, offers an array of Ponceño architectural styles, which often incorporate neoclassical details. The city underwent a massive restoration preceding the celebration of its 300th anniversary in 1996. See "Ponce," in chapter 8.

o **Museo de Arte de Ponce** (Ponce): This museum has the finest collection of European and Latin American art in the Caribbean, and its architecture, as well as its collection, heralds both the classical and the modern. The modern additions flow into the original museum structure, which has been called the "Parthenon of the Caribbean." The permanent collection is arranged by theme, rather than by date and school, which makes a visit to the museum livelier than the more academic arrangement typical in other museums. See p. 151.

o **The City of San Germán:** Founded in 1512, this small town in the southwestern corner of Puerto Rico is Puerto Rico's second-oldest city. Thanks to a breadth of architectural styles, San Germán is also the second Puerto Rican city (after San Juan) to be included in the National Register of Historic Places. Buildings, monuments, and plazas fill a 36-acre (15-hectare) historic zone. Today's residents descend from the smugglers, poets, priests, and politicians who once lived here in "the city of hills," so-called because of the mountainous location. See "San Germán," in chapter 7.

o **Iglesia Porta Coeli (San Germán):** The main attraction of this ancient town is the oldest church in the New World. It was originally built by Dominican friars in 1606. The church resembles a working chapel, although mass is held here only three times a year. Along the sides of the church are treasures gathered from all over the world. See "San Germán," in chapter 7.

o **Puerto Rico Museum of Art (San Juan):** This museum features interesting traveling shows and a growing permanent collection emphasizing local artists in impressive surroundings—a restored 1920s classic in Santurce. There are beautiful botanical gardens outside, and a theater exhibits cutting-edge films and performances of all types. There are day workshops, open to the public, and children's activities held here nearly every weekend. See p. 91.

THE best GOLF COURSES

o **Río Mar Beach Resort & Spa: A Wyndham Grand Resort** (Río Grande; ✆ 787/ 888-6000): Two world-class golf courses are located here in the shadow of El Yunque rainforest along a dazzling stretch of coast. The entire 6,782 yards (6,201m) of Tom and George Fazio's Ocean Course has seaside panoramas and breezes, and fat iguanas scampering through the lush grounds. The other course, a 6,945-yard (6,351m) design by golf pro Greg Norman, follows the flow of the Mameyes River through mountain and coastal vistas. See p. 131.

o **Dorado Beach Resort & Club** (Dorado; ✆ 787/796-8961 or 787/626-1006): With 72 holes, Dorado has the highest concentration of golf on the island. Of the many courses here, Dorado East is our favorite. Designed by Robert Trent Jones, Sr., it was the site of the Senior PGA Tournament of Champions throughout the 1990s. See p. 135.

o **El Conquistador Resort & Golden Door Spa** (Fajardo; ✆ 787/863-1000): This sprawling resort on Puerto Rico's northeast corner features 18 holes of par 72 golf with spectacular Atlantic Ocean views from its Arthur Hills Golf Course. See p. 195.

- **Palmas del Mar Country Club** (Humacao; © **787/285-2221**): Lying on the east coast on the grounds of a former coconut plantation, the Palmas del Mar resort boasts the second-leading course in Puerto Rico—a par-72, 6,803-yard (6,221m) layout designed by Gary Player. Some crack golfers consider holes 11 through 15 the toughest five successive holes in the Caribbean. There's also an 18-hole championship-caliber course designed by Rees Jones. See p. 200.
- **Trump International Golf Club** (Río Grande; © **787/657-2000**): Located on 1,200 acres (486 hectares) of glistening waterfront, the club comprises two recently improved 18-hole golf courses designed by Tom Kite that allow you to play in the mountains, along the ocean, among the palms, and in between the lakes. Its bunkers are carved from white silica sand. See p. 130.

PUERTO RICO IN CONTEXT

2

Puerto Ricans are intensely proud of their culture, a rich brew of Taíno Indian, Spanish, African, and American influences, and most relish showing off the best of it. Yet visitors will be just as struck at the worldliness of most Puerto Ricans as they are by the beat of salsa music, the symphony of flavor in a seafood stuffed mofongo, or the long line of master island painters, print makers, and song writers. That too results from its historic forging from several distinct world cultures.

For more than a century, Puerto Rico's political life has been dominated by its century-old ties to the United States. Those ties have been largely beneficial, and most Puerto Ricans cherish their U.S. citizenship and want to maintain the current political relationship, either through continued commonwealth status or statehood. A smaller percentage favor outright separation from the United States to make Puerto Rico a sovereign nation (the pro-independence party gubernatorial candidate usually gets 5 percent of the vote). Yet the relationship with the United States is also the source of island society's central anxiety, which centers on the need for a permanent political status.

Millions of Puerto Ricans have flocked stateside over the last 70 years in search of economic and educational opportunities and an improved quality of life, and they continue to do so. In fact, Puerto Ricans living stateside now surpass the number living on the island: roughly 5 million, versus about 3.6 million. But for most stateside *boricuas,* their allegiance still belongs to their island homeland, which means frequent trips during vacations and holidays. A sizeable number of Puerto Rican passengers are on most planes from the U.S. arriving at Luis Muñoz Marín International Airport in San Juan. They will burst into applause upon touchdown on Puerto Rican soil. Many others return to Puerto Rico after retiring.

The first wave of island migrants during the 1940s and 1950s largely settled in and around New York, and came seeking blue-collar jobs and the hope for a better future for their families. Today, the typical migrant is more likely a highly educated professional moving to south or central Florida pursuing greater career advancement opportunities and an improved quality of life.

Puerto Rican writer René Marqués, who came of age in the 1940s and 1950s when Puerto Rico was modernizing into an industrial economy and getting a big dose of U.S. influence, spoke of the dual nature of his island, which nevertheless contributed to its uniqueness. "Puerto Rico has two languages," he claimed, "and two citizenships, two basic philosophies of life, two flags, two anthems, two loyalties."

PUERTO RICO TODAY

Puerto Rico often makes headlines in U.S. news media, and daughters and sons of the island, from pop stars Ricky Martin and Marc Anthony to actors Benicio Del Toro and Jennifer López, have given U.S. and world audiences a taste of the enormous talent of this small island, which is also evident in the storied ledger of island baseball sluggers and boxing champs, from Roberto Clemente to Felix Trinidad. Of course, the news is not always good, and recent struggles with economic issues have also drawn headlines.

Puerto Rico, however, also draws attention because it is among the most developed destinations in the Caribbean and a true regional hub for transportation and telecommunications, with a modern infrastructure and a diversified economy, as well as a cultural and entertainment capital.

A Changing Economy

Puerto Rico is the easternmost of the Greater Antilles and the fourth largest island in the Caribbean after Cuba, Hispaniola (which comprises the Dominican Republic and Haiti), and Jamaica. The island is located at the crossroads between North and South America, at just 3½ hours airtime from New York, 60 minutes from Caracas, and only 4 days sailing from Atlantic ports in the U.S. and ports in the Gulf of Mexico. The Puerto Rican territory includes three other small islands, Vieques, Culebra, and Mona, as well as numerous islets.

Some 3.6 million people live in Puerto Rico, approximately one-third of them within the San Juan metropolitan area. The island, with an area of 3,435 square miles (9,000 sq. km)—110 miles long by 39 miles wide—has a mountainous interior and is surrounded by a wide coastal plain where the majority of the population lives. Rainfall averages 69 inches (175cm) per year and year-round temperatures range from 74°F (23°C) in the winter to 81°F (27°C) in the summer.

The island actually lost population during the last 10 years, one of a handful of U.S. jurisdictions to do so, according to the latest U.S. Census figures. It's a sign of the island's long-standing recession, which began in 2006 and continues today. With more than 4 million Puerto Ricans living stateside, it is now the first time there are more Puerto Ricans living in the continental U.S. than on the island.

Relationship with the United States

Puerto Rico came under the European sphere of influence in 1493, when Christopher Columbus landed here. Shortly thereafter, the island was conquered and settled by the Spaniards. It remained a Spanish possession for 4 centuries.

The territory of Puerto Rico was ceded to the United States upon signature of the Treaty of Paris, on December 10, 1898, a pact which ended the Spanish-American War. Puerto Ricans have been citizens of the United States since 1917. In 1950, after a long evolution toward greater self-government for Puerto Rico, the Congress of the United States enacted Public Law 600, which is "in the nature of a compact" and which became effective upon its acceptance by the electorate of Puerto Rico. It provides that those sections of existing law, which defined the political, economic, and fiscal relationship between Puerto Rico and the United States, would remain in full force. It also authorized the people of Puerto Rico to draft and adopt their own Constitution. The Constitution was drafted by a popularly elected constitutional convention, overwhelmingly approved in a special referendum by the people of Puerto Rico, and approved by the United States Congress and the president of the United States, becoming effective upon proclamation of the governor of Puerto Rico on July 25, 1952.

Puerto Rico's relationship with the United States is referred to herein as commonwealth status.

The United States and the Commonwealth of Puerto Rico (the "Commonwealth") share a common defense, market, and currency. The Commonwealth exercises virtually the same control over its internal affairs as do the 50 states. It differs from the states, however, in its relationship with the federal government. The people of Puerto Rico are citizens of the United States but do not vote in national elections. They are represented in Congress by a Resident Commissioner who has a voice in the House of Representatives but no vote. Most federal taxes, except those such as Social Security taxes, which are imposed by mutual consent, are not levied in Puerto Rico. No federal income tax is collected from Puerto Rico residents on income earned in Puerto Rico, except for certain federal employees who are subject to taxes on their salaries. The official languages of Puerto Rico are Spanish and English.

The 51st State?

The New Progressive Party wants to make Puerto Rico the 51st state, but the opposition is strong, both on the island and in Congress. In a nonbinding two-question political plebiscite held in November 2012, 53.97 percent of voters said they were against continuing Puerto Rico's current commonwealth territory status. A second question had voters choose among "nonterritorial" alternatives to the current status, with 61.13 percent voting for statehood, 33.34 percent voting for Puerto Rico becoming a nation in a free association with the U.S. and 5.49 percent voting for independence. Some 26 percent of ballots cast were left blank to protest that the status quo commonwealth status was left off the second ballot.

The current administration of Gov. Alejandro García Padilla is of the Popular Democratic Party, which backs the continued commonwealth status. It has called for a new status vote among all options by 2017, but the party will have to define specifically the commonwealth political status, and it must be approved by the federal government as Constitutionally acceptable. The Puerto Rican Independence Party typically achieves less than 5 percent of popular support in gubernatorial elections. These three parties have dominated island politics of the last 6 decades.

PUERTO RICO POPULATION & POP CULTURE

The inhabitants of Puerto Rico represent a mix of races, cultures, languages, and religions. They draw their heritage from the original native population, from Spanish royalists who sought refuge here, from African slaves imported to work the sugar plantations, and from other Caribbean islanders who have come here seeking jobs. The Spanish they speak is a mix, too, with many words borrowed from the pre-Columbian Amerindian tongue as well as English. Even the Catholicism they practice incorporates some Taíno and African traditions.

About 3.6 million people live on the main island, making it one of the most densely populated islands in the world. It has an average of about 1,000 people per square mile, a ratio higher than that of any of the 50 states. There are now more Puerto Ricans living stateside as there are on the island. If all of the estimated 5 million stateside Puerto Ricans were to all return home, the island would be so crowded that there would be virtually no room for them to live.

When the United States acquired the island in 1898, most Puerto Ricans worked in agriculture; today most jobs are industrial. One-third of Puerto Rico's population is concentrated in the San Juan metropolitan area.

When the Spanish forced the Taíno peoples into slavery, virtually the entire indigenous population was decimated, except for a few Amerindians who escaped into the remote mountains. Eventually they intermarried with the poor Spanish farmers and became known as *jíbaros*. Because of industrialization and migration to the cities, few *jíbaros* remain.

Besides the slaves imported from Africa to work on the plantations, other ethnic groups joined the island's racial mix. Fleeing Simón Bolívar's independence movements in South America, Spanish loyalists headed to Puerto Rico—a fiercely conservative Spanish colony during the early 1800s. French families also flocked here from both Louisiana and Haiti, as changing governments or violent revolutions turned their worlds upside down. As word of the rich sugar-cane economy reached economically depressed Scotland and Ireland, many farmers from those countries also journeyed to Puerto Rico in search of a better life.

During the mid–19th century, labor was needed to build roads. Initially, Chinese workers were imported for this task, followed by workers from countries such as Italy, France, Germany, and even Lebanon. American expatriates came to the island after 1898. Long after Spain had lost control of Puerto Rico, Spanish immigrants continued to arrive on the island. The most significant new immigrant population arrived in the 1960s, when thousands of Cubans fled from Fidel Castro's communist state. The latest arrivals in Puerto Rico have come from the Dominican Republic.

Islanders are most known for their contributions to popular music, and visitors here will no doubt see why. Sometimes, the whole island seems to be dancing. It's been that way since the Taínos, with music an important aspect of their religious and cultural ceremonies.

Young Puerto Ricans have developed their own *rock en español* and Latin pop sound, and a recent musical craze born in Puerto Rico is reggaeton, an infectious blend of rap, reggae, and island rhythms, often accompanied by x-rated hip shaking. Daddy Yankee put the music on the world map with his hit "Gasolina"; other well-known island artists in the genre are the duo Wisin y Yandel and Don Omar. Vico C is a local rapper credited with being a pioneer for today's reggaeton stars.

Puerto Rico is still dominated by salsa, a mix of African, Caribbean, and North American rhythms. Salsa bands tend to be full orchestras, with brass sections and several percussionists. The beat is infectious and nonstop, but salsa dancing is all about smooth gyrations and style.

The late Tito Puente, a Latin Jazz master, was instrumental in the development of the music along with singer Ismael Miranda. Puerto Rican salsa won world-wide fame in the late 1970s and early 1980s through groups such as the Fania All Stars, who paired Héctor Lavoe, Rubén Blades and Willie Colón, and El Gran Combo, who still performs today after 40 years together. Famous contemporary practitioners are Gilberto Santa Rosa and Marc Anthony. Actress and singer Jennifer López, Anthony's ex-wife, is another of Puerto Rico's most famous descendants. Their pet project, the biopic "El Cantante," based on Lavoe's life, was filmed in Puerto Rico and New York in 2007.

Jennifer López is not the only *borinqueña* to make a mark on the world stage: A total of four Puerto Rican women have won the Miss Universe competition, most recently Zuleyka Rivera in 2006.

The most famous Puerto Rican singer, however, is still probably pop star Ricky Martin, who continues to be a hometown favorite and sells out shows during his frequent island performances. Other famous island musicians currently include Rene Pérez of Calle 13 and Tego Calderon, who work the reggaeton genre while exploring other island and world beats, reggae band Cultura Profetica, female rocker Kany Garcia, *salseros* Gilberto Santrosa and Victor Manuel and rock bands Fiel a la Vega and La Secta All Stars.

Puerto Ricans have also made their mark in professional sports, particularly baseball. The most famous, of course, was Roberto Clemente, who is still a local legend and a role model for young ball players. Other recent stars who have retired include Iván Rodríguez, Bernie Williams, Jorge Posada and Carlos Delgado. Current professional baseball players from Puerto Rico include Carlos Beltrán, Yadier Molina, Javier López and Alex Cintrón.

Languages

Spanish is the language of Puerto Rico, although English is widely spoken, especially in hotels, restaurants, shops, and nightclubs that attract tourists. In the hinterlands, however, Spanish prevails.

If you plan to travel extensively in Puerto Rico but don't speak Spanish, pick up a Spanish-language phrase book. The most popular is "Berlitz Spanish for Travelers," published by Collier Macmillan. There's also "Frommer's Spanish Phrasefinder," a pocket guide with basic phrases to help you try to blend in with the locals.

Religions

The majority of Puerto Ricans are Roman Catholic, but religious freedom for all faiths is guaranteed by the Commonwealth Constitution. There is a Jewish Community Center in Miramar, and there's a Jewish Reformed Congregation in Santurce. There are Protestant services for Baptists, Episcopalians, Lutherans, and Presbyterians, and there are other interdenominational services.

Although it is predominantly Catholic, Puerto Rico does not follow Catholic dogma and rituals as assiduously as do the churches of Spain and Italy. Because the church supported slavery, there was a long-lasting resentment against the all-Spanish clergy of colonial days. Island-born men were excluded from the priesthood. When Puerto Ricans eventually took over the Catholic churches on the island, they followed some guidelines from Spain and Italy but modified or ignored others.

Following the U.S. acquisition of the island in 1898, Protestantism grew in influence and popularity. There were Protestants on the island before the invasion, but their numbers increased after Puerto Rico became a U.S. colony. Many islanders liked the idea of separation of church and state, as provided for in the U.S. Constitution. In recent years, Pentecostal fundamentalism has swept across the island. There are some 1,500 Evangelical churches in Puerto Rico today.

As throughout Latin America, the practice of Catholicism in Puerto Rico blends native Taíno and African traditions with mainstream tenets of the faith. It has been said that the real religion of Puerto Rico is *espiritismo* (spiritualism), a quasi-magical belief in occult forces. Spanish colonial rulers outlawed spiritualism, but under the U.S. occupation it flourished in dozens of isolated pockets of the island.

Students of religion trace spiritualism to the Taínos, and to their belief that *jípia* (the spirits of the dead—somewhat like the legendary vampire) slumbered by day and prowled the island by night. Instead of looking for bodies, the *jípia* were seeking wild fruit to eat. Thus arose the Puerto Rican tradition of putting out fruit on the kitchen table. Even in modern homes today, you'll often find a bowl of plastic, flamboyantly colored fruit resting atop a refrigerator.

Many islanders still believe in the "evil eye," or *mal de ojo.* To look on a person or a person's possessions covetously, according to believers, can lead to that individual's sickness or perhaps death. Children are given bead charm bracelets to guard against the evil eye. Spiritualism also extends into healing, folk medicine, and food. For example, some spiritualists believe that cold food should never be eaten with hot food. Some island plants, herbs, and oils are believed to have healing properties, and spiritualist literature is available throughout the island.

EATING & DRINKING

Some of Puerto Rico's finest chefs, Wilo Benet and Alfredo Ayala, have based their supremely successful careers on paying gourmet homage to their mothers' and grandmothers' cooking. A whole new generation of rising culinary artists is following in their footsteps by putting Puerto Rico's *comida criolla* at the front and center of their Nuevo Latino experimentation.

Comida criolla, as Puerto Rican food is known, is flavorful but not hot. It can be traced back to the Arawaks and Taínos, the original inhabitants of the island, who thrived on a diet of corn, tropical fruit, and seafood. When Ponce de León arrived with Columbus in 1493, the Spanish added beef, pork, rice, wheat, and olive oil to the island's foodstuffs.

The Spanish soon began planting sugar cane and importing slaves from Africa, who brought with them okra and taro (known in Puerto Rico as *yautia*). The mingling of flavors and ingredients passed from generation to generation among the different ethnic groups that settled on the island, resulting in the exotic blend of today's Puerto Rican cuisine.

Its two essential ingredients are *sofrito,* a mix of garlic, sweet peppers, onion, and fresh green herbs, and *adobo,* a blend of dried spices such as peppercorns, oregano, garlic, salt, olive oil, and lime juice or vinegar, rubbed on pork or chicken before it is slowly roasted. *Achiote* (annatto seeds) is often used as well, imparting an orange color to many common Puerto Rican dishes. Other seasonings and ingredients commonly used are coriander, papaya, cacao, *níspero* (a tropical fruit that's brown, juicy, and related to the kiwi), and *apio* (a small African-derived tuber that's like a pungent turnip).

The rich and fertile fields of Puerto Rico produce a wide variety of **vegetables.** A favorite is the **chayote,** a pear-shaped vegetable called *christophine* throughout most of the English-speaking Caribbean. Its delicately flavored flesh is often compared to that of summer squash. Native root vegetables such as yucca, breadfruit, and plantain, called *viandas,* either accompany main meals or are used as ingredients in them.

If you're in Old San Juan and are looking for a noshing tour of the local cuisine, we highly recommend **Flavors of San Juan** (© **787/964-2447;** www.flavorsofsanjuan. com). See p. 99.

Rum: Kill-Devil or Whiskey-Belly Vengeance

Rum is the national drink of Puerto Rico, and you can buy it in almost any shade. Because the island is the world's leading rum producer, it's little wonder that every Puerto Rican bartender worthy of the profession likes to concoct his or her own favorite rum libation. You can call for Puerto Rican rum in many mixed drinks such as rum Collins, rum sour, and rum screwdriver. The classic sangria, which is prepared in Spain

STRANGE fruit

A variety of starchy root vegetables and fruits form a staple of island cuisine, not just in Puerto Rico but throughout the Caribbean. While cassava is native to South America, plantains and bananas are from Asia and yams from Africa.

Breadfruit stems from the South Pacific and its most legendary sailing adventures. During Capt. James Cook's explorations of the South Pacific in the late 1700s, West Indian planters were intrigued by his accounts of the bread-fruit tree, which grew in abundance on Tahiti. Seeing it as a source of cheap food for their slaves, they beseeched King George III to sponsor an expedition to bring the trees to the Caribbean. In 1787, the king put Capt. William Bligh in command of HMS *Bounty* and sent him to do just that. One of Bligh's lieutenants was a former shipmate named Fletcher Christian. They became the leading actors in one of the great sea yarns when Christian overpowered Bligh, took over the *Bounty,* threw the breadfruit

trees into the South Pacific Ocean, and disappeared into oblivion.

Bligh survived by sailing the ship's open longboat 3,000 miles (4,830km) to the East Indies, where he hitched a ride back to England on a Dutch vessel. Later he was given command of another ship and sent to Tahiti to get more breadfruit. Although he succeeded on this second attempt, the whole operation went for naught when the West Indies slaves refused to eat the strange fruit of the new tree, preferring instead their old, familiar rice.

Descendants of those trees still grow in the Caribbean, and the islanders prepare the head-size fruit in a number of ways.

In Puerto Rico, *tostones* (fried plantain slices) accompany most meat, fish, or poultry dishes, while *cassava escabeche* is the most frequent compliment to Puerto Rican barbecued chicken and roast pig. But *pana*, or breadfruit, is also served here as in the rest of the region in similar ways.

with dry red wine, sugar, orange juice, and other ingredients, is often given a Puerto Rican twist with a hefty dose of rum.

Today's version of rum bears little resemblance to the raw, grainy beverage consumed by the renegades and pirates of Spain. Christopher Columbus brought sugar cane, from which rum is distilled, to the Caribbean on his second voyage to the New World, and in almost no time rum became the regional drink.

It is believed that Ponce de León introduced rum to Puerto Rico during his governorship, which began in 1508. Under his reign, landholders planted large tracts with sugar cane. From Puerto Rico and other West Indian islands, rum was shipped to colonial America, where it lent itself to such popular and hair-raising 18th-century drinks as Kill-Devil and Whiskey-Belly Vengeance. After the United States became a nation, rum was largely displaced as the drink of choice by whiskey, distilled from grain grown on the American plains.

It took almost a century before Puerto Rico's rum industry regained its former vigor. This occurred during a severe whiskey shortage in the United States at the end of World War II. By the 1950s, sales of rum had fallen off again, as more and different kinds of liquor had become available on the American market.

The local brew had been a questionable drink because of inferior distillation methods and quality. Recognizing this problem, the Puerto Rican government drew up rigid standards for producing, blending, and aging rum. Rum factories were outfitted with the most modern and sanitary equipment, and sales figures (encouraged by aggressive marketing campaigns) began to climb.

No one will ever agree on what "the best" rum is in the Caribbean. There are just too many of them to sample. Some are so esoteric as to be unavailable in your local liquor store. But if popular tastes mean anything, then Puerto Rican rums, especially Bacardi, head the list. There are 24 different rums from Puerto Rico sold in the United States under 11 brand names—not only Bacardi, but also Ron Bocoy, Ronrico, Don Q, and many others. Locals tend to like Don Q the best.

Puerto Rican rums are generally light, gold, or dark. Usually white or silver in color, the biggest seller is light in body and dry in taste. Its subtle flavor and delicate aroma make it ideal for many mixed drinks, including the mojito, daiquiri, rum Collins, rum Mary, and rum and tonic or soda. It also goes with almost any fruit juice, or on the rocks with a slice of lemon or lime. Gold or amber rum is aromatic and full-bodied in taste. Aging in charred oak casks adds color to the rum.

Gold rums are usually aged longer for a deeper and mellower flavor than light rums. They are increasingly popular on the rocks, straight up, or in certain mixed drinks in which extra flavor is desired—certainly in the famous piña colada, rum and Coke, or eggnog.

Dark rum is full-bodied with a deep, velvety, smooth taste and a complex flavor. It can be aged for as long as 15 years. You can enjoy it on the rocks, with tonic or soda, or in mixed drinks when you want the taste of rum to stand out.

WHEN TO GO

Climate

Puerto Rico has one of the most unvarying climates in the world. Temperatures year-round range from 75° to 85°F (24°–29°C). The island is wettest and hottest in August, averaging 81°F (27°C) and 7 inches (18cm) of rain. San Juan and the northern coast seem to be cooler and wetter than Ponce and the southern coast. The coldest weather is in the high altitudes of the Cordillera, the site of Puerto Rico's lowest recorded temperature—39°F (4°C).

THE HURRICANE SEASON

The hurricane season, the curse of Puerto Rican weather, lasts—officially, at least—from June 1 to November 30. But there's no cause for panic. In general, satellite forecasts give adequate warnings so that precautions can be taken. The peaks of the season, when historically the most damaging storms are formed and hit the island, occur in August and December.

If you're heading to Puerto Rico during the hurricane season, you can call your local branch of the **National Weather Service** (listed in your phone directory under the U.S. Department of Commerce) for a weather forecast or check its website at http://forecast.weather.gov. The San Juan office branch of the NWS can be accessed through its website at (www.srh.noaa.gov/sju).

Other options include Weather Underground (www.wunderground.com/weather-forecast/US/PR/San_Juan.html) and Accuweather (www.accuweather.com/en/pr/puerto-rico-weather).

Average Temperatures in Puerto Rico

	JAN	FEB	MAR	APR	MAY	JUNE	JULY	AUG	SEPT	OCT	NOV	DEC
TEMP. (°F)	75	75	76	78	79	81	81	81	81	81	79	77
TEMP. (°C)	24	24	25	26	26	27	27	27	27	27	26	25

The "Season"

In Puerto Rico, hotels charge their highest prices during the peak winter period from mid-December to mid-April, when visitors fleeing from cold northern climates flock to the islands. Winter is the driest season along the coasts but can be wet in mountainous areas.

If you plan to travel in the winter, make reservations 2 to 3 months in advance. At certain hotels it's almost impossible to book accommodations for Christmas and the month of February.

A second tourism high season, especially for hotels and destinations outside San Juan, does take place in July, when most islanders take vacation.

Increasingly, however, Puerto Rico is a weekend getaway for many visitors and demand for hotel rooms and rates also rise on weekends as well.

SAVING MONEY IN THE OFF SEASON

While winter rates are still higher than summer rates at most properties, Puerto Rico is slowly becoming a year-round destination. Many hotel properties are moving towards a pricing scheme of charging a weekday and a weekend rate.

However, there still is an off season, which runs from late spring to late fall, when temperatures in the mid-80s Fahrenheit (about 29°C) prevail throughout most of the region. Trade winds ensure comfortable days and nights, even in accommodations without air-conditioning. Although the noonday sun may raise the temperature to around 90°F (32°C), cool breezes usually make the morning, late afternoon, and evening more comfortable here than in many parts of the U.S. mainland.

Dollar for dollar, you'll spend less money by renting a summer house or fully equipped unit in Puerto Rico than you would on Cape Cod, Fire Island, Laguna Beach, or the coast of Maine.

The off season in Puerto Rico—roughly from May through November (rate schedules vary from hotel to hotel)—is still a summer sale, with many hotel rates slashed from 20 to 40 percent. It's a bonanza for cost-conscious travelers, especially families who like to go on vacations together. In the chapters ahead, we'll spell out in dollars the specific amounts hotels charge during the off season.

But the off season has been shrinking of late. Many hotels, particularly outside of San Juan, will charge full price during the month of July and summer holiday weekends. Some properties, particularly guesthouses and small hotels in vacation towns such as Vieques and Rincón, have dispensed with off-season pricing altogether.

In San Juan, the trend among smaller properties is to charge higher rates on weekends and holidays than during the week, rather than seasonal fluctuations in price.

OTHER OFF-SEASON ADVANTAGES

Although Puerto Rico may appear inviting in the winter to those who live in northern climates, there are many reasons your trip may be much more enjoyable if you go in the off season:

○ After the winter hordes have left, a less-hurried way of life prevails. You'll have a better chance to appreciate the food, culture, and local customs.

○ Swimming pools and beaches are less crowded—perhaps not crowded at all. Again, some areas will be extremely crowded in July and on summer holiday weekends.

- Year-round resort facilities are offered, often at reduced rates, which may include snorkeling, boating, and scuba diving.
- To survive, resort boutiques often feature summer sales, hoping to clear the merchandise they didn't sell in February to accommodate stock they've ordered for the coming winter.
- You can often appear without a reservation at a top restaurant and get a table for dinner, a table that in winter would have required a reservation far in advance. Also, when waiters are less hurried, you get better service.
- The endless waiting game is over: no waiting for a rental car (only to be told none is available), no long wait for a golf course tee time, and quicker access to tennis courts and watersports.
- Some package-tour fares are as much as 20 percent lower, and individual excursion fares are also reduced between 5 and 10 percent.
- All accommodations and flights are much easier to book.
- Summer is an excellent time for family travel, not usually possible during the winter season.
- The very best of Puerto Rican attractions remain undiminished in the off season—sea, sand, and surf, with lots of sunshine.

OFF-SEASON DISADVANTAGES

Let's not paint too rosy a picture. Although the advantages of off-season travel far outweigh the disadvantages, there are nevertheless drawbacks to traveling in summer:

- You might be staying at a construction site. Hoteliers save their serious repairs and their major renovations until the off season, when they have fewer clients. That means you might wake up early in the morning to the sound of a hammer.
- Single tourists find the cruising better in winter, when there are more clients, especially the unattached. Families predominate in summer, and there are fewer chances to meet fellow singles than in the winter months.
- Services are often reduced. In the peak of winter, everything is fully operational. But in summer, many of the programs, such as watersports rentals, might be curtailed. Also, not all restaurants and bars are fully operational at all resorts. For example, for lack of business, certain gourmet or specialty dining rooms might be shut down until house count merits reopening them. In all, the general atmosphere is more laid-back when a hotel or resort might also be operating with a reduced staff. The summer staff will still be adequate to provide service for what's up and running.

HOLIDAYS

Puerto Rico has many public holidays when stores, offices, and schools are closed: New Year's Day, January 6 (Three Kings Day), Washington's Birthday, Good Friday, Memorial Day, July 4th, Labor Day, Thanksgiving, Veterans Day, and Christmas, plus such local holidays as Constitution Day (July 25) and Discovery Day (Nov 19). Remember, U.S. federal holidays are holidays in Puerto Rico, too.

If you are bothered by crowds, avoid visiting beach towns outside San Juan, including Vieques and Culebra, during Easter week and late July, when they are filled with local vacationers.

Puerto Rico Calendar of Events

JANUARY

Three Kings Day, island-wide. On this traditional gift-giving day in Puerto Rico, there are festivals with lively music, dancing, parades, puppet shows, caroling troubadours, and traditional feasts. January 6.

San Sebastián Street Festival, Calle San Sebastián, in Old San Juan. Nightly celebrations with music, processions, crafts, and traditional foods, as well as graphic arts and handicraft exhibitions. For more information, call ⓒ **787/721-2400.** Mid-January.

FEBRUARY

San Blas Half Marathon, Coamo. International and local runners compete in a challenging 13-mile (21km) half-marathon in the hilly south-central town of Coamo. Call **Delta Phi Delta Fraternity (ⓒ 787/509-6375)** or go to the website www.maraton sanblas.com. Early February.

Coffee Harvest Festival, Maricao. Folk music, a parade of floats, traditional foods, crafts, and demonstrations of coffee preparation in Maricao, a 1-hour drive east of Mayagüez. For more information, call ⓒ **787/838-2290** or 787/267-5536. Second week of February.

Carnival Ponceño, Ponce. The island's Carnival celebrations feature float parades, dancing, and street parties. One of the most vibrant festivities is held in Ponce, known for its masqueraders wearing brightly painted horned masks. For more information, call ⓒ **787/284-4141.** Mid-February.

Casals Festival, Performing Arts Center in San Juan. *Sanjuaneros* and visitors alike eagerly look forward to the annual Casals Festival, the Caribbean's most celebrated cultural event. When renowned cellist Casals died in Puerto Rico in 1973 at the age of 97, the Casals Festival was 16 years old and attracting the same class of performers who appeared at the Pablo Casals Festival in France, founded by Casals after World War II. When he moved to Puerto Rico in 1957 with his wife, Marta Casals Istomin (former artistic director of the John F. Kennedy Center for the Performing Arts), he founded not only this festival but also the Puerto Rico

Symphony Orchestra to foster musical development on the island.

Ticket prices for the Casals Festival range from $15 to $75. Discounts are offered to students, people 60 and older, and persons with disabilities. Tickets are available through the **Luis A. Ferré Performing Arts Center** (ⓒ **787/620-4444), Ticket Center** (ⓒ **787/792-5000),** or the **Puerto Rico Symphonic Orchestra** in San Juan (ⓒ **787/721-7727).**

Information is also available from the **Casals Festival** (ⓒ **787/721-8370;** www.festcasalspr.gobierno.pr). The festivities take place from late February to early March.

MARCH

Emancipation Day, island-wide. Commemoration of the emancipation of Puerto Rico's slaves in 1873, held at various venues. March 22.

Puerto Rico Open is more than just a PGA golf tournament, with parties, cultural activities, fashion shows and culinary fest part of a week-long extravaganza in mid-March.

APRIL

Saborea, El Escambrón Beach, San Juan. A weekend culinary extravaganza every April sponsored by the Puerto Rico tourism board, Saborea brings together island flavors and chefs and draws global culinary stars. Call ⓒ **787/751-8001,** or visit www.saborea puertorico.com. April 10-12, 2015.

Good Friday and Easter, island-wide. Celebrated with colorful ceremonies and processions.

José de Diego Day, island-wide. Commemoration of the birthday of José de Diego, the patriot, lawyer, writer, orator, and political leader who was the first president of the Puerto Rico House of Representatives under U.S. rule. April 17.

Sugar Harvest Festival, San Germán. This festival marks the end of the island's sugar harvest, with live music, crafts, and traditional foods, as well as exhibitions of sugarcane plants and past and present harvesting techniques. Late April.

MAY

Condado Culinary Fest, Av. Ashford, Condado. Restaurants and cafes along oceanfront drive take the tables and chairs outside and offer special promotions on culinary creations and libations. There's music, art and other entertainment along the way. Very similar to the SoFo festival in Old San Juan and a very good time. Usually takes place in November. Call San Juan Department of Tourism & Culture at ℡ **787/721-0169** or 787/722-7079.

Puerto Rican Danza Week (Semana de la "Danza" Puertorriqueña), Convento de los Dominicos, Old San Juan. This week commemorates what is, perhaps, the most expressive art form in the Puerto Rican culture: danza music and dance. Throughout Danza Week, live performances and conferences are held at Convento de los Dominicos's indoor patio. The building is located on Old San Juan's Cristo Street. For information, call ℡ **800/866-7827** or 787/721-2400. Second week of May.

Heineken JazzFest, San Juan. The annual jazz celebration is staged at ParqueSixto Escobar. Each year a different jazz theme is featured. The open-air pavilion is in a scenic oceanfront location in the Puerta de Tierra section of San Juan, near the Caribe Hilton. For more information, check out the website www.prheinekenjazz.com, which has schedules and links to buy tickets and package information. End of May through the beginning of June.

JUNE

The Night of San Juan Bautista, islandwide. Puerto Rico's capital and other cities celebrate the island's patron saint with week-long festivities. At midnight, sanjuaneros and others walk backward into the sea (or nearest body of water) three times to renew good luck for the coming year. San Juan hosts several events, from music fests to sports events, for several days before and after the holiday. The night of June 23.

Aibonito Flower Festival, at Road 721 next to the City Hall Coliseum, in the central mountain town of Aibonito. This annual flower-competition festival features acres of lilies, anthuriums, carnations, roses, gardenias, and begonias. For more information, call ℡ **787/735-3871.** Last week in June and first week in July.

JULY

Luis Muñoz Rivera's Birthday, islandwide. A birthday celebration commemorating Luis Muñoz Rivera (1829–1916), statesman, journalist, poet, and resident commissioner in Washington, D.C. July 20.

Loíza Carnival. This annual folk and religious ceremony honors Loíza's patron saint, John (Santiago) the Apostle. Colorful processions take place, with costumes, masks, and bomba dancers (the bomba has a lively Afro-Caribbean dance rhythm). This jubilant celebration reflects the African and Spanish heritage of the region. For more information, call ℡ **787/876-1040.** Late July through early August.

AUGUST

Cuadragésimo Cuarto Torneo de Pesca Interclub del Caribe, Cangrejos Yacht Club. This international blue-marlin fishing tournament features crafts, music, local delicacies, and other activities. For more information, call ℡ **787/791-1015.** Mid-August.

International Billfish Tournament, at Club Náutico, San Juan. This is one of the premier game-fishing tournaments and the longest consecutively held billfish tournament in the world. Fishermen from many countries angle for blue marlin that can weigh up to 900 pounds (408kg). For specific dates and information, call ℡ **787/722-0177.** Late August to early September.

OCTOBER

La Raza Day (Columbus Day), islandwide. This day commemorates Columbus's landing in the New World. October 10.

National Plantain Festival, Corozal. This annual festivity involves crafts, paintings, agricultural products, exhibitions, and sale of plantain dishes; neuvatrova music and folk ballet are performed. For more information, call ℡ **787/859-3060.** Mid-October.

NOVEMBER

Start of Baseball Season, throughout the island. Six Puerto Rican professional clubs compete from November to January. Professionals from North America also play here. The city's Hiram Bithorn Stadium is also a frequent host for Major League Baseball series; in 2010, it was host to several New York Mets–Florida Marlins games.

Festival of Puerto Rican Music, San Juan. An annual classical and folk music festival, one of its highlights is a *cuatro*-playing contest. (A *cuatro* is a guitarlike instrument with 10 strings.) For more information, call ✆ **787/721-5274.** First week in November.

Jayuya Indian Festival, Jayuya. This fiesta features the culture and tradition of the island's original inhabitants, the Taíno Indians, and their music, food, and games. More than 100 artisans exhibit and sell their works. There is also a Miss Taíno Indian Pageant. For more information, call ✆ **787/828-2020.** Second week of November.

Puerto Rico Discovery Day, islandwide. This day commemorates the "discovery" by Columbus in 1493 of the already inhabited island of Puerto Rico. Columbus is thought to have come ashore at the northwestern municipality of Aguadilla, although the exact location is unknown. November 19.

DECEMBER

Old San Juan's White Christmas Festival, Old San Juan. Special musical and artistic presentations take place in stores, with window displays. December 1 through January 12.

Puerto Rico Heritage Artisans Fair, San Juan. The best and largest artisan fair on the island features more than 100 artisans who turn out to exhibit and sell their wares. The fair includes shows for adults and children, and traditional food and drink. It's held at the beautiful Luis Muñoz Rivera Park in Puerta de Tierra and is sponsored by the government.

Las Mañanitas, Ponce. A religious procession that starts out from Lolita Tizol Street and moves toward the city's Catholic church, led by mariachis singing songs to honor Our Lady of Guadalupe, the city's patron saint. The lead song is the traditional Mexican birthday song, "Las Mañanitas." There's a 6am Mass. For more information, contact **Ponce City Hall** (✆ **787/284-4141**). December 12.

Lighting of the Town of Bethlehem, between San Cristóbal Fort and Plaza San Juan Bautista in Old San Juan. This is the time that the most dazzling Christmas lights go on, and many islanders themselves drive into San Juan to see this dramatic lighting, the finest display of lights in the Caribbean at Christmas. During the Christmas season.

Hatillo Masks Festival, Hatillo. This tradition, celebrated since 1823, represents the biblical story of King Herod's ordering the death of all infant boys in an attempt to kill the baby Jesus. Men with colorful masks and costumes represent the soldiers, who run or ride through the town from early morning, looking for the children. There are food, music, and crafts exhibits in the town square. For more information, call ✆ **787/898-4040.** December 28.

SoFo Culinary Festival, Old San Juan. Held twice a year, in the summer and autumn, during which restaurants on La Fortaleza Street open their doors to offer food and live music. Mid-August and mid-December. Call San Juan Department of Tourism & Culture at ✆ **787/721-0169.**

Year-Round Festivals

In addition to the individual events described above, Puerto Rico has two yearlong series of special events.

Many of Puerto Rico's most popular events are during the **Patron Saint Festivals** (*fiestas patronales*) in honor of the patron saint of each municipality. The festivities, held in each town's central plaza, include religious and costumed processions, games, local food, music, and dance.

For more information about all these events, contact the **Puerto Rico Tourism Company** (✆ **800/866-7827** or 787/721-2400), La Princesa Building, Paseo La Princesa 2, Old San Juan, PR 00902.

For an exhaustive list of events beyond those listed here, check http://events. frommers.com, where you'll find a searchable, up-to-the-minute roster of what's happening in cities all over the world.

RESPONSIBLE TRAVEL

Puerto Rico is still struggling to find a balance between development and protecting its beautiful natural resources, a none-too-easy task on a small tropical island of 4 million residents.

Finding the right path towards sustainable development, however, is now a core concern of the tourism industry, government officials, and community and environmental groups. Gone are the days of uncontrolled beachfront development, constructing on flood zones, and allowing industry to flout environmental rules. Yet, there's a fierce debate over the specifics of the evolving sustainable development vision between environmental groups and development interests.

All sides, however, agree that protecting Puerto Rico's natural resources is essential to future prosperity. Hotels, restaurants, and tour operators have all taken note, and have introduced water conservation measures, green gardening techniques, increased use of locally grown produce, and guided tours given with a deep knowledge and respect of island culture and history. Water conservation, embracing greener forms of energy production, and protection of the island's coast and waterways are all current drives by broad sectors of island societies.

Visitors can help by visiting and supporting island nature reserves and beaches. Also, stay at a resort and play golf at a course that takes water-conserving gardening measures and recycles its waste water. Take a tour with a company that uses best

---

MORE sustainable TRAVEL RESOURCES

In addition to the resources for Puerto Rico listed above, the following websites provide valuable wide-ranging information on sustainable travel.

o **Responsible Travel** (www. responsibletravel.com) is a great source of sustainable travel ideas; the site is run by a spokesperson for ethical tourism in the travel industry. **Sustainable Travel International** (www.sustainable travelinternational.org) promotes ethical tourism practices, and manages an extensive directory of sustainable properties and tour operators around the world.

o **Carbonfund** (www.carbonfund. org), **TerraPass** (www.terrapass. org), and **Cool Climate** (http:// coolclimate.berkeley.edu) provide

info on "carbon offsetting," or offsetting the greenhouse gas emitted during flights.

o **Greenhotels** (www.greenhotels. com) recommends green-rated member hotels around the world that fulfill the company's stringent environmental requirements. **Environmentally Friendly Hotels** (www.environmentallyfriendly hotels.com) offers more green accommodation ratings.

o **Volunteer International** (www. volunteerinternational.org) has a list of questions to help you determine the intentions and the nature of a volunteer program. For general info on volunteer travel, visit **www.volunteerabroad.org** and **www.idealist.org**.

practices like focusing on local culture and the environment and economically benefits the community, like Acampa Nature Adventure Tours (www.acampapr.com). For more information, contact the Puerto Rico Hotel & Tourism Association (www.prhta.org), which is a member of the World Heritage Alliance (which promotes such cultural and environmental tourism) and promotes green practices by industry members. Another source is the government Puerto Rico Tourism Company (www.prtourism.com).

The Puerto Rico chapter of the Sierra Club (www.puertorico.sierraclub.org) is a great resource for environmental information on Puerto Rico, including marine corals, sea turtles, and endangered birds, and delivers up-to-the-minute news on current environmental battles, such as the drive to protect a miles-long stretch of beachfront between Luquillo and Fajardo known as the Northeast Ecological Corridor.

The website also has a large excursions and events section with information on fairs, turtle and rare Puerto Rican parrot trips, and visits to nature reserves. There is something going on every weekend.

Most of the site is in Spanish, except for the excellent section on the ongoing battle to preserve the Northeast Ecological Corridor (www.sierraclub.org/corridor), a nesting ground for endanger sea turtles that stretches across 7 miles of virgin white beachfront in the shadow of El Yunque Rainforest.

Animal lovers can give some love and help find new homes for dogs and cats rescued from the streets or abusive homes through the Save a Gato (cats; www.saveagato.org) or Save a Sato (dogs; www.saveasato.org) foundations. The groups are looking for volunteers to transport pets to new homes by taking them on flights back home. You can also adopt yourself, or just contribute to the groups' rescue efforts. As the proud padre of a bona-fide *sato* and *gato,* I'll argue they are the most loveable pets in the world.

SUGGESTED PUERTO RICO ITINERARIES

Puerto Rico may be a small island, but with its diverse geography and abundance of natural and cultural attractions, visitors rarely see all it has to offer, which takes some doing. You won't find a more vibrant city than San Juan, with its cutting-edge culinary and clubbing scenes; and its beaches (and year-round temperatures) put those of Miami and South Florida to shame. Puerto Rico is always warm, and it has those postcard perfect white-sand beaches lined with palm trees and sparkling blue sea that are the real draw for any visit to the Caribbean.

You can explore Old San Juan; discover that unspoiled beach town or remote mountain village; or go big-wave surfing, spelunking, or deep sea fishing. There are world-class performances and thriving locals arts and music scenes, as well as the most varied dining of any Caribbean destination. With all that going on, it will take some planning to get the most out of your stay, no matter how long that is.

We list a "Puerto Rico in 1 Week" tour and a "Puerto Rico in 2 Weeks" tour, for those with more time. Of course these itineraries can also be customized for shorter stays and special interests. If you've been to Puerto Rico before and have already visited San Juan and El Yunque, you'll find a number of new ideas, such as the pastoral Panoramic Route, the lure of the Spanish Virgin Islands, and the beaches of the west coast, from Guánica in the southwest through Isabela in the northwest.

Puerto Rico has an advanced highway system, but if you go the least bit off the beaten path (and sometimes you won't have much choice, if you want to see anything other than urban centers), you will venture on to some narrow, swooping rural highways offering difficult driving conditions. Take along a detailed road map, and remember to blow your horn as you turn dangerous curves in the mountains.

The itineraries that follow take you to some major attractions with some surprise discoveries. The pace may be a bit breathless, so skip a town or sight occasionally for some chill-out time—after all, you're on vacation.

One thing to keep in mind, you can base yourself out of San Juan for longer time periods, seeing much of the island in separate day trips from the capital. See chapter 1, "The Best of Puerto Rico," for some ideas.

Puerto Rico is a natural travel hub to the Caribbean, and too many visitors skip it altogether en route to other sun-bleached spots. There are, however, Caribbean connoisseurs who have combined their vacations with a few day layovers in San Juan for decades, and now love the city like an old friend, having come to know it a bit better over time. This is also another great way to experience Puerto Rico.

So remember, use any of these itineraries as jumping-off points for your own custom-made trip that more closely matches your interests or schedule.

THE REGIONS IN BRIEF

For a small island, Puerto Rico is a big place, with astounding geographic diversity squeezed into its 110×35-mile (177×56km) landmass. Beautiful beaches encircle its coastline, which fronts both the rough Atlantic, making for among the biggest waves in the region, and the tranquil waters of the Caribbean Sea, a sailor's and diver's paradise.

Puerto Ricans are great hosts, eager to entertain and intensely proud of their island's natural beauty, their culture, and their achievements as a people.

San Juan

The largest and best-preserved complex of Spanish colonial architecture in the Caribbean, Old San Juan (founded in 1521) is the oldest capital city under the U.S. flag. Once a lynchpin of Spanish dominance in the Caribbean, it has three major fortresses, miles of solidly built stone ramparts, a charming collection of antique buildings, and a modern business center. The city's economy is the most stable and solid in all of Latin America.

San Juan is the site of the official home and office of the governor of Puerto Rico (La Fortaleza), the 16th-century residence of Ponce de León's family, and several of the oldest places of Christian worship in the Western Hemisphere. Its bars, restaurants, shops, and nightclubs attract an animated group of fans. In recent years, the old city has become surrounded by densely populated modern buildings, including an ultra-modern airport, which makes San Juan one of the most dynamic cities in the West Indies.

The Northwest: Arecibo, Rio Camuy, Rincón & More

A fertile area with many rivers bringing valuable water for irrigation from the high mountains of the Cordillera, the northwest also offers abundant opportunities for sightseeing. The region's districts include the following:

AGUADILLA Christopher Columbus landed near Aguadilla during his second voyage to the New World in 1493. Today the town has a busy airport, fine beaches, and a growing tourism-based infrastructure. It is also the center of Puerto Rico's lace-making industry, a craft imported here many centuries ago by immigrants from Spain, Holland, and Belgium.

ARECIBO Located on the northern coastline a 2-hour drive west of San Juan, Arecibo was originally founded in 1556. Although little remains of its original architecture, the town is well known to physicists and astronomers around the world because of the radar/radio-telescope that fills a concave depression between six of the region's hills. Equal in size to 13 football fields and operated jointly by the National Science Foundation and Cornell University, it studies the shape and formation of the galaxies by deciphering radio waves from space.

RINCÓN Named after the 16th-century landowner Don Gonzalo Rincón, who donated its site to the poor of his district, the tiny town of Rincón is famous throughout

Puerto Rico for its world-class surfing and beautiful beaches. The lighthouse that warns ships and boats away from dangerous offshore reefs is one of the most powerful on Puerto Rico.

RIO CAMUY CAVE PARK   Located near Arecibo, this park's greatest attraction is underground, where a network of rivers and caves provides some of the most enjoyable spelunking in the world. At its heart lies one of the largest known underground rivers. Aboveground, the park covers 300 acres (121 hectares).

UTUADO   Small and nestled amid the hills of the interior, Utuado is famous as the center of the hillbilly culture of Puerto Rico. Some of Puerto Rico's finest mountain musicians have come from Utuado and mention the town in many of their ballads. The surrounding landscape is sculpted with caves and lushly covered with a variety of tropical plants and trees.

Dorado & the North Coast

Dorado, directly east of San Juan, is actually a term for a total of six white-sand beaches along the northern coast, reached by a series of winding roads. Dorado is the island's oldest resort town, home to storied golf courses, casinos, and resorts, the oldest of which is being transformed into a sumptuous Ritz Reserve property that perfectly suits its coastal plantation setting.

Several large hotel resorts have opened along the northwest of San Juan all the way down through Mayagüez. Rincón, Aguada, Aguadilla, and Isabella all have large hotels. The area offers beautiful beaches, natural wonders, and interesting attractions such as the Arecibo Observatory and the Río Camuy Cave Park.

The Northeast: El Yunque, a Nature Reserve & Fajardo

East of San Juan (see above) is a beautiful world of rain forest, stunning coastal waters, nature reserves, and posh resorts. Several world-class golf courses are located here, and there are ample sailing and watersports activities. It's home to both a rainforest and a bioluminescent bay, not to mention one of the largest leatherback turtle nesting areas on U.S. soil.

EL YUNQUE   The rainforest in the Luquillo Mountains, 25 miles (40km) east of San Juan, El Yunque is a favorite escape from the capital. Teeming with plant and animal life, it is a sprawling tropical forest (actually a national forest) whose ecosystems are strictly protected. Some 100 billion gallons of rainwater fall here each year, allowing about 250 species of trees and flowers to flourish.

FAJARDO   There are still small and sleepy areas of this town, founded as a supply depot for the many pirates who plied the nearby waters, but it has also grown up and is home to world-class resorts and attractions. There are several marinas in town, and the waters off its coast are a sailor's paradise, with beautiful offshore cays and coral reef.

LAS CABEZAS NATURE RESERVE   About an hour's drive from San Juan, this is an important and beautiful coastal natural reserve. Established in 1991 on 316 acres (128 hectares) of forest, it has mangrove swamp, offshore cays, coral reefs, freshwater lagoons, and a rare, bioluminescent bay—a representative sampling of virtually every ecosystem on Puerto Rico. There are a visitor center, a 19th-century lighthouse (El Faro) that still works, and ample opportunity to forget the pressures of urban life.

Puerto Rico

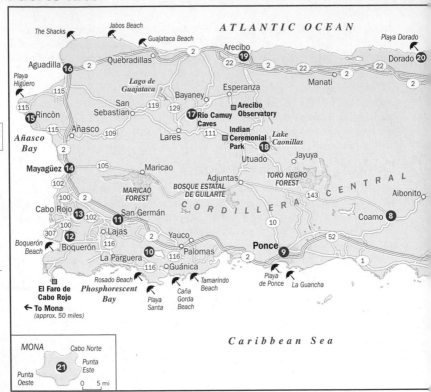

El Conquistador Resort & Golden Door Spa in Fajardo near Las Croabas, a fishing village on the northeastern tip of Puerto Rico's north coast, has a commanding perch overlooking the place where the Atlantic and Caribbean meet.

It has a water park and private island paradise with sandy beaches and recreational facilities. Challenging El Conquistador are the Rio Mar and Gran Melía properties in Río Grande, which are also top-of-the-line resorts.

The Southwest: Ponce, Mayagüez, San Germán & More

One of Puerto Rico's most beautiful regions, the southwest is rich in local lore, civic pride, and natural wonders.

BOQUERON Famous for the beauty of its beach and the abundant birds and wild-life in a nearby forest reserve, this sleepy village is now ripe for large-scale tourism-related development. During the early 19th century, the island's most-feared pirate, Roberto Cofresi, imperiled the residents' lives along the Puerto Rican coastline from a secret lair in a cave nearby.

CABO ROJO Established in 1772, Cabo Rojo reached the peak of its prosperity during the 19th century, when immigrants from around the Mediterranean, fleeing

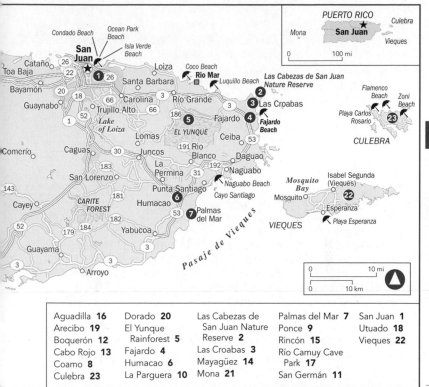

Aguadilla **16**	Dorado **20**	Las Cabezas de San Juan Nature Reserve **2**	Palmas del Mar **7**	San Juan **1**
Arecibo **19**	El Yunque Rainforest **5**		Ponce **9**	Utuado **18**
Boquerón **12**			Rincón **15**	Vieques **22**
Cabo Rojo **13**	Fajardo **4**	Las Croabas **3**	Río Camuy Cave Park **17**	
Coamo **8**	Humacao **6**	Mayagüez **14**		
Culebra **23**	La Parguera **10**	Mona **21**	San Germán **11**	

revolutions in their own countries, arrived to establish sugar-cane plantations. Today, cattle graze peacefully on land originally devoted almost exclusively to sugar cane, and the area's many varieties of exotic birds draw bird-watchers from throughout North America. Even the offshore waters are fertile; it's estimated that nearly half of all the fish consumed on Puerto Rico are caught in waters near Cabo Rojo.

LA PARGUERA   Named after a breed of snapper *(pargos)* that abounds in the waters nearby, La Parguera is a quiet coastal town best known for the phosphorescent waters of *La Bahía Fosforescente* (Phosphorescent Bay). Here, sheltered from the waves of the sea, billions of plankton (luminescent dinoflagellates) glow dimly when they are disturbed by movements of the water. The town comes alive on weekends, when crowds of young people from San Juan arrive to party the nights away. Filling modest rooming houses, they temporarily change the texture of the town as bands produce loud sessions of salsa music.

MAYAGÜEZ   The third-largest city on Puerto Rico, Mayagüez lies on the middle of the west coast, with beautiful beach areas to its north and south. While the city lacks its own beach, it is home to a few top quality hotels and has numerous attractions, including a zoo and botanical garden, so it's a good place to explore the west coast. Its history of disaster—including a great fire in 1847 and a 1918 tsunami—has allowed the city to forge a unique architectural identity, a blending of the distinct styles in vogue during the different eras of rebuilding the city has undergone throughout its history. The city has a beautiful waterfront park and promenade near the renovated historic district surrounding Plaza Colón, its main square that has a monument to Christopher Columbus. The town is known as the commercial and industrial capital of Puerto Rico's western sector and has a large University of Puerto Rico campus, which also helps spark the local cultural and entertainment scene.

PONCE   Puerto Rico's second-largest city, Ponce has always prided itself on its independence from the Spanish-derived laws and taxes that governed San Juan and the rest of the island. Long-ago home of some of the island's shrewdest traders, merchants, and smugglers, it is enjoying a renaissance as citizens and visitors rediscover its unique cultural and architectural charms. Located on Puerto Rico's southern coast, about 90 minutes by car from the capital, Ponce contains a handful of superb museums, one of the most charming main squares in the Caribbean, an ancient cathedral, dozens of authentically restored Colonial-era buildings, and a number of outlying mansions and villas that, at the time of their construction, were among the most opulent on the island.

SAN GERMÁN   Located on the island's southwestern corner, small, sleepy, and historic San Germán was named after the second wife of Ferdinand of Spain, Germaine de Foix, whom he married in 1503. San Germán's central church, Iglesia Porta Coeli, was built in 1606. At one time, much of the populace was engaged in piracy, pillaging the ships that sailed off the nearby coastline. The central area of this village is still sought out for its many reminders of the island's Spanish heritage and colonial charm. With a large university and historic district, and its ideal location, the town is beginning to wake up to its tourism potential after a long sleep. Several fine restaurants have opened recently, and the pace of renovation in the old district is on the rise.

The Southeast: Palmas del Mar & More

Southeastern Puerto Rico has large-scale tourism developments but is also home to the island's wildest and least developed coastline, which runs from Guayama—which has one of the most picturesque town centers on the island—to the steep cliff sides of Yabucoa.

COAMO   Although today Coamo is a bedroom community for San Juan, originally it was the site of two different Taíno communities. Founded in 1579, it now has a main square draped with bougainvillea and one of the best-known Catholic churches on Puerto Rico. Even more famous, however, are the mineral springs whose therapeutic warm waters helped President Franklin D. Roosevelt during his recovery from polio. The springs were also said to inspire the legend of the Fountain of Youth, which in turn set Ponce de León off on his vain search for them, leading him north to Florida.

HUMACAO   Because of its easy access to San Juan, this small, verdant inland town has increasingly become one of the capital's residential suburbs.

PALMAS DEL MAR   This sprawling vacation and residential resort community outside Humacao has great golf, tennis, and other amenities. The Equestrian Center at Palmas is the finest riding headquarters in Puerto Rico, with trails cutting through an old plantation and jungle along the beach.

Called the "New American Riviera," Palmas del Mar has 3 miles (4.8km) of white-sand beaches and sprawls across 2,800 acres (1,133 hectares) of a former coconut plantation—now devoted to luxury living and the sporting life. There are several different communities within Palmas, with both luxury homes and townhouses, as well as hotels and time share and vacation club rentals. The resort is ideal for families and has a supervised summer activities program for children ages 5 to 12.

The Offshore Islands: Culebra, Vieques & More

Few *norteamericanos* realize that Puerto Rico is host to two offshore island towns, which are among the most beautiful and, until recently, undiscovered locations in the Caribbean. Neither Vieques nor Culebra has a traffic light or fast food restaurant, and neither is likely to get either soon, despite the world-class lodging and tourist facilities beginning to appear on both islands, which have become known as the Spanish Virgin Islands.

Puerto Rico also has several islands within its jurisdiction that are intriguing nature reserves.

CULEBRA & VIEQUES   Located off the eastern coast, these two islands are among the most unsullied and untrammeled areas in the West Indies, even though Vieques is being belatedly discovered. Come here for sun, almost no scheduled activities, fresh seafood, clear waters, sandy beaches, and teeming coral reefs. Vieques is especially proud of its phosphorescent bay, Mosquito Bay, which is among the world's best. Each island town has miles of coastline and sailing and snorkeling offshore. Although the sister Spanish Virgin Islands remain laid back, they have become increasingly sophisticated in lodging and dining options, which today are top-notch.

MONA   Remote, uninhabited, and teeming with bird life, this barren island off the western coast is ringed by soaring cliffs and finely textured white-sand beaches. The island has almost no facilities, so visitors seldom stay for more than a day of swimming and picnicking. The surrounding waters are legendary for their dangerous eddies, undertows, and sharks.

Much closer to the coast, just off Rincón, is **Desecheo,** another nature reserve with great beaches and great diving offshore.

CAYO SANTIAGO   Lying off the southeastern coast is the small island of Cayo Santiago. Home to a group of about two dozen scientists and a community of rhesus monkeys originally imported from India, the island is a medical experimentation center run by the U.S. Public Health Service. Monkeys are studied in a "wild" but controlled environment. They provide scientific researchers both insight into their behavior, as well as a source of experimental animals for medical research into such maladies as diabetes and arthritis. Visitors are barred from Cayo Santiago, but you can often glimpse the resident primates if you're boating offshore.

PUERTO RICO IN 1 WEEK

If you budget your time carefully, you can see some of the major highlights of Puerto Rico in just 1 week. Naturally, most of your time will be spent in **San Juan,** the capital, but you'll also have time to visit **El Yunque** (a rainforest) and a beautiful beach, probably **Luquillo** right to the east. There also will be time for days spent in **Ponce,** Puerto Rico's second city, the beautiful beaches of the southwest, the historic town of **San Germán,** and a side trip to an offshore island or the northwest coast. *Start: San Juan.*

Days 1 & 2: San Juan ★★★

Take a flight that arrives in San Juan as early as possible on **Day 1.** Check into your hotel and, if it's sunny, head for the pool or beach directly, stopping only for maybe a pick-me-up coffee and a pastry to go. As surely as there will be hours of sunshine every day on your trip here, at certain times of the year, it can also cloud

Suggested Puerto Rico Itineraries

The Best of Puerto Rico in 1 Week

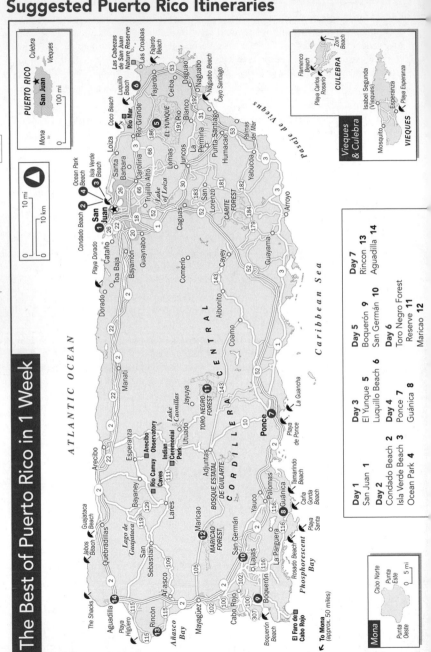

Day 1
San Juan **1**

Day 2
Condado Beach **2**
Isla Verde Beach **3**
Ocean Park **4**

Day 3
El Yunque **5**
Luquillo Beach **6**

Day 4
Ponce **7**
Guánica **8**

Day 5
Boquerón **9**
San Germán **10**

Day 6
Toro Negro Forest
Reserve **11**
Maricao **12**

Day 7
Rincón **13**
Aguadilla **14**

The Best of Puerto Rico in 2 Weeks

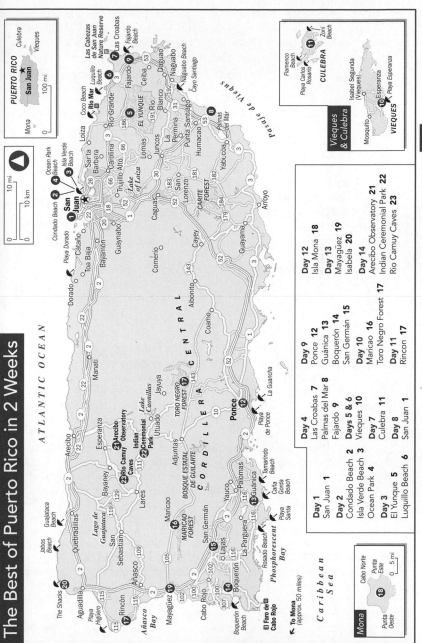

SUGGESTED PUERTO RICO ITINERARIES | Puerto Rico in 1 Week

Day 1
San Juan **1**

Day 2
Condado Beach **2**
Isla Verde Beach **3**
Ocean Park **4**

Day 3
El Yunque **5**
Luquillo Beach **6**

Day 4
Las Croabas **7**
Palmas del Mar **8**
Fajardo **9**

Days 5 & 6
Vieques **10**

Day 7
Culebra **11**

Day 8
San Juan **1**

Day 9
Ponce **12**
Guánica **13**
Boquerón **14**
San Germán **15**

Day 10
Maricao **16**
Toro Negro Forest **17**

Day 11
Rincon **17**

Day 12
Isla Mona **18**

Day 13
Mayagüez **19**
Isabela **20**

Day 14
Arecibo Observatory **21**
Indian Ceremonial Park **22**
Rio Camuy Caves **23**

up for a few hours, so we always recommend enjoying the sun while it's shining (even if it's for an hour or so).

After a quick swim and some sunshine, you can still spend the afternoon in Old San Juan, enjoying some sightseeing and shopping. A 2-hour walking tour covers the important churches, forts, and other highlights. Add another hour or so because you'll want to shop while you explore, and probably stop for refreshment—a rum drink or fresh fruit frappe—at one of the Old City's famous watering holes. The city is also one of the shopping meccas of the Caribbean, with bargains galore, lots of local arts and crafts, and high-profile retail shops.

Visit one of the area's many fine cafes and restaurants for an early dinner. Then return to your hotel for an early evening and a well-deserved rest.

On **Day 2,** with shopping and sightseeing behind you, prepare for a full day in the sun. Most hotel and resort pools are great, and the beaches in San Juan are glorious white-sand, turquoise-water affairs. For many visitors, that's why they came to San Juan in the first place. Depending on the location of your hotel, the finest beaches are **Condado Beach** (p. 101), **Isla Verde Beach** (p. 101), and **Ocean Park Beach** (p. 101). Enjoy the watersports activities along the beaches of the Greater San Juan area. See the "Diving, Fishing, Tennis & Other Pursuits" section, beginning on p. 100. Of course, there's nothing wrong with spending a day at the beach.

Make it a point tonight to enjoy some of the nightlife of the capital, either bar-hopping, taking in the club or music scene, or going casino gambling. San Juan is one of the nightlife capitals of the Caribbean. There's likely a lot going on right around your hotel; Old San Juan, Condado, and Isla Verde are centers of activity. See the "San Juan Nightlife" section, beginning on p. 117.

Day 3: El Yunque ★★★ & Luquillo Beach ★★★

While still based in San Juan, drive east for 25 miles (40km) to **El Yunque** for a morning visit. This 28,000-acre (11,331-hectare) attraction is the only tropical rainforest in the U.S. National Forest Service system. Stop first at **El Portal Tropical Forest Center** (p. 127) for maps and guidance. You're faced with a choice of hiking trails or else driving through. Unless you engage in extensive hiking, you can see some of the forest's greatest beauty in time for lunch.

After a visit to the rainforest, head north toward the town of Rio Grande and follow the signs to **Luquillo Beach** in the east. There are many roadside signs and kiosks where you can enjoy a tasty but inexpensive lunch. Shaded by tall coconut palms, the beach is crowded on weekends. Surfing, kayaking, diving, and snorkeling are just some of the activities you can enjoy here, along with the golden sands of the beach itself. There are also refreshment stands and a bathhouse, as well as toilets. Return west to San Juan for a final night.

Days 4 & 5: Ponce & the Southwest Coast ★★

Leave San Juan on the morning of **Day 4** and drive 75 miles (121km) southwest to the city of **Ponce,** the island's "second city." Take Route 1 south to Highway 52, and then continue south and west to Ponce, following the road signs. Allow at least 1½ hours for the drive. Once in Ponce, check into a hotel for 2 nights.

For orientation and to see the historic city, see "Ponce," on p. 145, which includes a stopover at **Parque de Bombas,** the famous firehouse, on the city's gorgeous central plaza. You can spend another few hours strolling through the historic downtown, visiting museums and cathedrals. Another of Ponce's chief attractions, which can easily absorb 2 hours of your time, is the **Museo de Arte de Ponce,** which recently underwent a beautiful makeover. (p. 151).

After some shopping and a local lunch in the old town, continue on one of the beach towns to the west, along Route 116: **Guánica, La Parguera,** or **Boquerón.** Heading to the coast today will mean more time for fun in the sun the next day because Ponce has no real beach. The only reason to stay in Ponce is to go out for a great meal and enjoy the entertainment at the **Ponce Hilton,** maybe squeezing in a round of golf or some pool time in the afternoon before dinner. (If it's a weekend, there could be a concert at the nearby **La Guancha,** a public marina and boardwalk where harborfront restaurants serve up local treats and drinks.)

Guánica's three lodging options—**Copamarina Beach Resort, Mary Lee's By the Sea,** and **Hotel 1812**—are among the best in their class for the region, and the town has seven spectacular beaches. La Parguera and Boquerón arc considered the "Cape Cod of Puerto Rico," with ample simple, clean lodging options, from small hotels to guesthouses.

If you head out of Ponce on Day 4, you will also be able to spend 2 hours in the afternoon exploring the **Guánica State Forest,** the best-preserved subtropical ecosystem on the planet. There are 750 plants and rare tree species that grow here, and many trails descend to the beautiful coastline. Grab a fresh seafood meal at a local restaurant by your hotel, which may be accompanied by live music.

On **Day 5,** you'll want to head to the beach because the finest on the island are all around you. In Guánica, go to **Caña Gorda** or **Playa Santa;** your best bet in La Parguera is to take a boat to **Mata La Gata** islet offshore, while the public beach at Boquerón has tranquil waters, white sand, and a healthy grove of palm trees running behind the beach.

In the afternoon, take a drive to the historic city of San Germán or farther on to Mayagüez. Make sure to drive by **El Faro de Cabo Rojo,** a lighthouse at Puerto Rico's southernmost corner, for a look. It's on a dramatic, blissfully isolated coastal perch.

In San Germán, the town's major attractions, including **Iglesia Porta Coeli** and **San Germán de Auxerre,** are in its historic downtown, a beautiful array of Spanish colonial and turn-of-the-20th-century buildings. If you go to Mayagüez, visit its beautiful downtown plaza, and then either its zoo or botanical gardens. Have dinner before heading back to your hotel.

Day 6: Mountain Retreat ★★

It's time to head up to the mountains, because you can't spend a week in Puerto Rico without spending a night at one of its country mountain retreats.

You can visit the **Toro Negro Forest Reserve** (p. 166), a 7,200-acre (2,914-hectare) park straddling the highest peak of the Cordillera Central, north of Ponce. Visit Lake Guineo or take a hike to the beautiful Juanita waterfalls. You should also have time to visit the other area forest reserve, **Monte Estado State Forest** in Maricao. There are fine country inns near both reserves. Most also offer traditional Puerto Rican fare. Have a restful night in the clean mountain air.

Day 7: Rincón & the Northwest ★★★

Get up early and begin driving up the west coast north of Mayagüez to **Rincón.** After checking in at a hotel, hit one of the town's famous beaches. If you surf or windsurf, today's the day for it because you are in the surfing capital of the

Puerto Rico in 1 Week

Caribbean. If it's summer, and the surf is down, then the snorkeling is great. Most hotels and guesthouses have fine pools as well.

If it's winter, consider spending some time whale-watching, as it's the season they breach right offshore. It's also possible to rent a boat to take you to **Desecheo Island** (just offshore) or the much longer trek to **Mona Island,** some 40 miles off the coast. Called "the Galápagos of the Caribbean," the island is inhabited by giant iguanas and three species of endangered sea turtles, among other rare plant, animal, and marine life. (If you want to squeeze this in on a 1-week trip, it would be best to eliminate the mountain retreat or the second day in the southwest.)

Rincón has a number of fine bars and restaurants, with great food and live entertainment. So make sure you have a great meal and some fun on your final night. And you'll want to be sure to watch the sun go down, which is a beautiful thing on the west coast of Puerto Rico.

The following morning, you'll find that it's only a 98-mile (158km) drive northeast back to San Juan, the hub of all the island's major transportation. The nearby Aguadilla airport, however, also has international flight service, so you could squeeze in some more beach time or another attraction (say the **Camuy Caves** or the **Arecibo Observatory**) if you do not have to return to San Juan before flying out.

PUERTO RICO IN 2 WEEKS

This tour, the longest in this chapter, is also the most recommended. It encapsulates the very essence of the island—it's "Puerto Rico in a Nutshell." Because of the island's small size, you can visit not only its three major cities (**San Juan, Ponce,** and **Mayagüez**) but also its greatest attraction, the **El Yunque** rainforest; its finest beach, **Luquillo;** its offshore islands, **Vieques** and **Culebra;** and even its most intriguing man-made attractions, such as the alien-hunting **Arecibo Observatory.** To start, follow the first 3 days of the "Puerto Rico in 1 Week" itinerary above (San Juan on Days 1 and 2, El Yunque and Luquillo Beach on Day 3), then head to Las Croabas to begin Day 4. *Start: San Juan.*

Days 1, 2 & 3: San Juan, El Yunque ★★★ & Luquillo Beach ★★★

Follow the first 3 days of the "Puerto Rico in 1 Week" itinerary above.

Day 4: Las Croabas & Palmas del Mar

The northeast corner of Puerto Rico is a water- and sports-enthusiast's dream, with sailing, golf, and all sorts of outdoor pursuits. It's not cheap, but it's worth every cent to check into **El Conquistador Resort & Golden Door Spa** (p. 195) for the day, taking advantage of its vast array of facilities and restaurants, as well as its water park, health club, spa, children's programs, and watersports equipment.

Using the resort as a base, you can explore **Las Cabezas de San Juan Nature Reserve** (p. 193), with its famous lighthouse, "El Faro," and untrammeled tropical forest and beaches. There's a marina on site and several more in town, including the **Puerto del Rey** (the Caribbean's largest and most modern marina). There a beautiful white-sand, public beach, **Playa Seven Seas,** and a short hike from here is **Playa Escondido (Hidden Beach)** and **Playa El Convento,** the start of a

7-mile undeveloped strip of land. See p. 194 for more coverage of these sandy strips.

The resort has several fine restaurants, and the village of Los Croabas, a quaint fishing port, has several simple but high-quality seafood restaurants.

Another option would be to continue driving south along the east coast to **Humacao** and the nearby resort of **Palmas del Mar,** where you can participate in the best-organized sporting activities in eastern Puerto Rico, ranging from vast tennis courts to scuba diving and golf, along with deep-sea fishing (see coverage beginning on p. 199). Palmas also has 3 miles (4.8km) of exceptional white-sand beaches, all open to the public. There are also a large number of places for lunch and dinner at the resort and a good, affordable seafood restaurant serving freshly caught fish.

If you can't afford the prices of these large resorts, there are several smaller inns throughout this area, from Luquillo to Naguabo.

Days 5 & 6: Vieques ★

Regardless of where you are based for the night, arrive early at the port of Fajardo on Puerto Rico's eastern coast for a 1-hour ferryboat ride to the island of **Vieques,** the largest of the so-called Spanish Virgin Islands (it is, in fact, a U.S. territory). Check into a hotel here for 2 nights. Resorts and small inns come in all price ranges (coverage of hotels begins on p. 208).

A stopover in Vieques might be the most idyllic spot in your vacation, as the island offers 40 beautiful, white-sand beaches, all open to the public. See **"Beaches,"** with coverage beginning on p. 214. Lazy days in the sun aren't the only activities on the island. You can tour the luminous waters of **Phosphorescent Bay,** join mountain-bike excursions, go fishing from a kayak, take snorkeling trips, or go scuba diving. **Fort Conde de Mirasol Museum** (p. 216) is an interesting museum housed in a historic fort, and federal authorities operate two wildlife refuges on former military lands. At night, Vieques offers a wide range of bars and good restaurants, the best available on any of Puerto Rico's offshore islands.

Day 7: Culebra ★

From Vieques, you can also ferry or fly over to close-by Culebra, which is far more offbeat and undiscovered than Vieques. Though still undeveloped, Culebra facilities have seen substantial upgrades in recent years, and there are many more quality rooms available over the last few years.

Like Vieques, Culebra is chock-full of white-sand beaches, and you can explore the **Culebra Wildlife Refuge** (p. 218). Also snorkel here, or kayak, fish, sail, or hike. The best way to explore the island is to rent and drive a jeep—although most visitors prefer to hang out for the day on one of Culebra's beaches. The main beach is the mile-long (1.6km) **Flamenco Beach,** an arcing cove with vibrant water and clean sand. The next morning, return by ferry to the port of Fajardo for a continuation of the tour.

Day 8: San Juan ★★★

On the morning of **Day 8,** leave Culebra by flying back to San Juan for an overnight stopover. Because the city is so vast and so filled with amusements, try to use the time to mop up all the shopping, attractions, and nightlife options you missed on your first visit. See chapter 6 for all the possible options, including outdoor pursuits, awaiting you.

Day 9: Ponce & the Southwest ★★

On the morning of **Day 9,** leave San Juan and drive south to Ponce, the chief city on the southern coast. Follow the suggestions as outlined in Day 4 and Day 5 of "Puerto Rico in 1 Week" (see above).

Day 10: Mountain Retreat ★★

Follow the suggestions for Day 6 of "Puerto Rico in 1 Week," above.

Day 11: Rincón & the Northwest ★

For suggestions, refer to Day 7 in "Puerto Rico in 1 Week," above. However, save a separate day for Isla Mona (see below), which richly deserves it.

Day 12: Isla Mona ★★★

Boat excursions over to this island are not as organized as they should be, but it's worth the trouble to get to Mona, even enduring a difficult sea crossing across Pasaje de la Mona. Coverage begins on p. 173. Most visitors use Mayagüez (covered earlier) as their base for exploring Mona Island, returning to the mainland for the night. Other, more adventurous travelers camp out on the island. Lying some 50 miles (80km) off the Puerto Rican mainland, Mona has been called the Jurassic Park of the Caribbean.

A nature reserve since 1919, Mona has been uninhabited for the past half-century except for day-trippers. Every species from fish-eating bats to wild goats and pigs live here. And of course, the giant iguanas. The environment is beautiful, but potentially hostile because of its wildness. Department of Natural and Environmental Resources rangers are on hand to offer advice and guidance. There are toilets and saltwater showers at Playa Sardinera, but visitors need to bring fresh water. You can go camping, but the itinerary assumes you'd rather return to the comfort of a hotel room in Mayagüez.

Day 13: Mayagüez & the Northwest

Squeeze in some chill time by the pool in this west-coast suburban city. Go explore the beautifully restored downtown area. Highlights include the elegant central **Plaza Colón,** dominated by a monument of Christopher Columbus, surrounded by 16 bronze statues of courtly ladies, and the historic **Yaguez Theater, City Hall,** and **Post Office.** Two huge fires and an earthquake at the turn of the 20th century destroyed much of the city three different times, but there's much fine architecture from the 1920s and later.

You'll also want to visit the city's zoo, **Puerto Rico National Parks Zoo,** or its **Tropical Agriculture Research Station** (p. 171), next to the Mayagüez Campus of the University of Puerto Rico. Anyone can walk through this site for botanical research, whose grounds feature towering bamboo, wild fruit trees, and the various plant species grown here.

After lunch, as you head north out of the city, drive by its historic harbor and warehouse district with a restored Customs House from the 1920s.

You'll be going to the beautiful towns of the northwest coast, most probably **Isabela** (p. 185), with abundant affordable lodging options right near the coast, about 30 miles (48km) north. It's so close, you'll have time for a quick swim at whatever beach is right outside your hotel or at its pool. There are no bad beaches here.

A kind of alternative-lifestyle vibe accompanies the town's surf culture, so the young and young at heart will find great entertainment and live music at area bars.

Day 14: Arecibo ★, Indian Ceremonial Park & Rio Camuy Caves ★★★

As you head east for your return to San Juan, you can take in three wonders of Puerto Rico. The **Observatorio de Arecibo** (p. 137), the world's largest and most sensitive radar/radio-telescope, searches the night sky for extraterrestrial life in the universe beyond. In Karst Country, the **Caguaña Indian Ceremonial Park** in Utuado (p. 142) was built by the Taíno Indians a thousand years ago. The grandest attraction of all, the **Rio Camuy Caves** (p. 138), contains the third-largest underground river in the world. With proper timing, all three of these attractions can be explored in 1 day, with time still left for the final drive back into San Juan. Arm yourself with a good map and explore the coverage of these attractions in chapter 7 before heading here.

Following your visits, continue to San Juan, at a distance of some 68 miles (109km) to the west. But remember, it's probably also possible to book a flight into San Juan and out of Aguadilla, especially during the winter high tourism season. Again, this would buy you another afternoon on the beach at Isabela.

SAN JUAN BASICS

All but a handful of visitors to Puerto Rico arrive in San Juan, the capital city. It is the political base, economic powerhouse, and cultural center of the island, home to about one-third of all Puerto Rico residents. With Isla Verde's palm-fringed aquamarine coast, the Spanish colonial romance of Old San Juan, and the modern elegance of Condado's oceanside boulevard, San Juan offers big-city fun and the pleasures of a tropical retreat. It takes in stride all it has to offer: postcard-perfect beaches, thriving arts and nightlife scenes, and sophisticated dining. A great place to party, it also has cultural treasures, such as the gothic San Juan Cathedral, or the gardens of Casa Blanca. Top sport-fishing grounds and surf breaks are right offshore.

4

THINGS TO DO Explore sentry-towers and dungeons at El Morro fortress, which rises above the swirling Atlantic from the rocky base of Old San Juan. Walk the old city's cobblestone streets, lined with Spanish colonial balconies dripping with bougainvillea, which are chock-full of cultural sites. Visit Puerto Rican masters Francisco Oller and Rafael Tufino at Santurce's Museo de Arte de Puerto Rico. Discover that life really is a beach here as you watch kiteboarders catch air at low-key Ocean Park or parasail above the beautiful crowd on Isla Verde's golden sands.

SHOPPING Old San Juan's narrow streets bustle with boutiques and funky shops, factory outlets, jewelry stores, and exclusive galleries. The city's local artwork is also on offer here, whether contemporary prints or antique *santos* wood carvings; it's competitively priced and top-notch quality. Plaza del Mercado, Santurce's traditional marketplace, sells tropical fruit, Santeria potions, and classic salsa and bolero recordings. Plaza las America, the Caribbean's largest shopping center, has Macy's, P. F. Chang's, and all the amenities of a village.

RESTAURANTS & DINING Be sure to taste *comida criolla's* (traditional Puerto Rican cuisine's) warm flavors at a San Juan *fonda* (basic restaurant), but there's more than tropical comfort food here. Peruvian ceviche houses, French bistros, and sushi emporiums blanket San Juan, home to the restaurants of celebrity chefs Wilo Benet, a "Top Chef" guest judge, and Roberto Trevino, an "Iron Chef" competitor, who take traditional Latino food to new heights. There's plenty to eat in the well-worn tourist areas, but much of the culinary action is in downtown Miramar and Santurce and the Hato Rey financial district.

NIGHTLIFE & ENTERTAINMENT   Nightlife starts late, with high-rollers rolling the dice in San Juan's casinos and Latin beats pulsing from beach bars along the city's golden coastline, which stretches from Condado through Isla Verde and beyond. In Old San Juan, head uphill along Calle Cristo to Calle San Sebastián for its famed mix of bohemian bars and cafes, with live Spanish pop and salsa music. To get into the clubs and discos, be sure to dress to impress. On Sunday nights, sip rum cocktails and watch the sun set over Old San Juan at the evocative Paseo de la Princesa, which winds along the city's main harbor.

ORIENTATION

The second-oldest city in the Americas (behind Santo Domingo in the Dominican Republic), the charming historic district Old San Juan has some of the best examples of Spanish colonial architecture in the hemisphere as well as stunning Art Deco and other types of buildings from the early 20th century. From La Fortaleza (the governor's mansion) to the two landmark Spanish forts to the Catedral de San Juan, the wonders of the city are all a short walk from each other.

New San Juan has its charms as well, particularly evident in its more storied residential architecture in Santurce, Miramar, and Río Piedras. The coastal areas are more modern, where parts of Condado and Isla Verde feel like a more intimate Miami Beach, with rows of luxury hotels and condominiums and fat golden beaches. The two main beach districts have low-key corners, however, and the residential Ocean Park community separates them. A few guesthouses are scattered amid the luxury homes fronting San Juan's best beach.

There are crime and traffic problems, and the effects of a long recession have taken their toll, with shuttered businesses and vacant, newly built luxury condominiums. Tourism is on the rise, however, and Puerto Rico is partially battling its economic challenges by offering well-heeled investors and retirees incredible tax breaks as well as vacation-property incentives and other attractions.

The waterfront district from Old San Juan to the Miramar Convention District is being renovated, with a bayside park on the edge of Old San Juan hosting attractions like the New York Trapeze School and regular concerts and other entertainment events. With a light-rail train system, bus and ferry lines, a coliseum, and a state-of-the-art convention center, San Juan is moving toward the future. New projects promise to take the mass transit line farther west along the northern coast and farther into metropolitan San Juan, connecting the financial district with the urban downtown Santurce area, the developing Convention District, and onward to Old San Juan.

Visitors can pretty easily live off the bus and Urban Train system and get where they want to go throughout the tourism districts of Isla Verde, Condado, and Old San Juan as well as the other main San Juan districts: Miramar, Santurce, Hato Rey, and Río Piedras. Taxis are plentiful and economically priced and are a must at night. Renting a car while staying in San Juan rarely makes sense.

Old San Juan is a 7-square-block area that was once completely enclosed by a wall erected by the Spanish centuries ago. The most powerful fortress in the Caribbean, this fortified city repeatedly held off would-be attackers. By the 19th century, however, it had become one of the Caribbean's most charming residential and commercial districts. Today, it's a setting for restaurants, shops, and a large concentration of art galleries and museums. Most of the major resort hotels are located nearby, along the Condado beachfront and at Isla Verde (see "Where to Stay," later in this chapter). But the Old City has several first-rate hotels and inns as well.

San Juan Orientation

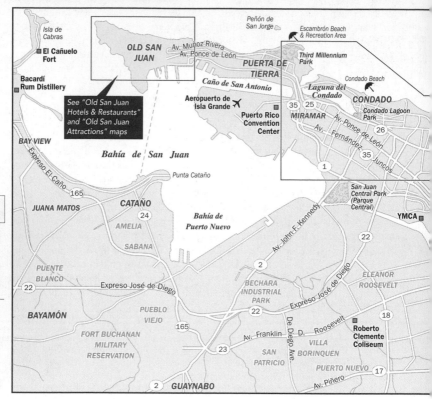

Arriving by Plane

Visitors from overseas arrive at **Luis Muñoz Marín International Airport,** the major transportation center of the Caribbean. The airport is on the easternmost side of the city, conveniently located near the Isla Verde, Condado, and Old San Juan tourist districts.

The airport offers such services as a tourist-information center, restaurants, hair stylists, coin lockers for storing luggage, bookstores, banks, currency-exchange kiosks, and bars. A number of shops sell souvenirs, local rums, and coffees for last-minute shopping for gifts for folks back home.

GETTING FROM THE AIRPORT TO THE CITY

BY TAXI   Some of the larger hotels outside San Juan send vans to pick up airport passengers and transport them back to the property, but they charge separately for this service. In San Juan, you'll probably opt to take a taxi to your hotel (buses at 75¢ are cheap but not very timely or practical). Dozens of taxis line up outside the airport to meet arriving flights, so you never have to wait. There are set fares for destinations within San Juan; for other destinations, the cost of the trip should be determined by the taxi meter. The island's **Puerto Rico Tourism Company** (**Transportation Division;** ✆ **787/999-2100** or 253-0418) establishes the flat rates between the Luis Muñoz Marín

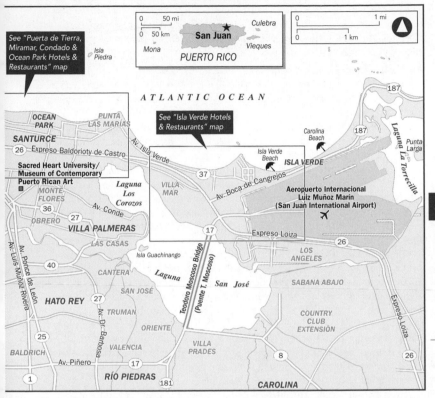

See "Puerta de Tierra, Miramar, Condado & Ocean Park Hotels & Restaurants" map

See "Isla Verde Hotels & Restaurants" map

4

SAN JUAN BASICS | Orientation

International Airport and major tourist zones: From the airport to any hotel in Isla Verde, the fee is $10; to any hotel in the Condado district, the charge is $15; and to any hotel in Old San Juan, the cost is $19. Taxi service from the airport is quite well regulated, with a dispatcher handing you a ticket detailing your costs. These also include baggage costs (50¢ for each of the first three bags, then $1 per bag), and a 10 to 15 percent tip is expected.

Travel time can vary widely, depending on traffic conditions, with late-afternoon and early morning traffic jams common during commuting hours Monday through Friday. With no traffic delays, Condado is only a 12-minute drive from the airport, but if you get stuck in one of the island's legendary *tapones,* as traffic jams are called here, it could take up to an hour. Old San Juan, the farthest destination, is about a 20-minute ride without traffic.

BY LIMOUSINE   There are more than enough reputable limousine rental companies to choose from, but arrangements must be made beforehand, since limousines don't sit at the airport like taxis. You must arrange pickup in advance, or call once you get in. A simple pickup from the airport to your hotel ranges in cost from $100 to $125. Most vehicles fit six passengers comfortably. Your driver will meet you outside the baggage-claim area.

BY PUBLIC CAR   Public cars, called *públicos,* are either vans or large sedans that are shared by passengers. The ride can sometimes be crowded and take longer the more passengers there are. They are a bargain for budget travelers who have to travel a distance from the airport and do not want to rent a car. It will cost you $20 to get to Ponce and $10 to Caguas, plus baggage fee. You'll probably have to take a public bus to pick up the público line, however.

BY CAR   All the major car-rental companies have kiosks at the airport. Although it's possible to rent a car once you arrive, your best bet is to reserve one before you leave home. They provide transportation to your car. See the "Getting Around" section of chapter 11 for details.

To drive into the city, head west along Route 26, or the Baldorioty de Castro Expressway, which cuts just south of San Juan's Atlantic coastline. Immediately to your right, you will see an Isla Verde exit, and soon the towering oceanfront condominiums of Isla Verde are visible to the right. The road cuts through the Santurce section at the heart of San Juan. You'll see exits for Condado. All hotels have parking lots open to the public, and several lots are visible from the main roads in the area—both Ashford Avenue and Isla Verde Avenue in Condado. The road then passes by the Condado Lagoon and crosses into Puerta de Tierra near the Caribe Hilton. The road at this point becomes Avenida Muñoz Rivera, as it passes a beautifully landscaped park of the same name on one side, followed by the El Escambrón public beach. The Third Millennium Park is on the opposite side. The road then climbs a bluff overlooking the Atlantic coastline, offering a dramatic view of waves crashing against the rocky shoals.

Here, you will pass the capitol building on your left, and then the historic Spanish fortress Fort San Cristóbal at the entrance of Old San Juan. If you continue straight down into the city along Calle San Sebastián, the northern border of Plaza Colón, you will find parking at **La Cochera** near Plaza de Armas, which is the closest to the center of the historic district. Another option is to turn right and take the northern coastal road to **Ballaja,** where there is parking. If you plan on visiting the San Sebastian Street area or El Convento hotel, these two options work best.

If you plan on hanging around the jumping SoFo section near La Fortaleza, you may want to head straight at the stop sign in front of Plaza Colón, taking the street that passes beside the Tapia Theater. Right behind the theater, where the road intersects with Calle Recinto Sur, is the large **Paseo Portuario** parking garage (© **787/722-2233**). Bear right for the entrance. Farther down the one-way street is the city-run **Doña Fela** parking garage (© **787/722-3558**), intersection Recinto Sur and Calle. Another option at Plaza Colón is to turn left at Plaza Colón as if exiting the city. Take your first two rights, which will turn you around again past the Treasury Building, and park your car in another **Covadonga Parking Garage** (© **787/721-6911**) on the left. Operating hours vary, but they are open at least until midnight during weekdays and 3am weekends. Prices vary, with municipal-run lots cheaper than private lots, but figure on paying $1 per hour at municipal lots and up to $3.50 at private lots.

BY BUS   Those with little luggage can take a bus at a cost of 75¢. You need to hop on the 40 or the 45, taking it one stop to Isla Verde. From there, you can take the 5, which runs through Isla Verde, swings towards Condado near Avenida de Diego, and then heads into Old San Juan. To go farther into the Condado, you should switch to 21 at the Parada 18, or Stop 18, bus transfer station, or get off at the Calle Loiza and Avenida De Diego stop and transfer there.

Visitor Information

The Puerto Rico Tourism Company office at **Luís Muñoz Marín Airport** (✆ **787/791-1014** or 787/721-2400, ext. 5216 or 5223) is open daily from 9am to 7pm. In Old San Juan, the Tourism Company operates an information center at La Casita, at Plaza de la Darsena, Old San Juan, near Pier 1, where the cruise ships come in (✆ **787/722-1709**). This office is open daily from 9am to 5:30pm.

City Layout

Metropolitan San Juan includes the walled Old San Juan at the end of a long peninsula, Puerta de Tierra, the narrow bridge of land between San Juan Bay and the Atlantic Ocean that connects the Old City with the rest of San Juan. You can take a bridge into Condado, a narrow strip of land between the ocean and a lagoon, or continue on to the beautiful residential Miramar neighborhood, where the once seedy waterfront section is being revamped into the world-class Convention Center District and related leisure development. The city also includes Santurce, its traditional downtown area, which has also been experiencing revitalization in recent years, with large theaters and old apartment buildings being polished up so that the sector is starting to shine again like it did in its 1940s heyday. The Hato Rey financial district has taken on an almost futuristic look with its elevated Tren Urbano and distinctive Puerto Rico Coliseum, which has something exciting going on just about every week. Río Piedras is both the site of the University of Puerto Rico and one of the best street markets in the Caribbean.

The Condado strip of beachfront hotels, restaurants, casinos, and nightclubs is separated from Miramar by a lagoon. Isla Verde, another resort area, is near the airport, which is separated from the rest of San Juan by an isthmus. Ocean Park is a charming residential neighborhood between the two that has a great beach.

FINDING AN ADDRESS   Finding an address in San Juan isn't always easy. You'll have to contend not only with missing street signs and numbers but also with street addresses that appear sometimes in English and at other times in Spanish. The most common Spanish terms for thoroughfares are *calle* (street) and *avenida* (avenue). When it is used, the street number follows the street name; for example, the El Convento hotel is located at Calle del Cristo 100, in Old San Juan. Locating a building in Old San Juan is relatively easy. The area is only 7 square blocks, so by walking around, it's possible to locate most addresses. Also, *sanjuaneros,* for reasons I've yet to determine, still use the stop numbers, or *paradas,* from a trolley that stopped running back in the 1950s as a reference point for directions. For example, *parada* 18 is at the heart of Santurce. In general, the higher the stop number, the farther its distance from Old San Juan.

STREET MAPS   "*¡Qué Pasa!,*" the monthly tourist magazine distributed free by the tourist office, contains accurate, easy-to-read maps of San Juan and the Condado that pinpoint the major attractions.

The Neighborhoods in Brief

Old San Juan   Home to among the hemisphere's finest restorations of Spanish colonial fortresses and buildings, the Old City is all the more beautiful for its dramatic location sprawled across a headland on the western end of an *isleta,* or peninsula that splits the roaring Atlantic Ocean from San Juan Bay. It's encircled by water; on the north is the Atlantic Ocean and on the south and west is the tranquil San Juan Bay. The historic Spanish wall built to hold off attacks still circles the city, which is filled with beautiful churches, shady plazas, majestic promenades, and wonderful residences and gardens. It's a robust cultural and commercial district with theaters, galleries, clubs, bars, and restaurants, and some of the most interesting shops in the region. There are fine lodgings with sundecks and pools, so you can work on your tan and stay in the city if that's your thing.

Puerta de Tierra Translated as "land gateway," Puerta de Tierra lies just east of the old city walls of San Juan. It is split by Avenida Ponce de León and interconnects Old San Juan with the Puerto Rican "mainland." Founded by freed black slaves, the settlement today functions as the island's administrative center and is the site of military and government buildings, including the capitol and various U.S. naval reserves. It is dominated by the green **Luis Muñoz Rivera Park,** and the oceanfront **Third Millennium Park** and adjacent **El Escambrón public beach.** Its southern end is home to a rough and tumble neighborhood with a few interesting eateries.

Miramar Miramar is an upscale residential neighborhood, with a small business district and a large port across San Juan Bay. It has two marinas where fishing boats and yachts lie at anchor. The whole harborside area is being redeveloped, spearheaded by the state-of-the-art Puerto Rico Convention Center and the Sheraton Puerto Rico Convention Center Hotel. Adjacent luxury retail, office, and residential units are scheduled, as government planners look to renovate the bayside coast all the way to Old San Juan. It's also the site of Isla Grande Airport, where you can board flights to the islands of Vieques and Culebra.

Santurce The historic downtown center is undergoing a revival, and now hosts some of San Juan's best museums and cultural attractions, most popular and cutting edge restaurants and nightspots, while offering traditional experiences like the central Plaza Mercado marketplace.

Condado Linked to Puerta de Tierra and Old San Juan by a bridge built in 1910, the Condado is back in vogue again, something it has been, off and on, since being known as

the "Riviera of the Caribbean," in the 1920s. It roared back to life in the 1960s and 1970s and has done so again today. Several restored hotels and other properties have undergone dazzling renovations along this district wedged between the Atlantic Ocean and the Condado Lagoon, with the most recent being the Legendary Vanderbilt Hotel in 2012. One of the most coveted neighborhoods in Puerto Rico, there are resort-style hotels and charming guesthouses tucked away along quiet streets and right on the beach.

The beautiful oceanfront **Window of the Sea Park** is at the center of the area; it opens onto the Atlantic Ocean and is fronted by gleaming townhouses and luxury towers, home to glamorous residences, restaurants, and designer fashion stores. These include Gucci and Salvatore Ferragamo, luxury condos, and Budatai, one of the island's best restaurants. The former La Concha has opened next door after a 10-year renovation, and luxury condos are being built in the former Vanderbilt hotel nearby. Luxury hotels and more modest guesthouses fill the sector, as do wonderful restaurants of all types.

One central road, **Avenida Ashford,** runs through Condado, which, at night especially, still evokes something of Miami Beach, with its restored Art Deco properties and modern luxury condos and hotels. The area is popular with locals, the gay community, and visitors.

Ocean Park Dividing the competitive beach resort areas of the Condado and Isla Verde, Ocean Park is a beachfront residential neighborhood with probably the prettiest and most low-key beach in San Juan. The beaches are wide here, and the sun beats down on the beach longer because there are few large condominiums. It's great for windsurfing and kite-sailing, games of paddle ball, and body surfing. The tree-covered streets are filled with beautiful suburban homes, a charming mix of Malibu, Spanish, and Caribbean influences.

The white, arching **Ultimate Trolley Beach** delineates the border between Ocean Park and Punta Las Marias. Adjacent to that, the neighborhood of **Santa Teresita,** with its share of equally stunning residences, has an equally nice park, **Barbosa Park.** The park is usually filled with soccer and basketball players. There are tennis courts, a baseball field, and a track, which are always a beehive of activity.

The beach disappears into a rock formation at **Punta Las Marías,** which is a gated community open to pedestrian visitors during the day. But unless you're a windsurfer using one of the neighborhood's famed launching points, your experience of the area will likely be confined to the **string of fine restaurants along Calle Loíza,** right before it turns into Avenida Isla Verde. The neighborhood is also popular with the gay and lesbian community, residents and visitors alike.

Isla Verde   East of the Condado, en route to the airport, Isla Verde—technically a part of the municipality of Carolina but in spirit more a part of San Juan—is larger than the Condado and probably has more hotels. Here there is also an oceanfront row of luxury condos and hotels along a main oceanfront boulevard. But where Condado may score higher with its restaurants, shops, and its older and more artful architecture, Isla Verde wins hands down in the beach department—you'll find a wide, clean, white-sand beach running the full length of the neighborhood just off its main strip. The main road here is called **Isla Verde Avenue. Pine Grove Beach,** a favorite with sailors and surfers, is located east of where the main beach ends. After Isla Verde is a municipal public beach and then the undeveloped area of **Piñones,** with its rural coastal charms.

Don't come here for history or romance. Two features put Isla Verde on the tourist map: some of San Juan's best beaches and its most deluxe hotels. This district appeals to travelers who like a hotel to offer everything under one roof: entertainment, vast selections of dining, convenient shopping, pools, and an array of planned activities.

Hato Rey   The city's financial district, the Wall Street of the West Indies, occupies several streets. There are high-rises, a large federal complex, and many business and banking offices.

The sector has been transformed by the **Puerto Rico Coliseum** and the **Tren Urbano,** which snakes through the towers of capitalism on elevated tracks. The new arena gets top acts (it's had the Rolling Stones, Paul McCartney, and Britney Spears). There's also the **Fine Arts Cinema,** with art and foreign films, luxury seats, gourmet food, and yes, beer and wine.

The sector also contains the huge **Luis Muñoz Marín Park,** with miles of cycling and jogging paths, picnic areas, and fields, interrupted by scores of small ponds and islands of tropical vegetation. The park also features a top-notch amphitheater and a cable car ride.

Río Piedras   South of Hato Rey and Santurce, this is the site of the **University of Puerto Rico,** whose buildings look like an Ivy League school except for the tropical vegetation. It's dominated by the landmark **Roosevelt Bell Tower,** named for Theodore Roosevelt, who donated the money for its construction. It's a top-notch institution than can boast beautiful grounds as an added attraction.

There's also a large shopping area surrounding the **Río Piedras Marketplace** (selling fresh fruit and vegetables) and the pedestrian walkway Paseo de Diego, lined with shops, eateries, and bargains galore. The shops attract travelers from across the Caribbean.

The **UPR Botanical Gardens** are located here as well, with a beautifully arranged array of tropical trees and plants.

Suburban San Juan   The San Juan sprawl has enveloped surrounding towns, reaching all the way down south into Caguas. Neighboring Bayamón, Guaynabo, and Carolina are practically considered part of the city, however. Guaynabo and Caguas have fine arts centers with top-name acts and full cultural performances, while Bayamón has such family activities as a bicycle linear park (a long, winding bike path along the Bayamón River) and the **Luis A. Ferré Science Technology Park.** Visitors will also likely go to Cataño to visit the **Bacardi Rum Plant.** It's a modest community built right across the bay from Old San Juban.

GETTING AROUND

BY TAXI   There is a flat-rate system for most destinations within San Juan, which is effective, and if you're caught in impenetrable traffic, it might actually work to your advantage. The island's **Puerto Rico Tourism Company (Transportation Division; ℰ 787/999-2100** or 253-0418) establishes flat rates between well-traveled areas within San Juan. From Luis Muñoz Marín International Airport to Isla Verde, $10; to Condado, $15; and to Old San Juan, $19.

There are also set fees from the cruise-ship piers outside of Old San Juan to set destinations: Isla Verde, $19; Condado, $12; and Old San Juan, $7. You will also be charged $1 per bag. Metered fares start off with an initial charge of $1.75, plus $1.90 per mile, and a 10¢ charge for each 25 seconds of waiting time. Tolls are not included in either fare. Normal tipping supplements of between 10 and 15 percent of these fares are appreciated.

But while meters are supposed to be used, on most trips outside the zoned rates, drivers will probably offer you a flat rate of their own devising. San Juan cabbies are loath to use the meter, more to do with ripping off the house or the taxman than the customer because more often than not, the quoted price is fair. But feel free to refer to the established flat rate (if it applies) or ask him to turn on the meter. Drivers normally comply immediately. If they refuse, you can get out and refer the driver to the Tourism Company Transportation Division numbers cited above. But if the quoted price seems fair (use the $19 flat rate for the airport to Old San Juan as a guide), it's probably easier to go ahead and pay it.

Taxis are invariably lined up outside the entrance to most of the island's hotels, but if they're not, a staff member can almost always call one for you. If you want to arrange a taxi on your own, some reliable operators in San Juan are **Metro Taxis** (ℰ **787/725-2870** or 725-3280), the **Rochdale Cab Company** (ℰ **787/721-1900**), and the **Major Cab Company** (ℰ **787/723-2460** or 723-1300).

You no longer have to negotiate a fare with the driver, usually at a flat rate, for trips to far-flung destinations within Puerto Rico. There are also now established fees for taxi rides from San Juan to island destinations. Some examples, from San Juan: Fajardo, $80; Ponce, $125; and Mayagüez, $160. The complete list is available at the Puerto Rico Taxi website (www.cabspr.com/tour.html).

BY BUS   The **Metropolitan Bus Authority** (ℰ **787/250-6064** for route information) operates buses in the greater San Juan area. Bus stops are marked by upright metal signs or yellow posts that say PARADA. The bus terminal is the dock area in the same building as the Covadanga parking lot next to the Treasury Department. Fares are 75¢.

Most visitors will find the bus service, comfortable, reliable and economic, but the MBA has a way to go in becoming a user-friendly enterprise. A big example is the differing information regarding Route Numbers posted on buses, official bus route maps and schedules (which are nearly impossible to find) and bus stops. The important thing to keep in mind is the bus route numbers. The lettered prefix is what is often marked differently. For example, the A5 and T5 are the same as the 5 bus route. A recent MBA route map discarded the lettered prefix, and we are doing the same, which seemed the most prudent course given the situation. However, be aware that the bus routes in this section will often be accompanied by lettered prefixes, either A, B, C or T, among others.

Beyond the discrepancies, officials were also considering schedule changes in late 2014. It's a good idea to check your itinerary with the driver or fellow passengers before boarding.

Three routes are particularly useful for tourists, those that carry San Juan passengers from Old San Juan to other San Juan tourism districts: The **5** goes to downtown Santurce, Ocean Park and Isla Verde; the **21** down Condado's Ashford Avenue and then on to downtown San Juan, the city's financial district Hato Rey and the Plaza Las Americas mall; and the **53,** which heads to the Convention Center District, then down Condado's oceanfront drive and on into Isla Verde. Call for more information about routes and schedules. The private **MetroBus** operates a few key express routes from Old San Juan to Río Piedras for 50¢.

Any bus marked ATI hooks up with the Tren Urbano, probably at its Sagrado Corazón Station, which is its last stop into the city. The Urban Train ticket cost 75¢ but officials are proposing to increase them to $1.50. Riders get one free transfer between the two systems per ticket.

ON FOOT   This is the only way to explore Old San Juan. All the major attractions can easily be covered in a day. If you're going from Old San Juan to Isla Verde, however, you'll need to rely on public transportation.

BY TROLLEY   When you tire of walking around Old San Juan, you can board one of the free trolleys that runs through the historic area. Departure points include the Covadonga, La Puntilla, Plaza de Armas, and the two forts, but you can board along the route by flagging the trolley down (wave at it and signal for it to stop) or by waiting at any of the clearly designated stopping points. Relax and enjoy the sights as the trolleys rumble through the old and narrow streets. The city has also begun operating a trolley along Loiza Street near Ocean Park, in Río Piedras and other areas.

BY LIMOUSINE   San Juan has nearly two dozen limousine rental companies, so there are more than enough reputable companies to choose from. There is a wide range of luxury vehicle rentals, called *limosinas* (their Spanish name), available, from Lincoln Town Car limousines to deluxe stretch Hummers. A simple pickup from the airport to your hotel ranges in cost from $100 to $125. Rentals for other standard trips range from about $70 to $125 per hour, with most cars seating six passengers comfortably. Many firms use drivers who hold tour-guide permits, and limousine operators often give tours of Old San Juan, El Yunque, or other sites to small groups or families. If the driver or another guide leaves the vehicle to tour a specific place by foot, it will cost another $15 to $25 hourly.

BY RENTAL CAR   See "Getting Around," in chapter 11, for details—including the benefits of car travel as well as the special challenges driving poses in Puerto Rico.

BY FERRY   The **Acuaexpreso** (© **787/494-0934**) ferry connects Old San Juan with the industrial and residential community of Cataño, across the bay. Ferries depart daily every 30 minutes from 6am to 9pm. The one-way fare to Cataño is 50¢. Departures are from the San Juan Terminal at Pier 2 in Old San Juan. However, it's best to avoid rush hours because hundreds of locals who work in town use this ferry. The ride lasts 6 minutes. Service on a second route between Old San Juan and the Hato Rey financial district has restarted with a $1 fare. Ferries run from 6:30am to 6:30pm Monday through Thursday and 6:30am to 8:30pm Friday through Sunday. The Hato Rey ferry terminal, adjacent to the Puerto Rico Coliseum and the Urban Train line, hosts popular bars and restaurants, as well as periodic concerts.

BY PUBLIC CAR   Public cars, called *públicos,* are either vans or large sedans that are shared by passengers. Though they can be crowded and uncomfortable, more often than not, they are quite comfortable and spacious. And they are a bargain for budget travelers who have to travel a distance from the airport and do not want to rent a car.

San Juan Mass Transit: Tren Urbano

Tren Urbano links San Juan to the Hato Rey financial district and Rio Piedras, home to the University of Puerto Rico, the Medical Center, and an increasing number of research and science facilities. It goes on to the western suburbs of Guaynabo and Bayamón. The system provides an easy mode of transportation through the most congested areas of metropolitan San Juan. During rush hour (5–9am and 3–6pm), the train operates every 8 minutes; otherwise, it runs every 12 minutes. There is no service daily from 11:20pm to 5:30am. The fare is 75¢ one-way and includes a transfer to buses. Officials proposed in late 2014 increasing the fare to $1.50 and cutting back service hours during non-peak hours and weekends. It's a beautiful ride and gives tourists a different experience of the city; the train passes on an elevated track through the modern, Hato Rey financial district, plunges underground in Río Piedras, and then snakes through upscale suburban neighborhoods, with tropical foliage and pools in many backyards. The fare includes a transfer because a special class of buses has been created to link up with particular Tren Urbano routes. The train and accompanying buses keep special expanded schedules during big events, such as festivals in Old San Juan. They also extend schedules when big acts play at the Puerto Rico Coliseum or big events take place at the Convention Center. The Metro Urbano, a bus rapid transport project, connects to Tren Urbano's westernmost station in Bayamón from suburbs farther west. For more information, call *©* **866/900-1284,** or log onto www.dtop.gov.pr/transporte_urbano/index.asp.

Most public cars travel set routes at prices far below what taxis would charge. You should consider taking one from the airport if you're traveling on a budget to areas outside of San Juan.

In San Juan, *público* departure and arrival points include the airport, right outside Old San Juan near Plaza Colón, and by the Río Piedras public marketplace. Every town on the island has at least one area where *públicos* congregate.

If you are traveling out on the island, you also can look them up in the telephone book and Yellow Pages under *la linea,* which are public cars that will pick you up where you are staying and bring you to a specific destination at an agreed-upon price. A 2-hour drive from San Juan to Guánica costs $25 one-way. Because you travel with other passengers, you may have to wait until the driver takes them to their destinations first. He will pick up and drop off passengers according to what is best for his route and schedule.

BY BIKE **Rent the Bicycle,** Calle Del Muelle, Capitolio Plaza 205, San Juan (*©* **787/602-9696**), is at the entrance of the Old San Juan bayside waterfront. They rent bikes for $27 per day ($17 for half a day) and also conduct several tours throughout San Juan ($39–$79). The two best are the Piñones and the San Juan city and beach tours. **Paradise Rentals** (in Old San Juan at Pier 2 and in Condado at Condado Village, 1214 Ashford Av.; *©* **787/413-2222**) rents electric bicycles, or E-bikes, which allow you to decide whether to pedal or not. Three hours costs $50, with each additional hour $15. Guided tours (Old San Juan for an extra $25) and self-guided audio tours (for an extra $15) are available. Bicycles are $35 per day and $10 per hour. Scooters cost $75 for 3 hours for the driver and an extra $35 per passenger.

[FastFACTS] SAN JUAN

Airport See "Arriving by Plane" and "Getting from the Airport to the City," earlier in this chapter.

American Express Call the company's local toll-free customer service line: © 800/327-1267.

Banks Local banks have branches with ATMs in San Juan that function on U.S. networks. Branches are open Monday to Friday 8:30am to 4pm, with select branches open Saturday 9am to noon. Bank branches in malls are open Saturday 8:30am to 6pm and Sunday 9am to 3pm.

Bus Information See "Getting Around," on p. 48. For information about bus routes in San Juan, call © 787/294-0500 or 250-6064.

Car Rentals See "Getting Around," in chapter 11. If you want to reserve after you've arrived in Puerto Rico, try Avis, Budget, or Hertz, or the local agencies Charlie Car Rental or Target Car Rental.

Consulates Many countries maintain honorary consulates here, mostly to try to drum up mutually beneficial trade on the island, but they can be of assistance to travelers. **Great Britain**'s consulate can be reached through (© 787/850-2400; britishconsulatesanjuan@yahoo.com). The consulate for **Canada** is at Av. Ponce de León 268, Ste. 1111, Hato Rey (© 787/759-6629; canadaprvi@aol.com),

and is open only by appointment. **Spain**'s consulate is located at Mercantil Plaza, 2nd floor, Av. Ponce de León, Hato Rey (© 787/758-6090; consulespana@isla.net), while the **Switzerland**'s consulate is at 816 Calle Dianam (© 787/977-0286; swiss consulate.pr@onelinkpr.net).

Currency Exchange The unit of currency is the U.S. dollar. Many large banks provide currency exchange at some branches, and you can also exchange money at the Luis Muñoz Marín International Airport. See "Money & Costs," in chapter 11.

Drugstores One of the most centrally located pharmacies is **Puerto Rican Drug Co.,** Calle San Francisco 157 (© 787/725-2202), in Old San Juan. It's open Monday to Friday from 7:30am to 9:30pm, Saturday 8am to 9:30pm, and Sunday 8:30am to 7:30pm. **Walgreens,** Av. Ashford 1130, Condado (© 787/725-1510), is open 24 hours. There are also other Walgreens throughout the city, one in practically every neighborhood. There are other locations in Old San Juan, Miramar, Isla Verde, and on Calle Loiza near Ocean Park. **CVS Pharmacy,** Paseo Gilberto Concepcion de Gracia 105 (© 787/725-2500), is located near the cruise-ship docks in Old San Juan and is open 7am to midnight daily. It also was about to

open a megastore at the Marriott Resort & Stellaris Casino in Condado, right across the street from Walgreen's megastore.

Emergencies In an emergency, dial © 911. Or call the local police (© 787/343-2020), fire department (© 787/343-2020), ambulance (© 787/766-2222), or medical assistance (© 787/754-2550).

Eyeglasses Services are available at **Pearle Vision Express,** Plaza Las Americas Shopping Mall (© 787/753-1033). Hours are Monday to Saturday from 9am to 9pm and Sunday from 11am to 5pm. **Tropical Vision,** Calle La Fortaleza 308 (© 787/723-5488), is located in Old San Juan.

Hospitals Ashford Presbyterian Community Hospital, Av. Ashford 1451 (© 787/721-2160), maintains a 24-hour emergency room.

Internet Access If you have a laptop or other wireless device, there are Internet hotspots throughout the city at food courts in malls, Starbucks, Burger King, McDonalds, and historic plazas in Old San Juan. Most hotels and guesthouses also have Wi-Fi service for guests.

Police Call © 787/343-2020 for the local police.

Post Office In San Juan, the **General Post Office** is at Av. Franklin Delano Roosevelt 585 (© 800/275-8777 or 787/622-1758). If you don't know your address in San Juan, you can ask that your mail be sent here "c/o General Delivery." This main branch is open Monday to Friday from 5:30am to 6pm, Saturday from 6am to 2pm. A letter from Puerto Rico to the U.S. mainland will arrive in about 3 to 4 days. See chapter 11, "Fast Facts," for more information.

Restrooms Restrooms are not public facilities accessible from the street. It's necessary to enter a hotel lobby, cafe, or restaurant to gain access to a toilet. Fortunately, large-scale hotels are familiar with this situation, and someone looking for a restroom usually isn't challenged during his or her pursuit.

Safety At night, exercise caution when walking along the back streets of San Juan, and don't venture onto the unguarded public stretches of the Condado and Isla Verde beaches at night. Few muggings take place in tourist areas, but the usual precautions exercised in any city apply at night.

Salons Most of San Juan's large resort hotels, including the Condado Plaza, the Marriott, and the Sheraton Old San Juan Hotel, maintain hair salons. Los Muchachos, in Old San Juan, has an army of stylists cutting and sprucing walk-in traffic as well as appointments.

Taxis See "Getting Around," earlier.

Telephone, Computer & Fax There are international call, Internet, and fax and mail services available at stores near the cruise-ship docks (catering mostly to crew). Long distance calling cards are widely available in drugstores and variety shops. For more information, see "Staying Connected," in chapter 11.

WHERE TO EAT

San Juan's fine dining scene is the most varied and developed in the Caribbean. City restaurants serve up excellent Spanish, French, American, Italian, Chinese, Mexican, and Asian cuisines. For more on Puerto Rican food, see "Eating and Drinking," in chapter 2.

While tasty Puerto Rican food has always been widely available on the island, in recent years, it has moved front and center, as many of the island's most talented chefs are bringing their native cuisine to new heights at some of its trendier eating establishments.

Yet a big part of the island's culinary appeal is its diversity. San Juan has some of the best steakhouses in the world (BLT Steak, the Palm, Morton's of Chicago, plus a number of superb local Latino steakhouses specializing in grilled meats). Seafood plays a big role in many restaurants, as expected, but what may surprise the visitor is the quality and variety of Asian, Lebanese, Arabian, and cutting-edge Peruvian restaurants there are, to name a few.

The resort hotels along Condado and Isla Verde house excellent restaurants, among them some of the island's finest. But you will miss out on some unique and memorable dining experiences if you don't search beyond the hotel establishments.

Spanish *panaderías,* or bakeries, have fresh baked goods, fat deli sandwiches, and traditional Spanish entrees such as *caldo gallego* and *arroz con pollo.* You get strong and tasty Puerto Rican coffee, fresh juices, and frappes as well. *Fondas,* basic restaurants with just a counter or a few tables, serve tasty local food at rock-bottom prices. The city is one of the fast-food capitals of the world, with all the familiar American brands, but also more obscure regional favorites. Street-food aficionados will also find solace in San Juan.

The restaurants listed in this chapter are classified first by area and then by price, using the following categories: **Expensive,** from $50 per person; **Moderate,** from $25 to $50 per person; and **Inexpensive,** under $25 per person. These categories reflect prices for an appetizer, a main course, a dessert, and a glass of wine.

For much more on Puerto Rico's food scene, see chapter 2.

Old San Juan

For the locations of Old San Juan restaurants, see the "Old San Juan Hotels & Restaurants" map, on p. 55.

EXPENSIVE

Aguaviva ★★ SEAFOOD   Sexy blue lighting, a floor patterned after ocean waves, lamps shaped like jellyfish: Yup, you've got an "under the sea" theme going here. But the restaurant's masterful designer has managed to make what could have been hokey "Little Mermaid" decor look hip and trendy. The food, too, is cutting edge, putting creative spins on classic Latin fish dishes. On the raw seafood front, you'll be cheating yourself if you don't get one of the ceviche tasting plates (we're big fans of the tomato mahi mahi and the tiger's milk prawns). The orzo paella is another stand-out, as is the grilled red snapper with *mofongo*. Wash it all down with a pitcher of watermelon sangria, and you'll be set. One warning though: If the fruit of the sea is not your thing, go elsewhere; Aguaviva serves few alternatives.

Calle Fortaleza 364. ✆ **787/722-0665.** Reservations not accepted. Main courses lunch $10–$30, dinner $17–$34. Lunch daily 11am–4pm; dinner Mon–Wed 6–11pm, Thurs–Sat 6pm–midnight, Sun 4–11pm. Bus: Old City Trolley.

Carli's Fine Bistro & Piano ★★★ INTERNATIONAL   Owner Carli Muñoz was a member of the Beach Boys from 1970 to 1981 (he has a gold record on the wall to prove it). He's also played piano with rock artists like Wilson Pickett, the Association, and Jan and Dean; and jazz greats like Charles Lloyd, Chico Hamilton and George Benson. These days Carli plays nightly at his bistro with a changing lineup of local musicians and visiting friends from across the globe. It's unique musical magic every night, with Carli always on, and bringing in the crowds. Carli's biggest hit, however, may just be his bistro; its food is, quite simply, a melody of flavor. Through such dishes as pan seared, almond amaretto grouper, roasted New Zealand rack of lamb, and righteous rib-eye steaks, the kitchen has yet to miss a note. The trio of risottos is a particular favorite of our among the main courses. The rhythm gets underway early with fun Puerto Rican fritters, the ceviche of the day, tuna carpaccio and escargot options. After the meal, Carli and his grand piano and the kitchen's variations on the crème brûlée will keep you in the groove. The quality of the music makes this restaurant's reasonable pricing a really incredible bargain.

Edificio Banco Popular, Calle Tetuán 206, off Plazoleta Rafael Carrión. ✆ **787/725-4927.** Reservations recommended. Main courses $18–$34. Mon–Fri 3:30–11pm, Sat 4–11:30pm. Bus: Old City Trolley.

Marmalade Restaurant and Wine Bar ★ INTERNATIONAL   We're no fans of the ultra-contemporary decor here, but the airport lounge feel may be appropriate for Chef Peter Schintler, who has traveled the globe to discover the flavors on which his wonderful cuisine is anchored. His fare is best experienced through the changing tasting menus with wine pairings. Groups can travel on a 15-course journey, which recently included crispy paella bites and garden-style beef tenderloin and Hawaiian sea bass (vegetarians get their own well-curated menus). Flavors like almond pomegranate and roasted peanut lime permeate the offerings, and the house white bean soup with Pancetta shavings is downright outrageous.

Calle Fortaleza 317. ✆ **787/724-3969.** Tasting menus $69–$89 per person; main courses $25–$36. Mon–Thurs 6pm–midnight, Fri–Sat 6pm–2am, Sun 6–10pm. Bus: Old City Trolley.

Parrot Club ★★ NUEVO LATINO/CARIBBEAN   A lone standout in a neglected sector of Old San Juan when it first opened in 1996, The Parrot gave birth to the entire SoFo restaurant district that today surrounds it, an exuberant area with cobbled stoned streets lined with restaurants, bars, plazas, music and happy people. Since then, this vibrant Nuevo Latino eatery has relied on inventive updates of Puerto Rican and Latino classics, and the warmest and smoothest wait staff in the city, to stay relevant. Among the stars of the menu here are passion fruit cocktails, plantain crusted mahi mahi and the restaurant's wildly delicious burger, topped with the main ingredients of a Cubano sandwich: roast pork, Virginia ham, and Swiss cheese. The menu has grown increasingly varied and sophisticated throughout the years, but this place is still built on good, friendly service, a hopping bar scene and bold and flavorful Latino cooking. *Note:* The Parrot's owners/creators, Emilio Figueroa and Gigi Zaferos, are also behind Dragonfly, Toro Salao, and Aguaviva in the neighborhood, so if you have trouble getting in here, try one of those.

Calle Fortaleza 363. ℂ **787/725-7370.** Reservations not accepted. Main courses $10–$23 lunch, $18–$29 dinner. Daily 11am–4pm and 6–11pm. Closed 2 weeks in Sept. Bus: Old City Trolley.

Toro Salao ★★ SPANISH TAPAS   We love the "salty bull" and its Spanish tavern interior, but choose either a seat at the bar or at the tables on the terrace out front which are both abuzz with life (the restaurant's angular interior leaves many dining areas

San Juan's Intoxicating Coffee

A coffee break in Old San Juan might last an afternoon. *Taza* (cup) after *taza* of Puerto Rico's rich brew will make you abandon Jamaican Blue Mountain coffee or Hawaiian Kona forever. The rich local coffees are from beans grown in Puerto Rico's lush, mountainous heartland, in towns such as Adjuntas and Jayuya, Maricao, and Las Marías. There are a growing number of fashionable cafes that offer fine local coffees, as well as gourmet brands from around the world. However, just about anywhere you go that serves coffee will serve a rich local brew (including Starbucks, McDonald's, and Burger King!).

Try **Caficultura** (ℂ **787/723-7731**), a gorgeous new spot on a shady corner of Plaza Colón; the **Cuatro Sombras** (Calle Recinto Sur 259; ℂ **787/724-9955**), a great cafe and microroastery; or the **Cuatro Estaciones** (Plaza de las Armas; no phone), the outdoor cafe on the western end of Old San Juan's central plaza, adjacent to the State Department.

Joaquin Pastor grows delicious coffee on his farm in Ciales, harvests, and then hand roasts the beans before bringing it to his Old San Juan cafe, **Finca Cialitos** (Calle San Justo 150; ℂ **939/207-9998**). This award-winning coffee is grown on the northern outskirts of the Toro Negro cloud forest and is as rich as the landscape in which it was born. Get immersed in the coffee-making process and enjoy the final, perfect result of a coffee made with pure passion and hard work. It's all about customized care, which brings out the coffee's natural characteristics, drawn from its particular region, according to Joaquin.

Outside the Old City, right in the heart of the Santurce Arts District, is **Hacienda San Pedro** (Av. De Diego 318, Santurce; ℂ **787/993-1871;** www.cafehsp.com), which roasts on site the delicious coffee grown at the owners' family plantation in Jayuya. When ordering, ask for *café con leche* (with milk), *puya* (unsweetened), *negrito con azúcar* (black and sweetened), or *cortao* (black with a dash of milk).

Old San Juan Hotels & Restaurants

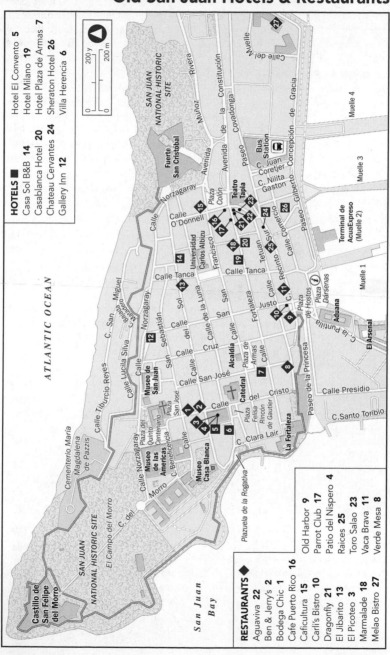

HOTELS ■
Casa Sol B&B **14**
Casablanca Hotel **20**
Chateau Cervantes **24**
Gallery Inn **12**
Hotel El Convento **5**
Hotel Milano **19**
Hotel Plaza de Armas **7**
Sheraton Hotel **26**
Villa Herencia **6**

RESTAURANTS ◆
Aguaviva **22**
Ben & Jerry's **2**
Bodega Chic **1**
Cafe Puerto Rico **16**
Caficultura **15**
Carli's Bistro **10**
Dragonfly **21**
El Jibarito **13**
El Picoteo **3**
Marmalade **18**
Melao Bistro **27**
Old Harbor **9**
Parrot Club **17**
Patio del Nispero **4**
Raices **25**
Toro Salao **23**
Vaca Brava **11**
Verde Mesa **8**

feeling remote). The varied menu includes mahi mahi tacos, arugula and goat cheese flatbread, and Greek olive and the claypot chicken among a number of globally inspired tapas and entrees. The Old City's finest pitcher of Sangria is another reason you'll want to linger.

Calle Tetuan 367. © **787/722-3330.** Reservations not accepted. Tapas $6–$25; main courses $16–$25. Mon–Sat 6pm–midnight. Bus: Old City Trolley.

MODERATE

Bodega Chic ★ FRENCH BISTRO   Perhaps the premiere spot for brunch in the Old City, this bistro's blend of classic French cuisine with Mediterranean and Caribbean herbs and flavors, along with reasonable prices and down-to-earth service and atmosphere, make it a good bet any time. Algerian chef-owner Christophe Gourdain trained with star chef Jean-Georges Vongerichten and offers wonders such as baked goat cheese *croustillant* (in crispy pastry), hangar steak with sautéed potatoes and string beans, flavorful mussels Provençal, and delectable braised lamb shank. The *frites* (fried potatoes) can't be beat. Kudos to the friendly wait staff who give savvy advice on the menu, as well as on other places to see and things to do in San Juan. This is one of the Old City's unexpected pleasures.

Calle Cristo 51. © **787/722-0124.** Reservations recommended. Main courses $15–$26. Tues–Fri 6pm–midnight, Sun 11:30am–4pm. Bus: Old City Trolley.

Café Puerto Rico ★ CREOLE/PUERTO RICAN   This small and friendly restaurant offers flavorful bargains and outdoor seating right on Plaza de Colón. Inside, the room has a welcome, old-fashioned ambiance thanks to ceiling fans, beamed ceilings, and tile floors, and the constant whir of a blender mixing up tropical fruit drinks. The menu features hearty regional fare. Top options include whole red snapper, paella, and chicken and rice. Of course, if you need a break during a day of strolling Old San Juan's winding streets, don't wait for dinner—lunch is enjoyable here and the bar serves up reasonably priced tropical drinks, sangria, and wine.

Calle O'Donnell 208. © **787/724-2281.** Main courses $10–$21. Mon–Sat noon–3pm and 5:30–10:45pm, Sun noon–9pm. Bus: Old City Trolley.

Dragonfly ★★ LATIN/ASIAN FUSION   The addictive Latin-Asian food here has kept this restaurant-lounge sizzling for years on the Old City's dining scene—a "hipster hotspot" since before the term was invented. The decor, with its mirrored, red-walled interior, outfitted with Shanghai lanterns and ornate curtains and furnishings, has a seductive power, just like the *platos* (plates), served here do. They measure somewhere between a tapa and a large appetizer portion in size and are best shared, about two per person. Ones to try include Peking duck nachos, Asian churrasco, *amarillo* (sweet plaintain) dumplings in citrus dipping sauce, tempura rock shrimp tacos, Peking duck, and Chino Latino lo mein with Puerto Rican *chicharrones* (fried chicken bites). There's also a full sushi bar and an ever-packed lounge area, for before dinner or after.

Calle Fortaleza 364. © **787/977-3886.** Reservations not accepted. Entrees $10–$28. Mon–Wed 6–11pm, Thurs–Sat 6pm–midnight. Bus: Old City Trolley.

El Picoteo ★★ SPANISH   A gorgeous spot to soak up the splendor of Old San Juan, the neighborhood's oldest tapas bar is still its tastiest and most authentic. The restaurant unfolds across the blooming terraces of the Spanish Colonial facades of Hotel El Convento, with a view to its historic courtyard and the action out on Calle Cristo. This is old school Spanish tapas akin to what you'd find at bar in San Sebastian,

Spain: fat shrimp in garlic sauce, spicy *papas bravas,* Spanish tortilla, or fresh octopus ceviche. El Picoteco also serves complete meals, including a solid paella. The restaurant's champagne-laced sangria is a whole other reason to come. A pleasant place for dinner or lunch, it's also a great stop for a cold drink and snack during a break from sightseeing or shopping in the Old City.

In El Convento Hotel, Calle del Cristo 100. 📞 **787/723-9202.** Reservations recommended. Main courses $6–$32; paella $20–$35. Tues–Sun noon–midnight. Bus: Old City Trolley.

Melao Bistro ★★ CARIBBEAN FUSION   This unpretentious bistro on the outskirts of the old city right on the bay consistently delivers flavorful food with friendly service at great prices. The lobster raviolis and fresh ceviche make for a great start to your meal, and you can't go wrong with the grilled trio of shrimp, chicken, and churrasco; the tamarind salmon; or mahi mahi in the lemon caper sauce. Daily specials, which always include a Puerto Rican classic, offer the best deals. The restaurant overlooks the new waterfront Bahia Urbana Park, which makes this a great stop before or after one of the many concerts and other events hosted there.

Cond. Capitolio Plaza, Ste. 201, Calle del Muelle, Viejo San Juan. 📞 **787/721-7160.** Main courses $7.95–$25. Mon–Tues 11:30am–3pm, Wed–Thurs 11am–10pm, Fri 11:30am–11pm, Sat 3–11:30pm. Bus: Old City Trolley.

Old Harbor Brewery Steak and Lobster House ★ AMERICAN   The perfect spot to bring your father, this microbrewery and traditional surf and turf spot offers simple, flavorful classics in a refined mariner atmosphere. Pick your own Caribbean spiny lobster from the tank and tell the kitchen to prepare it with the citrus *beurre blanc* sauce, or go for the filet mignon or rib-eye. There are also Kobe and Angus steak options, burgers, and—because you are in Puerto Rico—mofongo stuffed with seafood or steak. The Santo Viejo pilsner and Coqui lager are both pleasant brews, and there are options for pale ale and stout lovers, but we like the Taina seasonable beer the best. With a formal bar, classy brew vats and smart dining room, the Old Harbor is at home in its building, a former New York Federal Bank Branch that dates from the 1920s.

Calle Tizol 202 (near Recinto Sur). 📞 **787/721-2100.** Reservations recommended. Platters and main courses $13–$38. Daily 8am–7pm. Bus: Old City Trolley.

Patio del Nispero ★ INTERNATIONAL   This dreamy restaurant, in the flowering Spanish colonial courtyard of Old San Juan's most exquisite historic hotel, offers a deliciously cool respite during a day of site-seeing, or a romantic sojourn in the evening. Have a leisurely meal or drink in the shadow of the hotel's century-old nispero tree. The menu is a traditional mix of American, Puerto Rican, and continental dining options, but while the tune may be familiar, the kitchen never misses a note, and we've enjoyed everything from Eggs Benedict to the stuffed mofongo to the filet mignon. Drinks, from the ginger mojito to *cafe con leche,* are also first rate. Prices are inflated by the atmosphere, but it's perfectly fine to linger over drinks.

In the El Convento hotel, Calle del Cristo 100. 📞 **787/723-9020.** Reservations not necessary. Sandwiches $7.50–$29. Daily 6:30–3pm and 6–10pm. Bus: Old City Trolley.

Raíces ★★ PUERTO RICAN   Step in and immerse yourself in the rich flavors of *comida criolla* with all its traditional accompaniments from the folkloric skirts and shirts of the wait staff to the Puerto Rican music pumping through the rustic dining room (it has a countryside look, its walls hung with art by locals artists and artisans). If you're with a group, the mixed Puerto Rican appetizer platter is a great introduction to this cuisine: stuffed fried plantain fritters, codfish fritters, and assorted *empanadas* (turnovers) of beef, chicken, fish or shellfish. Don't pass up the plantain soup though; it's the embodiment of simple deliciousness as is the stuffed mofongo entrée (a garlicky plantain casserole filled with Creole chicken, shrimp, breaded pork, skirt steak, or mahi mahi). While prices are not cheap, the kitchen knows its stuff. Sure there's a level of show at this place, fueled by its location near the cruiseship docks. Raíces started in Caguas, way off the beaten tourist path, however, and all its locations have a strong local following. Rest assured, the *comida criolla* here is the genuine article.

Calle Recinto Sur 315. ℭ **787/289-2121.** Reservations not necessary. Main courses $10–$26. Mon–Fri 11am–4pm and 6–11pm, Sat 11am–11pm, Sun noon–10pm. Bus: Old City Trolley.

Vaca Brava ★ STEAK/PUERTO RICAN   This big, loud Puerto Rican steakhouse offers huge platters of grilled meat, friendly service, and, often, live music. Born in the mountain town of Barranquitas, Vaca Brava brought its countryside aesthetic to the city with *jíbaro* cowboys and cowgirls with big smiles serving the meals. There are individual steak, chicken, rib, and other dishes, but the place's fame rests on its grilled-meat platters for groups, like the Totem de la Vaca, which is flank steak rolled around chicken breast, then wrapped in bacon and covered with cheese or BBQ sauce (don't think about the calorie count, just order and enjoy), or the Totem de la Chillo, which is red snapper stuffed with steak and served with chimichurri sauce over a bed of mofongo. The huge dining room tables in the spacious spot are also made for groups, and you can order a mini-keg of Medalla, the local beer, to wash it all back. Head here when you're in the mood for loud fun.

Calle Recinto Sur 253. ℭ **787/723-3700.** Reservations not accepted. Main courses $13–$35; platters $30–$53. Mon–Thurs 11am–11pm, Fri–Sat 11am–midnight, Sun 11am–10pm. Bus: Old City Trolley.

Verde Mesa ★★★ HEALTHY GOURMET   Healthy eating is the focus here, but you likely won't be concentrating on that as you tuck in to the refined, toothsome food prepared here. Meals are served in a handsome country dining room, with fresh flowers and antique furnishings, and the owners welcome guests like old friends. If you are looking for a quick bite, go elsewhere; this is an experience to savor, and the kitchen prepares everything to order and won't be rushed. Seasonal fresh herbs and produce drive the offerings, with daily specials accounting for many, including fresh daily seafood specials, like mahi mahi ceviche or salmon stewed with fresh pumpkin. The couscous Niçoise, with fresh tuna, olives and asparagus, is out of this world, and the Verde Mesa rice, with vegetables, walnuts, and cranberries, is side dish that goes with everything. Save room for dessert, with daily inspirations like mango tart or vegetarian chocolate cake. Also, try a house cocktail, like the Rum Green Infusion with basil, lemon and cucumber. The table turnover is slow here; but they'll take your phone number and call your cell when your table is ready.

Calle Tetuán 107, Old San Juan. ℭ **787/390-4662.** Reservations not accepted. Main courses $12–$24. Mon–Sat 6–10pm. Bus: Old City Trolley.

INEXPENSIVE

Ben & Jerry's Cafe ★ ICE CREAM/CAFE   We all know the Vermont-based chain Ben & Jerry's (who can resist a cone of Chunky Monkey or Imagine Whirled Peace?), but this cafe goes well beyond ice cream. In fact, it serves one of San Juan's best brunches (all the way until 2pm). Offerings include an Acai bowl, with granola, bananas and berries; the "Godfather" omelet, with sundried tomato, pesto and mozzarella cheese; or chocolate chip pancakes and Belgium waffles. The brunch menu is limited at the Old San Juan location, which has free Wi-Fi, great music, and magazines, and special events like poetry readings and children's story telling. The Condado location (next to La Concha Hotel) has ice cream and great ocean side views from Ventana del Mar plaza.

Ventana del Mar, Condado del Cristo 61. ℭ **787/977-6882.** Ice cream and meals $3.95–$11. Sun–Wed 9am–10pm, Fri–Sat 9am–11pm. Bus: B21, C53. Calle del Cristo 61, Old San Juan. ℭ **787/977-6882.** Ice cream and meals $3.95–$11. Sun–Wed 11am–10pm, Fri–Sat 11am–11pm. Bus: Old City Trolley.

Caficultura ★ CAFE   You'll sing the praises of Puerto Rico's rich coffee at this spot on Plaza Colon, with its open double doors, high wooden ceilings, tiled floors, and walls adorned by prints by Rafael Tufino. The cooked food is notable, too, thanks to its self-titled "market kitchen" which uses mostly local produce. Among the tasty breakfast and lunch offerings are coconut French toast, scrambled eggs with pico de gallo and avocado to sweet potato crêpe with cheese and chicken sausage. As for the baked goods and sandwiches, they're not quite up to the level of the breakfasts. The barristers here, though are true artists though they do take their time. The outside tables are a great spot to people watch when you are not in a hurry.

Calle San Francisco 401, Plaza Colón Old San Juan. ℭ **787/723-7731.** Breakfast and lunch $3.50–$18. Daily 8am–6pm.

El Jibarito ★★ PUERTO RICAN   Real homemade Puerto Rican food is served here by friendly faces at reasonable prices in a pleasant dining room. Run by the same family for decades, the restaurant pays homage to the Old City and island country life with large murals, and the sound of fresh fruit and vegetables being chopped wafts through the Puerto Rican music from its blooming courtyard. This is your best shot at trying authentic *comida criolla*, whether its Boricua comfort food like stewed goat or breaded steak, a scrumptious mofongo stuffed with shrimp in sweet tomato sauce, or fried red snapper. Fried plantains, yellow rice with pigeon peas, or white rice with pink beans accompany the meals, along with a simple salad and garlic bread. They inevitably end with cheesecake or flan. Locals love this place.

Old San Juan, Calle del Sol 280. ℭ **787/725-8375.** Reservations not necessary. Main courses $8–$23; sandwiches and snacks available. Daily 10am–9pm. Bus: Old City Trolley.

Puerta de Tierra

For the locations of restaurants in Puerta de Tierra, see the map "Puerta de Tierra, Miramar, Condado & Ocean Park Hotels & Restaurants" on p. 61.

EXPENSIVE

Lemongrass Restaurant ★ PAN ASIAN   The dining room is the closest the Caribe Hilton compound gets to a Zen meditation temple—guests eat pond side in the midst of outdoor tropical gardens, with the singing tree frogs overhead. It's perfect for a romantic night out (have dinner with friends or the kids elsewhere). The Asian Latino fusion thing is so often done badly, but the mix is smooth here and many of the dishes sing, including the salmon and asparagus in ginger cream sauce and the skirt steak over miso and scallion risotto. You'll do better with the Asian entrees rather than the uninspired Latino ones (like the tamarind ribs). In fact, appetizers are much more adventurous than main courses, with Vietnamese fajitas, curry rice calamari, and tempura artichokes among the meal's high points. So you might consider making a meal entirely of starters. Also on site: a modern, elegant bar with champagne lounge. *Warning:* Service can be very slow.

Puerta de Tierra, Caribe Hilton, Calle Los Rosales. ℭ **787/724-5888.** Reservations recommended. Main courses $25–$32. Daily 5:30–10:30pm. Bus: 21.

INEXPENSIVE

El Hamburger ★ LIGHT FARE Smoke pours from this wooden burger shack from before noon through late evening every day, and from the counter issue juicy grilled burgers and flavorful hot dogs, golden onion rings and fries, and freezing cold beer. A favorite stop for hungry *sanjuaneros,* whether they're right from the beach or on the way out to party, El Hamburger always attracts a crowd. Part of the appeal may be the brash salsa blaring from the jukebox and the wooden walls covered with posters of Puerto Rican pop stars from across the years. There's also generous condiment selection, a rarity in Puerto Rico, not to mention the ocean breeze and the picture postcard scene of the palm trees on Atlantic bluff outside. You may try, but once bitten, it's hard to pass this tasty bargain up.

Av. Muñoz Rivera 402. ✆ **787/721-4269.** Reservations not accepted. Burgers from $3.50. Cash only. Sun–Thurs 11am–11pm, Fri–Sat 11am–1am. Bus: 5, M1.

Condado

For the locations of Condado restaurants, see the map "Puerta de Tierra, Miramar, Condado & Ocean Park Hotels & Restaurants" on p. 61.

EXPENSIVE

Budatai ★★ LATIN/ASIAN A beautiful spot, overlooking the Ventana del Mar park, Budatai is one of those few restaurants that successfully fuse Latino and Asian cuisine into something that tastes great, as opposed to just sounding good on paper. Highlights include the seared tuna with taro tots, halibut with sausage and clams, and the filet mignon with Asian potatoes and mushrooms. The crusted asparagus appetizer is excellent, as are the Geisha and Godzilla sushi rolls. This was the first restaurant opened by Chef Roberto Trevino, who has built up Food Network and James Beard credentials over his career (he now owns several other places in Condaded). The dining room is an understated beauty and the rooftop bar and lounge is an extraordinary location with a tanned and buff crowd.

Av. Ashford 1056, Condado. ✆ **787/725-6919.** Main courses $24–$40. Mon–Wed 11:30am–11pm, Thurs–Sat 11:30am–midnight, Sun 11:30am–10pm. Bus: 5, 53.

Casa Lola Criollo Kitchen ★★ PUERTO RICAN This mansion-turned-restaurant, on the Condado Lagoon, offers tasty reinventions of Puerto Rican dishes, with a menu as bold as its colorful interior. Chef Roberto Trevino's take on the cuisine of his adopted island home is less an homage to the classics than fresh creations inspired by the *comida criolla* palette. That means risotto with fried chicken chunks and roast pork in chimichurri sauce, or bouillabaisse *criollo,* a flavorful sweet tomato seafood stew of fresh cod, monkfish, shrimp, crawfish, clams, and mussels and served with grilled baguette. The filet mignon, in an aged rum sauce with vegetable caviar, is another inspired mash-up. Some of the best appetizers stick closer to the Puerto Rican playbook, like roast pork croquettes, *acalpurrias* stuffed with *ropa vieja,* and fried fresh fish bites with spicy lemon sauce. The sangria is unique and delicious and the red velvet cake perfectly executed. *Tip:* Try to get a seat overlooking the lagoon.

Ave. Ashford 1096, Condado. ✆ **787/998-2918.** Reservations recommended. Main courses $19–39. Daily 11:30am–1am. Bus: 21.

Perla ★★ SEAFOOD The food lives up to its dramatic setting, and that's no easy task. Shimmering reflections of water and light surround this seashell-shaped restaurant on the beach, and waves of blue undulate across its pale dining room. It's an architectural wonder and a breathtaking temple to the ocean and all the luscious food

Puerta de Tierra, Miramar, Condado & Ocean Park Hotels & Restaurants

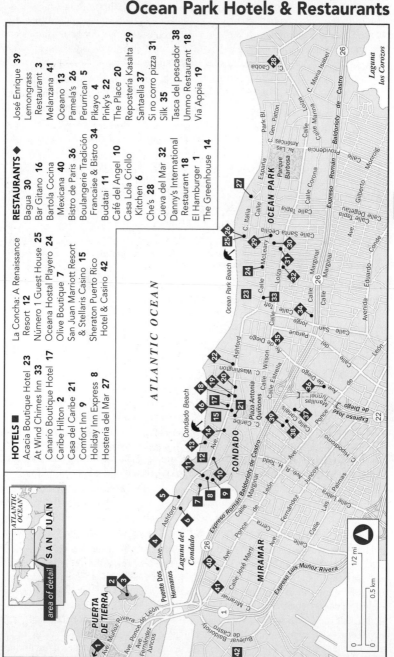

HOTELS ■

Acacia Boutique Hotel **23**
At Wind Chimes Inn **33**
Canario Boutique Hotel **17**
Caribe Hilton **2**
Casa del Caribe **21**
Comfort Inn **9**
Holiday Inn Express **8**
Hosteria del Mar **27**

La Concha: A Renaissance
  Resort **12**
Número 1 Guest House **25**
Oceana Hostal Playero **24**
Olive Boutique **7**
San Juan Marriott Resort
  & Stellaris Casino **15**
Sheraton Puerto Rico
  Hotel & Casino **42**

RESTAURANTS ◆

Bagua **30**
Bar Gitano **16**
Bartola Cocina
  Mexicana **40**
Bistro de Paris **36**
Boulangerie Tradición
  Francaise & Bistro **34**
Budatai **11**
Café del Angel **10**
Casa Lola Criollo
  Kitchen **6**
Che's **28**
Cueva del Mar **32**
Danny's International
  Restaurant **18**
El Hamburger **1**
The Greenhouse **14**

José Enrique **39**
Lemongrass
  Restaurant **3**
Melanzana **41**
Oceano **13**
Pamela's **26**
Perurrican **5**
Pikayo **4**
Pinky's **22**
The Place **20**
Reposteria Kasalta **29**
Santaella **37**
Si no corro pizza **31**
Silk **35**
Tasca del pescador **38**
Ummo Restaurant **18**
Via Appia **19**

we harvest from it. Perla's version of surf and turf, with a filet mignon served in a bacon port reduction and a lobster tail in a classic *beurre blanc* sauce, is extraordinary, as is the seared red snapper with a tomato chutney and polenta fries. Surprisingly, there are wonderful non-seafood plates here as well, like the veal noisettes with white truffle potatoes. Along with *a la carte* are worthwhile three- and five-course tasting menus with wine pairings. The desserts are mostly traditional and heavy, but we do think the tropical fruit sorbet trio offers a refreshing end to a great meal.

At Hotel La Concha, Av. Ashford 1077. ✆ **787/721-7500,** ext. 6800. Reservations recommended. Main courses $25–$60. Sun–Thurs 6–10pm, Fri–Sat 6–11pm. Bus: 21, 53.

Pikayo ★★★ PUERTO RICAN FUSION   Celebrity chef Wilo Benet has been bringing Puerto Rican cuisine to new heights since the 1990s and there's no sign of him, or his restaurant, slowing down. Through a number of physical moves and menu overhauls, Pikayo has remained at the vanguard of San Juan's culinary scene. The latest incarnation of the Condado Plaza eatery has "pikadera" section with extensive hot and cold offerings; look here for appetizers or to make an entire meal tapas style. Beef tenderloin *alcapurrias* with garlic aioli, gouda cheese with guava sauce, risotto de *gandules* with *chicharron* (peas and crispy chicken), Portuguese octopus with shallot sauce, and *jamon serrano,* are just a few of the pikadera offerings. Entrees like the South American sea bass and spicy chorizo emulsion are solid as well. Save room for some decadence at the end, with dessert options such as tiramisu with pecan brandy sauce, chocolate tart with peanut butter ice cream, or pistachio carrot cake with mascarpone frosting and Mandarin jam.

At the Conrad Condado Plaza, Ashford 999. ✆ **787/721-6194.** Reservations recommended. Main courses $34–$42. Daily 6–11pm. Bus: 21, 53.

Perurrican ★★ PERUVIAN   This is a tale of two restaurants. Score a table on the ocean side terrace, and your meal will be a happy one thanks to the lovely views, cooling breezes and food. But woe betide you if you're assigned an inside table. Not only will you be deprived of views, your enjoyment of the meal will be marred by the constant whirr of activity and acoustics that do not allow for conversation between dinner companions. You also have two uneven choices in the food here, which is a mix of Peruvian and Puerto Rico choices. The closer you stick to the Peruvian side of the menu, the better off you will be. Start with a ceviche or the *jalea mixta* a combination of golden fried seafood, yuca fries, Andean corn, and salsa *criolla.* For entrees, try *saltado* (stir-fry served over French fries and white rice) and *tacu tacu* (a crunchy rice, bacon, and bean dish) that both come with a choice of seafood, steak, or chicken.

Ave. Ashford 1045, San Juan Beach Hotel, Condado. ✆ **787/725-3030.** www.perurrican.com. Reservations not necessary. Main courses $13–$30. Mon 11:30am–9pm, Tues–Thurs 11:30am–10pm, Fri 11:30am–11pm, Sat noon–midnight, Sun noon–10pm. Bus: 21, 53.

Ummo Restaurant ★ ARGENTINE GRILL   The specialty here is grilled meats and fish platters, Argentinian style. But there's something for everyone thanks to a full pasta and seafood menu and several grilled vegetable mixes. All is served in a restaurant that's both handsome (dark wood and deep earth tones) and refreshingly unpretentious (the dining room mingles with the long bar area, where soccer games are on television, and live musicians perform several nights a week). The meats used here are top end and are grilled to perfection, making for satisfying meals. For starters, look to the asparagus and chorizo and arugula dumplings. And be sure to order a side of the creamy potatoes with your entrée, a highlight of any meal here. There is a front terrace overlooking Ashford Avenue, a great option if the weather is nice.

Av. Ashford 1351, Condado. ☏ **787/722-1700.** Reservations recommended. Main courses $17–$59. Daily 11am–1am. Bus: 21.

MODERATE

Most main courses in the restaurants below are at the low end of the price scale. These restaurants each have only two or three dishes that are expensive, almost invariably involving shellfish.

Bar Gitano ★ SPANISH TAPAS The food, like the ambience, is authentically Spanish here, so get ready for pitchers of refreshing sangria, tantalizing tapas plates and perfect paella. Back to those tapas, we think you can't go wrong with the tomato bread, spicy papas bravas, sweet peppers stuffed with cheese, and the unique meatballs and clam and mussels stew. Unless it's oppressively hot or looks like rain, take a seat on the front terrace with a view of the action on beachside Ashford Avenue, lined with bars, restaurants, shops, hotels and condos. Check for live flamenco shows and other performances, held on select Thursday and Sunday evenings.

Av. Ashford 1302. ☏ **787/294-5513.** Reservations recommended. Main courses $21–34; tapas $4–17. Mon–Wed 11:30am–11pm, Thurs–Sat 11:30am–midnight, Sun 11:30am–10pm. Bus: 5, 21.

The Greenhouse ★ INTERNATIONAL If you have a late night craving for French onion soup, or a smoked salmon meal, this is the place to be. This late-night eatery, and its vast menu, has been a part of Condado's night scene for 40 years. Every late-night dreamer who ever amounted to anything in San Juan (and the many more who never did) has dined here at some point over the decades, the predecessors of today's always interesting, and sometimes loopy, regulars. Service is sometimes friendly and sometimes brusque, but the crowd is always interesting, and the food usually worth the wait. The Greenhouse is known for its delicious black bean soup. *Be warned:* It's often crowded.

Av. Ashford 1200. ☏ **787/725-4036.** Main courses $8–$39. Sun–Thurs 11:30am–2am, Fri–Sat 11:30am–4am. Bus: 21.

Oceano ★★ INTERNATIONAL This sleek restaurant-lounge on the beach is the perfect spot to break from the sun for a cool tropical drink or tasty snack. The short, simple beach menu trots the globe, but hits all the tropics-friendly spots from an Asian chicken wrap to Ahi tuna tacos to plantain crusted calamari. A lunch menu widens to offer a few sandwiches and entrees, and the dinner menu brings in vegetarian and shrimp pad-Thai plates and some tasty entrees, like guava roast pork. It's a nice place for a sunset dinner, but don't wait much longer to eat. When night falls, the volume turns up and Oceano becomes more lounge than restaurant. Service is spotty, but it hardly matters given the setting (get a table on the beachfront patio). The crowd's as fashionable as the establishment.

2 Calle Vendig. ☏ **787/724-6300.** Main courses $15–$36, sandwiches and snacks $10–$24. Sun and Tues–Wed noon–midnight, Thurs noon–1am, Fri–Sat noon–2am. Bus: 21, 53.

INEXPENSIVE

Café del Angel ★ CREOLE/PUERTO RICAN Looking for a tasty, inexpensive *comida criolla* in the middle of the Condado tourist district? Look no further: Café del Angel is *the* choice from noon to late night. If you had a Puerto Rican grandma, this is what her food would taste like. The mofongos are a specialty, but all the Puerto Rican platters are good. Stick to those rather than the sandwiches and boiler plate U.S. alternatives, which are just okay. Service is friendly, and the bar (and bartender) gets increasingly entertaining as the evening wears on.

Av. Ashford 1106. ☏ **787/643-7594.** Main courses $7–$20. Wed–Mon 11am–10pm. Bus: 21.

Danny's International Restaurant ★ PIZZA/CAFE   Danny's offers tasty and economical American-style breakfast and thick pizzas, with inventive topping like seafood (mussels, calamari, shrimp, and octopus) and veggies (broccoli, spinach, mushroom, onions, sweet peppers, olives, fresh garlic). For breakfast, they serve the best eggs over easy with ham and hash browns in Condado. Later in the day, stick with the pizzas over the other options on the menu (you'll thank me).

Av. Ashford 1351. ☏ **787/724-0501** or 724-2734. Reservations not accepted. Breakfast $5.95–$14; pizza $15–$26. Sun–Thurs 7am–1am, Fri–Sat 7am–2am. Bus: 21, 10.

Pinky's ★★ CAFE/DELI   Moving between several locations in and around Condado over the years, Pinky's has retained a reputation for the best wraps and fruit frappes in town, and it just as well known for its healthy, flavorful, and filling breakfasts. I usually stick with the hard–to–beat classic surfer wrap (turkey, mozzarella, basil, tomato, onion, and pesto mayo), but there's a delicious Asian Ahi tuna wrap as well as one with grilled filet mignon. For breakfast try the drunken pilot, velvety scrambled eggs with goat cheese, spinach, and mushrooms. The only bad thing about this popular place is there's never enough room for all the patrons. Now, even with two locations in Condado (including near Ventana del Mar park), that glitch remains.

Av. Ashford 1451, Ste. 100-B, Condado. ☏ **787/222-5222.** Wraps and specialty sandwiches $3–$11; breakfast $2–$11. Daily 7am–9pm. Bus: 5, 1.

The Place at Condado ★★ BURGERS/PIZZA/ARTESANAL BEER   Delish burgers, fries, pizza, wings and more are on offer in this family-friendly spot with rustic dining, patio dining, and a bar and beer garden. Speaking of the bar, it carries an ample collection of craft beers from around the world. There's music (both the background soundtrack and regular live performances) and sports on the many TVs. We're particular fans of the thin crust pizzas, the wings, and the gourmet burgers, which are served on brioche and ciabatta buns, and sided by thin cut, golden fries and onion rings.

Av Ashford 1368, Condado. ☏ **787/722-0124.** Reservations recommended. Burgers and pizza $3–$15. Sun and Wed–Thurs 11:30–10pm, Fri–Sat 11:30am–midnight. Bus: 5.

Via Appia ★★ PIZZA/ITALIAN   This is red sauce heaven, from the clams *posillipo* to the sausage and peppers to the baked ziti to the linguini and clam sauce. The Julius Cesar sub is actually New Jersey-style with the oregano, oil, and vinegar just right, and the pizza here pays much more attention to the tomato sauce than most versions in San Juan, just like at the Jersey Shore boardwalk. There are tasty steaks, other continental classics such as chicken *Francaise,* and Italian favorites liked baked chicken parmigiana. Several affordable wines are available by the glass, and the house sangria packs a punch. Half the place is a non-descript deli and the other half a more refined bar and dining area, but you want to sit at the terraces out front, regardless of which side of the restaurant it fronts. The view and food are the same.

Av. Ashford 1350. ☏ **787/725-8711.** Pizza and main courses $9–$30. Mon–Fri 11am–11pm, Sat–Sun 11am–midnight. Bus: 5, 3, 1

Miramar

For the locations of restaurants in Miramar, see the map "Puerta de Tierra, Miramar, Condado & Ocean Park Hotels & Restaurants," on p. 61.

MODERATE

Bartola Restaurante ★ MEXICAN   Tortillas and guacamole are lovingly made on site at this stellar and authentic Mexican restaurant. Highlights of the menu include superb fish and pork tacos, grilled steak, grouper ceviche, and the many vegetarian options. End it all with hot fried churros with chocolate caramel sauce. Big flavors keeps this small restaurant packed.

Av. Ponce de Leon 701, Edif. Centro de Seguros, Ste. 108, Miramar. © **787/963-1298.** Main courses $11–$14. Mon–Wed noon–3pm and 6–10pm, Fri–Sat noon–11pm, Sun noon–10pm. Bus: 5.

Melanzana Bistro & Pizzeria ★★ ITALIAN   As cool as a Sophia Loren flick, this Mediterranean beauty serves up delicious Napolitano cuisine (the chef's home-town) with flavors that match the vibrant bar area and fashionable dining room. The offerings extend far beyond the delicious, authentic brick oven pizza, but these crispy creations will satisfy hardcore fans and win over new converts. That brick oven also perfectly toasts a selection of upscale calzones, another excellent choice. Or you could go for the velvety seafood risotto, potato-leek-truffle oil soup, eggplant with peppers, tuna carpaccio, or lamb meatballs. The veal chop and dorado blew us away on our last visit, and the coffee panna cotta and tiramisu made us break our "no dessert" rule. Really, it's hard to find losers on the menu here.

Av, Ponce de Leon 650, Miramar. © **787/722-1010.** Main courses $15–$35. Mon–Thurs noon–10pm, Fri noon–11pm, Sun 1–10pm. Bus: 5, M1.

Santurce & Ocean Park

For the locations of restaurants in Santurce and Ocean Park, see the map "Puerta de Tierra, Miramar, Condado & Ocean Park Hotels & Restaurants," on p. 61.

EXPENSIVE

Bagua ★★★ PUERTO RICAN FUSION   This bright little beach bar and bistro surprises with its inventive tapas and entrees, as well as its specialty cocktails and excellent sangria. The delicate coconut *arepa* filled with crab salad and the trio of stuffed miniature mofongos should not be missed, but neither should the "paella cro-quette" and passion fruit chicken wings, or the unique "tachoviche," a plantain taco filled with a fresh fish ceviche. For entrees, the jerk chicken and grilled octopus are standouts, and the filet mignon and grilled grouper are a few cuts above other versions I've tried in San Juan. The bar area on the first floor can get crowded, but you'll be able to spread out a bit more on the second floor, especially if you are with a group. Don't worry, the great classic reggae flows upstairs, too.

Calle María Moczo 51, Santurce. © **787/200-9616.** Main courses $13–$25. Mon–Tues and Thurs 11:30am–10pm, Fri–Sat 11:30am–11pm, Sun 11:30am–9pm. Bus: 5.

Bistro de Paris ★★ FRENCH   Classic French fare in a refined but relaxed set-ting, with breezy expert service—those are the lures at the adorable bistro. Yes, it can get hot and noisy on the front terrace, but the cheery dining rooms, with the charm of the French countryside, are a lovely experience. As is the food: Bistro de Paris has some of the best steaks in town (whether it's the churrasco or steak au poivre) and scrumptious seafood like Meunière trout and shrimp flambé. The bistro also gets the simple things right, with dreamy versions of the salad Niçoise, croque-monsieur, and French onion soup, not to mention awesome sides from ratatouille to potatoes au gra-tin. The warm pear tart is an exquisite end to the meal, but you will have to wait for it. Bistro attracts visitors to Puerto Rico, but it also has a loyal clientele of local

road food: RESTAURANTS ON WHEELS

Long before the current food truck trend gripped metropolises across the United States, Puerto Ricans were munching down *tripletas* (steak, roast pork, and ham and cheese sandwiches) and plate-fuls of stewed rabbit and rice and beans from lunch trucks and roadside kitchens built from converted school buses. Hard core road-food aficionados, who don't mind a little car exhaust with their lunch, might want to scout out the culinary offerings weekdays along the marginal roads surrounding both sides of Ken-nedy Avenue, which snake through auto-mobile dealers and swampland, as well as the rough and tumble ports area.

Most visitors, however, will want to stick to the new generation of gourmet food trucks, which are "upscaling" the experience for the mainstream, serving tasty food at affordable prices, ranging from $3 to $12.

One of the newest on the scene is **Vagón,** Calle Labra 302 (Corner Calle Ribot; (C) **787/515-4415;** Mon–Tues 11am–3pm, Wed 11am–9pm, Thurs–Fri 11am–11:30pm, Sat noon–9pm). Serving SoCal-style Mexican in downtown San-turce, the place got so popular that it morphed into a full-scale restaurant on the spot with outdoor seating. Fresh Baja fish tacos and other delights await; with live music on some nights.

The famed churrasco sandwich at **El Churry,** Avenida Isla Verde, Punta Las Marias (in front of Pepin Cafe; (C) **787/525-2552;** Wed 7pm–2am, Thurs–Sat 7pm–4am), has been drawing *sanjuaneros* with late-night munchies for years now. Grilled in the Argentine style, the sandwich is served with lettuce, tomatoes, ketchup, and mayo, with the obligatory order of fries and a soda included.

A permanent fixture on the city's late-night scene, **Los Monkeys,** at the Shell Station on the corner of Avenida De Diego and Calle Wilson, Santurce (Thurs–Sat evenings until 4am), serves up killer gourmet burgers and a luscious *tri-pleta,* among other options. There's always good music and happy people. Across from the open-all-night Super-max, it caters to the crowd stumbling out of the nearby Plan B and Bar Bero bars.

El Naqui, PR-24, near Metro Office Park, Guaynabo ((C) **787/407-3737;** Mon–Fri 11am–3pm, Sat noon–4pm), serves scrumptious grilled Asian steak kabobs, bourbon-smoked ribs, and hand-cut fries with garlic and fresh herbs, along with daily chef specials.

There are several food stands and trucks set up beside Plaza Darsenas in Old San Juan along the bayside boule-vard where the cruise-ship docks start. They sell everything from fresh fruit frappes to fried codfish fritters to tasty Mexican food.

---

politicians and power-brokers, professionals, and attorneys. San Juan's elite brunch here on weekends with their families. It's the perfect place to lunch after or before a visit to the Puerto Rico Art Museum across the street

Plaza de Diego, Av. José de Diego 310. (C) **787/998-8929.** Reservations recommended. Main courses $23–$38; weekend brunch $5–$19. Mon–Wed 11:30am–11pm, Thurs–Sat 11:30am–1am, Sun 11am–10pm. Bus: 5.

Jose Enrique ★★★ PUERTO RICAN   This hip restaurant by the Plaza del Mer-cado serves fresh, fantastic Puerto Rican food. It's named for the owner, one of the island's hottest your chefs. You'll pay for the experience and will have to wait for a meal, but it's worth every dime and you can wander around the open-air bars surrounding the traditional marketplace, abundant with flowers, fruits, and shiny vegetables, until the table is ready. The simple but attractive bar and dining room has high ceilings and tiled floors, a fitting home for the young chef's straightforward approach, keeping close to traditional island recipes, but wowing with the delivery. The changing daily menu is driven by the offerings at the adjacent fresh fruit and vegetable marketplace as well as what's fresh from local fishermen. On any given day, you'll find offerings such as grilled swordfish and malanga mash in a tropical fruit chutney, beef stew with white rice and tostones, tender and tasty rib-eyes and skirt steaks, and pork in a tomato fondue. The restaurant is a 12-minute walk from the Marriott in Condado, which you can do in the daylight and the early evening, but grab a cab going home at night to avoid the remote side streets you'll have to cross on the way.

Calle Duffaut 176, Santurce. ✆ **787/725-3518.** Entrees $12–$58. Sun–Thurs 11:30am–11pm, Fri–Sat 11:30am–midnight. Bus: 5.

Pamela's ★ CARIBBEAN FUSION   This beachfront restaurant's perfect location is matched by its delicious offerings. Grab a table right under the palm trees on the beach, if you can (if the weather's inclement, indoors is charming as well). And what will you eat? How about the grouper ceviche in a pineapple ginger marinade, chorizo in a passionfruit red wine sauce, or the clam and mussel casserole? Those are only some of the terrific starters. For entrees, there's scrumptious paella risotto; pan-seared mahi mahi with coconut curry fennel broth; and a killer French cut pork chop, crusted with yuca *mofongo*, in sundried tomatoes and guava chutney.

In the Número 1 Guest House, Calle Santa Ana 1, Ocean Park. ✆ **787/726-5010.** Reservations recommended. Lunch $8–$24; main courses $25–$29. Daily noon–3pm and 7–10:30pm. Tapas daily 3–7pm. Bus: 5, 53.

Santaella ★ COMIDA CRIOLLA FUSION   Eating here is a refined dining experience thanks to the gorgeous dining room, which is wrapped around a tropical garden in an interior courtyard. The menu here takes its rhythms from *comida criolla* but fuses that culinary vocabulary with sophisticated techniques and tastes from other cultures. So you might find yourself grazing on goat cheese quesadilla with honey and white truffle oil, roast pork and sausage au gratin with local root vegetables, or a curry beef stew shepherd's pie. The menu is extensive and can be a bit confusing. *Tip:* Santaella gets very lively on Thursday and Friday nights and so might not be appropriate for a quiet meal.

Calle Canals 219, Santurce. ✆ **787/725-1611.** Reservations recommended. Main courses $15–$40. Tues–Fri 11:30am–11pm, Sat 6:30–11pm. Bus: 5.

Silk ★★ PAN ASIAN   Top-notch Chinese food fills the menu at Silk, along with a complete sushi selection. The fare is fresh and delicious, and the big dining and bar areas, as well as the outside terrace, are tasteful and comfortable. The dark and roomy interior, brushed with Chinese red, has a sophisticated SoHo feel to it, and Silk does the classics—steamed dumplings, sesame noodles, Vietnamese spring rolls fried rice and lo-mein—with seasoned authority. We're particularly fond of the sizzling Mongolian, the fiery Kung Pao chicken, the scrumptious fried ice cream and, from the sushi menu, the Golden Dragon and Rock rolls. Our only quibble is that portions are smaller than your typical Chinese restaurant (in Puerto Rico most dishes come with fried rice and French fries) and prices are higher.

Av. de Diego 105, Gallery Plaza, Santurce. ✆ **787/721-1200.** Main courses $14–$39. Mon–Thurs 11am–11pm, Fri 11am–midnight, Sat noon–midnight, Sun noon–10pm. Bus: 5.

MODERATE

Boulangerie Tradición Francaise & Bistro ★ FRENCH   It's worth hunting down this out of the way country cafe (btw. Condado and Ocean Park) for its heavenly breakfasts (French toast with fresh fruit or the chunky French tortilla with ham and roasted potatoes) and exquisite almond croissants, baguettes, Napoleon pastries, and fresh fruit tarts. Throughout the day it offers surprising array of French classics like bouillabaisse, boeuf bourguignon, and cod filet in an artichoke sauce, and there's a number of delicious European–style sandwiches and pasta dishes. Excellent French roast coffee and Orangina are also served here.

Calle Taft 174. ② **787/721-6272.** Main courses $15–29; sandwiches $6.25–$11; breakfast $3.50–$13. Tues–Sun 7am–10pm. Bus: 5.

Cueva del Mar ★★ PUERTO RICAN/SEAFOOD   A locals' favorite, Cueva del Mar is a boisterous, fun restaurant with some of the best, and most affordable, seafood on the island. Go *bien criolla* with the *asopao de camarones* (shrimp rice stew), or the red snapper in *alcaparra* sauce, or stay more down island with the grouper in coconut sauce. It's all good. The *mofongo,* whether you have it stuffed with seafood in a *criolla* sauce or the churrasco, or as a side to anything, is particularly good, with a crunchy outer shield and perfectly a balanced, smooth interior. Not a fish fan? The chicken fricassee and roast pork are top notch, too. The kindly waiters will walk you through the menu and make sure you get something that delights your taste buds.

Santurce: Calle Loiza 1904, ② **787/726-8700.** Old San Juan: Calle Recinto Sur 205. ② **787/725-8700.** Reservations recommended. Main courses $13–$40. Sun–Thurs 11am–9:30pm, Fri–Sat 11am–11pm. Bus: 5.

Repostería Kasalta ★★ SPANISH/PUERTO RICAN   Repostería Kasalta is one of the best examples of the eponymous *pandarerias* across San Juan. These Spanish bakeries/delicatessens have cold cuts and Serrano hams, wonderful cheeses, roasted peppers, ceviches, big breakfast sandwiches, and fresh baked *pan de agua* and pastries. Kasalta's sandwiches—from the Cubano (roast pork, sweet ham, Swiss cheese and pickles, and mustard) to the beefsteak with arugula, tomato, and Gruyere—are among the finest in the city, and so is its *caldo gallego* soup. The Spanish entrees and tapas are top notch, and the fresh baked bread and pastries are among the tastiest in San Juan. President Barack Obama's quick stop here with Gov. Alejadro Garcia Padilla is immortalized with photos and a presidential special.

Av. McLeary 1966. ② **787/727-7340.** Reservations not accepted. Full American breakfast $3.50–$8.50; soups $3–$6; sandwiches $4.50–$15; entrees $5–$22. Daily 6am–10pm. Bus: 5, 53.

Tasca del Pescador ★★★ SEAFOOD   This small, always-packed restaurant across the street from the Santurce Plaza del Mercado has the best fresh seafood in the city. Start out with the seafood stuffed pepper, mixed seafood ceviche or the cod fritters. The seafood paella is excellent and will feed two, and there are rich seafood stews. The heart of the menu is a changing list of fresh catches of the day, none of which is likely to disappoint. Great Puerto Rican side dishes like perfectly fried *tostones* and flavorful *mofongo* round out the meal.

Calle Dos Hermanos 178. ② **787/721-0995.** Reservations not accepted. Entrees $12–$24. Tues–Sun 11am–6pm. Bus: 5.

Si No Corro Pizza ★★ PIZZA/WINE BAR   This neighborhood pizzeria is almost always crowded as it serves delicious pizza and pasta at extremely reasonable prices. You›ll want to try some appetizers—everything from the grilled chorizo to the mussels are excellent. The rustic style pizza is among the best in town (and San Juan is perhaps the best pizza town in the Caribbean) with such specialty combos pies as the Gardel (grilled chorizo, chimichurri, roast peppers, and red onion), the Mediterranean (eggplant, anchovies, olives, and basil), and the ultra-meaty La Loren (spicy Italian sausage, grilled and Spanish chorizo, bacon, and pepperoni). Pay attention to the daily specials: The pastas are just as good as the pizza. Si No Corro offers a good, reasonably priced wine selection; end your meal with tiramisu or gelato.

Calle Loiza 1917, Santurce. ✆ **787/998-2925.** Pasta $10–$15; pizza $13–$18. Sun–Thurs 11:30am–11pm, Fri–Sat 11:30am–midnight. Bus: 5.

Near Ocean Park

For the locations of these restaurants, see the map "Puerta de Tierra, Miramar, Condado & Ocean Park Hotels & Restaurants," on p. 61.

EXPENSIVE

Che's ★ ARGENTINEAN   One of the oldest Argentine steakhouses in the area, Che's is still one of the best. If you're driving, this is a good choice, since it has a big parking lot. Che's offers several steak options, along with sausage, chicken, and ribs. It also has a basic seafood selection, like lime halibut and garlic shrimp, several breaded veal and chicken cutlet options, and classic pastas. The place is causal and airy, perfect for families and no-fuss dining.

Calle Caoba 35. ✆ **787/726-7202.** Reservations recommended for dinner. Main courses $15–$30. Sun–Thurs 11:30am–10:45pm, Fri–Sat noon–midnight. Bus: 5.

Isla Verde

For the locations of restaurants in Isla Verde, see the map "Isla Verde Hotels & Restaurants," on p. 71.

EXPENSIVE

BLT Steak ★★ STEAKHOUSE   Leave it to a French chef, Laurent Tourondel, to recapture and update the extravagance of the American steakhouse. Here he offers outsized renditions of old-school classics, with very tasty results. The bone-in sirloin for two is a decadent treat, but so is hanger steak and rib-eye and the porterhouse for two, not to mention the grilled tuna. Diners have a choice of sauces including very flavorful chimichurri, béarnaise, peppercorn, and horseradish. And as at any good steakhouse, there are several toothsome potato options, including au gratin and jalapeno mashed potatoes. Leave room for the killer desserts.

In the Ritz-Carlton San Juan Hotel, Spa & Casino, Av. de los Gobernadores (State Rd.) 6961, no. 187, Isla Verde. ✆ **787/253-1700.** Reservations required. Main courses $22–$88; fixed-price menus $45–$75. Sun–Thurs 6–10:30pm, Fri–Sat 6–11pm. Bus: 5.

Koko ★ CARIBBEAN   The delicate and delicious Pan Caribbean cuisine served here meshes with the serene, nature-inspired decor, delivering one smooth dining experience. You'll see what we mean if you try the Jamaican picadillo dumplings, calypso fish tacos, or coconut tempura shrimp—three fine ways to open a meal. Move on to spiced rum pork tenderloin, red snapper with curried coconut risotto, or one of the daily specials. We must say, it's inspiring to see young local chefs looking to the wider Caribbean for inspiration, and the results are very flavorful here. Koko also houses a popular rum bar and lounge.

At El San Juan Hotel & Casino, Av. Isla Verde 1660. ✆ **787/791-7078.** Reservations not accepted. Main courses $23–$46. Daily 4pm–midnight. Bus: 5.

DINING WITH kids

Puerto Ricans love children and are more likely to bring them out to dinner than in many other countries. As a result, most restaurants are used to dealing with children and are prepared to handle them. Likewise, large family groups going out to restaurants are very common. The **Ciao Mediterranean Café** (below), right on the beach in Isla Verde, is a great place for lunch, especially if you're enjoying the beach. Pizzas, pastas, salads, and sandwiches are offered at reasonable prices. Big families will also appreciate the **Vaca Brava** (p. 58) *criollo* steakhouse with large enough platters, tables, sides, desserts, and flavors to handle any crew. There's also enough place to run around at **Brother Jimmy's BBQ** (below) on the roof of the El San Juan Hotel. Kids will also enjoy the food and ambience at **The Place** (p. 64) as much as their parents do. **El Jibarito** and **Raíces** are family friendly and local, and the **Parrot Club** (p. 54) has the tastiest kid's menu in town.

MODERATE

Brother Jimmy's BBQ ★ BARBECUE Brother Jimmy's spreads across the 8,000 square foot roof of El San Juan Hotel, serving its signature southern BBQ. For starters, we like the spinach and artichoke dip, the fried pickles and green tomatoes. Most move on next to chicken and ribs, country fried steak and sliced brisket. The bar specializes in over–the–top cocktails, and there are televisions everywhere, including a giant 25-foot screen, for sports, sports and more sports.

In El San Juan Hotel & Casino, Av. Isla Verde 6063. ℂ **787/791-1000.** Main courses $11–$27. Mon–Fri 5pm–midnight, Sat–Sun noon–midnight. Bus: 5.

INEXPENSIVE

Ciao Mediterranean Café ★ MEDITERRANEAN Yes this is one of those poolside hotel restaurants that serve flavorful but uninspired dishes based on the tastes of a generic U.S. tourist. Like those other establishments, Ciao's location is so perfect you often just don't mind paying more just so you won't have to leave. Even among hotel pool bars, this place is special, spreading across a boardwalk beneath palm trees and lined with blooming tropical plants that fronts the wide, golden Isla Verde beach. A long bar with seats runs the length of the restaurant from the beach side; it's a great spot to take a break from the sun. The food here is also a cut above most pool bar cafes, marked by influences from Spanish, Greek and Moroccan cuisine. It's helpful to know about when you want something good to eat without leaving the beach.

In the InterContinental San Juan Resort & Casino, Av. Isla Verde 5961. ℂ **787/791-6100.** Reservations recommended for dinner. Pizzas and salads $8–$20; main courses $12–$20. Daily 11:30am–11pm. Bus: 5.

Mi Casita ★ PUERTO RICAN Conveniently located near major hotels, Mi Casita specializes in Puerto Rican and American food, including U.S.-style breakfast. If you haven't tried mofongo (stuffed with shrimp or churrasco, arroz con pollo) you may want to here, as they do a good version of it. The menu covers a broad range, from Puerto Rican classics to cheeseburger platters. Don't visit during the height of lunch or dinner rush hour: Service backs up, and wait times balloon.

Plazoleta Isla Verde, Av. Isla Verde. ℂ **787/791-1777.** Main courses $8.95–$21. Daily 7:30am–10:30pm. Bus: 53, 5.

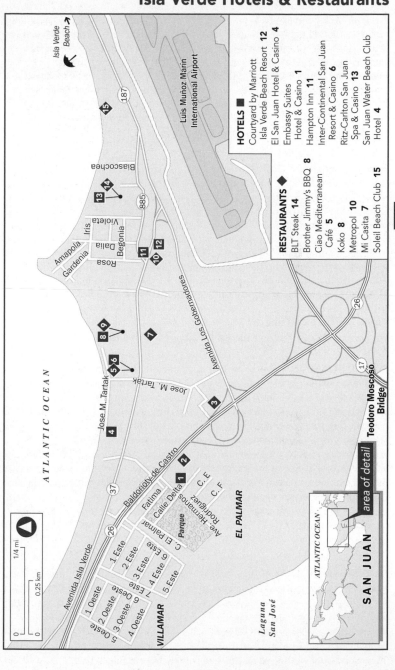

Isla Verde Hotels & Restaurants

HOTELS ■

Courtyard by Marriott
Isla Verde Beach Resort **12**
El San Juan Hotel & Casino **4**
Embassy Suites
Hotel & Casino **1**
Hampton Inn **11**
Inter-Continental San Juan
Resort & Casino **6**
Ritz-Carlton San Juan
Spa & Casino **13**
San Juan Water Beach Club
Hotel **4**

RESTAURANTS ◆

BLT Steak **14**
Brother Jimmy's BBQ **8**
Ciao Mediterranean
Café **5**
Koko **8**
Metropol **10**
Mi Casita **7**
Soleil Beach Club **15**

ATLANTIC OCEAN

Luis Munoz Marin
International Airport

Isla Verde Beach

Biascochea

Violeta
Iris
Begonia
Amapola
Dalia
Gardenia
Rosa

Avenida Los Gobernadores

Jose M. Tartak

Baldorioty de Castro

EL PALMAR

VILLAMAR

Avenida Isla Verde

Laguna
San José

Fatima
Calle Delta
Ave. Hermanos
Rodríguez
Parque
C. El Palmar
C. E
C. F

1 Oeste
2 Oeste
3 Oeste
4 Oeste
5 Oeste
6 Oeste
1 Este
2 Este
3 Este
4 Este
5 Este
6 Este
7 Este

Teodoro Moscoso
Bridge

ATLANTIC OCEAN

area of detail

SAN JUAN

1/4 mi
0.25 km

Metropol ★ CUBAN/PUERTO RICAN   This local institution has been serving tasty Cuban and Puerto Rican food in a family setting for a half-century. The menu is extensive, and portions are large. It includes dozens of steak and chop selections, paella and stuffed mofongo, asopao and roast pig, and all sorts of fresh fish and seafood options. All come with local side dishes like rice and black beans, sautéed yucca and *tostones*. If you have trouble deciding from among all the options, try the Fiesta Cubano, which is a selection of traditional island dishes: congri, tamale, pork, cassava, Latin pot roast, and shredded beef. On Sunday afternoon, Puerto Rican families in their Sunday best usually fill the dining room for celebrations of all sorts. The atmosphere, tasty home-style Latin cooking and low prices all harken back to a delicious past.

Club Gallistico, Av. Isla Verde. ✆ **787/791-4046.** Main courses $11–$37. Daily 11:30am–11:30pm. Bus: 53, 5.

Panadería España Repostería ★ BAKERY/DELI/SPANISH   If you are staying in Isla Verde and you want a real Spanish bakery, your best bet is to hoof it over the highway bridge to Panadería España, which makes strong coffee, a delicious Cubano sandwich (roast pork, Swiss cheese, pickles, and mustard), and specialties like *caldo gallego* soup, seafood paella, and braised chorizo. There's also fresh orange juice and baked delights such as lighter than air *pan de aqua* (the Caribbean version of the baguette), oversized cookies, and delicious cheese pastries simply called *quesitos*. A simple dining area fronts the deli and bakery counters and small kitchen.

Centro Comercial Villamar, Marginal Baldorioty de Castro. ✆ **787/727-3860.** Soups and tapas $4–$6; sandwiches $5–$8. Daily 6am–10pm. Bus: 5.

Near Isla Verde

For the location of this restaurant, see the map "Isla Verde Hotels & Restaurants," on p. 71.

Soleil Beach Club Piñones ★★ CARIBBEAN   This rustic oceanfront bar and restaurant has food as delicious as the view from its oceanfront terrace and second floor open air dining room. The laid-back beach vibe (you can hear the waves and smell sea salt from where you sit) and flavorful cuisine is an intoxicating mix that will have you lingering. The surf and turf (a grilled mix of shrimp, calamari, fresh fish filet, Angus skirt steak, chicken breast, and chorizo) is especially good, and this is a great spot to try the Caribbean lobster served in a *beurre blanc* sauce. The grilled fish kabobs, seafood avocado salad and coco curry chicken are other good options. The bar draws a crowd on weekend afternoons and early evenings, and the extensive appetizer offerings make it a great spot for drinks and snacks, as well.

Soleil Beach Club, Carretera 187, Km 4.6, Piñones. ✆ **787/253-1033.** Reservations recommended. Dinner main courses $13–$39; lunch specials $7–$10. Sun–Thurs 11am–11pm, Fri–Sat 11am–2am. Call ahead to arrange free transportation to and from your hotel in the Soleil Beach Club van.

Hato Rey

El Cairo Restaurant ★★ MIDDLE EASTERN   Tasty food, beautiful belly dancers and friendly service are reason enough this ranks as our favorite among San Juan's many great Middle Eastern restaurants, but the haremlike decor is also an attraction. We stick to the standard grilled kabobs, falafel, hummus, and tabbouleh, but the grilled lamb shank and keiba will not disappoint and neither will the tasty curry dishes. There's no better way to end a meal than with the wonderful baklava.

Calle Ensenada 352 (corner Av. Franklin Delano Roosevelt). ℂ **787/273-7140.** Reservations recommended Fri–Sun evenings. Main courses $12–$30. Sun and Tues–Thurs noon–10pm, Fri–Sat noon–11pm. Bus: 21.

Il Nuovo Perugino Enoteca ★★★ ITALIAN   This ultra-chic wine bar and restaurant is housed in what looks like a plush seashell. The creations by chef and owner Franco Seccarelli are as inspired as the setting. We love the pasta, from penne with pancetta in vodka sauce to the *paccheri alla matriciana,* and entrees, which range from veal scaloppini to parsley lamb chops to halibut in yellow pepper sauce, hit uncanny highs. There is also rich risotto and heavenly desserts, as well as friendly, efficient service.

Popular Center, Atrium Second Floor, Hato Rey. ℂ **787/722-5481.** Reservations recommended. Main courses $25–$41. Mon 11:30am–3pm, Tues–Sat 11:30am–10:30pm. Bus: 21.

WHERE TO STAY

Whatever your preferences in accommodations—a beachfront resort or a place in historic Old San Juan, sumptuous luxury or an inexpensive base from which to see the sights—you can find a perfect fit in San Juan.

In addition to checking the recommendations listed here, you might want to contact a travel agent; there are package deals galore, which can save you money and match you with an establishment that meets your requirements. Before talking to a travel agent, however, you should refer to our recommendations about how to select a room in Puerto Rico (p. 226).

Most hotels have air-conditioned rooms. We've pointed out the hotels that don't have them. They are mostly small guesthouses on the beach with a mix of rooms with air and rooms without.

Increasingly, hotels and guesthouses have Wi-Fi in the rooms and throughout the property and often offer it free of charge. We'll specify free Wi-Fi, where that's the case, and otherwise list when it's free in specific areas. Otherwise, expect a daily charge.

Taxes & Service Charges

All hotel rooms in Puerto Rico are subject to a tax that is not included in the rates given in this book. At casino hotels, the tax is 11 percent; at noncasino hotels, it's 9 percent. At government-sponsored country inns, called *paradores puertorriqueños,* you pay a 7 percent tax. Some hotels add a 10 percent service charge; if not, you're expected to tip for services rendered. Once confined to the larger properties, a growing number of hotels (including high-end guesthouses) are also applying a resort fee or hotel fee, which can range from 10 to 20 percent of the cost of your room per night. The fees are ostensibly to offset the costs of facilities, such as a pool or health club, but it is also a way of hoteliers trying to keep their listed prices as low as possible. We've listed the specific fees for each property here because of the prevalence of this practice, and the hefty rates some properties are charging. When you're booking a room, it's a good idea to ask about these charges anyway.

Old San Juan

Old San Juan, home to some of the most exquisitely restored Spanish architecture in the hemisphere, still plays a central role in the life of contemporary San Juan. Lodging options include boutique hotels and basic budget rooms and everything in between.

BEST FOR: Visiting art and antiques galleries, historic and cultural sites, shopping, dining, and nightlife.

DRAWBACKS: Beaches are a cab or bus ride away and there are no good resort-style pools in the Old City.

For the locations of hotels in Old San Juan, see the map on p. 55.

EXPENSIVE

Chateau Cervantes ★

The location at the Cervantes couldn't be better…and worse. On a street in the heart of Old San Juan, with the free trolley stop right outside, it's just a 5-minute walk from the cruise ship docks (making it a top choice for those who are combining sea and land vacations). However that central location means it gets a lot of traffic and noise, both day and night. As well, the standard rooms are lilliputian at just 200 square feet. But they're cunningly designed to feel larger (with just the furnishings guests' need) and all rooms feature a soothing color palette, pretty balconies and, for the bedding, luxurious Egyptian cotton sheets and custom mattresses. All this in a Spanish Colonial mansion with wrought iron balconies and arched windows and doorways—a charming and lovely space. We must also give a shout-out to the staff who are an especially hardworking and caring group. The nightly rate includes a sit-down continental breakfast at Panza restaurant at ground level.

Calle Recinto Sur 307, Old San Juan. ✆ **787/724-7722.** www.cervantespr.com. 12 units. Summer standard $130, suites $181–$192, presidential suite $870. Winter standard $162, suites $200–$300, presidential suite $910. Parking is at public lots across the street. Bus: Old City Trolley. **Amenities:** Restaurant, smoke-free rooms, Wi-Fi.

Hotel El Convento ★★★

One of the most storied hotels in all the Caribbean, El Convento was constructed in 1651 as a Carmelite nunnery, the first nunnery in the Americas. Though the original building was torn down and rebuilt in 1854, the historic ambiance of the place still harkens back to those early colonial times, thanks to such details as the Tuscan columns that guard the entrance, the exquisite latticed choir and the preserved historic details throughout. The inner courtyard, riotous with bougainvillea and leafy palms, holds one of the oldest trees in the city (it reached 300 several years back). Rooms are sumptuous steps back in time, with high ceilings striped with wooden beams, handmade tiles, pretty balconies, velvet settees and other elegant antiques. But don't worry, if you're more into fun in the sun than history, you'll be well taken care of here, too. On the roof is a splash pool, Jacuzzi and sundeck (all have incredible vistas over the city); and guests have beach access at El Convento's sister property. El Convento holds three restaurants, including a highly convivial tapas bar (reviewed on p. 56). There's even a state-of-the-art fitness center. If any place ever embodied the phrase "best of both worlds" this would be it.

Calle del Cristo 100, San Juan. ✆ **800/468-2779** or 787/723-9020. www.elconvento.com. 68 units. Winter $240–$330 double, $645 suite; summer $150–$240 double, $595 suite. $1,130 deluxe suite. Hotel fee 18 percent. Parking $20. Bus: Old City Trolley. **Amenities:** 4 restaurants, 3 bars, fitness center, Jacuzzi, small rooftop plunge pool, Wi-Fi.

Sheraton Old San Juan Hotel & Casino ★

The area in the direct vicinity of the cruiseship docks is not the best neighborhood to stay in Old San Juan, and while the Sheraton is comfortable, it lacks that Old City charm that mark other nearby options, many of which are more affordable than the Sheraton. The rooftop pool is the biggest in the neighborhood but still small by island standards, with a cramped sunbathing area. A huge casino dominates the ground floor and the lobby is often busy with cruise traffic. Bottom line, this is a good option only if you have to/or want to spend a lot of time in Old San Juan and need the accouterments of a full service hotel. There is nothing particularly unpleasant about the Sheraton, just nothing that makes it much of an attraction in and of itself. If you do stay here, walk up a block to SoFo and some of the best restaurants in all of San Juan for meals.

Calle Brumbaugh 100, San Juan. ℂ **800/325-3535** or 787/721-5100. www.sheraton.com. 240 units. Winter $189–$239 double, $239–$369 suite, $599 presidential suite; off season $169–$199 double, $240–$319 suite, $469 presidential suite. 11 percent resort fee. Valet parking $21. Bus: Old City Trolley. **Amenities:** 2 restaurants, 3 bars, casino, fitness center, Jacuzzi, outdoor pool, room service, smoke-free rooms, rooms for those w/limited mobility, Wi-Fi.

MODERATE

Casablanca Hotel ★★   The Casablanca offers that rarest of hotel amenities: real charm. Public spaces are filled with quirky, and often beautiful, works of pop art, along with a mash-up of contemporary and antique furnishings and big mosaic tiles. Rooms have as individual a feel; each is different, but all feature four-poster beds (with excellent mattresses), unconventional art on the walls, fun pieces of furniture (a brightly colored contemporary lamp here, an elaborately carved antique desk there), small balconies (in most) and a sense of fun. The hotel is set in the heart of the exuberant SoFo restaurant and retail district, which means guests can walk to pretty much everywhere in Old Town. The rooftop has a sundeck and stone bathing pools, an excellent spot to work on your tan without leaving the Old Town. Best of all is the staff, a charismatic bunch who know all there is to know about San Juan and go out of their way to help guests. The only downside to staying here (and it will be a serious one for some)? This five-story hotel has no elevator, so if you have a mobility impairment you'll want a guarantee that you're on the first floor.

Calle Fortaleza 316, San Juan. ℂ **787/725-3436.** www.hotelcasablancapr.com. 35 units. High season $149–$239; low season $120–$219. Prices include taxes and continental breakfast. Bus: Old City Trolley. **Amenities:** Reading lounge, free pass to nearby gym, rooftop terrace and stone plunge pools, free Wi-Fi.

Casa Sol Bed and Breakfast ★★   The Old City's first true B&B, Casa Sol is a beautiful, historic private home, elegantly furnished in a Spanish style, with charming hosts in Eddie and Tisha. Right in the middle of the historic sector, it makes a pleasant base to explore its forts, shops, galleries and cathedrals, as well as its restaurants, bars and clubs. The spot has a "quiet" policy from 8pm to 7am, meaning guests are asked to not to engage in loud conversations (or, er, other loud activities) should they come home late, so this is clearly not the spot for everyone. Those looking for a serene retreat, and a local view of living here, will be charmed by the stay. All the rooms are handsomely appointed, but the ones overlooking the interior patio are best.

Calle Sol 316, Old San Juan. ℂ **787/980-9700** or 787/399-0105. www.casasolbnb.com. 5 units. $168–$210. Rates include breakfast. Bus: Old City Trolley. **Amenities:** Spacious interior courtyard, bicycles, concierge and tour services, in-house cash laundry, free Wi-Fi.

Gallery Inn at Galería San Juan ★★   The drop-dead gorgeous lair of artist Jan D'Esopo, this centuries-old mansion looms over city, and boasts spectacular views from its rooftop wine deck of the steep Atlantic coast on one side and across Old San

Juan rooftop to the bay and beyond, on the other side. Jan's fine clay and bronze sculptures, paintings and prints adorn this highly bohemian, character-filled house, with its interior gardens and patios, fountains and tropical birds and a small waterfall pool. Guests are free to ramble through the 50-plus room inn, which spirals up seven levels. Much of the owner's work is on exhibit in the guest rooms. Yes, some of the bathrooms are dated and you'll see a scruff mark every once in a while on a wall. But most overlook those flaws (which don't show that the place isn't clean, it is—very!) because they feel privileged to be staying in such a unique environment.

Calle Norzagaray 204–206, San Juan. © **866/572-ARTE** (2783) or 787/722-1808. www.thegallery inn.com. 22 units (some with shower only). Off season $135–$165 double, $205–$250 suite; winter $195–$265 double, $310–$390 suite. 11 percent hotel fee. Off-season specials available. Rates include continental breakfast. 5 free parking spaces, plus street parking. Bus: Old City Trolley. **Amenities:** Breakfast room, vast public areas, free Wi-Fi in common areas.

Hotel Milano ★ This reasonably priced hotel in the middle of Old San Juan is clean and comfortable with modern amenities. The rooms are functional, but not charming, and they give no hint of the architectural grandeur of Old San Juan. That being said, the rooftop terrace, where continental breakfast is served, has great views and the rates are more than fair (usually).

Calle Fortaleza 307, San Juan. © **877/729-9050** or 787/729-9050. www.hotelmilanopr.com. 30 units. Winter $105–$185 double; off season $95–$145 double. 7 percent service charge. Continental breakfast $5.35. Bus: Old City Trolley. **Amenities:** Rooftop terrace cafe, free Wi-Fi, public computer in lobby.

Villa Herencia Hotel ★★ A stone's throw from El Convento, on perhaps Old San Juan's most iconic stepped street, this is another option for a romantic retreat where a centuries-old view of beauty still holds sway. Guests can luxuriate in a rooftop bath and soak up views of the Old City's blissfully crooked skyline. They also linger in its courtyards and fountain-filled tropical gardens, as well as its library and dining room, adorned with works by painter Roberto Parilla. The eight guest rooms feature Venetian mirrors and Eastern European chandeliers, handcrafted furniture, antiques, plush beds, balconies overlooking interior courtyards, and windows opening to capture the sea breeze. This is a rarefied experience at a reasonable rate.

Caleta Las Monjas 23, San Juan. © **877/722-0989.** www.villaherencia.com. 8 units. Winter $150–$250 double; off season $125–$225 double. 9 percent hotel fee. Continental breakfast $5.35. Bus: Old City Trolley. **Amenities:** Rooftop terrace, meeting rooms, free Wi-Fi.

INEXPENSIVE

Hotel Plaza de Armas ★ We recommend this somewhat dowdy property because it offers a clean, comfortable good night's sleep in the heart of the historic zone at an economic rate, not an easy find these days. The staff is friendly and full of good tips and the hotel is set right on the Plaza del Armas, meaning it rubs shoulders with San Juan City Hall and the Puerto Rico State Department, and is close to everything a visitor might want to see. Pass up the continental breakfast (not included in the nightly rate) and dine at the Cafe Cuatro Estaciones on the Plaza with the locals instead. Alas, it does not have a pool or sundeck.

Calle San José 202, San Juan. © **877/722-9191.** www.sanjuan-plazadearmashotel.com. 30 units. Winter $165–$195 double; off season $115–$135 double. Rates include taxes. Bus: Old Town Trolley. **Amenities:** Onsite bistro, smoke-free rooms, rooms for those w/limited mobility, Wi-Fi.

In **Condado** and **Isla Verde,** rates range from $525 a week for a studio to $2,250 a week for a deluxe, modern, three-bedroom condo. **San Juan Vacations,** Cond.

ROOM WITH A LOCAL'S VIEW: apartment RENTALS

Despite the explosion of Old City hotel and guesthouse rooms over the past few years, one of the best ways to experience the city remains getting a furnished apartment for a short-term rental. Many are restored, historic quarters with beautiful rooftop terraces or verdant interior courtyards, or both. During your vacation, you'll get a great sense of what it feels like to live in this enchanted city, and you'll normally save money (especially if yours is a large group).

Prices range from $500 weekly for a basic studio to $2,500 weekly for a three-bedroom, restored colonial beauty with rooftop terrace and ocean views. Short-term rentals are assessed a 7 percent tax, and many require a minimum 3- or 4-night stay. Cleaning fees are also assessed, which can range from $50 to $75.

The expert in Old City short-term rentals is **Vida Urbana,** Calle Cruz 255, Old San Juan ((*C* **787/587-3031;** www.vidaurbanapr.com), a spinoff of Caleta Realty, a veteran in this field. Years ago, I found a three-bedroom apartment through Caleta, a place near Catedral de San Juan, with huge adjoining living and dining rooms and a rooftop terrace running the length of the apartment. We loved it. We had a reception there, and a group of about eight friends stayed there for the week. A comparable apartment would cost around $1,500 for the week today. There are two lovely apartments for rent above the gallery and gift shop **Bóveda,** Calle Cristo 209, Old San Juan ((*C* **787/725-0263;** www.boveda.info), with artful, bright decor in a restored colonial building, complete with interior garden courtyard and balconies with double-door entrances. A cool tropical vibe flows through the duplex ($1,000 weekly) and studio suite ($500 weekly).

Marbella del Caribe, Ste. S-5, Isla Verde ((*C* **800/266-3639** or 787/727-1591; www.sanjuanvacations.com), is the biggest name in the business. We've also worked through **Ronnie's Properties,** Calle Marseilles 14, Ritz Condominium, Ste. 11-F, San Juan (www.ronniesproperties.com).

Puerta de Tierra

Stay in Puerta de Tierra only if you have a desire to be at the Caribe Hilton. When you stay in Puerta de Tierra, you're sandwiched halfway between Old San Juan and the Condado, but you're not getting the advantages of staying right in the heart of either.

BEST FOR: Families and other visitors who want a "resort" type of vacation and plan to spend as much time as possible at the Hilton, which has topnotch facilities and a private beach, as well as the mammoth Luis Muñoz Rivera Park and the Third Millennium Park, which are beautiful places during the day but mostly deserted at night.

DRAWBACKS: The neighborhood is not safe to walk around at night, requiring a rental car or taxi if you decide to venture off the grounds.

For the location of hotels in Puerta de Tierra, see the map on p. 61.

Caribe Hilton ★★ With its own beach (the only private one in San Juan) and large swatches of tropical gardens, the Caribe Hilton is still one of San Juan's finest properties in a city full of them. The infinity pool (plus two other pools), wide variety of restaurants (from Morton's to Quiznos) and picturesque Caribe Terrace bar and lounge, where the piña colada is said to have been born, are a large part of its appeal. The Caribe does have its challenges, however (and a 2014 renovation program suggests that staff is addressing them). First off there's a wide gulf between the quality of the rooms in the old and new towers. In the former, you're likely to experience slow elevators, cranky plumbing and dated decor. In the new, well, everything is newer, spiffier and up to Hilton's usual standards (so ask to change towers if you're not pleased with your digs). The Caribe's other problem is less fixable and that's its location, a neighborhood that is a nowhere man's land after dark, with very little commerce in the area anytime. Sure you can take a cab back home from Condado or Old San Juan after an evening meal, but all those cab fares do start to add up. Still, the views from the hotel are great, as is that private beach and because there are so many rooms to fill here, the Caribe often discounts deeply (do a thorough web search before booking).

Calle Los Rosales, San Juan. ℂ **800/445-8667** or 787/721-0303. www.caribe.hilton.com. 812 units. Winter $249–$299 double, $399–$749 suite; off season $105–$229 double, $412–$2,474 suite. Rates don't include taxes or 18 percent resort fee. Children 16 and under stay free in parent's room (maximum 4 people per room). Valet parking $23; self-parking $17. Bus: 5, 21. **Amenities:** Beach, 3 pools, 5 restaurants, 2 bars, babysitting, children's activities and playground, health club, room service, smoke-free rooms, rooms for those w/limited mobility, free Wi-Fi.

Condado

A wave of renovation has polished this landmark of the island's Tropical Modernism movement into San Juan's answer to South Beach, with designer boutiques and trendy restaurants, upscale jewelers and spas along Ashford Avenue, and its gorgeous beachfront filled with beautiful people and fashionistas.

BEST FOR: Those who want to mix their fun in the sun with some cosmopolitan shopping, dining, and partying. The area draws a young crowd and GLBT travelers. It has good bus connections into Old San Juan, and taxis are plentiful.

DRAWBACKS: The surf can become rough, and the beach is shorter and narrower than those at Ocean Park and Isla Verde.

For the locations of hotels in Condado, see the map on p. 61.

EXPENSIVE

La Concha: A Renaissance Resort ★★★   This fab beach hotel is a shining example of Puerto Rico's tropical modernism architecture movement. It first opened in December 1958, and underwent a sweeping rehabilitation and makeover for its 50th birthday, staying true to the original design while updating the property to current standards and tastes. The structure was built to incorporate the natural elements surrounding it into the hotel, and sea breezes and the beach light are ever present in its public areas, especially elegant and open white marble lobby, which has gurgling fountains and river ponds, and blends into the outdoor terraces, tropical gardens and leveled pool areas outside. The rooms are restrained, with updated Mid-Century-Modern-style furnishings and seek to make the most of their view, especially ocean side rooms. The hotel has an enviable location in the center of Condado and adjacent to the Ventana del Mar park and a fine beach. It attracts a young urban crowd, as well as locals to its casino, bars and restaurants. This is a very lively spot.

Av. Ashford 1077, San Juan. ℂ **877/524-7778** or 787/721-7500. www.laconcharesort.com. 248 units. Winter $299–$359 double, $399–$499 suite; off season $199–$269 double, $299–$409 suite. 18 percent resort fee. Valet parking $20; self-parking $15. Bus: C53, B21. **Amenities:** 6 restaurants, 2 bars, 3 pools, room service, rooms for those w/limited mobility, Wi-Fi.

Olive Boutique Hotel ★★   The Olive combines Mediterranean luxury and warm service to create a hotel so appealing, most guests forget it's not on the beach. The decor is inspired by the owners' travels, which means a mélange of contemporary French, Italian, Moroccan and Spanish influences. How does that translate? You'll see a lot of wrought iron lamps and chandeliers, chicly distressed wooden walls, modesty–be-damned all-glass bathrooms (in some guestrooms) and a canny mix of antiques with more contemporary pieces throughout the hotel. All in all, the guestrooms (and beds) are wonderfully comfortable, though the standard suites are on the small side. The rooftop terrace and bar-cafe are another key lure, with breath-taking views and a fun, adult ambiance.

Calle Aguadilla 55, Condado. ℂ **877/705-9994.** www.oliveboutiquehotel.com. 15 units. $229–$269, plus $45 nightly resort fee and 9 percent hotel room tax. Rates include continental breakfast. Valet parking $21. Bus: 5. **Amenities:** Rooftop terrace, business center services, free Wi-Fi.

San Juan Marriott Resort & Stellaris Casino ★★   We love this place for its super friendly staff, great location, and open and functional design, evident in public areas, from the lobby to the oceanside pool and sun terrace. That openness also informs the guest rooms' design which features spacious siting areas, oversized bathrooms and balconies. Anyway you turn outside the hotel you will find fine bars, shops and restaurants. The lobby bar often has Latin big band performances and the casino is popular and busy. The poolside restaurant and bar are top notch. A favorite with families, it's one of the best big hotels in Condado, period.

Av. Ashford 1309, San Juan. ℂ **800/228-9290** or 787/722-7000. www.marriott.com. 525 units. Winter $289–$349 double, $369–$414 suite; summer $195–$255 double, $285–$305 suite. Resort fee 18 percent. Valet parking $20; self-parking $16. Bus: B21, A5. **Amenities:** 3 restaurants, 3 bars, babysitting, casino, health club, Jacuzzi, 2 pools, room service, sauna, 2 tennis courts, rooms for those w/limited mobility, Wi-Fi.

MODERATE

Comfort Inn   This family-oriented hotel has small, bland hotel rooms and a small swimming pool but offers good rates (surf the Internet for discounts as well as looking at air/hotel packages) and is near a great beach and newly renovated oceanfront plaza with open-air restaurants and lots of nice spots to hang out. Each room has either one or two queen-size beds, and each has a tub-and-shower bathroom. Some additionally have sofas that convert into beds for children.

Calle Clemenceau 6, Condado, San Juan. ℂ **800/858-7407** or 787/721-0170. www.comfortinn.com. 50 units. $119 double; $189 suite. $5 per person hotel fee. Parking $15. Bus: 21 or 10. **Amenities:** Outdoor pool, computers with high-speed Internet, rooms for those w/limited mobility, free Wi-Fi.

INEXPENSIVE

Acacia Boutique Hotel ★   A half block from the beach, this cozy residence has bright guest rooms with simple furnishings and small bathrooms with showers. There is a great rooftop terrace, hot tub and sundeck and a tropical garden. Guests can use the pool at Wind Chimes Inn across the street. As at the Wind Chime, the main draw here is the quiet beach, which is wide, safe and shaded by tall palms and almond trees.

Calle Taft 8, Condado, San Juan. ℂ **787/725-0668.** www.acaciaboutiquehotel.com. 15 units (shower only). Winter $175–$275 double; summer $125–$225 double. 5 percent service fee. Parking $10. Bus: A5 or B21. **Amenities:** Pool, gardens, free Wi-Fi.

At Wind Chimes Inn ★   The fact that this guest house is a block from the beach, instead of directly on it, may give some pause, but this is one of the best guesthouses in the area, and steps away from probably the best stretch of beach in Condado (the swatch from Parque del Indio to Ocean Park). The same can be said for its nearby sister property, the Acacia Boutique Hotel. A Spanish colonial-era manor Wind Chimes has a small pool and a tiled courtyard, plus a nice cafe/bar for guests. There are 22 differently sized rooms, each with kitchens, ceiling fans, and air conditioners. Beds are comfortable, but some of the quarters could use a bit of TLC. They not dirty, just dated. Final perk: the setting in a nice, residential area with lots of good restaurants and bars.

Av. McLeary 1750, Condado, San Juan. ℭ **800/946-3244** or 787/727-4153. www.atwindchimesinn. com. 22 units (shower only). Winter $207–$259 double; off season $99–$130 double. 5 percent service fee. Parking $10. Bus: 21, 5. **Amenities:** Bar, outdoor pool, room service, rooms for those w/limited mobility, free Wi-Fi.

Canario Boutique Hotel ★
This perfectly positioned lodging is one of the biggest bargains in Condado. A block from the beach and near all shops, restaurants, bars and parks, the location couldn't be better. So what if calling it a "boutique hotel" is stretching the truth a hair? This is, in reality, a very simple motel, with tiny rooms and no amenities beyond the included breakfast. Still, for the price and the level of maintenance (it's very clean), we think it's a solid choice for budgeteers.

Av. Ashford 1317, Condado, San Juan. ℭ **800/533-2649.** www.canariohotels.com. Bus: 21, 5. **Amenities:** Patio, whirlpool, free Wi-Fi, included breakfast.

Casa del Caribe ★
Let's get the negatives out of the way first: Rooms here are dowdy and dated, and the Internet is turtle slow. But when you get over those downsides, we think you'll like Casa del Caribe, especially at the low price you'll likely be paying (surf the Internet). A half a block from bustling Ashford Avenue, this quiet, 1940's era guesthouse is hidden away behind garden walls and under towering shade trees. The veranda and tropical courtyard are lovely, the air-conditioning in the guestrooms works well and the mattresses are comfy. Most importantly, you're in the middle of Condado, just a 2-minute walk to beach and top hotels and restaurants.

Calle Caribe 57, El Condado, San Juan. ℭ **787/722-7139.** www.casadelcaribebedandbreakfast. com. 13 units. Winter $85–$155 double; off season $65–$129 double. 5 percent room service fee. Rates include continental breakfast. Parking $10. Bus: B21. **Amenities:** Smoke-free rooms, 1 room for those w/limited mobility, free Wi-Fi, kitchens in some rooms.

Holiday Inn Express ★
This economic Condado alternative has a good location (just off bustling Ashford Av.), and while it lacks the charm of many area guest houses in the same price range, service is consistent and the hotel has a small, shady pool. Make sure your room has a balcony that opens up to a water view (the hotel is near the Condado Lagoon and the Windows on the Sea Park).

Calle Marinao Ramirez Bages 1, Condado, San Juan. ℭ **888/465-4329** or 787/724-4160. www. ichotels.com. 115 units. Winter $139–$209 double; off season $139–$279 (weekend surcharges apply). $5.50 service fee. Rates include continental breakfast. Parking $15. Valet $16. Bus: B21. **Amenities:** Health club, pool, whirlpool, Wi-Fi.

Miramar

Miramar, a residential neighborhood, is very much a part of metropolitan San Juan, and a brisk 30-minute walk will take you where the action is. Regrettably, a good beach is about a mile away. It's also home to the new Convention Center District, two marinas, and a commuter airport.

BEST FOR: Visitors who come to Puerto Rico to attend an event at the Convention Center located here.

DRAWBACKS: It's far from the beach, has few hotels and rooms, and few tourist attractions or amenities except for a string of fine restaurants and some interesting shops.

For the location of hotels in Miramar, see the map on p. 61.

Sheraton Puerto Rico Hotel & Casino ★   Most of the guests who stay here do so to attend events at the adjacent Puerto Rico Convention Center. But we have to give the hotel props for its facilities, which include the island's largest casino, and a superb spa and health club. The casino draws a crowd, and there are popular restaurants onsite, like Texas de Brazil. On weekends, there is as likely to be a DJ show or concert taking place at the Convention Center as a convention. We also like the looks of the Sheraton, its stylish guestrooms and common area, that handsome (and massive skylight) and its vast windows. All that being said, the hotel is a long walk to the best beaches, restaurants and nightlife (most guests rent a car or resign themselves to a lot of time in taxis and buses). Bottom line: Unless you're here for a convention, you'll likely want to stay in a more happening neighborhood, despite the hotel's strengths.

200 Convention Blvd., San Juan. © **866/932-7269** or 787/993-3500. www.sheratonpuertorico hotelcasino.com. 503 units. Winter $275–$285 double, $369–$375 suite; off season $149–$169 double, $197–$242 suite; $369–$2,619 Governor's suite; $469–$3,320 President's suite. Resort fee 16 percent. Children 16 and under stay free in parent's room (max. 4 people per room). Valet parking $22; self-parking $16. Bus: C53. **Amenities:** 3 restaurants, 2 bars, babysitting, casino, health club, room service, complete spa, smoke-free rooms, rooms for those w/limited mobility, Wi-Fi.

Santurce & Ocean Park

Santurce is the traditional downtown area of San Juan, and Ocean Park is a beautiful oceanfront neighborhood wedged in between the Condado and Isla Verde tourism districts. Santurce has been undergoing a revival, with Art Deco theaters and beautiful apartments being renovated; it's now the home to the city's best museums, performing arts center, and increasingly, among its best clubs and pubs. Ocean Park is a beautiful neighborhood, filled with palm trees and gorgeous homes, and has the city's most charming beach, fronted by low-slung homes and guest houses rather than the towering luxury condominiums and resorts that line Condado and Isla Verde. There are no suitable hotel rooms in downtown Santurce, but Ocean Park has some of the best guesthouses in the city.

BEST FOR: Visitors who want to feel the sand between their toes as much as possible, and prefer an intimate inn to a big hotel or resort.

DRAWBACKS: No resort-style swimming pools. The area is quiet at night and you need a cab to go to Condado, Isla Verde, or Old San Juan after sundown.

EXPENSIVE

Número Uno Guest House ★★★   The best guesthouse in Ocean Park has plush, stylish guestrooms with snazzy oversized bathrooms, handsome public areas, and an excellent on-site restaurant and bar. Not enough? Numero Uno fronts the best stretch of beach in San Juan, bar none. Yes, it's a public beach but wonderfully low key, pristine and friendly. The staff (a terrific bunch) set up loungers for guests there free of charge, and are happy to serve meals and cocktails to those lounging on the sands. Inside the guesthouse area are gurgling fountains and tropical gardens, along with the mosaic-tiled dining room, patios, and terraces. Get your reservations here very early, as the same guests tend to return year after year.

Calle Santa Ana 1, Ocean Park, San Juan. © **866/726-5010** or 787/726-5010. www.numero1guest house.com. 13 units (shower only), including economy, oceanview, jr. suites, and apts. High season

$139–$239 double, $590 penthouse; low season $99–$179 double, $550 penthouse. Hotel fee 15 percent. Rates include continental breakfast. Free street parking. Bus: C53, A5. **Amenities:** Restaurant, bar, outdoor pool, limited room service, rooms for those w/limited mobility, Wi-Fi.

MODERATE

Hosteria del Mar ★   A 2014 upgrade has improved this property immensely, but we still suggest you splurge for an ocean-view room, with either a balcony or terrace, right on San Juan's most low-key beach. It's well worth the extra $40 especially since rooms are comfortable but a bit drab, something you won't notice if you are on the beach side. Suites and efficiencies with kitchen facilities are also available. Uvva, the onsite restaurant is fired up from 8am to 10pm, with everything from healthy wraps to steaks on the menu. There is seating inside, on a sundeck or down along the beach, making it easy to linger on property.

Calle Tapía 1, Ocean Park, San Juan. ✆ **877/727-3302** or 787/727-3302. www.hosteriadelmarpr. com. 27 units. Year-round $139–$179 double, $279 apt. Children 11 and under stay free in parent's room. Self-parking on the street in a gated beachfront community with security. Dogs under 40 lb. allowed in room for $25 per night. Bus: 5. **Amenities:** Restaurant, room service, Wi-Fi.

INEXPENSIVE

Oceana Hostal Playero ★   A block from the best beach in the city, this is an affordable option for those looking to spend their days on the beach and their nights eating and partying nearby. Other than that, there's not much special about the place: Rooms are dowdy if clean (though you will see scuff marks on the walls and other signs of wear and tear). Suites have kitchens and can sleep up to six. The property has a small pool and sundeck, outdoor patio, and a nice health food restaurant.

Av. McLeary 1853, Ocean Park, San Juan. ✆ **787/728-8119.** 17 units (some shower only, some tub only). Winter $188–$228 double, $248–$488 suite; off season $155–$195 double, $218–$418 suite. $10 per night hotel fee. Rates include continental breakfast. Free parking. Bus: A5 or A7. **Amenities:** Small pool, restaurant, free Wi-Fi.

Isla Verde

The fat golden beach here is mighty fine, and the top hotels fronting it have verdant landscaping, large pools, watersports of all sorts, and lounge chairs along the beach. The top restaurants and clubs at the hotels alone make Isla Verde a great nightlife spot, but there are numerous stand-alone restaurants, pubs, and clubs of top quality. It's also the nearest vacation spot to the airport. Its main drag is filled with U.S.-based or -styled stores and restaurants, and there are many local spots as well.

BEST FOR: Visitors who want to stay at a resort-style hotel; spend as much time on the beach as possible; and want to be entertained and wined and dined near their hotel.

DRAWBACKS: Isla Verde is the least cultural part of San Juan, and Avenida Isla Verde is like many other overdeveloped roadways in the U.S., with strip malls and towering condominiums. If you want to discover what Puerto Rico is like, you have to leave the neighborhood.

EXPENSIVE

El San Juan Hotel & Casino: The Waldorf Astoria Collection ★★   The El San Juan doesn't shy away from glamour. Its 13,000 square-foot casino is served by tuxedo-clad croupiers and aglitter with crystal chandeliers. The opulent lobby, hand-carved of marble and mahogany, is ground zero to a number of popular bars and restaurants, for decades a place to see and be seen, with local celebrities rubbing shoulders with well-heeled travelers from around the globe. The fab pool area features swim-up bars and waterfalls. And though the designers can't take credit for Mother Nature's handiwork, the beach is everything a vacationer would want: broad, pristine golden sands, bedecked with loungers. It, and the resort's tropical gardens, are shaded by hundreds of towering palm trees and century-year-old banyans. Guest rooms are done in either bright tropical or subdued earth tones; all are well equipped electronically and have comfortable beds and furnishings, with cutting edge bathrooms and amenities. But no place is perfect, and some guests do complain about the noise from the planes arriving and departing from the airport (which is quite close by).

Av. Isla Verde 6063, San Juan. © **888/579-2632** or 787/791-1000. www.luxuryresorts.com. 382 units. Winter $199–$249 double, $299–$399 suite; off season $149–$179 double, $199–$299 suite. Resort fee 18 percent. Valet parking $21; self-parking $16. Bus: A5, C53. **Amenities:** 7 restaurants, 4 bars, babysitting, casino, children's programs, health club, 2 outdoor pools, room service, sauna and steam room, spa, tennis courts, watersports equipment/rentals, rooms for those w/limited mobility, Wi-Fi.

InterContinental San Juan Resort & Casino ★

The Intercontinental's best features are its wonderful pool and the surrounding pool area (with waterfalls and swim-up bars), its pristine beach and the oceanside Ciao Mediterranean Café, which rambles across a beachfront boardwalk. The on-site spa is also a winner, with an expert staff and treatment spaces both indoors and out. A heavy-handed wrist-band policy, however, is annoying to most guests and dampens the desired tranquil vibe. Rooms are comfortable and functional, if somewhat conservatively decorated. The InterContinental is close to other area resorts, restaurants, bars, and shops. Guests can easily walk anywhere within Isla Verde.

Av. Isla Verde 5961, Isla Verde. © **800/468-9076** or 787/791-6100. www.ichotelsgroup.com. 402 units. Winter $281–$318 double, $344–$719 suite; off season $209–$270 double, $453–$626 suite. 18 percent resort fee. Children 15 and under stay free in parent's room. Valet parking $25; self-parking $20. Bus: 5, 53. **Amenities:** 3 restaurants, lounge, babysitting, health club, pool, room service, sauna, scuba diving, whirlpool, rooms for those w/limited mobility, Wi-Fi.

Ritz-Carlton San Juan Spa & Casino ★★★

San Juan's most sumptuous resort is set on 8 beachfront acres and once you're here, there's really no reason to leave. The beach is special one, with areas of wading pools perfect for infants, protected swatches with tranquil water, and areas with small but consistent surf of from 1- to 3-foot waves, perfect spots to learn to surf with a great onsite surf school. Surfing is just one of the many offered water sports; the Ritz also runs a topnotch kid's club. Great dining, including outposts of New York City's BLT Steak and Il Mulino, is a prized feature of the resort. The large guest rooms, with ocean or garden views, have extra-comfy beds and sofas swathed in fine linens, and marble bathrooms. The ninth floor boasts preferred accommodations and a private Ritz-Carlton Club lounge with personal concierge staff.

Av. de los Gobernadores (State Rd.) 6961, No. 187, Isla Verde. © **800/241-3333** or 787/253-1700. www.ritzcarlton.com. 416 units. Winter $529–$729 double, $749–$1,279 suite; off season $229–$359 double, $429–$1,279 suite. Resort fee 16 percent. Valet parking $25; self-parking $17. Bus: 5. **Amenities:** 5 restaurants, 3 bars, nightclub, babysitting, Caribbean's largest casino, children's program, health club, large pool, room service, spa, 2 tennis courts, rooms for those w/limited mobility, Wi-Fi.

MODERATE

Courtyard by Marriott Isla Verde Beach Resort ★★

A large property close to the airport, Courtyard by Marriot is right on the beach at Pine Grove, a spot favored for beach lovers for its fine white sand and gentle blue water. With a wraparound veranda lined with massive hammocks and beach chairs, laid-back is the driving force at this property; it's blessed with a spacious pool area and beachfront, and a large indoor bar and dining area. The lobby is a bit cold feeling, but you can learn to dance salsa or surf here, and there are a number of restaurants plus a casino and nightclub on site. Be warned that even with double-paned windows, noise from the nearby airport can still be an issue. However, for the price, you're getting the same golden sands as the ritzier hotels down the avenue, which may be worth the minor inconvenience.

Boca de Cangrejos Avenida 7012, Isla Verde. ℂ **800/791-2553** or 787/791-0404. www.sjcourtyard. com. 293 units. Winter $279–$329 double, $354–$454 suite; off season $185–$260 double, $260–$360 suite. 18 percent hotel fee. Valet parking $20; self-parking $15. Bus: M7. **Amenities:** 3 restaurants, ice-cream parlor, bar, casino, free Wi-Fi.

Embassy Suites Hotel & Casino ★

This all-suites property has primo accommodations, but it's 2 long blocks from the beach, which is hard to overcome even with the (arguably) better quality of rooms and service here. Oversized rooms are well equipped with excellent beds and plush extras like usable fridges, sitting rooms and microwaves. The public areas, with palms and fountains, are darn nice, as is lagoon-style pool. There are also a nice range of dining options on site from El Patio, which serves tapas and sangria, to a branch of Outback Steakhouse.

Calle José M. Tartak 8000, Isla Verde, San Juan. ℂ **800/362-2779** or 787/791-0505. www.embassy suites.com. 299 suites. Winter $159–$169 1-bedroom suite, $259 2-bedroom suite, $650 presidential suite; off season $139–$149 1-bedroom suite, $239 2-bedroom suite, $650 presidential suite. Rates include breakfast and free happy hour 5:30–7:30pm. Valet parking $20; self-parking $16. Bus: 5 or 21. **Amenities:** 2 restaurants, 3 bars, small casino, health club, pool, room service, rooms for those w/limited mobility, Wi-Fi.

Hampton Inn

Across Isla Verde Avenue a 10-minute walk from the beach, this moderately priced property rubs shoulders with the finest resorts in the area and is within walking distance of the best bars, restaurants, and casinos in Isla Verde. The guest rooms are surprisingly stylish, with plush beds and sofas and other extras, and breakfast is included, adding to the value, and making it popular for families on a budget. The pool is pleasant, but guests will more likely want to hang at the beach. There's not much going on here, but it's a comfortable home base.

Av. Isla Verde 6530, Isla Verde. ℂ **800/HAMPTON** (426-7866) or 787/791-8777. http://hampton inn3.hilton.com. 201 units. Winter $244–$254 double, $264–$284 suite; off season $159–$169 double, $189–$199 suite. Rates include breakfast bar. Parking $10. Bus: 5, 45. **Amenities:** Bar, babysitting, health club, high-speed Internet, pool, whirlpool, rooms for those w/limited mobility, free Wi-Fi.

Howard Johnson Hotel

This property offers clean modern rooms in the Isla Verde beach district at an economic rate, a block away from a great beach and the boulevard that is home to the biggest hotels, restaurants and clubs in the district. There's a small pool and health club, but most guests will want to head straight to the fat golden beach across the street. If you don't want to linger in your hotel room, instead maximizing nightlife and beach time, you won't regret returning to it when it's finally time for bed. A great local pizzeria is on site.

Av. Isla Verde 4820, Isla Verde. ℂ **787/728-1300.** www.hojo.com. 115 units. Winter $140–$185 double, $210 suite; summer $98–$124 double, $145 suite. Parking $7. Bus: A\5. **Amenities:** 2 restaurants, health club, pool, rooms for those w/limited mobility, free Wi-Fi.

San Juan Water Beach Club Hotel ★★

Hipster heaven, the San Juan Water Beach Club is *almost* a beachfront resort (you have to walk on a small path next to the parking lot to get to the sands but can see the water from most guestrooms). Rooms are sleek aqua-and-white affairs, with polished stone floors, rainfall showers and I-Pod docking stations. Unfortunately, they have little closet and dresser space, and the walls are thin, so noise between rooms can be a problem. The lobby and lounges are trendy affairs, with projections that make the walls look watery, and billowing curtains and artwork that carry on the ocean theme. The property has a hopping 11th-floor bar with the Caribbean's only rooftop fireplace and beautiful dining and lounges areas, as well as a rooftop pool and sundeck.

Calle José M. Tartak 2, Isla Verde. © **888/265-6699** or 787/253-3666. www.waterclubsanjuan.com. 84 units. Winter $181–$258 double, $317 suite; off season $144–$225 double, $288 suite. Hotel fee 14 percent. Parking $15 daily. Bus: 5, 21. **Amenities:** Restaurant, 2 bars, fitness center, Jacuzzi, outdoor rooftop pool, room service, smoke-free rooms, rooms for those w/limited mobility, Wi-Fi.

SAN JUAN ATTRACTIONS

The Spanish began to settle in the area now known as Old San Juan around 1521. At the outset, the city was called Puerto Rico ("Rich Port"), and the whole island was known as San Juan. Today, the streets are narrow and teeming with traffic, but a walk through Old San Juan—in Spanish, El Viejo San Juan—makes for a good stroll. It's the biggest and best collection of historic buildings, stretching back 5 centuries, in all the Caribbean, and you can do it in less than a day. Some visitors have likened it to a "Disney park with an Old World theme," since even fast food restaurants and junk stores are housed in historic buildings. In this historic 7-square-block area of the western side of the city, you can see many of Puerto Rico's chief sightseeing attractions and do some shopping along the way.

On the other hand, you might want to plop down on the sand with a drink or get outside and play. "Diving, Fishing, Tennis & Other Outdoor Pursuits," later in this chapter, describes the beaches and sports in the San Juan area.

SEEING THE SIGHTS

Forts

Castillo de San Felipe del Morro ★★★ HISTORIC SITE   Called "El Morro," this fort stands on a rocky promontory dominating the entrance to San Juan Bay. Constructed in 1540, the original fort was a round tower, which can still be seen deep inside the lower levels of the castle. More walls and cannon-firing positions were added, and by 1787, the fortification attained the complex design you see today. Both the English and the Dutch attacked this fortress repeatedly.

The U.S. National Park Service protects the fortifications of Old San Juan, which, together, have been declared a World Heritage Site by the United Nations. With some of the most dramatic views in the Caribbean, you'll find El Morro an intriguing labyrinth of dungeons, barracks, vaults, lookouts, and ramps. Historical and background information is provided in a video in both English and Spanish. The nearest parking is the underground facility beneath the Quincentennial Plaza at the Ballajá barracks (Cuartel de Ballajá) on Calle Norzagaray. Park rangers lead hour-long tours for free, although you can also visit on your own.

El Morro, along with Fort San Cristóbal (see below), forms the **San Juan National Historic Site.** Ancient underground tunnels originally

5

0

Old San Juan Attractions

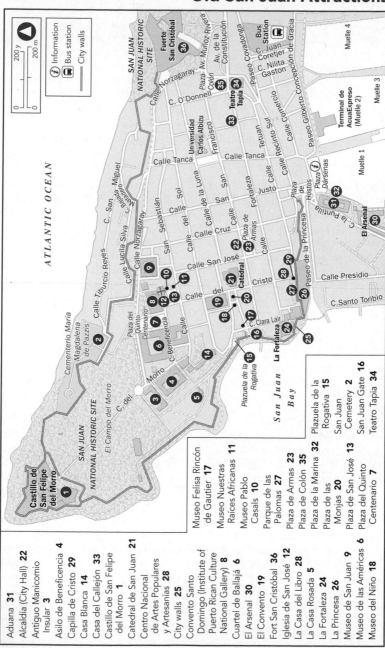

connected the forts, but today two modern trolleys ferry visitors back and forth. The walk, however, is beautiful along the oceanfront Calle Norzagaray. A museum at El Morro provides a history of the fort through exhibits of historic photographs and artifacts, written orientations, and a video presentation. A guided tour is offered hourly, but informational brochures allow you to walk around on your own while learning the story. There's also a gift shop. Make sure to walk out on the northernmost point, a narrow wedge overlooking the waves crashing into the rocky coast. The promenade circling the base of the fort is also worth exploring. The grounds of El Morro are a great spot to fly a kite, and families and children are out every weekend doing so. An annual kite festival is also held every March. You can buy a kite at stands right in front of the fort, or at Puerto Rico Drug or Walgreens on Plaza Colón.

At the end of Calle Norzagaray. ℂ **787/729-6960.** www.nps.gov/saju/index.htm. Admission $5 adults (16 and older), free for children 15 and under. Daily 9am–6pm. Closed Thanksgiving, Christmas, and New Year's. Parking $2 hourly. Bus: Old San Juan Trolley.

Fort San Cristóbal ★★★ CASTLE   Construction on this huge fortress began in 1634. The structure was reengineered in the 1770s, and is one of the largest ever built in the Americas by Spain. Its walls rise more than 150 feet (46m) above the sea—a marvel of military engineering. San Cristóbal protected San Juan against attackers coming by land in conjunction with El Morro, which protected the city from invaders by seas. The two are linked by a half-mile (.8km) of monumental walls and bastions filled with cannon-firing positions. A complex system of tunnels and dry moats connects the center of San Cristóbal to its "outworks," defensive elements arranged layer after layer over a 27-acre (11-hectare) site. To get the full scope, be sure to look at the scale model on display. Like El Morro, the fort is administered and maintained by the U.S. National Park Service. Be sure to see the *Garitadel Diablo* (the Devil's Sentry Box), one of the oldest parts of San Cristóbal's defenses, and famous in Puerto Rican legend. The devil himself, it is said, would snatch away sentinels at this lonely post at the edge of the sea. In 1898, cannons on top of San Cristóbal fired the first shots of the Spanish-American War in Puerto Rico during an artillery duel with a U.S. Navy fleet. Park rangers lead hour-long tours for free here, but wandering on your own is fun.

In the northeast corner of Old San Juan (uphill from Plaza de Colón, on Calle Norzagaray). ℂ **787/729-6960.** www.nps.gov/saju/index.htm. Admission $5 both forts, free for children 15 and under. Daily 9am–6pm. Bus: Free trolley from Covadonga station to the top of the hill.

Churches

Capilla de Cristo ★ CHURCH   Cristo Chapel was built to commemorate what legend says was a miracle. In 1753, a young rider lost control of his horse in a race down this very street during the fiesta of St. John's Day and plunged over the precipice. Moved by the accident, the secretary of the city, Don Mateo Pratts, invoked Christ to save the youth, and he had the chapel built when his prayers were answered. Today it's a landmark in the old city and one of its best-known historical monuments. The chapel's gold and silver altar can be seen through its glass doors. Because the chapel is open only 1 day a week, most visitors have to settle for a view of its exterior.

Calle del Cristo (directly west of Paseo de la Princesa). ℂ **787/722-0861.** Free admission. Tues 8am–5pm. Bus: Old City Trolley.

Catedral de San Juan ★★ CATHEDRAL   The spiritual and architectural centerpiece of Old San Juan began construction in 1540 as a replacement for a thatch-roofed chapel that was blown apart by a hurricane in 1529. Chronically hampered by a lack of funds and a recurring series of military and weather-derived disasters, it slowly evolved into the gracefully vaulted, Gothic-inspired structure you see today.

Joggers' Trail or Romantic Walk

El Morro Trail, a jogger's paradise, provides the Old City's most scenic views along San Juan Bay. The first part of the trail extends to the San Juan Gate. The walk then goes by El Morro and eventually reaches a scenic area known as Bastion de Santa Barbara. The walk passes El Morro's well-preserved walls, and the trail ends at the entrance to the fortress. The walkway is designed to follow the undulating movement of the ocean, and sea grapes and tropical vegetation surround benches. The trail is romantic at night, when the walls of the fortress are illuminated. Stop at the tourist office for a map, and then set off on the adventure.

Among the many disasters to hit this cathedral are the following: In 1598, the Earl of Cumberland led the British Navy in a looting spree; in 1615, a hurricane blew away its roof; in 1908, the body of Ponce de León was disinterred from the nearby Iglesia de San José and placed in a marble tomb near the transept, where it remains today (see the box "Ponce de León: Man of Myth & Legend," in chapter 2, for more about Ponce de León). The cathedral also contains the wax-covered mummy of St. Pio, a Roman martyr persecuted and killed for his Christian faith. The mummy has been encased in a glass box ever since it was placed here in 1862. To the right of the mummy is a bizarre wooden replica of Mary with four swords stuck in her bosom. After all the looting and destruction over the centuries, the cathedral's great treasures, including gold and silver, are long gone, although many beautiful stained-glass windows remain. The cathedral faces Plaza de las Monjas (the Nuns' Square), a shady spot where you can rest in front of Hotel El Convento.

Calle del Cristo 153 (at Caleta San Juan). ℂ **787/722-0861.** Free admission. Mon–Sat 8am–4pm, Sun 8am–2pm. Bus: Old City Trolley.

Museums

Many of the museums in Old San Juan close for lunch between 11:45am and 2pm, so schedule your activities accordingly if you intend to museum-hop.

Felisa Rincón Museum de Gautier ★★ MUSEUM   This museum is as quirky as the woman it honors, a trailblazer who assumed political power in 1946 and kept it through 1968, playing a hand in the astounding modernization and transformation of San Juan, the city she ruled as mayor, and the rest of Puerto Rico. The museum has many photographs, and other documents, charting her remarkable life and showing her with U.S. and world leaders as well as world-renowned artists. "Dona Fela" is remembered as an almost mythical figure—she had frozen snow brought to San Juan to celebrate Christmas—and the rooms are filled her furniture, gowns, hand-fans, headdresses and other treasured possessions, which bear testament to her good taste. But the heart of the exhibits are those that show her empathetic touch with the city's poor. Felisa Rincón was a serious leader with solid record of accomplishment, and that comes through. You'll pass by some of Old San Juan's greatest treasuries, the historic San Juan Gate and the San Juan Cathedral among others, to come to this little museum, but you won't see the best the city has to offer until you step inside.

Caleta de San Juan 51, at Recinto Oeste. ℂ **787/723-1897.** www.museofelisarincom.com. Free admission. Mon–Fri 9am–4pm. Bus: Old City Trolley.

San Juan Attractions

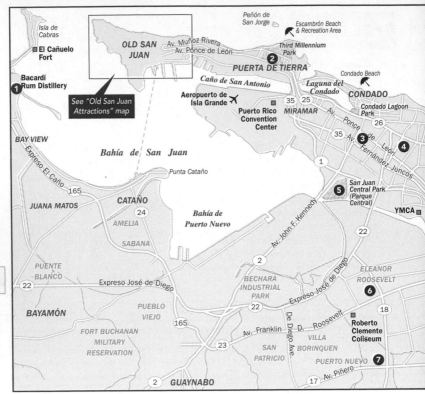

Galeria Nacional ★MUSEUM Located inside Old San Juan's Antiguo Convento de los Dominicos, a restored former convent, the Galeria Nacional has exhibits from the Institute of Puerto Rican Culture's vast holdings. These range from Spanish colonial religious art to important works by Puerto Rican masters José Campeche and Francisco Oller to pieces by Rafael Tufiño and others from the "generation of the 1950s," artists who excelled in painting and printmaking. The museum also stages exhibits by contemporary artists. The museum closed to the public in November 2013 for renovations and is slated to reopen by January 2015.

Antiguo Convento de los Dominicos, Calle Norzagaray 98 (corner Calle del Cristo behind Plaza San José), Caleta de San Juan 51, at Recinto Oeste. ☏787/977-2700. Admission $3, $2 children and seniors. Tues–Sat 9:30am–5:30pm, closed noon–1pm for lunch. Bus: Old City Trolley.

Luis Muñoz Marín Foundation ★ MUSEUM As the first elected governor of Puerto Rico, Luis Muñoz Marín enjoys somewhat the same position in Puerto Rican history that George Washington does for the mainland United States. Which makes this museum, a 30-minute drive south of San Juan, Puerto Rico's "Mount Vernon." A documentary acquaints visitors with the governor's life and achievements before they walk through Marín's study and library, and view his extensive art collection. Later most take the chance to relax in his tropical garden and gazebo. There's an historic archive; the shop and the grounds surrounding the foundation were restored in 2014.

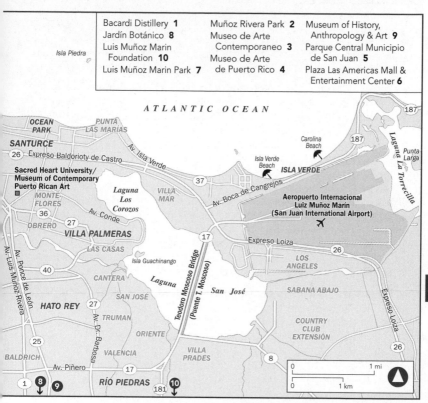

Bacardi Distillery **1**	Muñoz Rivera Park **2**	Museum of History,
Jardín Botánico **8**	Museo de Arte	Anthropology & Art **9**
Luis Muñoz Marin	Contemporaneo **3**	Parque Central Municipio
Foundation **10**	Museo de Arte	de San Juan **5**
Luis Muñoz Marin Park **7**	de Puerto Rico **4**	Plaza Las Americas Mall &
		Entertainment Center **6**

Marginal Rd. 877, Km 0.4, Trujillo Alto Expwy. ☏ **787/755-7979.** www.flmm.org/v2. Admission $6 adults, $3 children and seniors 60 and older. Tours Mon–Fri (reservations required) 10am and 2pm, Sat–Sun 10:30am and 1pm. Bus: 31 or public car from Plaza Colón (easier).

Museo de Arte de Puerto Rico ★★★ ART MUSEUM   Puerto Rico's pre-miere arts showcase since opening in 2000, the museum is serious about its role as a repository of the best in Puerto Rican art and in its ability to draw major shows from abroad to the island, featuring renowned international artists. Housed in an historic beauty in downtown Santurce, the museum is home to some of Puerto Rico's greatest stars, including classical masters Francisco Oller (1833–1917) and the late-18th-century master José Campeche, along with modern masters like Rafael Tufiño, Angel Botello, Arnaldo Roche Rabelle, and Antonio Martorell. There is a gorgeous sculpture and botanical garden behind the museum. There's also a great restaurant on site, and some of San Juan's best restaurants (like Bistro de Paris across the street) nearby.

Av. José de Diego 299, Santurce. ☏ **787/977-6277.** www.mapr.org. Admission $6 adults; $3 students, seniors, and children; free for children 4 and under and seniors over 75; free for all Wed 2–8pm. Tues and Thurs–Sat 10am–5pm, Wed 10am–8pm, Sun 11am–6pm. Bus: 5, 21.

Museo de Arte Contemporáneo de San Juan ★ MUSEUM   The city's contemporary art museum may be housed in a traditional, U.S.-style brick schoolhouse, but it showcases cutting edge contemporary art from Puerto Rico and throughout Latin America and the Caribbean. This forward-thinking entity also puts on intriguing events and groundbreaking performances, and runs a number of workshops.

Rafael M. de Labra Building, Corner Avs. Ponce de León and Robert H. Todd, Santurce. ✆ **787/977-4030.** www.museocontemporaneopr.org. Admission $5; $3 students with identification, children under 18, and people 60 and older; free for visitors 75 and over; last Wed of the month free admission during extended hours 4–9pm. Tue–Fri 10am–4pm, Sat 11am–1pm, Sun 1–5pm. Bus: ME, 5.

Museo de Historia, Antropología y Arte ★ MUSEUM   This small museum, at the University of Puerto Rico's main campus, makes a big impression with its broad-ranging Caribbean archeology collection and riveting works by Puerto Rican artists. It "Mona Lisa" is Francisco's Oller's "El Velorio," an 8-foot by 13 foot painting created in 1893 and depicting a wake at a rural island home; the painting has become emblematic of country living on the island. The museum's permanent collection has paintings, drawings, and prints from island and international artists, as well as sculpture, examples of popular art, historic documents, and artifacts. The whole she-bang is housed in a building designed in 1951 by architect Henry Klumb, one of a wave of international architects who came to the island to help build a modern Puerto Rico, mostly through public building commissions. Klumb, whose work is marked by open spaces and simple geometric patterns, won numerous commissions for the UPR.

Universidad de Puerto Rico Rio Piedras Campus, Av. Ponce de Leon, Rio Piedrase. ✆ **787/763-3939** or 787/764-0000, ext. 83080, 83086. Free admission. Mon–Fri 8am–noon and 1–4:30pm. Bus: ME.

Museo de Arte e Historia de San Juan ★ MUSEUM   Located in the city's centuries-old marketplace, the Museo hosts changing art and historic exhibitions, often featuring up–and–coming artists. The museum might has recently hosted everything from a huge Antonio Martorell installation to a children's art show. A local farmer's market takes place Saturday mornings until 2pm.

Calle Norzagaray 150. ✆ **787/724-1875.** Free admission, but donations accepted. Tues–Fri 9am–4pm, Sat–Sun 10am–4pm. Bus: To Old San Juan terminal, then the Old City Trolley.

Museo de las Américas ★★ MUSEUM   This museum celebrates art from Puerto Rico and throughout the Caribbean and Latin America. That encompasses everything from the carved figureheads of New England whaling ships to dugout canoes created by Carib Indians in Dominica to Puerto Rican *santos*, hand-carved wooden statues of the saints. This regional, Pan Caribbean approach is much too rare in Puerto Rico, which makes this museum all the more refreshing to visit. The Museo also hosts exhibits previously on display at the former Museo de Nuestras Raíces Africanas (Museum of Our African Roots). These focus on conquest and colonization and the African heritage running throughout Puerto Rico culture and the cultures of the Caribbean and Latin America. The museum wraps around a lovely Spanish colonial courtyard, which often is home to artisan fairs and weekend music performances.

Sala Cuartel de Ballajá, at Calle Norzagaray and Calle del Morro. ✆ **787/724-5052.** www.museolasamericas.org. Admission $3 students with ID; $2 children 12 and under, students, and seniors 65 and older. Tues–Sat 9am–noon and 1–4pm, Sun noon–5pm. Bus: Old City Trolley.

Historic Sights

In addition to the forts and churches listed earlier, you might want to see the sites described below.

San Juan Gate ★★★ (Calle San Francisco and Calle Recinto Oeste) was built around 1635, just north of La Fortaleza, several blocks downhill from the cathedral. It was the main point of entry into San Juan if you arrived by ship in the 17th and 18th centuries. The gate is the only one remaining of the several that once pierced the fortifications of the old walled city. For centuries, it was closed at sundown to cut off access to the historic Old Town. (Bus: Old City Trolley.)

Plazuela de la Rogativa ★★★ (Caleta de las Monjas), a little plaza with a statue of a bishop and three women, commemorating one of Puerto Rico's most famous legends. In 1797, from across San Juan Bay at Santurce, the British held Old Town under siege. That same year they mysteriously sailed away. Later, the commander claimed he feared that the enemy was well prepared behind those walls; he apparently saw many lights and believed them to be reinforcements. Some people believe that those lights were torches carried by women in a *rogativa,* or religious procession, as they followed their bishop. (Bus: Old City Trolley.)

The **city walls** ★★★ around San Juan were built in 1630 to protect the town against both European invaders and Caribbean pirates. The city walls that remain today were once part of one of the most impregnable fortresses in the New World and even today are an engineering marvel. Their thickness averages 20 feet (6m) at the base and 12 feet (3.7m) at the top, with an average height of 40 feet (12m). At their top, notice the balconied buildings that served for centuries as hospitals and also residences of the island's various governors. Between Fort San Cristóbal and El Morro, bastions were erected at frequent intervals. The walls come into view as you approach from San Cristóbal on your way to El Morro. (Bus: Old Town Trolley.)

San Juan Cemetery ★, on Calle Norzagaray, officially opened in 1814 and has since been the final resting place for many prominent Puerto Rican families. The circular chapel, dedicated to Saint Magdalene of Pazzis, was built in the 1860s. Aficionados of old graveyards can wander among marble monuments, mausoleums, and statues, marvelous examples of Victorian funereal statuary. Because there are no trees, or any other form of shade here, it would be best not to go exploring in the noonday sun. In any case, be careful—the cemetery is often a venue for illegal drug deals and can be dangerous. (Bus: Old City Trolley.)

Alcaldía (City Hall) ★ GOVERNMENT BUILDING The City Hall, with its double arcade flanked by two towers resembling Madrid's City Hall, was constructed in stages from 1604 to 1789. Still in use, this building comprises a tourist-information center downstairs plus a small art gallery on the first floor.

Calle San Francisco. © **787/724-7171.** Free admission. Mon–Fri 8am–5pm. Closed holidays. Bus: Old City Trolley.

Casa Blanca ★★ HISTORIC HOME This rustic residence is in perhaps the Old City's choicest location, atop a verdant hilltop overlooking the Atlantic coastline at the entrance to San Juan Bay, housed the family of Puerto Rico's first governor, Juan Ponce de Leon, for 2.5 centuries after his death in 1519, then became a residence for first Spanish, and then American military officers. Today, a museum bearing the Conquistador's name takes visitors back in time in a meandering tour through what 16th-through 18th-century furnishings, dress, and kitchen utensils from the time looked like. The simple Spanish colonial structure is made beautiful by its furniture, paintings, and other works of art. Yet, its vast garden, dense with spraying fountains, singing birds, and colorful tropical trees and plants, is its finest feature.

Calle San Sebastián 1. © **787/725-1454.** Admission $3. Wed–Sun 8am–4:30pm. Bus: Old City Trolley.

El Arsenal ★ ARCHITECTURE The Spaniards used a shallow craft to patrol the lagoons and mangroves in and around San Juan. Needing a base for these vessels, they constructed El Arsenal in the 19th century. It was at this base that they staged their last stand; flying the Spanish colors until the final Spaniard was removed in 1898, at the end of the Spanish-American War. Changing art exhibitions are held in the building's three galleries.

La Puntilla. $\mathcal{C}$ **787/723-3068.** Free admission. Wed–Sun 8:30am–4:30pm. Bus: Old City Trolley.

La Casa del Libro ★ MUSEUM   This museum spotlights the arts of printing and bookmaking, with century-old prints and rare books on display, some 500 years old, and a library full of beautiful books and graphics. In 2014, it was operating out of temporary quarters (Calle Fortaleza 319, corner Callejón de la Capilla) while a renovation was taking place.

Calle del Cristo 255. $\mathcal{C}$ **787/723-0354.** Free admission. Tues–Sat 11am–4:30pm. Bus: Old City Trolley.

La Fortaleza ★ HISTORIC BUILDING   The office and residence of the governor of Puerto Rico is the oldest executive mansion in continuous use in the Western Hemisphere, and it has served as the island's seat of government for more than 3 centuries. Its history goes back even further than that to 1533, when construction began on a fortress to protect San Juan's Spanish settlers during raids by Carib tribesmen and pirates. The original medieval towers remain, but as the edifice was subsequently enlarged into a palace, other modes of architecture and ornamentation were also incorporated, including baroque, Gothic, neoclassical, and Arabian. La Fortaleza has been designated a national historic site by the U.S. government. Proper attire is required (informal okay).

Calle Fortaleza, overlooking San Juan Harbor. $\mathcal{C}$ **787/721-7000,** ext. 2211. Free admission. 30-min. tours of the gardens and building (conducted in English and Spanish) given every half-hour. Mon–Fri 9am–3:30pm. Bus: Old City Trolley.

Teatro Tapía ★ THEATER   Standing across from the Plaza de Colón, this is one of the oldest theaters in the Western Hemisphere, built about 1832. In 1976, a restoration returned the theater to its original appearance. Much of Puerto Rican theater history is connected with the Tapía, named after the island's first prominent playwright, Alejandro Tapía y Rivera (1826–82). Various productions—some musical—are staged here throughout the year, representing a repertoire of drama, dance, and cultural events.

Av. Ponce de León. $\mathcal{C}$ **787/721-0180.** Prices vary. Access limited to ticket holders at performances (see "San Juan Nightlife," later in this chapter). Bus: A5, B21, any other to Old San Juan Station.

Historic Squares

In Old San Juan, **Plaza del Quinto Centenario (Quincentennial Plaza)** ★★ overlooks the Atlantic from atop the highest point in the city. A striking and symbolic feature of the plaza, which was constructed as part of the 1992–93 celebration of the 500th anniversary of the discovery of the New World, is a sculpture that rises 40 feet (12m) from the plaza's top level. The monumental sculpture in black granite and ceramics symbolizes the earthen and clay roots of American history and is the work of Jaime Suarez, one of Puerto Rico's foremost artists. From its southern end, two needle-shaped columns point skyward to the North Star, the guiding light of explorers. Placed around the plaza are fountains, other columns, and sculpted steps that represent various historic periods in Puerto Rico's 500-year heritage.

TAKING DAY breaks

You'll probably want to plan on a good lunch during a full day of sightseeing and shopping in Old San Juan (see chapter 5), but the Old City has other ways to take a break than from a trip to the restaurants and cafes listed in the previous chapter, whether for a refreshing drink or snack or a full body massage.

Anam Spa Cocktail Lounge ★

(Calle Cristo 259 A-1, Corner Calle Tetuan, Old San Juan; ✆ **787/962-4579**) Spoil yourself with a foot massage and flavorful sangria after hours of site seeing in the Old City at this spa-bar-lounge in a gorgeous colonial mansion looking out above San Juan Bay. Open daily 11am to 7pm.

Marilyn's Place ★★ (Calle San

Francisco 100, Old San Juan; ✆ **787/724-0444**) An oasis at the heart of Old San Juan, this outdoor cafe behind the State Department off Plaza de Armas is surrounded by tropical vegetation and is a cool, shady respite from the heat of the city. Open Monday to Thursday 11am to 9pm and Friday to Sunday 11am to 11pm.

El Convento Hotel ★★★ (Calle

Cristo 100, Old San Juan; ✆ **787/723-9020**) There are two good options for a civilized break tucked into the public areas of this historic hotel: at a terrace table at El Picoteo or down in the courtyard Patio del Nispero. Both are excellent restaurants with great food, but are also enchanted spaces for a cool refreshing drink during a break from site seeing.

Nono's ★ (Calle San Sebastian 100,

Old San Juan; ✆ **787/725-7819**) With an enviable location on the corner of Cristo and San Sebastian streets across from the Plaza San Jose, this classic bar is ideal for people watching while you enjoy a refreshing drink.

Sweeping views extend from the plaza to El Morro Fortress at the headland of San Juan Bay and to the Dominican Convent and San José Church, a rare New World example of Gothic architecture. Asilo de Beneficencia, a former indigents' hospital dating from 1832, occupies a corner of El Morro's entrance and is now the home of the Institute of Puerto Rican Culture. Adjacent to the plaza is the Cuartel de Ballajá, built in the mid–19th century as the Spanish army headquarters and still the largest edifice in the Americas constructed by Spanish engineers; it houses the Museum of the Americas.

Centrally located, Quincentennial Plaza is one of modern Puerto Rico's respectful gestures to its colorful and lively history. It is a perfect introduction for visitors seeking to discover the many rich links with the past in Old San Juan.

Once named St. James Square, or Plaza Santiago, **Plaza de Colón ★** at the main entrance to Old San Juan is at times bustling and busy, but also has a shady, tranquil section. Right off Calle Fortaleza, the square was renamed Plaza de Colón to honor the 400th anniversary of Christopher Columbus' so-called discovery of Puerto Rico, which occurred during his second voyage. Of course, it is more politically correct today to say that Columbus explored or came upon an already inhabited island. He certainly didn't discover it. But when a statue here, perhaps the most famous on the island, was erected atop a high pedestal, it was clearly to honor Columbus, not to decry his legacy. There are some benches beside a newspaper stand in a shady part of the plaza that make a great place to sit. You can grab something cool to drink from a corner store.

Plaza de Las Armas ★ is located at the heart of Old San Juan. The main square is home to San Juan City Hall, built in 1789 as a replica of the Madrid City Hall, and the Puerto Rico State Department, in a beautiful colonial building from the 18th century. The plaza also has a fountain (which, unfortunately, is usually not working), with four statues representing the four seasons, and some gazebos and a cafe. The Cuatro Estaciones, or Four Seasons, cafe is a nice spot for a strong cup of coffee or a cold drink. In a recent renovation, large trees were planted in the plaza, which provides blissful shade in several spots.

The **Paseo de la Princesa** ★★ is a wide bayside promenade with outstanding views. The walkway runs along the bay beneath the imposing Spanish colonial wall that surrounds the Old City. It takes its name from a prominent building along it, La Princesa, a former prison in the 1800s that has been blissfully restored and now houses the Puerto Rico Tourism Company Headquarters. The sexy fountain at its center, "Raíces" or "Races," shoots powerful streams of water over the bronze naked Adonises and Amazon warrior goddesses riding huge horses and fish; you'll get wet if you get too close. Spanish artist Luis Sanguino undertook the work as part of the 500th anniversary of San Juan's founding. The statue is meant to show the Taíno, African, and Spanish roots of Puerto Rico and its people. Farther along, the promenade bends around the bay and passes a shaded area before heading down to San Juan Gate. The new El Morro trail, which goes around the base of the fortress, is actually an extension of this promenade. There are food and drink vendors and often artisans selling their crafts, especially at the start of the route near the cruise-ship docks. Enter near the cruise-ship docks at the corner of Recinto Sur and Calle La Puntilla or via the San Juan Gate (Calle San Francisco and Calle Recinto Oeste).

Parks & Gardens

Bahía Urbana ★ PARK/GARDEN   This long-term development project aims to remake the coastline of San Juan Bay between Old San Juan and the Convention Center in Miramar from a seedy waterfront into a vibrant tourism and entertainment mecca, with world class hotels, high-end retail and residential spaces, and an open shoreline with waterfront restaurants, promenades, and yacht moorings. The first step towards this vision was the renovation of the decaying port zone surrounding piers 7 and 8 on the border between Puerta de Tierra and Old San Juan into a bayside park, surrounded by water and green areas and connected to Old San Juan via a pedestrian bridge. The park hosts concerts and other special events and is home to a fine restaurant and trapeze school.

Jardín Botánico ★ PARK/GARDEN   Administered by the University of Puerto Rico, Jardín Botánico is a lush tropical garden with some 200 species of vegetation. You can pack a picnic lunch and bring it here if you choose. The orchid garden is exceptional, and the palm garden is said to contain some 125 species. Footpaths blaze a trail through heavy forests opening onto a lotus lagoon.

Barrio Venezuela (at the intersection of rtes. 1 and 847), Río Piedras. ℂ **787/765-1845.** Free admission. Daily 6am–6pm. Bus: 19.

Luis Muñoz Marín Park ★ PARK/GARDEN   This 140-acre (57-hectare) park is the best-known, most frequently visited children's playground in Puerto Rico—although it has equal appeal to adults. Conceived as a verdant oasis in an otherwise crowded urban neighborhood, it's a fenced-in repository of swings, jungle gyms, and slides set amid several small lakes and rolling green fields. Here you'll also find an incomparable view of San Juan. A small-scale cable car carries passengers aloft at

Seeing the Sights | SAN JUAN ATTRACTIONS

10-minute intervals for panoramic views of the surrounding landscape ($2 per person).

Av. Piñero, at Hato Rey. ℂ **787/763-0787.** Free admission for pedestrians; parking $3 Wed–Sun 8am–6pm. Bus: 17.

Luis Muñoz Rivera Park ★ PARK/GARDEN   This 27-acre (11-hectare) park, frequently confused with Luis Muñoz Marín Park (see above), is a green rectangle in the middle of Puerta de Tierra. You'll drive by the seaward-facing park on your way to San Juan. It was built 50 years ago to honor Luis Muñoz Rivera, the Puerto Rican statesman, journalist, and poet. It's filled with picnic areas, wide walks, shady trees, landscaped grounds, and recreational areas. There's a children's playground that's filled with fun on weekends. Its centerpiece, El Pabellon de la Paz, is sometimes used for cultural events and expositions of handicrafts. A new pedestrian and bicycle path connects the park with the oceanfront Tercer Milenio, or Third Millennium Park, across Avenida Muñoz Rivera. The Commonwealth Supreme Court is located at the eastern side of the park.

Btw. aves. Muñoz Rivera and Ponce de León. ℂ **787/721-6133.** Free admission; parking $3. Daily 24 hr. Bus: 5.

Parque Central Municipio de San Juan ★★ SPORTS COMPLEX   This mangrove-bordered park was inaugurated in 1979 for the Pan-American Games. It covers 35 acres (14 hectares) and lies southeast of Miramar. Joggers appreciate its labyrinth of trails, and a long boardwalk runs along mangrove canals. It boasts 20 tennis courts, four racquetball courts, a full track-and-field area with stadium bleachers, exercise trails, and children's play area. A golf course is being developed on an adjacent former landfill and an Olympic standard diving and swimming arena was completed several years ago. Fat, huge iguanas slither from the mangrove-choked channels and into the park's pathways.

Calle Cerra. ℂ **787/722-1646.** Free admission for pedestrians; parking $2. Mon–Thurs 6am–10pm, Fri 6am–9pm, Sat–Sun 6am–7pm. Bus: 1.

Sightseeing Tours

If you want to see more of the island but you don't want to rent a car or manage the inconveniences of public transportation, perhaps an organized tour is for you.

   Rico Suntours, Calle Pesante 15, San Juan (ℂ **787/722-2080**), and **Travel Services, Inc.,** Calle Loiza 1199 (ℂ **787/982-1200**), are two of the largest tour operators and destination management companies in Puerto Rico, managing a range of tours for groups and individuals, and able to custom-make tours as well. They both have several volunteer-tourism offerings, whether you want to serve homeless people living on the streets or pitch in with a community project in the adjacent coastal community of Loiza. **Castillo Sightseeing Tours & Travel Services,** 2413 Calle Laurel, Punta La Marias, Santurce (ℂ **787/791-6195**), maintains counters at the Ritz-Carlton San Juan, the Verdanza Hotel, and ESJ Towers. With a fleet of air-conditioned buses, the company's tours include pickups and drop-offs at hotels as an added convenience.

   Sunshine Tours (ℂ **787/647-4545**) and **Amador Island Tours** (ℂ **787/397-1881**) have similar offerings. One of the most popular half-day tours travels along the northeastern part of the island to El Yunque. It departs most days of the week between 8:30 and 9am, lasts 4 to 5 hours, and costs about $59 per person, $77 if you take one of the more extensive hiking tours. Another favorite is a city tour of San Juan that departs daily around 1pm. The 4-hour trip costs around $59 per person and includes a stop at

THE BEST PLACES TO SEE PUERTO RICAN art

With its dozen or so museums and even more art galleries, Old San Juan is the greatest repository of Puerto Rican arts and crafts, although the city's single most important museum is probably the Museo de Arte de Puerto Rico in downtown Santurce. In the Old City, galleries sell everything from pre-Columbian artifacts to paintings by such well-known artists as Angel Botello, who died in 1986, and Rafael Tufiño, who died in 2008. There's also contemporary traditional crafts, such as *santos*, the hand-carved wooden saints the island is known for. Galleries also show a large cast of talented established and up-and-coming contemporary artists.

Art openings at galleries are usually big affairs, with wine and cheese receptions, and occasionally live music or theatrical performances. A cluster of galleries is spread along Calle Cristo and Calle San José, which is 1 block east. For specific galleries, see "Art," later in this chapter. Old City art museums, meanwhile, are clustered around its northern Atlantic coast, like the **Galería Nacional** (p. 90), which mixes lively contemporary shows with greatest hits from the deep Institute of Puerto Rican Culture vault, and the **Museo de las Américas** (p. 92), which romps across the New World.

Santurce, however, is equally important as the Old City, now that it has some of the island's top museums. The impressive **Museo de Arte de Puerto Rico** (p. 91) has the catalog of Puerto Rican artists and attracts world-class international exhibits within regal surroundings. The **Museo de Arte Contemporáneo** (p. 91) gets crazily creative from its perch in a converted brick schoolhouse.

Take the trek out to the University of Puerto Rico Rio Piedras campus to visit the **Museum of History, Anthropology & Art** (p. 92), home to the Francisco Oller's incredible "El Velorio," which focuses on a wake held at a country home in the 19th century, and so much more.

Outside San Juan, the greatest art on the island can usually be seen at the **Museo de Arte de Ponce** (p. 151). In addition to such European masters as Reubens, Van Dyck, and Murillo, the museum features works by Latin American artists, including Diego Rivera. Following a $30 million renovation, it erected the majestic and colorful "Brushstrokes in Flight," a 25-foot-high sculpture by Roy Lichtenstein, outside its front entrance.

the Bacardi Rum Factory. Other trips include the Arecibo Observatory and the Camuy Caves, as well as snorkeling and offshore beach excursions on plush catamarans.

Few cities of the Caribbean lend themselves so gracefully to walking tours. You can embark on these on your own, stopping and shopping en route. The best, of course, is a walking tour of Old San Juan. There are several suggested routes from which to choose, or you could go and get lost and cover the entire mile-square historic sector. (See the "Old San Juan Attractions" map, on p. 87.) There are also guided tours available. One of the most informative is by **Legends of Puerto Rico** (© **787/605-9060;** www.legendsofpr.com), which hosts personalized tours, specializing in entertaining cultural and nature adventure tours. **Sunshine Tours** (© **787/698-9667;** www. puerto-rico-sunshinetours.com) also has experienced, knowledgeable guides. **San Juan Oculto,** or Hidden San Juan (© 787/748-7248; www.fusamp.org; $20 suggested donation), is a monthly walking tour through Old San Juan to visit important, and largely unknown, architectural and historic buildings and other works. The project is undertaken in coordination with the University of Puerto Rico's School of Architecture.

For a fantastic overview of authentic Puerto Rican cuisine, we highly recommend the walking/noshing tour, **Flavors of San Juan,** Old San Juan walking food tour (© 787/964-2447; www.flavorsofsanjuan.com; $70; no children under 18; daily 2-hr. tours at 5pm). Itineraries vary, but samples may include *tostones, mofongo,* tapas at a Spanish restaurant (where the owner serenaded us a cappella), rum or beer samples, and possibly a mojito and French fries at a French bistro. There are also 3-hour cooking classes ($99) and a rum and bites tour ($40).

Especially for Kids

Puerto Rico is one of the family-friendliest islands in the Caribbean, and many hotels offer family discounts. Programs for children are also offered at a number of hotels, including day- and night-camp activities and babysitting services. Trained counselors at these camps supervise children as young as 3 in activities ranging from nature hikes to tennis lessons, coconut carving, and sand-sculpture contests.

Teenagers can learn to hip-hop dance Latino-style with special salsa and merengue lessons, learn conversational Spanish, indulge in watersports, take jeep excursions, or scuba-dive in some of the best diving locations in the world. All the major hotels have full children's programs, so it might depend on what you are looking for. Top city hotels such as **InterContinental San Juan Hotel & Casino** (p. 83), the **Ritz-Carlton San Juan** (p. 83), the **San Juan Marriott & Stellaris Casino** (p. 79), and the **Caribe Hilton** (p. 77) have great pool facilities for kids, day-camp activities, watersports, and other sports equipment, play areas for little kids, and video arcades or other activities for teens.

Children love **El Morro Fortress** (see "Forts," earlier in this chapter) because it looks just like the castles they have seen on TV and at the movies. On a rocky promontory, El Morro is filled with dungeons and dank places and also has lofty lookout points for viewing San Juan Harbor. The grounds around the fort also make for great kite flying. The city's historic plazas offer their own possibilities, such as running through the gushing fountains of Quincentennial Plaza or feeding the pigeons at Plaza de Armas.

Luis Muñoz Marín Park (see "Parks & Gardens," above) has the most popular children's playground in Puerto Rico. It's filled with landscaped grounds and recreational areas—lots of room for fun in the sun. And kids love the short cable-car ride.

Kids—from teens to toddlers—adore the Caribbean's largest mall, **Plaza Las Americas** (© 787/767-5202; www.plazalasamericas.com), especially on a rainy day, which has all the familiarity of the mall back home, with its movie theaters and food courts, but is probably a whole lot more glamorous.

Museo del Niño (Children's Museum) ★★
When you need a plan for a rainy day or the kids needs some pint-size entertainment, head straight to this newly renovated interactive museum that rambles throughout a centuries-old villa. It's set on a shady plaza and easy to spot by the playful sculpture by Jorge Zeno out front. Inside, hands-on exhibits on nature, science, and health mix fun with education. Don't miss the broadcast studio where families can create their own news reports, an arts and crafts workshop using recycled materials, and the rooftop play space.

Calle del Cristo 150. © **787/722-3791.** www.museodelninopr.org. Admission $5 adults, $7 children 15 and younger. Tues–Thurs 9am–3:30pm; Fri 9am–5pm; Sat–Sun 12:30–5pm. Bus: Old City Trolley.

THE CATHEDRAL OF rum

Just across the bay from Old San Juan, the Barcardi distillery is the world's largest rum producer, turning out 100,000 gallons of the tropical drink enhancer daily. And the **Casa Bacardi Visitor Center,** Carretera 165, Cataño (© **787/788-8400**), is where you can find out all about this "Cathedral of Rum." Fun and informative tours take 90-minutes and cover the entire rum making process from sugar cane to bottle. At the end of the tour, cozy up to the Art Deco bar for your choice of rum beverage.

Several tour buses ply the route between the Barcardi distillery and major hotels a part of tour packages, but you can also take a ferry from Old San Juan to Catano, and then a publico or taxi to the plant in no time. Tours of the visitors center cost $12 and include one drink. This is a lot of fun, but don't plan it in advance. It's best seized on an otherwise wasted rainy afternoon or morning, and can be arranged in a snap.

DIVING, FISHING, TENNIS & OTHER OUTDOOR PURSUITS

Active vacationers have a wide choice of things to do in San Juan, from sunning on the beach to kite sailing to surfing. There are numerous land sports to do under the sun, such as tennis and bicycle touring. Most beachside hotels, of course, offer on-site watersports activities, which are also available for nonguests (see chapter 4).

The Beaches

Some San Juan beaches can get crowded, especially during summer and holiday weekends, but for most of the week, they are deliciously roomy. It's rare to find yourself alone on a beach in San Juan, but if you do, be careful. Petty crime is a reality you need to keep in mind. However, city beaches are usually very safe, friendly, and well-protected places. They are also surprisingly pretty: Ocean Park and Pine Grove are among the most charming beaches in all of Puerto Rico.

All beaches on Puerto Rico, even those fronting the top hotels, are open to the public. Public bathing beaches, with lifeguards and facilities, are called *balnearios* and charge for parking and for use of lockers and showers. Beach hours in general are 9am to 5pm in winter, to 6pm off-season. Most *balnearios* are operated by the Puerto Rico National Parks Company, with others operated by island municipalities. For all *balnearios,* entrance is free, but the parking lot carries a fee. Even when the beaches are closed, you can still enjoy them, but there won't be facilities open, lifeguards, or, in some cases, available parking.

There are two public beaches in the San Juan area with lifeguards, changing rooms, and showers. **El Escambrón public beach** (Av. Muñoz Rivera, Pda. 8—that is, *parada,* or stop 8—Puerta de Tierra; © **787/721-6133;** Wed–Sun and holidays 8:30am–5pm; parking $5) is right next to the Caribe Hilton and surrounded by two sprawling parks. There's a great swimming beach protected by reefs and rock formations jutting out of the water. The famed El 8 surf spot is just to the west, however. There's good snorkeling around the rocks with lots of fish. There's a snack bar and a full-scale restaurant located here. The other public beach is **Isla Verde public beach** (Av. Los Gobernadores, Carolina; © **787/791-8084;** Tues–Sun 8:30am–5pm; parking

$4), a huge expanse of white sand and tranquil waters between Isla Verde and Piñones. There are lifeguards; changing rooms, bathrooms, and showers; picnic areas and barbecue grills; and an on-site restaurant.

Famous with beach buffs since the 1920s, **Condado Beach** ★★ put San Juan on the map as a tourist resort. Backed up against high-rise hotels, it seems more like Miami Beach than any other spot in the Caribbean. All sorts of watersports can be booked at the activities desks in the hotels. A small beach near the Condado Plaza hotel is the only one with lifeguards, who are on duty from 8:30am to 5pm. There are also outdoor showers. The beaches in the rest of the Condado are much nicer, but because there are no lifeguards and the surf can get rough, particularly by the San Juan Marriott, swimmers should exercise caution. There are powerful riptides here that have been responsible for past drownings. There are no public toilets here. People watching is a favorite sport along these golden strands, which stretch from the Ventana del Mar Park to beyond the Marriott. The best stretch of beach in the Condado runs from the Ashford Presbyterian Hospital to Ocean Park. The area behind the Atlantic Beach Hotel is popular gay beach; the beach farther along, with Marriott guests and surfers, is also pretty but has extremely rough waters at times.

One of the most attractive beaches in the Greater San Juan area is **Ocean Park Beach** ★★★, a mile (1.6km) of fine, gold sand in a neighborhood east of Condado. This beach attracts young people and travelers looking for a guesthouse rather than a large hotel. The beach runs from Parque del Indio in Condado all the way to the Barbosa Park in the area known as El Ultimo Trolley, and offers paddle tennis, kiteboarding, and beach volleyball. You can grab lunch and refreshments from several area guesthouses, and vendors walk up and down the beach, selling cold beer, water, and soft drinks, and even snacks such as fried seafood turnovers. Farther east, there's no real beach at **Punta Las Marías,** but it's one of the favorite launch points for windsurfers.

Isla Verde Beach ★★ is the longest and widest in San Juan. It is ideal for swimming, and it, too, is lined with high-rise resorts a la Miami Beach. Many luxury condos are on this beachfront. Isla Verde is good for watersports, including parasailing and snorkeling, because of its calm, clear waters; many kiosks will rent you equipment, especially by the El San Juan. There are also cafes and restaurants at hotels and more reasonably priced individual restaurants nearby.

Isla Verde Beach extends from the end of Ocean Park to the beginning of a section called Boca Cangrejos. The most popular beach is behind the Hotel El San Juan and the InterContinental San Juan hotels. But Pine Grove beach, behind the Ritz-Carlton, is a great swimming beach and very popular as well, particularly with surfers.

Sports & Other Outdoor Pursuits

ADVENTURE   Go flying through the trees on a zip-line at **La Marquesa Original Canopy Tour Park,** La Marquesa Forest Reserve, Guaynabo (© **787/789-1598** or 444-0110). Costs vary depending on group size, but run around $99 per person including transportation to your hotel. The rate without transportation is $75. You'll get a bird's eye view of a tropical forest as you soar along suspended cables, from 10 to 70 feet (3–21m) high, traversing across 14 different platforms during the thrilling 2-hour tour. Speed demons, here's your shot at an adrenalin rush; but if you'd rather take it easy, you can control your speed with a brake grip. Being 50 feet (15m) up and leaping through the air is a rush, even with the harness strapped to the cable and the redundant safety features.

BIKE RENTALS   The best places to bicycle are in city parks such as Luis Muñoz Marín (Hato Rey) and Luis Muñoz Rivera (Puerta de Tierra). You can make it from Condado to Old San Juan driving mostly through the latter park. There are also bicycle trails; I recommend the coastal boardwalk running along Piñones, which is beautiful and safe, especially on the weekends, if a little beat up. There are bike rentals available in the area during weekends, although most San Juan streets are too crowded for bicycle riding. **Rent the Bicycle,** Calle Del Muelle, Capitolio Plaza 205, San Juan (✆ 787/602-9696), is at the entrance of the Old San Juan bayside waterfront. It rents bikes for $27 per day ($19 for a half-day) and also conducts several tours throughout San Juan (the Piñones boardwalk tour is a good option). **Paradise Rentals,** in Old San Juan at Pier 2 and in Condado at Condado Village, 1214 Ashford Ave. (✆ 787/413-2222), rents bicycles and electric bicycles, or E-bikes.

CRUISES   For the best cruises of San Juan Bay, go to Caribe Aquatic Adventures (see "Scuba Diving," below). Bay cruises start at $25 per person.

DEEP-SEA FISHING ★   Deep-sea fishing is top-notch here. Allison tuna, white and blue marlin, sailfish, wahoo, dolphinfish (mahi mahi), mackerel, and tarpon are some of the fish that can be caught in Puerto Rican waters, where 30 world records have been broken. Charter arrangements can be made through most major hotels and resorts. The big game-fishing grounds are very close offshore from San Juan, making the capital an excellent place to hire a charter. A half-day of deep-sea fishing (4 hr.) starts at around $650, while full-day charters begin at around $1,050. Most charters hold six passengers in addition to the crew.

There are three marinas in the San Juan metropolitan area, with fishing charters and boat rentals available at all three. The **Cangrejos Yacht Club** (✆ 787/791-1015) is right near the airport on Rte. 187, the road from Isla Verde to Piñones, while the two other marinas are next to each other near the Condado bridge and the Convention Center in Miramar: **San Juan Bay Marina** (✆ 787/721-8062) and **Club Nautico de San Juan** (✆ 787/722-0177). All the marinas are just minutes away from the hunting grounds for big game sports fish like tuna and marlin, so you'll spend most of your time in the water actually fishing.

Sea Born Fishing Charters has one of the most experienced crews in the business and a fine 45-foot air-conditioned deluxe Hatteras called the *Sea Born.* Contact the vessel directly at P.O. Box 9066541, Puerto de Tierra, San Juan (✆ 787/723-2292 or 787/309-6376) or email at seabornfishing@gmail.com. The crew members know their fishing and are very informative. They began their career with fishing stalwart Capt. Mike Benítez, who began the company and went on to become the most experienced operator in San Juan sailing out of Club Nautico. His crew is knowledgeable and informative, and the *Sea Born* is plush and comfortable. Fishing tours for parties of up to six cost $700 for a half-day excursion, $1,150 for a full day, with bottled water soft drinks, bait, crew and all equipment included. (See "Scuba Diving," below, for another deep-sea fishing option.) Another veteran outfit is **Castillo Fishing Charters** (✆ 787/726-5752), which has been running charters out of the San Juan Bay Marina since 1975. Capt. Joe Castillo runs the company with his son José Iván and daughter Vanessa, and they all know their stuff. The *Legend,* a 48-foot Hatteras, is also an excellent vessel built for fishing and comfort. Rates are $749 for a half-day (8am–noon or 1–5pm) and $1,177 full day (8am–4pm), and includes everything, plus soft drinks and water. Cpt. Omar Orraca at **Caribbean Outfitters** (✆ 787/396-8346), which operates out of the Cangrejos Marina, will take you deep sea fishing on a 35-foot Bertram, but also offers backcountry tarp fishing, and fly and bone fishing trips.

GOLF The city of San Juan has opened the **San Juan Golf Academy and Driving Range** (Marginal Av. Kennedy, entrance to San Juan Obras Publicas department; ℭ **787/771-8962** or 480-4580; $5 for 50 balls, $10 for 100 balls, clubs are also available; Tues–Sat 7am–9pm, Sun and holidays 11am–6pm). Besides the driving range, there are putting greens and chipping ranges and lessons are given.

In the San Juan suburb of Bayamón is the 9-hole **Río Bayamón Golf Course** (ℭ **787/740-1419**), a municipal course. Greens fees are $25 and include a cart, and rentals range from $15 for a simple set to $35 for a professional set. Lessons are also given.

The **Berwind Country Club** (ℭ **787/876-5380**) in Loiza is the nearest full-size course to the city. Built on a former coconut plantation, it's a beautiful place, with ocean views, towering palms, and frenzied tropical foliage, but it has not been well maintained and is not resort-level state, which is a shame given its water hazards and three of the toughest holes to finish on the island. Green fees, including a cart, are under $50 throughout the week. A resort project planned for adjacent to the course is stalled by financial problems. Call ahead; operating hours have become sporadic during weekdays.

The island's best golf courses are within a short drive of San Juan, including those clustered around Dorado to the west and Río Grande to the east (see chapter 6).

HORSE RACING Great thoroughbreds and outstanding jockeys compete year-round at **Camarero Racetrack,** Calle 65 de Infantería, Rte. 3, Km 15.3, at Canovanas (ℭ **787/641-6060**), Puerto Rico's only racetrack, a 20-minute drive east of the center of San Juan. Races begin at 2:45pm Monday, Wednesday, Friday, Saturday, Sunday, and holidays. There are from seven to nine races daily, and bets include Win, Place, the "Exacta," Daily Double, Trifecta, Superfecta, Pick Six, and Pick Three. The clubhouse has a fine-dining restaurant, the Terrace Room, which serves good steaks, seafood, and local cooking. The grandstand has free admission.

RUNNING The cool, quiet, morning hours before 8am are a good time to jog through the streets of Old San Juan. Head for the wide thoroughfares adjacent to El Morro and then San Cristóbal, whose walls jut upward from the flat ground. The seafront Paseo de la Princesa, at the base of the governor's mansion La Fortaleza, is another fine site. **San Juan Central Park** (Calle Cerra; exit from Av. Muñoz Rivera or Rte. 2; ℭ **787/722-1646**) has an excellent professional track in an outdoor track-and-field stadium with bleachers. There is a similar setup at **Parque Barbosa** right off the beach in Ocean Park. Condado's Avenida Ashford and the hard-packed sands of Isla Verde are busy sites for morning runners as well. The renovated Dos Hermanos Bridge connecting Condado to Puerta de Tierra has plenty of room for joggers and cyclists, and you can make a big loop around the Condado Lagoon or to Escambron Beach and the adjacent Luis Munoz Rivera Park.

SCUBA DIVING In San Juan, the best outfitter is **Caribe Aquatic Adventures,** Calle 19 1062, Villa Nevarez (ℭ **787/281-8858;** www.diveguide.com/p2046.htm). Its dive shop is open daily from 9am to 9pm. This outfitter will take you to the best local dive sites in the Greater San Juan area. A local dive in Puerta de Tierra costs $60. Other dives cost $125 per person, and a resort course for first-time divers costs $145, half-day lesson $95. Escorted dive jaunts to the eastern shore are also offered. Snorkeling lessons or tours lasting 1 hour and including basic equipment go for $55, and a two-tank dive costs $145.

Another good outfitter is **Ocean Sports.** Its main office is Av. Isla Verde 3086 (ℭ **787/268-2329;** www.facebook.com/oceansportspr). It offers diving courses and scuba diving and snorkeling trips in San Juan, off the east coast, and even out to Mona

Island. A two-tank dive off the east coast will run from $95 to $150. There are kayak and snorkeling trips around San Juan.

SNORKELING Snorkeling is better in the outlying portions of the island than in overcrowded San Juan. But if you don't have time to explore greater Puerto Rico, you'll find that most of the popular beaches, such as Luquillo and Isla Verde, have pretty good visibility and kiosks that rent equipment. Snorkeling equipment generally rents for $15. If you're on your own in the San Juan area, one of the best places is the San Juan Bay marina near the Caribe Hilton.

Watersports desks at the big San Juan hotels at Isla Verde and Condado can generally make arrangements for instruction and equipment rental, and can also lead you to the best places for snorkeling, depending on where you are in the sprawling metropolis. If your hotel doesn't offer such services, you can contact **Caribe Aquatic Adventures** (see "Scuba Diving," above), which caters to snorkelers and scuba divers alike.

Still, if you are staying in San Juan and want to go snorkeling, consider taking a day trip to Fajardo, where you'll get a real Caribbean snorkeling experience with tranquil, clear water and stunning reefs teaming with tropical fish. Several operators offer day trips (daily 10am–3:30pm) leaving from Fajardo marinas (most likely Villa Marina or Puerto del Rey), but transportation to and from your San Juan hotel can also be arranged. Prices start at around $69 per person, or $99 including transportation to and from San Juan. Even if you don't particularly want to snorkel, the trips are still worth it for a day of fun in the sun. The trips usually take place on large luxury catamarans, holding about 20 passengers or more. Most have a cash bar serving drinks and refreshments, a sound system, and other creature comforts. The boats know the best reefs and hot spots for bigger fish, and will plan the trip according to weather conditions and other variables. A huge reef extending east to Culebra protects the ocean off Fajardo's coast, which makes for calm seas with great visibility.

Inquire at your hotel desk about operators providing service there. There are many reputable companies. My friends and I have all been satisfied with the **Traveler** (✆ 787/863-2821), **East Island Excursions** (✆ 787/860-3434), and **Catamaran Spread Eagle II** (✆ 787/887-8821). **Erin Go Bragh Charters** (✆ 787/860-4401) offers similar day trips aboard a 50-foot sailing ketch, which is an equally pleasurable experience.

SPAS & FITNESS CENTERS The Ritz-Carlton San Juan Hotel, Spa & Casino ★, Av. de los Gobernadores 6961, No. 187, Isla Verde (✆ 787/253-1700), set a new standard of luxury in San Juan hotels. That special treatment is no more evident than at its spa, with state-of-the-art massages, body wraps and scrubs, facials, manicures, pedicures, and a salon guaranteed to make you look like a movie star. In an elegant marble-and-stone setting there are 11 rooms for pampering, including hydrotherapy and treatments custom-tailored for individual needs. The 12,000-square-foot (1,115-sq.-m)

Swimmers, Beware

You have to pick your spots carefully if you want to swim along many San Juan beaches, especially Condado Beach. The waters at the beach beside the Condado Plaza Hotel are calmer than in other areas because of a coral breakwater. The beach near the Marriott is not good for swimming because of rocks, a strong undertow, and occasional rip tides. There are no lifeguards except at public beaches. Ocean Park is better for swimming, but can still be hazardous when the tides kick up. Isla Verde beach is generally much calmer, especially at its eastern end. The surf off Piñones, farther east, may be the most treacherous of all.

spa features a 7,200-square-foot (2,195-sq.-m) outdoor swimming pool, male and female steam baths, a sauna, and a whirlpool. Treatment specialties include the latest in skin, touch, and soak therapies, and wellness salon services. Caribbean fruits and flowers, and botanical treatments culled from El Yunque rainforest are employed in the treatments. Two house specialties are the detoxifying coffee body scrub and coconut milk moisturizing session and a rainforest stone massage with passion fruit oil. Specialty sessions range in price from $130 to $275.

The 12,000-square-foot (1,115-sq.-m) Olas Spa at the **Caribe Hilton,** Calle Los Rosales (© **787/721-0303**), offers everything from traditional massages to more exotic body and water therapies, using such products as honey, cucumber, sea salts, seaweed, or mud baths. You can choose your delight among the massages, including one called "Rising Sun," traditional Japanese shiatsu that uses pressure applied with hands, elbows, and knees on specific body points. Among the body wraps is Firm Away, a super-firming, brown and green algae body cocoon therapy for a soft, toned, and smooth skin. Other services include manicures and pedicures, a full-service hair salon, and many day-spa packages.

The InterContinental San Juan Resort & Casino, Av. Isla Verde 5961 (© **787/791-6100**), also has a plush spa adjacent to its beautiful pool area that has breathtaking ocean views. The masseuses trained locally and throughout the world, are among the best in San Juan, with the spare tropical setting as mellow as the house Swedish massage. The Caribbean Wrap aims to improve skin condition over the long haul, while the After Sun Pampering Massage looks to improve its elasticity and smoothness.

El San Juan Hotel & Casino, Av. Isla Verde 6063 (© **787/791-1000**), offers a stunning panoramic view of San Juan and a sauna, a steam room, and luxury massages.

Zen Spa, Av. Ashford 1054, Condado (© **787/722-8433**), has a full range of massages, facial treatments, body wraps, and therapeutic services. It's open 8am to 7pm weekdays, 9am to 6pm weekends. Specialty massages, which start at $55 for 25 minutes, include a detoxifying massage and a combo Swedish and Shiatsu massage.

International Fitness, Av. Ashford 1131, Condado (© **787/721-0717**), is air-conditioned, well equipped, and popular with residents of the surrounding high-rent district. Besides weight and cardio machines, there is TRX, zumba, pilates, spinning, body combat, and other fitness classes. Entrance costs $15 for a gym visit, $18 to take a class. A 3-day visit is $40, 5-day $65, or $80 for a week. Hours are Monday to Thursday 5am to 10pm, Friday 5am to 9pm, and Saturday 9am to 7pm; closed Sunday.

Liv Fitness Club, at Gallery Plaza, Calle Loíza, Condado (© **787/998-4553**), is 1 block away from the oceanfront. This stylish, popular health club with a view charges $25 for walk-ins. There are free weights, machines, rows of cardio equipment, and studios hosting 50 classes weekly, like yoga, kickboxing, and sheer spinning insanity, included in the price of admission.

SURFING & PADDLEBOARDING Velauno, Calle Loíza 2430, Punta Las Marías in San Juan (© **787/728-8716;** www.velauno.com), has paddleboard rentals and gives tours and lessons. Prices are $100 for the first person's first hour, and $50 for each additional hour, while additional persons pay $50 the first hour and $25 each additional hour.

Former pro surfer William Sue-A-Quan and a few associates give lessons through his **Walking on Water Surfing School** (© **787/955-6059;** www.gosurfpr.com), working right on the beach at Pine Grove and also offering lessons through the Ritz-Carlton. He's a great teacher, and takes on students as young as 5 and as old as 75. Another pro, Carlos Cabrero, teams up with personal trainer, Victor Tort, to teach beginners and to

Sanjuaneros would never brag that their island city is the capital of the Caribbean, and in many ways it isn't, largely perhaps because residents are too busy looking northward to the U.S., rather than to opportunities with regional partners.

In many ways, however, San Juan can stake claim as one of the Caribbean's most vibrant and beautiful urban centers, with beaches and weather to put South Florida to shame; a lively music, arts, and performance and cultural scene; and an entertainment infrastructure that includes a world-class coliseum, convention center, and smaller amphitheaters and stages. Puerto Rican royalty (from Benicio del Toro to Marc Anthony and J-Lo to Ricky Martin) are regularly jetting in, but it's the local talent that will more likely wow visitors.

The Puerto Rico José Miguel Agrelot Coliseum (500 Ave., Arterial B, Hato Rey; *©* **787/265-4736;** box office Mon–Fri 10am–5pm), known locally as "the Choliseo," has hosted major performers like Shakira, Britney Spears, Paul McCartney, the Rolling Stones, and Billy Joel, and it regularly gets top-name Latino acts. The **Puerto Rico Convention Center** (100 Convention Blvd., San Juan; *©* **800/214-0420**) attracts all sorts of national groups as well as other entertainment events, and is another site for concerts and performances. Both venues have cafe-bars that have become hangouts for young urban professionals to let loose after work, especially on Thursday and Friday nights. A redevelopment of the ferry terminal into an entertainment and restaurant complex was also recently completed adjacent to the Coliseum, which not only increased mass transit options, but also provided another great entertainment option in the area. The new **Bahia Urbana Park** on the bay at the entrance to Old San Juan hosts periodic concerts and other events, as does the **Tito Puente** amphitheater in the bucolic surroundings of Luis Muñoz Marin Park.

Museo de Arte de Puerto Rico (p. 91) is a showcase of island art, but also hosts top-rate traveling exhibitions and has such amenities as a 5-acre (2-hectare) sculpture and botanical garden, and a 400-seat theater, named for Raúl Juliá, the late Puerto Rican actor.

Old San Juan has its **SoFo,** a once abandoned sector of La Fortaleza Street that is now buzzing with activity, home to some of Old San Juan's best restaurants, bars, and clubs. A play on the name of New York City's SoHo, SoFo purportedly refers to South Fortaleza Street. The name has stuck, even though it's geographically inaccurate, as the area is actually East Fortaleza Street. The **Parrot Club** (p. 54) is the original hot spot of the neighborhood, opening more than a decade ago with its brash and flavorful Nuevo Latino cuisine in a land of crusty

train practitioners to become experts. The **Puerto Rico Institute of Surf Kinesiology** (*©* **787/728-3377** or 222-4555; prisksurf@gmail.com) out of his **Tres Palmas surf shop** in Ocean Park. The lessons take place off "the point" in Condado behind Ashford Hospital. It's the best shop in town if you are actually interested in surfing equipment or other equipment like boogie boards and skateboards. There's no skimping on the fashion either. They operate an excellent summer surf camp, which kids can attend for weeklong stints.

TENNIS   Most of the big resorts have their own tennis courts for their guests. There are 20 public courts, lit at night, at **San Juan Central Park,** at Calle Cerra (Exit F on

Chinese restaurants and delis, run-down tourist shops, and dusty fabric stores. Today, these run-down businesses have been renovated. The area is a center for world cuisine, where you can find everything from French **Trois Cent Onze** to Indian **Tantra** (p. 122) to Asian Fusion **Dragonfly** (p. 56).

Naturally beautiful **Ocean Park,** dotted with a few low-key guesthouses and restaurants, attracts an eclectic set of trendsetters: students, surfers, gay people, and urban creatives from the East Coast who prefer its low-lying skyline and laid-back ambience over the big resorts and condos of Condado and Isla Verde.

The **Condado,** however, has undergone its own revival, with the renovation of La Concha hotel, the opening of some of the city's best restaurants (such as Budatai and the relocated Pikayo), the establishment of an oceanfront park, and a string of boutiques of the world's top names in fashion and jewelry.

The **Plaza de Mercado de Santurce** (near Calle Canals and Av. Ponce de León) is a traditional food market and a great place for tropical fruits and vegetables; and there's a bunch more oddities, such as old Puerto Rican music recordings, herbs, and religious artifacts involving santería. There are several good restaurants in the surrounding neighborhood (José Enrique's and La Tasca del Pescador) and several bars. The neighborhood is a swirl of activity from early in the day through late evening. On Thursday and Friday nights, large crowds gather as the streets are blocked off from traffic. Several spots have live music. It's a favorite after-work spot for locals and a lot of fun. Just join the crowd and meander from one spot to the next. Seafood fritters, chicken kebabs, and meat turnovers are sold from street vendors, and there is music everywhere.

The city also has several beautiful green parks with loads of activities during weekends. A plan to connect them via bicycle and pedestrian pathways is underway. It will build on the Parque Lineal Marti Coli, which stretches for nearly 2 miles (3.2km) along Caño de Martín Peña, from Hato Rey to Parque Central. Eventually this bicycle path will reach a distance of nearly 12 miles (19km), linking the Old City with Río Piedras. Biking, hiking, and jogging pathways are planned; one day bikers will be able to go along the breadth of San Juan without having to encounter traffic. In the meantime, enough trails have been completed for a memorable stroll.

At night, in Old San Juan at **Nuyorican Café** (p. 118), there's the sounds of salsa and Latin rhythms with an African beat, while **Yerba Buena** (p. 119) in Condado also hosts a big Latin jazz band as well as a house salsa band.

Rte. 2; © **787/722-1646**), open daily. Fees are $4 per hour, 6am to 10pm. There are also four racquetball courts here. **The Barbosa Tennis Club** (© **787/722-1646**) gives lessons at Parque Barbosa, at the Ultimo Trolley beach in Ocean Park, where eight courts are located. Court fees are $6 per hour per player. **The Isla Verde Tennis Club** (© **787/727-6490**) is open all week, weekdays from 8am to 10pm, Saturdays from 8am to 7pm, and Sundays from 8am to 6pm. Courts cost from $20 to $25 hour, and semiprivate lessons at $75 per hour.

KITE BOARDING & SAILING Kite boarding has long supplanted windsurfing along the San Juan coastline from Isla Verde through Ocean Park. Kite-boarding advice and lessons are available at **Velauno,** Calle Loíza 2430, Punta Las Marías in

San Juan ((C) **787/728-8716;** www.velauno.com). Their instructors will also rent equipment, with prices starting at about $75 daily. A 2-hour beginner's lesson costs $150. Also try **15 Knots Kiteboarding School,** Av. Isla Verde 4851, Isla Verde ((C) **787/362-7228**). It rents equipment and has lessons for all abilities; beginners can take a tandem kiteboard ride with an instructor.

SHOPPING

Because Puerto Rico is a U.S. commonwealth, U.S. citizens don't pay duty on items brought back to the mainland. And you can still find great bargains on Puerto Rico, where the competition among shopkeepers is fierce. Even though the U.S. Virgin Islands are duty-free, you can often find far lower prices on many items in San Juan than on St. Thomas. A local 7 percent sales and use tax is levied on most goods and services.

The streets of the Old City, such as Calle Fortaleza, Calle San Francisco, and Calle del Cristo, are the major venues for shopping. After years of trying, local restrictions on operating hours of stores, aimed at protecting small businesses and the religious nature of Sundays in Roman Catholic Puerto Rico, were finally relaxed in 2010. Shops and stores are now free to open any time except between 6am and 11am Sunday mornings. In general, malls in San Juan are open Monday to Saturday 9am to 9pm and Sunday from 10am to 7pm. In such tourism districts as Old San Juan, Condado and Isla Verde, some shops stay open even later, and many Old City retailers, restaurants and bars will open whenever cruise ships are at harbor, regardless of the hour. There are now more 24-hour grocery stores and pharmacies, and Walmart has also instituted the concept.

Native handicrafts can be good buys, including needlework, straw work, ceramics, hammocks, and papier-mâché fruits and vegetables, as well as paintings and sculptures by Puerto Rican artists. Among these, the carved wooden religious idols known as *santos* (saints) have been called Puerto Rico's greatest contribution to the plastic arts and are sought by collectors. For the best selection of *santos,* head for **Galería Botello** (see "Art," below), **Olé,** or **Puerto Rican Arts & Crafts** (see "Gifts & Handicrafts," later in this chapter).

Condado also has a lot of interesting shops, most of which line Avenida Ashford, along with the restaurants, hotels, and luxury condominiums. And the up and coming Calle Loíza, home on its Condado end to clubs and chic Oriental and Spanish restaurants, and on its Ocean Park end, the best Argentine neighborhood pizzeria in the world and a fabulous hippy vegan and fruit drink emporium. In between, running from De Diego Avenue in Condado to Calle Tapia in Ocean Park, Loíza Street is home to fashion designer shops and studios, fashion boutiques, pawnshops, and fabulous restaurants, from Greek to Peruvian to fish taco and fritter stands. Fitness studios, beauty salons, and flower, fruit and vegetable stands.

Puerto Rico's biggest and most up-to-date shopping mall is **Plaza Las Américas,** in the financial district of Hato Rey, right off the Las Américas Expressway. This complex, with its fountains and modern architecture, has more than 200 shops, including great local boutiques and the biggest names in retail and fashion. The variety of goods and prices is roughly comparable to that of large stateside malls. There are also several top-notch restaurants, a full cineplex, plus art galleries and food stores. If you want a break from the sun (or if it's raining), there are entertainment options here for all. If you are driving, the **Outlet 66 Mall** is not that much farther, and can be combined with a trip to El Yunque, a day fishing or snorkeling trip from Fajardo of a trip to northeast golf courses or beaches.

Unless otherwise specified, the following stores can be reached via the Old City Trolley. Likewise, store hours are noted only when they stray from those mentioned above.

Antiques

El Alcazar ★   Perhaps the largest antiques dealer in the Caribbean, this spot is a treasure chest of antique Puerto Rican furniture, silver, and artwork, porcelain, and statues of the saints hand-carved by local artists from wood. The finds here include stuff from the region, but also European art collections from majestic estates. Calle San José 103. ℂ **787/723-1229.** www.fortelezaantiques.com.

Art

Butterfly People ★   The arrangements are works of art, but some viewers may find the butterfly displays more creepy than beautiful. Preserved and suspended in creative arrangements inside airtight see through box frames, the enduring works get some of the worlds most beautiful butterflies from Indonesia and Malaysia and elsewhere in tropical Asia. Open weekends 10am to 6pm. Calle Cruz 257. ℂ **787/723-2432.** www.butterflypeople.com.

Galería Botello ★   The gallery hosts trailblazing work by contemporary artists but also is a homage to the late Angel Botello, who was born and raised in Galicia, Spain, but fled to the Caribbean, living for years in Haiti before making Old San Juan his home. The gallery is housed in the restored colonial mansion where he lived, and is filled with his paintings and bronze sculptures, as well the works by other contemporary artists and a collection of antique *santos,* wood statues of the saints hand-carved by skilled Puerto Rican artisans. Calle del Cristo 208. ℂ **787/723-9987.** www.botello.com.

Galería Exodo ★   A fresh gallery that explores boundaries and their dissolution in showcasing Puerto Rican and Caribbean artists working across cultural, geographic and political boundaries. It also champions art that explores the debilitating marginalization of indigenous and minority communities and the impact that exile has had on an artist's development. Dozens of artists have work displayed at any given time from across the Americas, including U.S. marginalized communities. A very vibrant collection that is fun and exhilarating. Calle Cristo 152 & 200B (Corner Calle San Francisco). ℂ **787/725-4252** or 784/723-4913. www.galeriaexodo.com.

The Gallery Inn ★★   The rambling gallery in a huge Spanish colonial inn focuses on the accomplished work Jan D'Esopo, a beautiful Connecticut-born artist who moved to Puerto Rico decades ago and never left. She has done man fine bronze sculptures of famous Puerto Ricans but her paintings and other sculptures are more engaging. Gorgeous oceanfront location. In the Gallery Inn, Calle Norzagaray 204. ℂ **787/722-1808.** www.thegalleryinn.com.

Haitian Gallery ★   The place for Haitian art in San Juan, where you can get playful jungle and warm Haitian landscape scenes, primitive sculptures, and enchanting handicrafts, and Technicolor Port au Prince street scenes. The art is vibrant and hopeful, even fun, often coming from the unlikeliest of places. There are also beautiful ethnic pieces from across the Americas, which are just as engaging. Lots of bargains in a range of $25 to $500. Open daily from 10am to 6pm. Calle Fortaleza 206. ℭ **787/721-4362.** Other location: Calle Fortaleza 367. ℭ **787/725-0986.** www.facebook.com/haitian.gallery. puertorico.

Obra Galería Alegría ★   For 15 years, this gallery has had the straight forward purpose of showing the best work possible of Puerto Rican artists and has delivered remarkably well on that premise. It shows the work of both important masters and respected contemporary artists. Artists include: Lorenzo Homar; Domingo García; Julio Rosado del Valle; Ángel Botello, José Campeche, Nick Quijano, Jorge Zeno, and Magda Santiago. It's open Tuesday through Saturday from 1:30pm to 5pm. Calle Cruz 301 (corner Recinto Sur). ℭ **787/723-3226.** www.facebook.com/obragaleria.

Books

Beta Book Café ★   This Andalusian book chain is filling the void left by the collapse of Borders, which had come to dominate the local book market before going out of business. Beta has a branch at Plaza Carolina and plans to open another location in Plaza Las Americas during 2015; in the space Borders ran its flagship store. The cafe-bookstore has a wide literature and nonfiction section, children's area, readings and special events, a great magazine and newspaper collection, and an excellent cafe. Plaza Carolina, Av. Jesús M. Fragoso, Carolina. ℭ **787/725-0592.** www.facebook.com/BetaBookcafe.

La Tertulia ★★   A bookstore with a wide selection of books and music in a large, beautiful setting, La Tertulia carries the latest hits in Spanish and English, plus nonfiction, fiction, and classics in both Spanish and English. It's open Monday through Saturday from 9am to 10pm and Sunday from 10am to 8pm. Recinto Sur 305, Old San Juan. ℭ **787/724-8200.**

Libros AC ★   This bookstore, which doubles as a bistro cafe, is part of the Renaissance of downtown Santurce, an exciting new building across from the towering Ciudadella residential and retail community close to the arts district near the art museum and the performing arts center. There are great titles, but a limited selection, with more Spanish than English books. The excellent, reasonably priced coffee and food will lure book lovers just the same, as will the excellent Wi-Fi connections, comfortable seats, and clean bathrooms. It's open Monday through Saturday from 9am to 10pm and Sunday from 10am to 8pm. Av Ponce De Leon 1501o, Santurce. ℭ **787/998-5132.** www.librosac.com.

The Poet's Passage ★★   Enchanting local poet Lady Lee Andrews is the hostess with the mostess at this cafe-bookstore-gallery, which showcases the work of her husband painter Nicolas Thomassin, which weaves into her poetry. There are poetry readings, exhibit openings, and other events. It's open Monday through Saturday from 9am to 10pm and Sunday from 10am to 8pm. Calle Cruz 203, Old San Juan. ℭ **787/567-9235.**

Carnival Masks

La Calle ★   This is the spot for to buy handmade, brightly painted masks (sometimes called *caretas*) that are worn by *vegigantes,* carnival revelers. The masks depict inspired creatures with horns and trumpet noses and bulging eyes, and other pagan

CARNIVAL masks

The most popular of all Puerto Rican crafts are the bright and festive **caretas**—papier-mâché masks worn at island carnivals. They may be a tangle of horns, fangs, and bulging eyes, but with their carnival colors and the laughing, costumed revelers, called **vegigantes,** who wear them, they are more about announcing party time than trying to be scary. The vegigantes wear bat-winged jumpsuits and roam the streets either individually or in groups.

The origins of these masks and carnivals may go back to medieval Spain and/or tribal Africa. A processional tradition in Spain, dating from the early 17th century, was intended to terrify sinners with marching devils, in the hope that they would return to church. Cervantes described it briefly in Don Quixote. Puerto Rico blended this Spanish procession with the masked tradition brought by slaves from Africa. Some historians believe that the Taínos were also accomplished mask makers, which would make this a very ancient tradition indeed.

The predominant traditional mask colors were black, red, and yellow, all symbols of hellfire and damnation. Today, pastels are more likely to be used. Each vegigante sports at least two or three horns, although some masks have hundreds of horns, in all shapes and sizes. Mask-making in Ponce, the major center for this craft, and in Loíza Aldea, a palm-fringed town on the island's northeastern coast, has since led to a renaissance of Puerto Rican folk art.

The premier store selling these masks is **La Calle** (p. 110). Masks can be seen in action at the three big masquerade carnivals on the island: the **Ponce Festival** in February, the **Festival of Loíza Aldea** in July, and the **Día de las Máscaras** at Hatillo in December.

inspirations of half man, half beast. There is also handcrafted jewelry, ethnic crafts, and a gallery of fine local artists. Calle Fortaleza 105. ☏ **787/725-1306.**

Cigars

The Cigar House & Lounge ★★ Puerto Rico's biggest cigar emporium just got a whole lot better with a cigar bar where you can enjoy a fine stogy and an excellent beer, whiskey or aged dark rum in air-conditioned comfort beneath a skylight. More than 300 brands from around the world are kept in a walk-in humidifier, including fine quality Dominican cigars and about six different brands using Puerto Rican leaf, but the top Nicaraguan brands here are among the best. A great ventilator system keeps the air fresh. Officially open from 10am to 10pm, but will stay open later if the crowd is still having fun. Calle Fortaleza 257. ☏ **787/723-5223.** www.thecigarhousepr.com.

Don Collin's Cigars ★ The renovated Old City digs are the perfect spot for this local cigar maker looking to give this Puerto Rican tradition a rebirth. The cigars are made in the oldest cigar factory in the Caribbean, using Puerto Rico-grown wraps and tobacco but mixing fine leaf from across the Caribbean and Latin American region. Open daily from 9am to 9pm. Calle Cristo 59. ☏ **787/977-2983.** www.don-collins.com.

Clothing & Beachwear

Costazul ★ Everything you might need for the beach for men, women, youths and children. This is quality stuff, name brands at reasonable prices, so it's worth a stop if you need to find need something for some fun in the something but want to make sure it's a keeper. Open Monday to Saturday 9am to 7pm, Sunday 11am to 5pm. Calle San Francisco 264. ℂ **787/724-8085.**

Hecho a Mano ★★★   Gorgeous exotic clothing for women, handmade jewelry, and other beautiful items line what has been one of Old San Juan's best boutiques for the last 2 decades. Fashion trends run from ethnic and indigenous to cutting edge cocktail dresses. The staff is as charming as the merchandise. Hecho a mano has grown from a single store in Old San Juan to about a dozen locations, including a shop on Condado's Ashford Avenue and at Plaza Las Américas. Open daily 10am to 7pm, Sunday from 11am to 7pm. Calle San Francisco 260, Old San Juan. ℂ **787/722-5322.** www. hechoamanoonline.com.

Mrs. and Miss Boutique ★   This is the for tropical clothing for women; the spot shimmers with silklike and soft cotton designs in a rainbow of colors and exotic patterns. Great spot for sun dresses, sarongs and other summery fashion that never goes out of style. Open daily 11am to 6pm. Calle Fortaleza 154. ℂ **787/724-8571.**

Nono Maldonado ★   The fashion boutique of one of the mavericks of Puerto Rico design, there is a full range of elegant, tasteful clothing for men and women with a fabulous collection of linen shirts. A former fashion editor at "Esquire" magazine, Maldonado has branched out recently into interior design and fragrances. Av. Ashford 1112. ℂ **787/721-0456.** www.nonomaldonado.com. Bus: 5.

Polo Ralph Lauren Factory Store ★   The great American clothing store moved into larger quarters by the cruiseship docks, but it still offers great prices on fine clothing from one of the world's iconic fashion brands. A lot of the merchandise is summer and spring wear suited to the tropics, but you'll find a wide variety, including swimsuits, shirts, dress suits, and a full collection of women's fashion. The best prices are on the on "irregular" merchandise that looks just fine. Open Monday to Saturday. 9amto 9pm, Sunday 11am to 7pm. Harbor Plaza, Paseo Gilberto Concepcion de Gracia 105. ℂ **787/724-1025.** www.ralphlauren.com.

Ruedo ★   With beautiful vintage clothing and accessories for women as well as offerings by young local designers, this Old City shop is fresh and fun. It's open Tuesday through Saturday 11:30am to 5pm. Calle Sol 201, Old San Juan. ℂ **787/466-3068.** www. facebook.com/ruedovintage.

Wet Boutique ★★   If you want to look great on the beach, stop in here for some of San Juan's most sizzling swimsuits, with designer bikinis and one-piece suits, as well as some trunks for guides. Erika, who possesses the charm of Helen Mirren, will guide you to the design that's just for you. Calle Cruz 150, Old San Juan. ℂ **787/722-2052.**

Chocolate & Spices

Casa Cortés Chocobar ★★★   Chocolate lovers, here's your Nirvana. This 2,500 square foot space's gleaming glass and marble is all about placing chocolate on a pedestal, with hundreds of artisan chocolate creations on display and a complete menu where chocolate plays a role in every dish, whether it's the house eggs Benedict with chocolate chili hollandaise sauce or the brie panini with chocolate hazelnut sauce. There is also wine and chocolate pairings and a tapas menu. The gorgeous spot was opened by the Cortés family to highlight its gourmet chocolate brand, which is made with cacao grown in the Dominican Republic and created in Puerto Rico. The restaurant has a great collection of local paintings; upstairs, there is a two-level gallery of the family's art collection, mostly pieces from across the Caribbean. The menu ranges from $7 to $16. Open Tuesday through Sunday 8am to 6pm. Calle San Francisco 210, Old San Juan. © **787/722-0499.** www.casacortespr.com.

Corné Port-Royal Chocolatier ★   Come here if you are looking for the world's best chocolate, which uses centuries-old Belgian recipes and the finest cocoa and ingredients available. The smell of chocolate in the store is hard to resist, but there are also delicious candies, cookies, jellies, and coffee for sale. Open Monday through Saturday 10am to 6pm. Calle San Justo 204, Old San Juan. © **787/725-7744.** www.corne portroyal.com.

Spicy Caribbee ★   Step in this shop to experience the flavors of the Caribbean in all their glories, with sauces and seasonings, teas and coffees, and jams and chutneys. Whether you are looking for a dusky Puerto Rican coffee, atomic habanero pepper sauce, or a complex jerk rub, you will find it here. There are also Caribbean soaps and fragrances, beautiful cookbooks and crafts, music CDs, and other gifts. For years, it's been one of the best stops in Old San Juan. Calle Cristo 154. © **787/725-4690.**

Discount Stores

Marshalls ★   You go to place for everything from luggage to beachwear to sunglasses, this U.S. discount store packs more bargains than perhaps any spot in Old San Juan. The place is always crowded. Locals love it for the cut rates on designer brands and kitchenware, and the store will resolve any tourist quandary from the need to replace a broken sandal to replacing that lost set of earrings. You can also find decent bathing suits for less than the prices here anywhere in San Juan. In Plaza de Armas, across from the City Hall, at Calle Rafael Cordero 154, Old San Juan. © **787/722-3020.**

Gifts & Handicrafts

Art-Furniture-Art ★   Reproductions of classic Caribbean and Spanish colonial furniture made a name for designer Diana M. Ramos, who has since moved on to works that are have a simple modern elegance. Form and function lie down together in this beautiful furniture gallery inside La Cochera parking garage, the only one at the heart of the Old City, a block behind Plaza de las Armas. Calle Luna 204, Old San Juan. © **787/722-4181.**

Barrachina ★   Old San Juan's biggest tourist trap is actually not too bad a spot to get stuck in for a while, especially if you are a cruise ship visitor with only a few hours to explore the Old City. Its Spanish colonial courtyard is charming, with a bar serving tropical drinks and there's an elegant dining room serving classic Puerto Rican fare and flamenco shows every night. Need that perfect gift? There's everything for sale: jewelry, perfume, cigars, rum, and other gifts. This Old San Juan institution lays claim to the invention of the piña colada back in 1963, but another local legend has it that the drink was actually invented earlier by a bartender at the Caribe Hilton. Calle Fortaleza 104 (btw. Calle del Cristo and Calle San José). © **787/725-7912.**

Bóveda ★★   There is a treasure trove of beautiful things from across the Americas: elegant clothing, native fabrics, finely crafted jewelry, housewares, and antiques. It's a fun place to shop with new coming in all the time and an engaging staff that clearly love this place. Calle del Cristo 209. © **787/725-0263.** www.boveda.info.

Ecléctica ★★   This global artisan shop brings you wonders of the world, and prides itself in engaging in fair trade practices and using sustainable materials. Exotic tablecloths and bed sheets, hand-carved jewelry boxes from mango wood and a whole line of tagua nut products from the South American rainforest, from buttons to earrings

shopping **FOR SANTOS**

The most impressive of the island's crafts are the *santos*, carved religious figures that have been produced since the 1500s. Craftspeople who make these are called *santeros*; using clay, gold, stone, or cedar wood, they carve figurines representing saints, usually from 8 to 20 inches (20–51cm) tall. Before the Spanish colonization, small statues, called *zemi*, stood in native tribal villages and camps as objects of veneration, and Puerto Rico's *santos* may derive from that pre-Columbian tradition. Every town has its patron saint, and every home has its *santos* to protect the family. For some families, worshipping the *santos* replaces a traditional Mass.

Art historians view the carving of *santos* as Puerto Rico's greatest contribution to the fine arts. The earliest figures were richly baroque, indicating a strong Spanish influence, but as the islanders began to assert their own identity, the carved figures often became simpler.

In carving *santos*, craftspeople often used handmade tools. Sometimes such natural materials as vegetable dyes and even human hair were used. The saints represented by most *santos* can be identified by their accompanying symbols; for example, Saint Anthony is usually depicted with the infant Jesus and a book. The most popular group of *santos* is the Three Kings. The Trinity and the Nativity are also depicted frequently.

Art experts claim that *santos*-making approached its zenith at the turn of the 20th century, although hundreds of *santeros* still practice their craft throughout the island. Serious *santos* collectors view the former craftsmen of old as the true artists in the field. The best collection of *santos* is found at **Puerto Rican Arts & Crafts** (see below).

Some of the best *santos* on the island can be seen at the Capilla de Cristo in Old San Juan. Perhaps at some future date, a museum devoted entirely to *santos* will open in Puerto Rico.

to tiny sculptures. Make sure to listen to the Tibetan wind chimes, which have a sound as beautiful as the Himalayans; there's also an incredible collection of Christmas ornaments. The fabulous collection also includes teak furniture and hand-carved wooden *santos*, and countless other gifts. The store has consolidated to one location from two, but the space is bigger and the collection as seemingly infinite. Calle O'Donnell 204, Plaza Colón. ✆ **787/721-7236.**

Mundo Taíno ★   Your go to place for authentic Puerto Rican souvenirs, whether it's dark rum, indigenous petroglyphs, or a soundtrack to El Yunque rainforest you're looking for. The fine art, music and book collection cuts beneath the surface of the skin of island culture, and the friendly, youthful staff is helpful and proud of their heritage, which is great to see. Calle San José 151, Old San Juan. ✆ **787/724-2005.**

Olé ★   A great spot to buy a Panama hat, with a huge array of styles and sizes so that you will undoubtedly find one to your liking that gives you a custom fit. There are nice hats for under $50, although most hats cost nearly twice and top-of-the-line hats can fetch more than $1,000. With a collection of local high quality paintings and prints, exquisite *santos* wood carvings, and hand crafted jewelry of fine silver and emeralds, however, this shop is about much more than a great hat. Calle Fortaleza 105. ✆ **787/724-2445.**

Puerto Rican Arts & Crafts ★★   Your go-to stop for fine Puerto Rican paintings, prints and sculptures, including the traditional wood carvings of the saints, and other traditional works, like the vibrant Ponce carnival masks, and a wealth of works using ancient petroglyphs of the Taínos. There are really high quality souvenirs, often superior versions of things served elsewhere, like homemade jewelry, silkscreens and gourmet products such as coffee, rum and sauces. The centuries-old colonial mansion that houses it all is a real charmer. Closes at 6pm Monday through Saturday and 5pm Sunday. Calle Fortaleza 204. ℰ **787/725-5596.** www.puertoricanart-crafts.com.

Vaughn's Gifts &Crafts ★ Its *raison d'etre* is the large collection of Panama and other tropical straw hats, but there's sizeable collection of Caribbean crafts and bric a brac. The shop has a stuck-in-the-past feel to it that's quaint because of the high quality of the merchandise. Calle Fortaleza 262. ℰ **787/721-8221.**

Jewelry

Bared & Sons ★ For a half century, this has been one of the island's top jeweler with an extraordinary collection of quality watches–from Rolex to Bvlgari–and exquisite gold jewelry with diamonds and gemstones. It specializes in engagement and wedding rings. It's gorgeous store is in a renovated historic building where you'll want to go for that one special gift, regardless the cost, not for hunting bargains. San Justo 206 (at the corner of Calle Fortaleza). ℰ **787/724-4811.**

Reinhold Jewelers ★★ This award winning store is a designer jewelry pioneer, emphasizing the artists who make the dazzling items on display, whether it's an intense blue sapphire creation or a delicate diamond balanced on gold. Works by the big names—from John Hardy to David Yurman—are all here, but Reinhold also works with up and coming local and regional artists. Its service and annual holiday catalog matches the quality of its merchandise. Adjacent to its flagship store at the main entrance to Plaza Las América, it operates the David Yurman design boutique, forming a dazzling expanse of jewelry that is a sight to be seen. The El San Juan Hotel Gallery location is also charming. Plaza Las Américas 24A, 24B, Hato Rey. ℰ **787/554-0528.** Other location at El San Juan Hotel Gallery, Isla Verde. ℰ **787/796-2521.** www.reinholdjewelers.com.

Kamel International Bazaar ★ Over the top costume jewelry and exotic designs dominate this shop, but there are quality gemstone pieces and beautiful Larimar semiprecious stones as well. The extensive collection of bracelets has you covered for anything and there's necklaces fit for Cleopatra. There's a campy Middle Eastern marketplace air to the place, but you can fine real bargains on great stuff. Beyond jewelry, there is fine linen clothing for men and women, paintings and crafts, and gorgeous handbags. Calle Cristo 154. ℰ **787/722-1455.** www.facebook.com/KamelInternationalBazaar.

A Dying Art: Old Lace

Another Puerto Rican craft has undergone a big revival just as it seemed that it would disappear forever: lace. Originating in Spain, *mundillos* (tatted fabrics) are the product of a type of bobbin lace-making. This 500-year-old craft exists today only in Puerto Rico and Spain.

The first lace made in Puerto Rico was called *torchon* (beggar's lace). Early examples of beggar's lace were considered of inferior quality, but artisans today have transformed this fabric into a delicate art form, eagerly sought by collectors. Lace bands called *entrados* have two straight borders, whereas the other traditional style, puntilla, has both a straight and a scalloped border.

The best outlet in San Juan for lace is **Linen House** (below).

Lace & Linens

Linen House ★★   Puerto Rico's best collection of lace linens, including bed sheets, shower curtains, table cloths, curtains, and lace doilies. The store specializes in creating lace details for weddings, including table settings and special setting for the cake. Beautiful stuff at reasonable prices. Calle Fortaleza 250, 104. ℂ **787/721-4219** or 725-6233. www.facebook.com/pages/The-Linen-House/75550768574.

Leather & Equestrian Accessories

Coach ★   A factory outlet of this famed chain of leather shops, you will find a wide selection of Coach merchandise as well as big discounts on close-out products. Special deals, such as 50 percent discount coupons for special periods, can drive prices down further. Calle Cristo 150. ℂ **787/722-6830.** www.coach.com.

Dooney & Bourke Factory Store ★   Another emporium for leather lovers that also offers great deals on its extraordinary collection of women's handbags and briefcases, as well as a full line of leather products. Great bargains can be had here, too. Calle Cristo 200, Old San Juan. ℂ **787/289-0075.** www.dooney.com.

Lalin Tack & Leather Shop ★   Founded by a Cuban cowboy in 1971, this store specializes in horse saddles and bridles, but also has an extensive collection of other leather items and cowboy boots and hats. Much of the merchandise is made in Puerto Rico, but Latin American goods are also part of the collection. The prices here are often better than the U.S., so a trip to the Puerto Nuevo suburb where this is located might be worth it, and it has a core international clientele, serviced by shipping. The store also sells leather and tools for leather artisans. Av. Piñero 1617, Puerto Nuevo. ℂ **787/781-5305** or 749-4815. www.lalins.com. Bus: B17.

Malls

The Outlet at Route 66 ★   Puerto Rico's biggest outlet mall is a quick trip to the east in in Canóvanas, on the road to El Yunque forest. A huge collection of big names discount stores—including Nike, Levi's, Guess, and the Gap—are housed in the enclosed mall. Good prices, especially during sales, and the bargains extend to the food court and movie theater here. At the Canóvanas exit to Route 66. Hwy. 3 18400, Barrio Pueblo, Canóvanas. ℂ **787/256-7040.** www.theoutletmall66.com. No bus.

Plaza Las Américas ★★   An oasis on a rainy day, the Caribbean's largest mall goes way beyond shopping with its own restaurant row, spas, a cinema, and beauty salons. Dining options range from The Cheesecake Factory and P.F. Chang's China Bistro to local finds like pizzeria Faccio's and gourmet salad and soup bar Ponte Fresco. There are always special events taking place, coffee festivals, car shows, musical performances, and fashion shows. It's a place to shop, for sure, with Macy's, Armani Exchange, Ann Taylor, Banana Republic, and 300 other stores. Av. Franklin Delano Roosevelt 525, Hato Rey. ℂ **787/767-5202.** www.plazalasamericas.com. Bus: 22.

Markets

Plaza del Mercado de Santurce ★★   Puerto Rico's traditional marketplace is filled with locally grown fruits and vegetables, medicinal herb shops, cafes serving coffee, fruit drinks, and Puerto Rican food and classic salsa and bolero musical recordings. The market is quite close to Condado and is surrounded by restaurants and bars. A popular hangout on Thursday and Friday evenings; an open air terrace that fronts it is a great spot to indulge in whatever it was you just bought inside. Calle Dos Hermanos at Calle Capitol, Santurce. (C) **787/723-8022.** Bus: A5.

SAN JUAN NIGHTLIFE

San Juan nightlife comes in all varieties. From the vibrant performing-arts scene to street-level salsa, and with casinos, discos, and bars, there's plenty of entertainment available almost any evening.

Island nightlife begins very late, especially on Friday and Saturday nights. Hang out until the late, late afternoon on the beach, have dinner around 8pm (9 would be even better), and then the night is yours. The true party animal will rock until the broad daylight. Many bars and nightclubs are open until 2am during the week, and 4am on weekends. Many clubs and some bars are closed on Mondays and Tuesdays.

"*¡QuéPasa!*," the official visitor's guide to Puerto Rico, lists cultural events, including music, dance, theater, film, and art exhibits. It's distributed free by the tourist office. Local newspapers, such as the English-language weekly "Caribbean Business" (which carries a daily website at www.caribbeanbusinesspr.com), often have entertainment information and concert and cultural listings, as do the Spanish-language "El Vocero," "El Nuevo Día," and "Primera Hora" daily newspapers. Also check the Ticketpop website (www.ticketpop.com), which lists upcoming major acts.

The Performing Arts

Centro de Bellas Artes ★   This cultural treasure lies at the heart of downtown Santurce, where Puerto Rico's finest performing artists, as well as world renowned performing artists perform. Make sure to find out what's going on when you are in town, or plan your visit to an event you want to see. The center's main stage, named after the legendary opera singer Antonio Paoli room, measures 62 by 50 feet and has a two-level auditorium that can seat nearly 2,000. Known for its fine acoustics, which are attributed at least in part to its suspended platform, the concert hall hosts operas, the traditional zarzuela, symphony concerts, ballet, and popular music concerts. The 800-seat René Marqués, also has great sound and lighting, and is the preferred spot for theatrical productions. The Carlos Marichal Theater is even more intimate, with 210 seats, a favorite with experimental productions. Av. Ponce de León 22. (C) **787/724-4747** or 725-7334 for the ticket agent. www.cba.gobierno.pr. Tickets $40–$200; 50 percent discounts for seniors. Bus: 5, M1.

Teatro Tapía ★   One of the oldest theaters in the Americas, the Tapia holds varied performances throughout the year, including holiday concerts and children's groups, drama and cultural events. It's located at the entrance to Old San Juan just south of Plaza Colon, its charming facade contributing to the overall allure of the district. Av. Fortaleza at Plaza Colón. (C) **787/721-0180.** Tickets $7–$30, depending on the show. Bus: Old San Trolley trolley.

The Club & Music Scene

Club Brava and Ultra Lounge ★   This ever chic spot has a big, blazing dance floor for shaking bodies, a balcony circling above for those who want to watch, and a low-key lounge area upstairs for smoother operators. With a great sound system and fashion police at the door, Brava attracts San Juan's rich, beautiful, and famous, as well as well-heeled travelers looking to dance. It's expensive (the $20 cover is just the beginning) and management wants you to "dress to impress," describing attire as "fashionably elegant." The party gets going late, and the DJ's mix of Latin, house, electronica, and other forms is always part of a good long groove. However, if you get started early on your night out, you'll probably have more fun dancing at the lobby bar. Open Thursday through Saturday from 10pm until 5am. In El San Juan Hotel & Casino, Av. Isla Verde 6063, Isla Verde. ℂ 787/791-2781. www.bravapr.com. Cover hovers around $20 depending on event; free for guests of El San Juan Hotel (just show room key). Bus: 5.

Downtown ★★   A great spot on the water in the middle of the city where you can experience live rock and other performances, televised sporting events, and great crowds. There are more than 100 tap beers from around the world and an extensive pub menu, which grows in appeal as the night presses on. Right by the ferry and Urban Train stops adjacent to the Puerto Rico Coliseum, known as El Choliseo, and there is ample and secure parking here. It's a favorite of young professionals toiling in the nearby financial district. Open Thursday through Saturday from 10pm until 5am. Hato Rey Ferry Terminal, Av Arterial B 125, Hato Rey. ℂ 787/523-6666. www.facebook.com/downtownpr. Cover changes with acts but hovers around $10for special performance only. Bus: M1.

La Piazza Terrace Club at Di Zucchero jm ★   The second floor of an Italian restaurant right across from the Marriott Hotel is transformed weekend nights into one of San Juan's best nightclubs, with DJs from Miami, Brazil, and Italy, flying in, and live bands also performing. The food at the Italian restaurant is quite good, and so is the late night menu served in the upstairs lounge. Unlike some city clubs, this spot attracts mixed age groups. The best part is you won't likely have to go far to get here. If you do, a big parking lot is adjacent and taxis and bus stops abound. 1210 Av Ashford, Condado ℂ 787/946-0835. www.dizuccheropr.com.

La Factoria ★★   The bartenders here are serious about their craft; there's a great cocktail, beer, and wine selection, and the food's quite good. Designer bar burgers, as well as bites such as lavender goat cheese balls and pork empanadas are paired with a solid wine list and inventive drink selection. Its "hidden" and "private" bars and rooms strike some as snooty, but as always, the regular folks bar is the place to be anyway. Calle San Sebastian 148 (corner Calle San Jose), Old San Juan. ℂ 787/594-5698. www.facebook. com/FactoriaLaSanse. Mon-Wed 6:30pm-3am, Thurs 6:30pm-4am, Fri-Sat 4pm-4am, Sun 4pm-3am.

La Concha Lobby Bar ★   The lobby of this revamped architectural gem celebrates every night, as guests and locals come out to play at the very heart of Condado. The Solera tapas restaurants and casino are adjacent, and right outside is the Ventana del Mar Park, lined with cafes and bars; Condado's finest boutiques and restaurants are right across the street. Actors and DJs often stay here and it's also a hotspot for local celebrities and San Juan's young and beautiful. 1077 Av. Ashford, Condado. ℂ 787/721-7500. www.laconcharesort.com.

Nuyorican Café ★★   It's no surprise the night before the Rolling Stones performed a show in Puerto Rico during their last tour, Mick Jagger and Keith Richards showed up around midnight here to hear some live salsa. The Nuyorican is the real deal, the spot to hear local music of high quality, with live bands playing salsa and Latin jazz, among other genres. The performance is usually inspired and the cover charge reasonable (below $10 unless something special). Throw in a great crowd, weekly evening salsa lessons, periodic theatrical performances, and tasty pizza and other food. This is about the music though. Don't expect snappy and flawless service. Calle San Francisco 312 (entrance down the alley), Old San Juan. ℂ 787/977-1276 or 366-5074. www.nuyoricancafepr.com.

Music While You Munch

Several restaurants in Old San Juan, and elsewhere throughout the city, have live music on certain days of the week. Knowing the schedule could help you decide on where to eat dinner. **The Parrot Club** has live Latin jazz and salsa a few nights weekly, as does **Bar Gitano** in Condado and **Koko** in Isla Verde. **Café Concierto** (📞 787/725-4927; www.carlicafeconcierto.com) has live jazz nightly at 9pm, while **Barrachina Restaurant** (p. 113) has a live flamenco music and dance show nightly. **La Playita** in Isla Verde hosts weekend troubadours and has a breathtaking view over the sea, while Condado's **Yerba Buena,** Av. Ashford 1350, Condado (📞 787/721-7500), has Latin Jazz on Monday nights and Cuban salsa Fridays.

Plan B ★ Live classic rock and televised sporting events rule this huge and popular watering hole, with three stages, five bars and a kitchen that cooks up pizza, wings and other tavern fare late into the night. You can see a live rock band, try to impress with karaoke, or watch the game of the moment on the big screen. The spot attracts young professionals and rock fans, especially on weekend nights. The cover bands are usually competent and entertaining, but sometimes fall flat. The crowd always rocks though. Open Tuesday to Sunday 5pm to 2am. Calle Loíza 509. 📞 **787/993-5468.** www.theplanbpr.com. Bus: A5.

The Bar Scene

Unless otherwise stated, there is no cover charge at the bars recommended below.

Amadeus Bistro Bar ★ Mostly Spanish and Puerto Rican classics are sang up with gusto in a nightly performance along with the excellent menu, whether a full meal or something light is what you are looking for. The 7pm show, which takes place Monday to Friday, is almost always as consistently good as the kitchen. It draws a crowd of local professionals unwinding after work in the evenings, and power brokers from the nearby financial district and federal courthouse who lunch here. Av. Chardón 350, Hato Rey. 📞 **787/641-7450.** www.amadeuspr.com. Bus: B21.

The Brick Haus ★ If sports TV, loud rock n roll, and craving quencher pub grub is you thing, you'll love this place, which is frequented by Coast Guard and cruise ship personnel, a young local crowd, and travelers. It's open late and is located in the SoFo restaurant district, near the cruise ships, Old San Juan taxi stand and bus stations and main parking lots. Calle O'Donnell 359, Old San Juan. 📞 **787/723-1947.** www.brickhaussportsbars.com. Bus: Old City Trolley.

Delavida Restobar ★ This great nightspot got a chic makeover and a much deeper menu after a recent name and ownership change that was all for the best. There's more entertainment too, with live guitar and reggae music nights, guest DJs, and parties for big concerts and sports events. The tapas at this "gastropub" are still great, but it's also a perfect dinner spot if you are hanging out at the nearby Placita, a string of open air bars surrounding the Santurce Marketplace. The interior bar and dining room are handsomely restored and the back deck is a dream. Callelturriaga 1361. 📞 **787/723-5577.** www.facebook.com/DLVRestobar. Tapas and entrees $7–$30. Tues-Thurs 11:30am–11pm, Fri 11:30am–midnight, Sat 6pm–midnight, Sun noon-8pm. Bus: 5.

Eight Noodle Bar Chinese ★ Come here for late night sticky rice and dumplings and the Chinese classics, as well as shrimp tempura and sushi. It's all fabulous and served at tables in one of the hotel's lobby areas, right outside the one of San Juan's most popular casinos. The people watching is great, with party animals from across town and the casino crowd drawn here by the intoxicating food served from 4pm to 4am daily. Av. Ashford 999, Condado Plaza Hotel, Condado. ℂ **787/723-8881.** www.condadoplaza.com.

El Batey ★★★ Puerto Rico's best dive is surrounded by architectural landmarks and historic treasures, with your bar stool a literal stone's throw from the Gothic San Juan Cathedral and the Caribbean's most gorgeous Spanish colonial hotel. Graffiti and business cards cover its cracked walls, along with aging drawings of local legends who once drank here, but the open air windows overlook the beautiful facades and crowds along the Old City's prettiest street. The jukebox sizzles with everything from Sinatra to the Clash, Charlie Parker to Bob Dylan, but the conversation at the bar will undoubtedly get your ear. The chattering eccentrics on any given night may include idealistic painters, jaded political operatives, investment bankers falling down to earth, and beautiful University of Puerto Rico students just starting or about to finish their night. The spot is on the short list of favorite bars of any *sanjuanero* worth hanging out with and also attracts an eclectic group of world travelers. El Batey has been cool since Allen Ginsberg read poetry here back in the 1950s. Calle Cristo 101. ℂ **787/725-1787.** No bus.

El Patio de Sam ★ The old Old San Juan is still alive at this nightspot, a bar and restaurant that has been drawing hipsters since Hunter S. Thompson hung out here in the early 1960s. The dining room is in a large interior courtyard surrounded by the work of fine local artists, including prints by masters from the famed Generacion de los 50s (Generation of the 1950s), greats like Rafael Tufino and Lorenzo Homar who worked and lived in or near San Juan for much of their lives. There's live music usually guitar players at the bar, but the chatter is always engaging, and while Puerto Rican food is served here, the burgers and bar food are a much better bet. Open daily noon to 1am. Calle San Sebastián 102. ℂ **787/723-1149.** Bus: Old Town Trolley.

El San Juan Hotel & Casino Lobby Bar ★★ A huge chandelier is suspended above the sunken oval-shaped bar at the center of this gorgeous hotel lobby, among the fines perches in the city to sip up some San Juan nightlife. Take a moment to take in the marble and burnished mahogany as you rub shoulders with locals and vacationers dressed for a night on the town. A swirl of activity surrounds the bar, as people dart in and out of a cluster of clubs and restaurants surrounding the space, and the adjacent casino, one of the finest in town. Open daily 6pm to 3am. In Old San Juan Hotel & Casino, Av. Isla Verde 6063, Isla Verde. ℂ **787/791-1000.** www.elsanjuanhotel.com. Bus: A5.

Ficus Mexican Bar & Grill ★ A popular spot for young professionals and conventioneers, this open air Tex-Mex bar sits beside the convention center and its huge fountain, an impressive setting. Sports events are broadcast on big televisions and there are DJ and other performances are select nights. Say yay to the jalapeño poppers if you like it spicy; fajitas and tacos hit the spot, too. Thursday through Saturday 5pm to 2am, Sunday 2pm to 10pm. At the Puerto Rico Convention Center, 100 Convention Blvd., Miramar. ℂ **787/641-7722.** www.ficusbarandgrill.com.

La Taberna Lupulo ★★ Craft beer aficionados hail this place as the real deal, with dozens of amazing beers within a collection that numbers 50 taps and 150 bottles, as well as a passionate and knowledgeable staff friendly enough to effortlessly guide you through it all. It's also probably the best bar in Old San Juan, a gorgeous space with high, beamed ceilings and wood double doors flung open to the street, and an open air Spanish colonial courtyard. The crowd is as captivating as the ambience, and there's great burgers and bar food, but there's rarely sufficient elbowroom at this popular spot to comfortably chow down. Come here for the brews, other top-notch libations, and the vibe. Monday to Friday 6pm to 2am, Saturday 1pmto 2am, Sunday noon to 2am. Calle San Sebastian 151, Old San Juan. ✆ **787/721-2772.** www.facebook.com/taberna lupulo. Bus: Old Town Trolley.

La Sombrilla Rosa ★ A nice neighborhood bar with daily happy hours, a relaxed atmosphere with friendly staff and patrons, and good music. Weekdays, until 3pm, it serves flavorful *comida criolla* at prices ranging from $5.50 to $8. At night, there are often beer and drink specials, music on the sound system, sports on TV, occasional live performances, and always interesting people from the neighborhood. Open from 9:30am to 3pm for lunch, then from 7pm to at least 3am nightly. Calle San Sebastián 154. ✆ **787/725-5656.** Bus: Old Town Trolley.

Mango's Ocean Park ★ There's fresh flavorful American, Caribbean, and Asian cuisine served here, but the fun and loud bar at this beach district spot is also a popular draw. This is one of the few places in Ocean Park to hang out, so there's a crowd from the beach community, making it a great spot to mingle with locals. There's live music and other special events, plus weekly drink and menu specials. Open Tuesday to Wednesday noon to 1am, Thursday to Sunday noon to 2am. Calle María Moczo 57 ✆ **787/998-8111.** www.mangosoceanpark.com. Bus: 5.

Mist ★ The Water Club hotel's rooftop bar overlooks the Isla Verde coastline, and the simple tropical decor of this sky high nest makes way for the breathtaking view, with seating dispersed in lounge areas around the pool. Renowned local and international DJs spin music and you can graze from a tapas menu served under the stars. It's

THE birth OF THE PIÑA COLADA

When actress Joan Crawford tasted the piña colada at what was then the Beach-combers Bar in the **Caribe Hilton** (p. 77), she claimed it was "better than slapping Bette Davis in the face."

One story has it that the famous drink is the creation of bartender Ramon "Monchito" Marrero, now long gone, who was hired by the Hilton in 1954. He spent 3 months mixing, tasting, and discarding hundreds of combinations until he felt he had the right blend. Thus, the frothy piña colada was born. It's been estimated that some 100 million of them have been sipped around the world since that fateful time.

Monchito never patented his formula and didn't mind sharing it with the world. Still served at the Hilton, here is his not-so-secret recipe:

2 ounces light rum
1 ounce coconut cream
1 ounce heavy cream
6 ounces fresh pineapple juice
½ cup crushed ice
Pineapple wedge and maraschino cherry for garnish

Pour rum, coconut cream, heavy cream, and pineapple juice in blender. Add ice. Blend for 15 seconds. Pour into a 12-ounce glass. Add garnishes.

The folks at Barrachina, meanwhile, insist a bartender employed with the restaurant, Ramón Portas Mingot, developed the drink that put the island on the world cocktail map.

a romantic spot. In the San Juan Water & Beach Club, Calle José M. Tartak 2. ✆ **787/728-3666.** www.waterbeachhotel.com. Bus: A5.

Pa'l Cielo ★   This spot might look like your typical *fonda* serving up local fare, but its bold color and decor are backed up by a cutting edge fusion of Far East, Peruvian, and Caribbean influences. Great cocktails and house music are always on tap, but live musical performances have given way to guest celebrity DJs and big sporting events. Hours have also been cut back to weekend evening (Fri–Sat 5pm–2am, Sun 4pm–1am). Calle Loíza 2056. ✆ **787/727-6798.** www.facebook.com/chinchorropalcielo. Bus: 5.

Rix on the Reef ★★★   This quintessential beach bar is located right at the sand, with a gorgeous view of the Atlantic and the San Juan coastline, and has cold beer at good prices, reggae and rock music jamming through the sound system, and some good conversation at the bar. This colorful, tin-roofed wooden shack is the perfect spot to soak in the gorgeous tropical coast regardless of the hour. There are often live bands on weekend nights, and during the day you can rent stand up paddle boards and kayaks from here and go swimming and snorkeling right out front. A great bar day and night, with a number of adjacent fish fritter and kebab stands. Just over the bridge from Isla Verde to Piñones (park in the first lot on your right after the bridge, and follow path under bridge to ocean will bring you right to the bar). The perfect city getaway 5 minutes away. Open Thursday through Sunday 11am to 11pm. Carr. 187, Lote B Torecilla, Piñones. No phone. www.rixonthereef.com. Bus: 45.

Solera ★★   Enjoy flavorful tapas and sangria, or just tall tropical drinks, from comfortable and secluded furnishings, surrounded by a tropical garden and towering palms and an infinity of stars beyond them. This restaurant unfolds between the cool marble lobby and the multi-leveled lush pool and terrace area of La Concha Hotel. Great bites like coconut calamari, pork dumplings and lobster wonton taquitos. The adjacent casino and lobby bar pulse all night long and then some. Everything is excellent except the bill. Av. Ashford 1077, San Juan. ✆ **787/721-7500.** www.laconcharesort.com. Bus: C53, B21.

Tantra ★   Sip a delicious flavored martini at the bar while taking in the gorgeous room, a mélange of exotic colors and furnishings, ethnic art and sculpture and Asian fabric, and the trans-Pacific rhythms. The menu and bar area are well suited for a few late munchies and drinks. There is belly-dancing Thursday to Saturday nights and always really fine world beat music being played. A recent menu revision has taken this restaurant back to its roots in Indian cuisine, with favorites like Chana masala, tandoori chicken, paneer curry, naan, and samosas. Purists quibble, but we really like the food. Puerto Rico anti-smoking restrictions have shut down the hookah lounge, but the water pipes are still there, part of the intricate collection of Far East artifacts that provide much of the charm of Tantra, which is housed in a beautifully restored Old San Juan mansion. The staff is friendly and charming. Calle Fortaleza 356. ✆ **787/977-8141.** Main courses $14–$29, Sampler Platters $60-75. Sun–Thurs 2pm–midnight; Fri–Sat 2pm–1am. Bus: Old City Trolley.

> ### Romantic Sunsets
>
> There is no better place on a Sunday night from 5:30 to 7pm to watch the sun set over Old San Juan than at Paseo de la Princesa. In this evocative colonial setting, you can hear local trios serenade you as the sun goes down. You might also opt to follow around the base of El Morro—it's a great place to share the moment with your lover.

Hot Nights in Gay San Juan

San Juan has probably the largest and most influential gay community in the Caribbean, and Puerto Rico is largely accepting and supportive of it. That fact was highlighted by the overwhelming support favorite son Ricky Martin received after announcing he was gay. Visitors have an ample range of gay- and lesbian-friendly establishments that provide opportunities to interact with locals and visitors alike. Some discos, known for their hot music and dancing, also draw straight couples as well. Many mainstream restaurants and nightclubs have core gay clientele, too, especially in the Condado, Santurce, and Old San Juan areas.

Circo Bar ★   The city's most popular gay club has great dance music, from 80s and 90s hits to cutting edge techno, with video and dance bars that stay pumping until after dawn, as well as a laid back lounge to get away from crowd and the noise. There are DJs, male dancers, and drag queen shows. It's one of the only spots in the city for guys to dance together, but like many gay clubs, it also attracts straight and lesbian couples as well as a good mix of locals and travelers and broad mix of age groups. Don't bother showing up until after midnight because nobody else does. Warm up for the evening with drinks at Splash or Tia Maria's, two popular gay bars in the area. A bit removed from the tourist district, so cab it here and back home. No cover. Open daily 9pm to 5am, even holidays. Calle Condado 650, Condado. ✆ **787/725-9676.** Bus: 21.

La Girafa Verde ★   San Juan's newest gay club is as delightful as its name (the green giraffe), and centrally located near the Museum of Puerto Rico Art along De Diego Avenue, which is experiencing a rebirth with new clubs, cafes, and nightspots. There are two levels of fun (a main disco dance floor and a rooftop party space), with DJs every night, drag shows, and other special events. It officially opens at 8pm, but the entertainment doesn't get underway in earnest until about 10pm, and the party really starts getting hot around midnight. Early birds will be rewarded with nightly happy hours until 10pm. It's a quick cab ride to the Condado area hotels from here.

La Rumba Party Cruise

La Rumba Party Cruise has been San Juan's party boat for more than a decade, a floating Latin dance club with two levels and neon lights that mixes salsa and merengue with other contemporary island rhythms and club beats. The sailing fiesta, with a cash bar and lounge space to chill, cruises into the early morning on weekend nights but the 2-hour sailings get underway as early as 7:30pm on Sundays, 9:30pm on Saturdays and 10:30pm Fridays. That's a good option for visitors that find San Juan the late start at city clubs too much but still want to dance. Departs from adjacent to Old San Juan's Pier 1 (Plaza Darsenas).

Schedules vary, but cruises tend to last 2 hours each, and depart every Friday at 10:30pm, 12:30am, and 2:30am; Saturday at 9:30pm, 11:30pm, 1am, and 2:30am; and every Sunday at 7:30, 9:30, and 11:30pm. The boat stays at dock for the first hour but then sails along the Old City Spanish colonial skyline, etched with fortress walls and cathedrals, and the breathtaking coast during its cruise. Cruises cost $14 per person (tax included). For reservations and more information, call ✆ **787/375-5211,** 263-2962, or 525-1288, or visit www.larumbacruises.com.

Open Thursday to Saturday 8pm to 6am (Sunday until 3am). Av. Ponce de León 1257, Santurce. ℭ **787/723-6643.** www.facebook.com/jirafaverde. No cover. Bus: 5, 1.

Tia Maria's Liquor Store ★   This neighborhood gay bar is a great spot for visitors to mix with the local community. A down to earth spot that is as open to women as it is to and men, it's a favorite spot for after work happy hour or a late night drink after dinner. Located in an up and coming neighborhood filled with new restaurants and bars, with one of the city's best gay clubs right across the street. This is a spot for fine conversation, but it's right near the action. Open Sunday to Thursday 11am to midnight; Friday to Saturday 10am to 2am. Av. José de Diego 326 (near the corner of Av. Ponce de León), Santurce. ℭ **787/724-4011.** Bus: 1, 5.

Casinos

Nearly all the large hotels in San Juan, Condado, and Isla Verde offer casinos, and there are other large casinos at some of the bigger resorts outside the metropolitan area. The atmosphere in the casinos is casual, but you still shouldn't show up in bathing suits or shorts. Most of the casinos open around noon and close between 2 and 4am. Guest patrons must be at least 18 years old to enter.

The 18,503-square-foot (1,719-sq.-m) **Ritz-Carlton Casino,** Avenue of Governors, Isla Verde (ℭ **787/253-1700**), combines the elegant decor of the 1940s with tropical fabrics and patterns. It features traditional games such as blackjack, roulette, baccarat, craps, and slot machines. In Old San Juan, try your luck at the **Sheraton Old San Juan Hotel & Casino,** Calle Brumbaugh 100 (ℭ **787/721-5100**), where five-card stud competes with some 240 slot machines and roulette tables. There's a stately gaming parlor just off the lobby at the **El San Juan Hotel & Casino** (one of the most grand), Av. Isla Verde 6063 (ℭ **787/791-1000**); and the **Condado Plaza Hotel & Casino,** Av. Ashford 999 (ℭ **787/721-1000**), remains one of the city's busiest and most exciting casinos. **La Concha's** (ℭ **787/721-7500**) Casino del Mar is right off the hotel's jamming lobby, and it's in keeping with its vanguard mix of high-tech and sleek design.

NEAR SAN JUAN

Within easy reach of San Juan's cosmopolitan bustle are superb attractions and natural wonders. With San Juan as your base, you can explore the island by day and return in time for a final dip before dinner and an evening on the town. Travelers looking for the ultimate Caribbean vacation experience, but who also want to be able to appreciate San Juan's cosmopolitan charms, will find some of Puerto Rico's best resorts within an hour's drive of San Juan. In Río Grande, there's the Río Mar Beach Resort and Spa, a Wyndham Grand Resort, and the Gran Mélia Golf Resort & Villas.

To the west, there is the **Dorado Beach, a Ritz Reserve Property,** a luxury resort that has risen on the site of a legendary property first fashioned by Laurance Rockefeller from the grounds of a breathtaking oceanfront coconut plantation, and home to some of the Caribbean's finest golf course.

Road improvements have cut the travel time from San Juan to other destinations and resorts covered in subsequent chapters. For example, you can get from San Juan to Fajardo and its mammoth **El Conquistador Resort & Golden Door Spa** in 45 minutes. Even the sprawling Palmas del Mar vacation community is within the 1-hour day trip test. While it's halfway down Puerto Rico's East Coast, it's accessible through two major highways. And Ponce is now a 90-minute drive, making it possible to visit the city in the morning, hit the beach in Guánica for 3 hours, and return to San Juan in the early evening.

Many of Puerto Rico's must-see sites lie much closer to San Juan, however. A bit more than an hour west of San Juan is the world's largest radar/radio-telescope, **Arecibo Observatory.** After touring this awesome facility, you can travel west to nearby **Río Camuy Cave Park,** for a good look at marvels below ground. Here you can plunge deep into the subterranean beauty of a spectacular cave system carved over eons by one of the world's largest underground rivers. The caves are part of a wider natural wonderland known as Karst Country, which you can also further explore, as well as an adjacent section of the central mountains laced with beautiful lakes.

Just 35 miles (56km) east of San Juan is **El Yunque National Forest,** the only tropical rainforest in the U.S. National Park System. Named by the Spanish for its anvil-shaped peak, El Yunque receives more than 100 billion gallons of rainfall annually. If you have time for only one side trip, this is the one to take. Waterfalls, wild orchids, giant ferns, towering tabonuco trees, and sierra palms make El Yunque a photographer's and hiker's paradise. Pick up a map and choose from dozens of trails graded by difficulty, including El Yunque's most challenging—the 6-mile (9.7km) El Toro Trail to the peak. The best one is probably the hike to La Mina Falls, a 45-minute walk through plush jungle, with interpretative nature signs explaining the

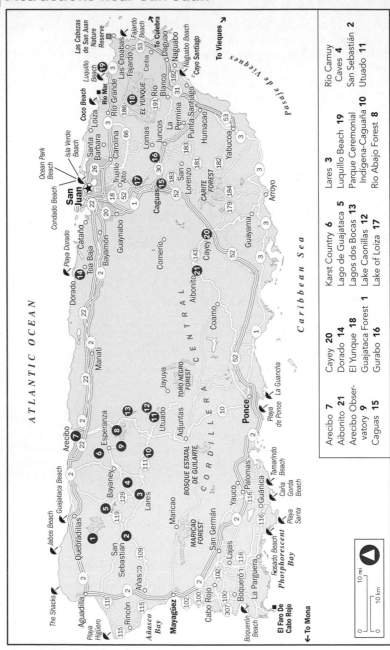

Arecibo **7**
Aibonito **21**
Arecibo Observatory **9**
Caguas **15**

Cayey **20**
Dorado **14**
El Yunque **18**
Guajataca Forest **1**
Gurabo **16**

Karst Country **6**
Lago de Guajataca **5**
Lagos dos Bocas **13**
Lake Caonillas **12**
Lake of Loíza **17**

Lares **3**
Luquillo Beach **19**
Parque Ceremonial
Indígena-Caguaña **10**
Río Abajo Forest **8**

Río Camuy
Caves **4**
San Sebastián **2**
Utuado **11**

foliage along the way. The trail ends at a beautiful spot where waterfalls crash into a wondrous natural pool in the mountain stream below. At El Yunque is El Portal Tropical Center, with 10,000 square feet (929 sq. m) of exhibit space, plazas, and patios. This facility greatly expands the recreational and educational programs available to visitors. La Coca Falls and an observation tower are just off Rte. 191.

Visitors can combine a morning trip to El Yunque with an afternoon of swimming and sunning on tranquil **Luquillo Beach.** Soft white sand, shaded by coconut palms and the blue sea, makes this Puerto Rico's best and best-known beach. Plan on having lunch, sampling local delicacies at a group of food kiosks right beside the public beach.

Fajardo, and its beautiful Caribbean coast, is about 15 minutes farther east. As noted previously, sailing and snorkeling trips off Fajardo are an easy day trip from San Juan through one of the luxury catamaran outfits that include transportation to and from San Juan area hotels (see chapter 6). Or you could visit undeveloped stretches of Fajardo beachfront, around **Las Cabezas de San Juan** nature reserve and **Seven Seas public beach,** on your own (see chapter 10).

Many visitors overlook trips to San Juan suburbs in the capital's backyard. Bayamón has a great science park and zoo, Guyanabo has an interesting sports museum, and Caguas a sprawling skate park and entertainment complex, and a botanical and cultural garden.

Central mountain towns, such as Cayey and Aibonito, are also accessible by day trip from the capital. Having a lunch of roast pork and other Puerto Rican delicacies and breathing in the clean mountain air is reason enough for a drive from the capital. A favorite spot is **Guavate,** a 45-minute drive south, where open-air barbecue restaurants are lined along a country road with a mountain stream of the Carite Forest as a backdrop.

EL YUNQUE ★★★

25 miles (40km) E of San Juan

The El Yunque rainforest, a 45-minute drive east of San Juan, is a major attraction in Puerto Rico. The El Yunque National Forest is the only tropical forest in the U.S. National Forest Service system. The 28,000-acre (11,331-hectare) preserve was given its status by President Theodore Roosevelt. Today the virgin forest remains much as it was in 1493, when Columbus first sighted Puerto Rico. Visit during the week, if possible, because weekends can be very crowded along popular trails and natural attractions.

Getting There

From San Juan, take Rte. 26 or the Baldorioty de Castro Expressway east to Carolina, where you will pick up Rte. 66 or the Roberto Sánchez Vilella Expressway, a toll road that runs east to Río Grande. You can now take the expressway to an exit at Palmer, the community at the base to El Yunque's main entrance, along Route 191. Take 191 for 3 miles (4.8km), going through the village of Palmer. As the road rises, you will have entered the Caribbean National Forest. You can stop in at the El Portal Tropical Forest Center to pick up information (see below).

Visitor Information

El Portal Tropical Forest Center, Rte. 191, Río Grande (✆ **787/888-1880**), is a 10,000 square-foot exhibition and information center, with three pavilions that offer exhibits and bilingual displays. The actor Jimmy Smits narrates a documentary called "Understanding the Forest." The center is open daily from 9am to 5pm; it charges an admission of $4 for adults and $2 for seniors and children under 12.

El Yunque is the most popular spot in Puerto Rico for hiking; for a description of our favorite trails, see "Hiking Trails," below. Hikers will find useful information at any of the park's visitor information centers or at the **El Yunque Catalina Field Office,** near the village of Palmer, beside the main highway at the forest's northern edge (© **787/888-1880**). The staff can provide material about hiking routes, and, with 10 days' notice, help you plan overnight tours in the forest. Camping permits are required but free. Several private guides give tours of El Yunque, but stick to the main trails and you can go on your own.

Exploring El Yunque

Encompassing four distinct forest types, El Yunque is home to 240 species of tropical trees, flowers, and wildlife. More than 20 kinds of orchids and 50 varieties of ferns share this diverse habitat with millions of tiny tree frogs, whose distinctive cry of *coquí* (pronounced "ko-*kee*") has given them their name. Tropical birds include the lively, greenish blue, red-fronted Puerto Rican parrot, once nearly extinct and now making a comeback. Other rare animals include the Puerto Rican boa, which grows to 7 feet (2.1m). (It is highly unlikely that you will encounter a boa. The few people who have are still shouting about it.)

El Yunque is the best of Puerto Rico's 20 forest preserves. The forest is situated high above sea level, with El Toro its highest peak. You can be fairly sure you'll be showered upon during your visit, as more than 100 billion gallons of rain fall here annually. However, the showers are brief, and there are many shelters. On a quickie tour, many visitors reserve only a half-day for El Yunque. But we think it's unique and deserves at least a daylong outing.

HIKING TRAILS   The best hiking trails in El Yunque have been carefully marked by the forest rangers. Our favorite, which takes 2 hours for the round-trip jaunt, is called **La Mina & Big Tree Trail,** and it is actually two trails combined. The La Mina Trail is paved and signposted. It begins at the picnic center adjacent to the visitor center and runs parallel to La Mina River. It is named for gold once discovered on the site. At La Mina Falls, there is a great waterfall and natural pool where you should take a dip. The mountain stream seems freezing at first, but becomes absolutely refreshing nearly instantaneously. Beyond the falls, the Big Tree Trail begins (also signposted). It winds a route through the towering trees of Tabonuco Forest until it approaches Rte. 191. Along the trail you might spot such native birds as the Puerto Rican woodpecker, the tanager, the screech owl, and the bullfinch.

Those with more time might opt for the **El Yunque Trail,** which takes 4 hours round-trip to traverse. This trail—signposted from El Caimitillo Picnic Grounds—takes you on a steep, winding path. Along the way you pass natural forests of sierra palm and *palo colorado* before descending into the dwarf forest of Mount Britton, which is often shrouded in clouds. Your major goal, at least for panoramic views, will be the lookout peaks of Roca Marcas, Yunque Rock, and Los Picachos. On a bright, clear day, you can see all the way to the eastern shores of the Atlantic.

DRIVING THROUGH EL YUNQUE   If you're not a hiker but you appreciate rainforests, you can still enjoy El Yunque. You can drive through the forest on Rte. 191, which is a tarmac road. This trail goes from the main highway of Rte. 3, penetrating deep into El Yunque. You can see ferns that grow some 120 feet (37m) tall, and, at any minute, you might expect a hungry dinosaur to peek between the fronds, looking for a snack. You're also treated to lookout towers offering panoramic views, waterfalls, picnic areas, and even a restaurant.

Where to Stay

Ceiba Country Inn ★★   By the time you read this review, a pool will have been added to Ceiba Country Inn's facilities, possibly the only amenity that was missing at this adorable little B&B. The rural setting couldn't be prettier (the views across the lush green mountains all the way down to the blue sea are stunning); the staff make each guest feel like a VIP; and the included breakfasts are scrumptious, particularly owner Michael's famous home-baked banana bread. Rooms are simply decorated but spotless and comfortable. Close to El Yunque and east coast beaches, there's plenty to do during the day; at night it's board games and books, and the symphony of coquís, the singing Puerto Rican tree frogs. The inn's bar has a television, and there's a small library and lounge and Spanish patio with free Wi-Fi connection.

Rd. no. 977, Km 1.2 Ceiba. (C) **888/560-2816** or 787/885-0471. www.ceibacountryinn.com. 9 units (all shower only). $95 double. Rate includes breakfast. Free parking. **Amenities:** Bar (guests only); free Wi-Fi in common areas.

El Yunque Rainforest Inn ★★★   An ideal honeymoon haven, this exquisite lodging has the perks of a vacation rental with the full-service of a B&B. That's because each guest gets their own elegantly decorated, two-bedroom villa, complete with patio, but still receives an absolutely delish breakfast each morning. The setting, right in the heart of the rainforest is idyllic: Guests can hike trails to a private waterfall and swimming hole, as well as to a secluded beach no-one else visits. There's neither air conditioning nor TV's, but you will miss neither, especially with the crystal clear Wi-Fi connection and the Inn's library of books and DVDs. Final perk: in-room spa treatments.

Rd. no. 186 Río Grande. (C) **800/672-4992** or 787/378-6190. www.rainforestinn.com. 3 villas. Doubles $160–$165, Villa for four $425. Free parking. **Amenities:** Bar; free Wi-Fi; included breakfast.

LUQUILLO BEACH ★★★

31 miles (50km) E of San Juan

Luquillo Beach is the island's best and most popular public stretch of sand. From here, you can easily explore El Yunque rainforest (see above). "Luquillo" is a Spanish adaptation of *Yukiyu*, the god believed by the Taínos to inhabit El Yunque.

Getting There

If you are driving from San Juan, take Rte. 26 or the Baldorioty de Castro Expressway east to Carolina, where you will pick up Rte. 66 or the Roberto Sánchez Vilella Expressway. The $1.50 toll road will take you farther along Rte. 3, putting you in Río Grand, and the exit for the Wyndham Rio Mar and Gran Melía Puerto Rico resorts.

A **hotel limousine** ((C) **787/888-6000**) from the San Juan airport costs $225 per carload to the Wyndham Río Mar Beach Resort and Spa. A taxi costs approximately $70. Hotel buses make trips to and from the San Juan airport, based on the arrival times of incoming flights; the cost is $78 per person round trip and $58 for child; $200 for a family of four, for transport to El Conquistador Waldorf Astoria in Fajardo.

Hitting the Beach

Luquillo Beach ★★, Puerto Rico's finest beach, is palm-dotted and crescent-shaped, opening onto a lagoon with calm waters and a wide, sandy bank. It's very crowded on weekends, but much better during the week. There are lockers, tent sites, showers, picnic tables, and food stands that sell a sampling of the island's *frituras* (fried fare), especially cod fritters and tacos. The beach is open from 8:30am to 5pm, Wednesday through Sunday, plus holidays.

You can also snorkel and scuba dive (see below) among the living reefs with lots of tropical fish. Offshore are coral formations and spectacular sea life—eels, octopuses, stingrays, tarpon, big puffer fish, turtles, nurse sharks, and squid, among other sea creatures.

Great Golf

The Río Grande–Fajardo area has become the golf hot spot in Puerto Rico, which itself is known as the Ireland of the Caribbean because of the number and quality of its greens.

While standard green fees are high, from $165 to $275, there are often special rates and guests usually are afforded discounts as well. Tom Kite and Bruce Besse designed two 18-hole courses for the **Trump International Golf Club Puerto Rico ★**, 100 Clubhouse Dr., Río Grande (© **787/657-2000**), adjacent to the well-recommended Gran Melía Puerto Rico (see below). You face a spectacular vista of fairways, lakes, and the Atlantic beyond, with two courses with their own character, which fan out from the Caribbean's largest clubhouse, which has been redone in the regal style of the Trump name. Luxury vacation villas, condominiums, and a beach club are being developed by Trump and his local partner Arturo Díaz.

The **St. Regis Bahia Beach Plantation Resort and Golf Club ★★**, Rte. 187, Km 4.2 (© **787/857-5800**), was given a renovation by Robert Trent Jones, Jr. The breathtaking 7,014-yard course, sprawling across some 480 acres (194 hectares) of lush beachfront, runs from the tip of Loiza River to the mouth of the Espíritu Santo River, overlooking a verdant green valley of El Yunque rainforest. The golf gets high marks, and the new luxury St. Regis resort only makes this spot all the better. Jones' father, Robert Trent Jones, Sr., designed the legendary Dorado Beach East golf course, and brother Rees Jones undertook the Palmas del Mar's Flamboyán course in 1999.

The **Wyndham's Río Mar Beach Resort ★** (see below) has two world-class courses that stretch out in the shadow of El Yunque rainforest along a dazzling stretch of coast. The entire 6,782 yards of Tom and George Fazio's Ocean Course has seaside panoramas and breezes, and fat iguanas scampering through the lush grounds. The other course, a 6,945-yard design by golf pro Greg Norman, follows the flow of the Mameyes River through mountain and coastal vistas. This is one of the better deals in the area with standard greens fees starting at $165 but offers as low as $99. **El Conquistador**'s golf offerings in nearby Fajardo are also well regarded, as are the greens in **Palmas del Mar** in Humacao (see chapter 9).

Watersports

Watersports kiosks at both the Wyndham Rio Mar Beach Resort and the Gran Melía Puerto Rico resorts have everything from Hobie Cats (about $100 per hour) to sea kayaks (about $15 per hour) for rent. Both properties have lots of beach and watersports activities on site, but your best bet for scuba diving and snorkeling is to head farther east to Fajardo for a scuba trip or a day-sailing and snorkeling adventure. **Dragonfly Adventures** (© **787/649-8040** at Gran Melía and **787/637-8600** at Rio Mar) arranges tours from either property to make it easy. There's a kayak eco-adventure, day-long snorkeling trip with picnic lunch and a sailing trip to Culebra on offer. **Sea Ventures Dive Centers** (© **800/739-3483** or 787/863-3483) at Fajardo's Puerto del Rey Marina is among the best bets for scuba diving. A two-tank discover dive package costs $150, while a two-tank dive for certified divers is $119 (both rates include gear).

Sports & Adventure

Hacienda Carabalí ★, Rd. no. 992, Km 4, Luquillo (© **787/889-5820** or 889-4954), is a 600-acre (243-hectare) ranch in the foothills of El Yunque rainforest that gives horseback riding, mountain biking, and all-terrain vehicle tours on trails running through the rainforest, along river banks, and the ocean coast. There's also a go-kart track and restaurant with entertainment. A 2-hour horseback-riding tour costs $65 per person, while a 1-hour tour is $37. The 1-hour ATV tour is $48 for the driver and $27 for the passenger, while a 2-hour tour is $91 for the driver and $54. The go-kart track costs $7.50 for a short ride ticket. If you have a group mountain tours can be arranged through an advanced reservation. Soar through the rainforest with the folks from **Yunque Zipline Adventure** ★ (© 787/242-3368), a fabulous, fun 3-hour tour costing $99 per person. The course is beautiful and includes the island's longest zip-line at 850 feet (259m). The tour also involves rappelling, so a moderate degree of physical fitness is required. There is a morning tour (leaving at 9am) and an afternoon tour (leaving at 2pm).

Where to Stay

Gran Melía Puerto Rico ★ Though it's not our favorite beach resort on the island, the Gran Melía does have some good points. It offers not one but two lovely pools, one of which is a handsome free-form pool with ocean views and a swim up bar (the other is usually quieter and is surrounded by cabanas). Rooms are quite spacious and have island flair (lots of mahogany woods, colorful walls, handsome furnishings) though the upkeep on the non-deluxe rooms could be improved (we'd suggest a renovation). The resort, which encompasses two nice golf courses and has expansive and lushly landscaped open areas (you have both the rainforest and the beach here), is eye-candy in spots. And those who like to keep busy will find more than enough to do here, from yoga classes, to watersports to merengue lessons to visits to the Melía's top-notch spa. All that being said there are some major disappointments, which range from the rocky, sub-standard beach to the uninspired food in the restaurants. And because the resort is relatively remote, guests without cars can feel a bit trapped here. Bottom line: If you get a great deal through a package (and the property works with many packagers), this could be a good choice, but don't go at the published rates.

Coco Beach Blvd. 1000, Río Grande. © **866/436-3542** or 787/809-1770. www.grand-melia-puerto-rico.com. 582 units. $195 double, $403–$466 suite, $317-391 Red Level. 18 percent resort fee. Parking $20 daily. **Amenities:** 6 restaurants; 3 bars; babysitting; fitness center; 2 golf courses; gym; kids' clubs; 2 outdoor pools; room service; spa; sauna; 3 lit tennis courts; smoke-free rooms; rooms for those w/limited mobility; Wi-Fi free in public areas, charge in rooms.

The Río Mar Beach Resort & Spa, a Wyndham Grand Resort ★★ Ideal for families and active vacationers, the Rio Mar sits on a splendid beach in the shadow of El Yunque rainforest. Its championship golf courses curve dramatically through the jungle and along the coast, and it offers ample water sports opportunities, and classic

Caribbean experiences, like horseback riding on the beach. We also have to give special kudos to the staff who run the excellent kid's club. The lush grounds, dotted with lakes, add to the appeal, as do the muted, earth and wood toned rooms. There are about a dozen restaurants and bars on premises and a casino, so you have a variety of dining options and some nightlife, but the place remains pretty low-key and you will likely want to eat some meals in nearby Luquillo and Fajardo.

Río Mar Blvd. 6000, Río Grande. © **877/636-0636** or 787/888-6000. www.wyndhamriomar.com. 600 units. High season $209–$269 double, $609–$969 suite. Off-season $169–$249 double, suite $569–$969. Resort fee 15 percent. Self-parking free. **Amenities:** 8 restaurants; 4 bars; casino; children's programs; deep-sea fishing; health club & spa; horseback riding nearby; outdoor pool; room service; sailing; 13 tennis courts; smoke-free rooms; rooms for those w/limited mobility, Wi-Fi free.

St Regis Bahía Beach ★★★ So near San Juan but so far away, this luxe resort hides in a rarified world of nearly 500 acres, encompassing a seaside forest, coconut grove, and an undeveloped coastline of white beach and swaths of wild sea grapes. Palm and almond trees tower overhead, while gorgeous lakes, canals, and gardens are spread across the lush grounds, and there are paths to walk, jog or ride bicycles along and take it all in. The narrow lagoon pool curves in a blue strip across the sun splashed esplanade with private cabanas and plush lounge chairs. The largest lake has a boathouse with standup paddle boards, kayaks and small sail boats, and the unspoiled 2-mile long beach is gorgeous. The resort is centered around the Plantation House, a place of Old World elegance, housing the reception center, the resort's signature restaurant **Fern** and the **St. Regis Bar,** with a stunning Arnaldo Roche Rabell painting hanging over the bar. **Reméde Spa** is topnotch with private massage villas that are perfect for couples. The St. Regis also offers world-class golf and tennis facilities and a complete children's program, including the nightly "S'mores and Stories," at an outdoor fireplace. Those who book here are treated to oversized rooms with plush comforts and edgy tech, all housed in low-key, hacienda-like villas spread across the property. Bahia Beach also has an advantage over resorts in Rio Grande and Fajardo in being closer to the international airport in San Juan.

Rte. 187, Km 4.2, Rio Grande. © **787/809-8000.** www.bahiabeachpuertorico.com. 139 units. High season $614–$764 double, $1,065–$1,010 suite; off-season $458–$548 double, $810–$1,510 suite. $60 resort fee. Valet parking only $22 guests, $28 nonguests daily. **Amenities:** 3 restaurants; 3 bars; butler service; fitness center; golf course; kids' clubs; outdoor pool; room service; sauna; spa; 2 lit tennis courts, smoke-free rooms; rooms for those w/limited mobility; Wi-Fi free.

Where to Eat

Barbakoa ★★ PUERTO RICAN On the road to El Yunque rainforest, this al fresco restaurant, set beside a river, serves creative takes on Puerto Rican food. What more could you want? Buckets of Medalla beer are served at the table and service is friendly. My favorites on the menu are the tamarind ribs, turkey in cilantro cream sauce, and the mahi mahi surf and turf are all good. If you don't want a full meal, it's a great stop after a hike in the rain forest for some cold beer and snacks, like mini yucca *mofonguitos* and grilled sausages. There's live jazz on Saturdays from late afternoon.

Rte.191, Km 1, Mameyes, Palmer, Rio Grande. © **787/888-8797.** www.barbakoarestaurant.com. Main courses $12–$35. Thurs–Mon noon–8pm.

Brass Cactus ★ AMERICAN This gringo pub is a favorite with locals and tourists, serving American standards (golden onion rings, tasty ribs, burgers, and steaks) in a friendly setting with sports on the television, American rock on the sound system, and memorabilia on the walls. Those not dining hang at the convivial bar, which offers a good beer selection, mango martinis, and wicked mojitos.

In the Condominio Complejo Turistico, Rte. 3, Marginal. © **787/889-5735.** www.thebrasscactus. com. Sandwiches, burgers $6.95–$9.95; entrees $12–$29. Sun–Thurs 11am–midnight; Fri–Sat 11am–2am.

Fern ★★ INTERNATIONAL   Star NYC-based chef Jean Georges Vongerichten is the master behind Bahia Beach's signature restaurant, so the menu is a "greatest hits" of the celebrity chef's food at his other restaurants. Not that we're complaining: The food is stellar, whether you try such appetizers as steamed shrimp salad in champagne dressing or the house version of a Mexican pizza. Standouts among the entrees include salmon with lime potatoes and cucumbers, and the charred coconut spicy chicken with pineapple. The "simply cooked" steak and fish (served with blistered peppers and spicy sauce) are also excellent. Guests can ante up for a six-course tasting menu ($86) or order a la carte. The restaurant is as swellegant as the food. In the morning, classy renditions of basic breakfast standards at eye-popping prices are on offer.

At the St. Regis Bahia Beach Resort, Rte. 187, Km 4.2, Rio Grande. © **787/809-8000.** www.bahia beachpuertorico.com. Reservations required. Main courses: breakfast $16–$28, dinner $32–$49. 7am–11:30am daily; Mon–Thurs 6–9pm; Fri–Sat 6–10pm; Sun brunch noon–4pm.

Molasses ★ AMERICAN/PUERTO RICAN   If you want to lunch at Bahia Beach, your best bet is this handsome room at the golf clubhouse, with panoramic views of the coast on the north, and Puerto Rico's misty green mountains to the south. There's fine Puerto Rican *mofongo* and fried red snapper, but also tasty sandwiches and salads. The restaurant is also open at night, a favorite spot of Bahia Beach residents, and is known for its steaks and seafood. It's not cheap but portions are surprisingly hearty, so don't be shy about sharing. Golfers can get a super early continental breakfast before tee-off.

At the St. Regis Bahia Beach Resort, Rte. 187, Km 4.2, Rio Grande. © **787/809-8049.** www.bahia beachpuertorico.com. Reservations recommended. Main courses $24–$42. Lunch Wed–Sun 11:30am–5pm; Dinner Sun–Thurs 6–9pm; Fri–Sat 6–10pm.

Palio ★ ITALIAN   This formal, traditional Northern Italian restaurant executes the classics with verve, but be prepared to pay for the experience. There's everything you'd expect: osso buco, seafood pasta fra diavolo, veal marsala, and fresh fish in a lemon caper sauce and all should be delish.

In the Wyndham Rio Mar Beach Resort and Golf Club, 6000 Rio Mar Blvd, Rio Grande. © **787/888-6000.** Reservations recommended. Main courses $262–$59. Daily 6am–11pm.

King's Seafood ★ SEAFOOD/PUERTO RICAN   Straight up seafood and Puerto Rican fare crafted from fresh ingredients with tried-and-true recipes: That's the appeal of King's (so ignore the decor, which looks like a primitive take SpongeBob's Krusty Krabb). The service friendly and it's a good place to try Caribbean lobster, fired red snapper, or *mofongo* stuffed with seafood.

Calle Fernandez García 1. © **787/889-4300.** www.kingsseafoodprcom. Main courses $12–$29; Tues–Thurs 11am–9pm, Fri 11am–10pm, Sat–Sun noon–10pm.

DORADO ★★

18 miles (29km) W of San Juan

Dorado—the name itself evokes a kind of magic—is a small town with some big resorts, a world of storied luxury hotels and villas unfolding along Puerto Rico's north shore west of San Juan. The **Dorado Beach, A Ritz Reserve Property** is the latest incarnation of Dorado's most famed resort that first opened its doors in 1958, a for decades operated as the luxury the Hyatt Cerromar and Hyatt Dorado Beach resorts. The site was originally purchased in 1905 by Dr. Alfred T. Livingston, a Jamestown, New York, physician, who developed it as a 1,000-acre (405-hectare) grapefruit-and-coconut plantation. Dr. Livingston's daughter, Clara, widely known in aviation circles as a friend of Amelia Earhart, owned and operated the plantation after her father's death. It was she who built the airstrip here. In 1955, Clara Livingston sold her father's 1,700-acre (688-hectare) Hacienda Sardinera to the Rockefeller family. Her former house, now called Su Casa, served as a golf clubhouse in the '70s and restaurant from 1982 to 2006, and remains on the property. The legendary resort hosted former presidents John F. Kennedy, Dwight Eisenhower, Gerald Ford, and George H. W. Bush, as well as athletic greats Joe Namath, Mickey Mantle, and Joe DiMaggio, and actresses Joan Crawford and Ava Gardner. Today, Dorado Beach remains at the forefront of luxury tourism. It was only the second site to win the Ritz Reserve brand, which signals distinctive boutique resorts with a deep connection to their particular corner of paradise.

Getting There

If you're driving from San Juan, take Expwy. 22 west. Take Exit 22-A to get on Rte. 165 north to Dorado. Alternately, you can take the meandering coastal route along Hwy. 2 west to Rte. 693 north to Dorado (trip time: 40 min.) You'll pass a couple interesting beaches and coastal lookouts, as well as fine spots to eat.

The Beaches

If you take this latter route, you'll want to detour down Rte. 870 in the Palo Seco area of Toa Alta. This narrow road runs through the middle of a narrow peninsula famous for the restaurants serving seafood and Puerto Rican cuisine running along it. At the end of the road is the **Parque Nacional Isla de Cabra** (Rte. 870, Toa Baja; ℂ **787/384-0542;** Wed–Sun and holidays 8:30am–5pm; parking $3), a fascinating spit of land at the mouth of San Juan Bay that has an incredible view of the Old City. The water here is not great for swimming, but there are play areas and green picnic areas with great views. There are also small restaurants and bars, everywhere a great coastal view and the whole area with great breezes. The area was a former leper colony built by the Spanish and then was a shooting range and training area for many decades for the police. There is a small fort within the park called **El Cañuelo** that was built to protect the entrance of the Bayamón River and back up the much larger El Morro across the bay, by providing crossfire to invading ships. This is a favorite picnic area for Sundays and a good spot to ride a bike or fly a kite.

There are also a few fine bathing beaches along this route before getting to Dorado. The best is probably **Cerro Gordo** public beach (Rte. 690, Vega Alta; ℂ **787/883-2730**), along with the **Manuel "Nolo" Morales** public beach along Dorado's "Costa del Oro," or "Gold Coast" (ℂ **787/796-2830**). Both charge $3 per car parking fee and keep the same hours as other public beaches and parks, Wednesday through Sunday and holidays, 8:30am to 5pm.

Where to Stay

Dorado's lodging options were severely limited when the two Hyatt properties shut their doors, but staying at the former Hyatt resort is still possible, and the Embassy Suites property is a unique, all-suites resort with great facilities.

WORLD-CLASS golf AT THE FORMER HYATT DORADO

The Hyatt Dorado Beach and Hyatt Cerromar hotels closed in 2006, but their world-class golf courses have remained open. The Ritz-Carlton Reserve Dorado Beach Hotel took over the site of the old Hyatt Dorado Beach in 2012. The resort's existing amenities are among the finest within any Caribbean resort destination: 3 miles of beaches; 72 holes of Robert Trent Jones, Sr. golf courses; 11 miles of Rockefeller nature trails; the Watermill water park; the Dorado Beach Fitness, Wellness, and Tennis Center; and Zafra (in the golf clubhouse) and West Beach dining venues. Additional amenities are at the **Dorado Beach, A Ritz Reserve**— Wind and Waves Center; Ambassadors of the Environment program from Jean Michel Cousteau; Spa Botanico; West Beach Club, and dining venues by Jose Andrés. If golf is your game, Dorado Beach Resort has you covered.

The courses, designed by Robert Trent Jones, Sr., match the finest anywhere. The two original courses, known as East and West, were carved out of a jungle and offer tight fairways bordered by trees and forests, with many ocean holes. The East Course was recently renovated by the designer's son, Robert Trent Jones, Jr. The Sugarcane and Pineapple (Top 50 in Caribbean) courses feature wide fairways with well-bunkered greens and an assortment of water traps and tricky wind factors. Each is a par-72 course. The longest course is 7,047 yards. On the Pineapple and Sugarcane courses, regular greens fees are $150, and on the East course it is $250. After 3pm, prices plunge to $60 and $100, respectively. The East course requires a caddy which costs $80. The West course remains closed for renovations with no reopening in sight. Courses are open daily from 7am until dusk. Golf carts are included.

Dorado Beach, A Ritz Reserve ★★★ The opening of this resort, along with the St. Regis Bahia Beach in Río Grande, set a new standard for hotels in Puerto Rico. Both properties have been developed to be in tune with the surrounding environment, so they're more low-key than the nightclub and casino centered atmosphere at most other Puerto Rican resorts. Dorado Beach is a truly remarkable piece of paradise, with a primordial beauty to the landscape, despite the fact that the resort's just 35 minutes from San Juan. The 1,400 acres of grounds include impressive nature trails, and all the rooms, including the restaurants, are close to the fabulous 3-mile coastline. Consider a room with a private plunge pool and outdoor shower, if you want to get especially close to nature. The rooms have all the comfort, style, and amenities you would expect from this chain, with awesome ocean views to boot. At the center of the complex is 1920s restored plantation house Su Casa, which is available for rent as a five-bedroom villa. The 5-acre Spa Botánico is a lush enclave within the resort. For info on the top-notch golf opportunities here, see the box above. *Tip:* While the west rooms are more conveniently located, the east side has less traffic.

Dorado Beach Drive 100, Dorado. (🎧 **787/626-1100.** www.ritzcarlton.com/en/Properties/Dorado Beach/Default.htm. 128 units. High season: $1,099–$1,799 guest rooms, $2,499–$3,698 suites. Low season: $699–$1,099 guest rooms, $2,099–$3,298 suites. $95 per room daily resort fee. Valet parking $19. **Amenities:** 2 restaurants; cafe; bar; health center; golf; pool; spa; room service; tennis court; rooms for those w/limited mobility, Wi-Fi free included in resort fee.

Embassy Suites Dorado del Mar Beach & Golf Resort ★ Highlights of this better-than-usual chain property include a swell beachfront location with a wonderful golf course designed by Puerto Rico legend Chi Chi Rodriguez; and a fabulous pool area which spills over to the coast. While some areas of the property are showing signs of wear and tear of late, the suites and condos are airy and tropical and most have ocean views, and the resort casino is usually rocking. All this will be particularly tempting if you get a good deal (and there are *many* on the Internet; surf around). The property is a favorite of families and golfers.

Dorado del Mar Blvd. 210, Dorado. ℭ **787/796-6125.** www.embassysuitesdorado.com. 174 units. $139–$199 2-room suites. An 18 percent resort fee is applicable to the quoted rates and includes high-speed Internet access, all local calls, 800 calls, incoming/outgoing faxes, B&W copies, and 1 hour of tennis. Valet parking $19; self-parking $12. **Amenities:** 3 restaurants; bar & grill; fitness center; golf; pool; massage; room service; tennis court; rooms for those w/limited mobility; Wi-Fi free.

Where to Eat

Grappa ★★ ITALIAN   A charming setting and Italian food (that tips its hat occasionally to the flavors of Puerto Rico): Those are the potent lures at Grappa. Chef Omar uses locally grown herbs and vegetables for super-fresh food; highlights of the menu include the superb risottos and classic pastas like the Bolognese and carbonara.

Calle Mendez Vigo 247, Dorado. ℭ **787/796-2674.** www.facebook.com/grapppr. Main courses $12–$30. Wed–Thurs and Sun 5–10pm; Fri–Sat 5–11pm.

El Vigia ★ SEAFOOD/PUERTO RICAN   The Isla de Cabras scene is an exceedingly local affair, and weekend afternoons are extremely lively, with many establishments hosting live bands or karaoke. Many seafood joints line the main road into Isla de Cabras, but this is our choice for its super-fresh fish and its way with such Puerto Rican classics as *mofongo* and *asopao* (we also appreciate the tasty sangria, though be careful, as it does have a kick). You can enjoy a meal on an oceanfront terrace, but you'll get wet if the seas or the skies are stormy (when that's the case head inside to the big, comfortable bar and dining room). El Vigla is a favorite spot for weddings and other celebrations.

Calle Manuel Enrique 130, entrance Isla de Cabras. ℭ **787/725-2736.** www.elvigiarestaurant.com. Main courses $12–$39. Daily 11am–9pm.

Mi Casa ★★★ SPANISH   Celebrity Chef José Andrés's handsome restaurant at the Ritz Reserve Dorado Beach is a worthy splurge. Known for avant-garde Spanish cuisine, here the chef incorporates Puerto Rican and Caribbean flavors into many of the dishes here (though his signature dishes do make an appearance on the menu). The delicious spiny Caribbean lobster *asopao* and the Guavate style roast pork with caramelized mango sauce are spectacular riffs on local specialties, and the big Delmonico rib-eye is to die for. Make sure to try the tomato bread at some point during your meal, which should end with the delightful passionfruit flan. For breakfast, the best dish is the *huevos a la cubana*, which the menu says is "Like José's mom made:" two fried eggs, sautéed rice, crispy bacon, caramelized banana, and tomato sauce. *Tip:* Ask for a terrace table overlooking the ocean; the ambiance in the main dining room doesn't come close to matching the outdoor space.

At the Dorado Beach, A Ritz Reserve, Dorado Beach Drive 100, Dorado. ℭ **787/278-7217.** www. ritzcarlton.com/en/Properties/DoradoBeach/Default.htm. Main courses $17–$70. Tues–Sat 7–10am breakfast; 6–10:30pm dinner.

Made in Puerto Rico ★ PUERTO RICAN   This homage to Puerto Rico's traditional fare offers specialties plates from across the island. We're talking *mofongo* with fried pork rind Bayamón style, Ponce's excellent variation on the ubiquitous sautéed dorado filet, and chicken fricassee recipe from the mountain town of Aibonito. It's a festive place: Servers wear folkloric dress and local music is played. The weekend buffet brunch is quite popular.

Made in Puerto Rico, Rte. 693, Km 8.5, Dorado. ℂ **787/626-6666.** Main courses $12–$20. Tues–Thurs 11am–10pm; Fri–Sat 11am–11pm; Sun 11am–9pm.

Zafra Restaurant ★ CARIBBEAN/CONTINENTAL   This beautiful restaurant at the Dorado Beach Golf Clubhouse has great views and serves early breakfasts, lunch, and dinner. For starters, its salads, soups, or seafood, either calamari or ceviche, while main course include boneless marinated duck, serrano ham crusted halibut and lamb chops with green beans and mashed potatoes. There's also salads and sandwiches on the lunch menu.

Dorado Beach Resort & Club, 500 Plantation Dr., Ste. 1, Dorado. ℂ **787/626-1054** or 626-1031. Main courses $28–$52. Fri–Sun 7am–11am; daily 11am–5:30pm; Wed–Sun 6–10pm; bar service daily 11am–close.

ARECIBO & CAMUY ★

68 to 77 miles (109–124km) W of San Juan

Getting There

Arecibo Observatory lies a 1¼-hour drive west of San Juan, outside the town of Arecibo. From San Juan, head west along four-lane Rte. 22 until you reach the town of Arecibo. At Arecibo, head south on Rte. 10; the 20-mile (32km) drive south on this four-lane highway is almost as interesting as the observatory itself. From Rte. 10, take Exit 75-B and follow the signposts along a roller-coaster journey on narrow two-lane roads. First you will go right on Rte. 652 and take a left on Rte. 651. Proceed straight through the intersection of Rte. 651 and Rte. 635, and then turn left at the cemetery onto Rte. 625, which will lead you to the entrance of the observatory.

On the same day you visit the Arecibo Observatory, you can also visit the Río Camuy Cave Park. The caves also lie south of the town of Arecibo. Follow Rte. 129 southwest from Arecibo to the entrance of the caves, which are at Km 18.9 along the route, north of the town of Lares. Like the observatory, the caves lie approximately 1½ hours west of San Juan.

Exploring the Area

To get to the **Observatorio de Arecibo** ★★, take Expwy. 22 heading east. Take Rte. 129 south toward Utuado for about 2.5 miles. Go left at the Texaco Station on to Rte. 635 for about 1.25 miles, then take a right at the crossroads to stay on Rte. 635, and follow the road for another 3.5 miles, when you'll have to turn right to remain on the road. Continue for another half mile, then take a left at the cemetery to Rte. 625. Follow road for about 3 miles until the entrance of the Observatory.

Dubbed "an ear to heaven," **Observatorio de Arecibo** ★★ (ℂ 787/878-2612; www.naic.edu) contains the world's largest and most sensitive radar/radio-telescope. The telescope features a 20-acre (8-hectare) dish, or radio mirror, set in an ancient sinkhole. It's 1,000 feet (305m) in diameter and 167 feet (51m) deep, and it allows scientists to monitor natural radio emissions from distant galaxies, pulsars, and quasars, and to examine the ionosphere, the planets, and the moon using powerful radar signals. Used by scientists as part of the Search for Extraterrestrial Intelligence (SETI), this is the same site featured in the movie "Contact" with Jodie Foster. This research effort speculates that advanced civilizations elsewhere in the universe might also communicate via radio waves. The 10-year, $100-million search for life in space was launched on October 12, 1992, the 500-year anniversary of Columbus's arrival on the shores of the New World.

Unusually lush vegetation flourishes under the giant dish, including ferns, wild orchids, and begonias. Assorted creatures, such as mongooses, lizards, and dragonflies, have also taken refuge there. Suspended in an outlandish fashion above the dish is a 600-ton (544,311kg) platform that resembles a space station. This is not a site where you'll be launched into a "Star Wars" journey through the universe. You are allowed to walk around the platform, taking in views of this gigantic dish. At the Angel Ramos Foundation Visitor Center, you are treated to interactive exhibitions on the various planetary systems and introduced to the mystery of meteors and educated about intriguing weather phenomena.

Visiting hours are Wednesday through Sunday and most holidays from 9am to 4pm, but during the Christmas season (Dec 15–Jan 15) and summer (June–July) visitors are welcome every day. The observatory is closed to visitors on eight holidays: Good Friday, Easter, Mother's Day, Father's Day, Thanksgiving, Christmas, New Year's, and Three Kings Day (Jan 6). There's a souvenir shop on the grounds. Plan to spend about 1½ hours at the observatory (Rte. 625 final, Arecibo; ✆ **787/878-2612;** www.naic.edu; admission $10 adults, $6 seniors and children).

Parque de las Cavernas del Río Camuy (Río Camuy Caves) ★★ (✆ **787/898-3100**) contains the third-largest underground river in the world. It runs through a network of caves, canyons, and sinkholes that have been cut through the island's limestone base over the course of millions of years. Known to the pre-Columbian Taíno peoples, the caves came to the attention of speleologists in the 1950s; they were led to the site by local boys already familiar with some of the entrances to the system. The caves were opened to the public in 1986. You need at least 2 hours for an adequate experience, but the more adventurous can take full-day tours exploring a part of the mysterious world with private tour operators.

Today, visitors explore most sites via the park trolley: a 200-foot-deep (61m) sinkhole, a chasm containing a tropical forest, complete with birds and butterflies and a huge water fall, and the entrance of Cueva Clara, the park's premiere cave, a 45-minute odyssey through a fascinating underworld of stalactites and sculpted cavern walls. Tres Pueblos Sinkhole is 65 feet (20m) wide and 400 feet (122m) deep; it's named for its location at the border of the towns of Camuy, Hatillo, and Lares (north at Km 2 on Rte. 129, from Rte. 111; ✆ **787/898-3100;** Wed–Sun and holidays 8am–5pm; admission $15 adults, $10 children 4–12; parking $3–$4, depending on vehicle).

Back down in Arecibo, a fun and interesting stop, especially if you are traveling with children, is the **Arecibo Lighthouse & Historic Park** ★ (Hwy. 655, El Muelle, Barrio Islote, Arecibo; ✆ **787/880-7540;** www.arecibolighthouse.com). Housed in a lighthouse built by the Spanish in 1898, this "cultural theme park" takes visitors on a history tour of Puerto Rico. But it's a very tactile tour, where you can actually walk through many of the exhibits. It really interests kids; it definitely found the kid in us! The slave quarters were riveting, the mammoth pirate ship was thrilling, and then there was the pirate's cave, with its alligators and sharks. Bring sun block, hats, and comfortable shoes and clothes. Tickets are $12 adults, and $10 children and seniors. The park is open 9am to 6pm weekdays and holidays, and 10am to 7pm on weekends. Parking costs $3.

Another unique place to visit while in Arecibo is the island's last remaining drive-in movie theater. About an hour's drive from San Juan, the **Auto Cine Santana** ★ (Exit 63 toward Rte. 2, left on Rte. 662; *©* **787/881-7869**) is a family-owned business that has been keeping alive the tradition of watching movies under the stars since 1957. For just $3 per person, it is a great alternative for a night out. Snack bar selections go beyond your typical popcorn, candy, and soda to include *alcapurrias* and fried turnovers, and a variety of fresh fruit juices. The featured films aren't usually blockbusters and are often dubbed in Spanish with English subtitles. The movie schedule is Monday, Wednesday, Thursday, at 8pm; Friday, Saturday and Sunday at 7:30 and 9:30pm.

Where to Eat

If you want to eat before heading back to the city, Arecibo is a good place, with several fine restaurants.

Salitre Mesón Costero ★★ SEAFOOD/PUERTO RICAN The terrace here, which overlooks the ocean, is one of the great sunset watching spots in the area. For your food, you'll have a wide range of choices, all of them solid, from grilled fresh fish and seafood, to steaks and tapas. We also recommend the stuffed *mofongo*, again available in a wide variety: fresh fish, shrimp, conch and lobster tail. The house take on Puerto Rican paella, *mamposteado de mariscos*, is also first rate. In short: authentic, home-style cooking with great flavor. When it gets crowded, expect long waits for food.

Rte. 681, Km 3.8, Barrio Islote, Arecibo. *©* **787/816-2020.** http://salitre.com. Main courses $14–$52. Sun–Thurs 11am–9pm, Fri–Sat 11am–11pm.

Picolo Restaurant ★ SEAFOOD/PUERTO RICAN Another no frills option in the waterfront area that's not quite as good as Salitre, but does fine by the fresh fish of the day and the typical Puerto Rican food, including rich seafood and chicken stews and *mofongo* stuffed with shrimp in sweet tomato sauce. The atmosphere and service can be lacking, but the fresh simple fare is tasty and at a good price.

Rte. 681, Km 0.3, Barrio El Pasaje, Arecibo. *©* **787/878-2303.** Main courses $7–$45. Mon–Sat 7am–9pm, Sun 10am–6pm.

KARST COUNTRY ★★

One of the most interesting areas of Puerto Rico is the large **Karst Country,** south of Arecibo. This otherworldly group of rock formations was created by the process of water sinking into limestone. As time goes by, larger and larger basins are eroded, forming sinkholes. *Mogotes* (karstic hillocks) are peaks of earth where the land didn't sink into the erosion pits. The Karst Country lies along the island's north coast, directly northeast of Mayagüez in the foothills between Quebradillas and Manatí. The region is filled with an extensive network of caves. The world's largest radio/radar telescope dish, the 20-acre (8-hectare) Arecibo Observatory (see above), rests within one of these sinkholes.

South of the Karst Country looms the massive central mountain region and Utuado at the heart of the massive Cordillera Central mountain range, which rides the island's back from east to west like an elevated spine.

The Karst Country area was deforested in the late 1940s; alluvial valleys and sinkholes were then used for pastures, shifting cultivation, and coffee plantations. In this region, most of the coffee sites were abandoned in the 1960s, and today most of these sites are covered with secondary forests. The recovery of these forests has been very rapid because of a close seed source—trees left on the steep slopes—and the presence of large populations of dispersers, mainly bats.

Getting There

The only way to explore the Karst Country, which is easy to reach from San Juan, is by car. Leave San Juan on the four-lane highway, Rte. 22, until you come to the town of Arecibo, a 1½-hour drive, depending on traffic. Once at Arecibo, take Rte. 10 south, in the direction of Utuado.

If you'd like a specific goal for exploring in the Karst Country, visit the Arecibo Observatory and the Río Camuy Caves, previewed above. However, you can also spend a day driving at random, exploring lakes and forests at your leisure. If you decide to go this route, make the commercial town of **Arecibo** your base. Although not of tourist interest itself, it is the capital of the Karst Country and the starting point from which you can drive south along many interesting and winding roads.

From Arecibo, you can take Rte. 10 south in the direction of Utuado (see "Central Mountains," below), which serves as the southern border to Karst Country. Along the way, you'll pass **Lagos dos Bocas ★**, one of the most beautiful lakes of the Karst Country, and a reservoir adjacent to the Río Abajo Forest. Lagos dos Bocas, which lies 12 miles (19km) south of Arecibo,

Get a Good Map
Arm yourself with the most detailed map you can find at one of the bookstores in San Juan. The free maps dispensed by the tourist office are not sufficiently detailed and do not show the tiny secondary roads you'll need to traverse for a motor tour of the Karst Country.

is in the mountains of Cordillera Central. Along with a nearby lake, **Lake Caonillas,** it is the main source of water for the North Coast Superaqueduct, which provides water for north coast towns stretching from Arecibo to San Juan.

Take time out at Lagos dos Bocas to ride one of the free government-operated **launches ★** that traverse the lake. Established as a taxi service for residents of the area, these launches can be used by sightseers as well. The launches leave from a dock along Rte. 123 on the west side of the lake, with departures scheduled every hour unless the weather is bad. It's a 30-minute ride across the lake to the other main dock. On weekends, modest wooden restaurants around the lake open to serve visitors, and the launch makes stops at them. Most have tasty snacks, fried turnovers, and the like, and cold drinks. **Rancho Marina ★** (Lago Dos Bocas, Utuado; ℂ **787/894-8034** or 787/630-2880) is your best bet for lunch (entrees $11–$17) with basic Puerto Rican dishes, from red snapper filet in a *salsa criolla* to breaded rabbit in a tropical sauce. It's open 10am to 6pm weekends and holidays. There's even mango tembleque for dessert! The launch will take you back to your car, and then you can continue your journey.

Head back down to Arecibo, and then take the expressway back to San Juan.

CENTRAL MOUNTAINS ★

Utuado marks the southern border of Karst Country. It's a municipality at the dead center of the island that sprawls across the spine of the Cordillera Central mountain range. To experience the island's Central Mountains, continue driving up into the mountains above Lago dos Bocas. After about 20 minutes you'll reach the **Casa Grande Mountain Retreat** (see below), which is open from 5 to 8:30pm every day. This establishment, a guesthouse and restaurant, serves upscale *comida criolla*—inspired dishes with vegetarian options. Café Casa Grande spills from a dining room and patio to a veranda overlooking a lush mountain valley. But you may want to spend the night if you dine too late. The property is reached via curving country roads, which can be tough to handle at night.

This is Utuado, a good base in the Cordillera Central massif overlooking the heartland of Karst. Utuado is a stronghold of *jíbaro* (country folk) culture, reflecting the mountain life of the island as few other settlements do.

Just south of here you'll hook up again with Rte. 111 going west to Lares. You'll almost immediately come to **Parque Ceremonial Indígena Caguana (Indian Ceremonial Park at Caguana)** ★, Rte. 111, Km 12.4. The site is signposted and need not take up more than 30 minutes of your time. Built by the Taíno Indians some 1,000 years ago, the site was used for both recreation and worship, and mountains near the Tanamá River encircle it. You can still see the outlines of the ancient *bateyes* (ball courts), which are bordered by carved stone monoliths decorated with petroglyphs (see "Life After Death: Taíno Burial & Ceremonial Sites," below). The best-known petroglyph is the much-photographed *Mujer de Caguaña,* a figure squatting in the position of an earth-mother fertility symbol. There is a small and very minor museum of Indian artifacts and skeletons on site. The site is open daily from 8:30am to 4:20pm. Admission is $2 for adults, $1 children (ages 6–13), $1 for seniors 60 and older. For more information, call ✆ **787/894-7325.**

From Lares, take Rte. 129 south to return to Arecibo, a good spot for a meal before taking the expressway back to San Juan (p. 137).

Where to Stay

Casa Grande Mountain Retreat ★★   This ain't Idaho, but it's your own private Utuado, where rooms are rustic cabins scattered along a mountainside with verandas and porches with stunning vistas of the more than 100-acre former hacienda, which is wild with tropical plants and trees. The resort has an onsite botanical garden, a yoga studio with daily classes, a fresh water swimming pools, and hammocks everywhere. An onsite cafe serves breakfast and dinner daily and late lunch on weekends; it's a mix of local and international food. At the Retreat, you'll find no telephones, air-conditioning, or television—this place is about decompression in a tropical mountain paradise. A ceiling fan does the trick in the simple rooms. A nature trail from the property offers a great hike through a tropical forest; horseback tours can also be arranged for guests.

P.O. Box 1499, Utuado. ✆ **888/343-2272,** 787/894-3900, or 894-3939. www.hotelcasagrande.com. 20 units. $126 double. 9 percent resort fee. From Arecibo, take Rte. 10 south to Utuado, then head east on Rte. 111 to Rte. 140; head north on Rte. 140 to Rte. 612 for ¼ mile (.4km). **Amenities:** Restaurant; bar; pool; free Wi-Fi.

The Southern Route to the Mountains

A much easier way to the Central Mountains from San Juan is to head south along the Luis A. Ferré Expressway, Hwy. 52, to **Cayey** and even farther up to **Aibonito.** You can take an afternoon drive and have dinner as the sun sets in the mountains; from some vantage points, the view goes all the way to the coast.

In fact, this path is well worn by *sanjuaneros* heading south with mountain air and food on their minds. Their first stop is usually **Guavate ★★**. Take the exit for Rte.

life after death: TAÍNO BURIAL & CEREMONIAL SITES

The **Taíno Indians** who lived in Puerto Rico before Europeans came here were ruled by *caciques*, or chiefs, who controlled their own villages and several others nearby. The Taínos believed in life after death, which led them to take extreme care in burying their dead. Personal belongings of the deceased were placed in the tomb with the newly dead, and bodies were carefully arranged in a squatting position. Near Ponce, visitors can see the oldest known Indian burial ground in the Antilles, the **Tibes Indian Ceremonial Center** (p. 153).

Even at the time of the arrival of Columbus and the conquistadores who followed, the Taínos were threatened by the warlike and cannibalistic Carib Indians coming up from the south. But though they feared the Caribs, they learned to fear the conquistadores even more. Within 50 years of the Spanish colonization, the Taíno culture had virtually disappeared, the Indians annihilated through either massacres or European diseases.

But Taíno blood and remnants of their culture live on. The Indians married with Spaniards and Africans, and their physical characteristics—straight hair, copper-colored skin, and prominent cheekbones—can still be seen in some Puerto Ricans today. Many Taíno words became part of the Spanish language that's spoken on the island even today. Hammocks, the weaving of baskets, and the use of gourds as eating receptacles are part of the heritage left by these ill-fated tribes.

Still standing near Utuado, a small mountain town, **Parque Ceremonial Indígena-Caguana (Indian Ceremonial Park at Caguana),** Rte. 111, Km 12.3 (© **787/894-7325**), was built by the Taínos for recreation and worship some 800 years ago. Stone monoliths, some etched with petroglyphs, rim several of the 10 *bateyes* (playing fields) used for a ceremonial game that some historians believe was a forerunner to soccer. The monoliths and petroglyphs, as well as the *dujos* (ceremonial chairs), are excellent examples of the Taínos' skill in carving wood and stone.

Archaeologists have dated this site to approximately 2 centuries before Europe's discovery of the New World. It is believed that the Taíno chief Guarionex gathered his subjects on this site to celebrate rituals and practice sports. Set on a 13-acre (5.3-hectare) field surrounded by trees, some 14 vertical monoliths with colorful petroglyphs are arranged around a central sacrificial stone monument. The ball complex also includes a museum, which is open daily from 8:30am to 4:20pm; admission is $2 for adults, $1 children (ages 6–13), $1 for seniors 60 and older.

There is also a gallery called Herencia Indígena, where you can purchase Taíno relics at reasonable prices, including the sought-after *Cemís* (Taíno idols) and figures of the famous little frog, the *coquí.* The Taínos are long gone, and much that was here is gone, too. This site is of special interest to those with academic pursuits, but of only passing interest to the lay visitor.

184, which winds through rolling farmland and farther up along a mountain stream flowing through the lush **Carite State Forest.** In addition to the eateries, the sector is famous for local arts and crafts and plants and flowers that are sold from stands along the roadway. While the area began gaining fame years ago for a cluster of restaurants outside the natural reserve's main entrance, the string of *lechoneras* has now extended along the entire route from the expressway. Indeed, **Los Amigos,** at the Expressway exit, is for those who want to dive in to the genuine experience, and make a quick escape. (On Sun afternoons, especially around Christmas season, traffic is often clogged along the country road.) It has among the best food we've had here, and though utterly drab (like a restaurant converted from a gas station), it draws a lively crowd from early on. A merengue band was getting the party started right when we last stopped in around 2pm on a Sunday, when patrons were already burning up the dance floor in between the cafeteria and the food stands in front of the open-air fire pits where whole pigs, chickens, and turkeys were being slowly roasted Puerto Rican style.

The best restaurants, however, have a certain rustic charm in addition to their utilitarian nature, and take advantage of the beautiful surroundings. **El Rancho Original** (Rte. 184, Km 27.5; ✆ **787/747-7296**) has outdoor bohios with tables beside a mountain stream cutting through the lush forest adjacent to the restaurant. Other noteworthy spots are **La Casa del Guanime** (Rte. 184, Km 27.8; ✆ **787/744-3921**), **Los Pinos** (Rte. 184, Km 27.7; ✆ **787/286-1917**), and **El Mojito** (Rte. 184, Km 32.9; ✆ **787/738-8888**). Most have live music on weekend afternoons, so whether your taste runs from salsa to merengue to local *jíbaro* country music or to something more contemporary, it may play a big role in your choice. Also, the road carves through a lush forest and a string of restaurants along its right-hand side is set in front of the mountain stream; several have dining rooms overlooking the stream and in the quieter ones its gurgling is the only music you'll hear.

The atmosphere is important, but the main thing about Guavate is the food: roast pork and chicken, fried rice and pigeon peas, boiled root vegetables soaked in oil and spices, and blood sausage. This is traditional Puerto Rican mountain food, but the level of the cooking keeps getting better every time we return. The roast turkey is a healthy alternative to the pig; it has recently been showing up *escabeche* style, drenched in olive oil, garlic and onions, roasted peppers, and herbs—absolutely delicious.

Just south of Guavate is the northern entrance to the **Carite Forest Reserve ★**, a 6,000-acre (2,428-hectare) reserve that spreads from Cayey to neighboring Caguas and San Lorenzo, and all the way down to Patillas and Guayama on the south coast. The forest ranges from heights of 820 to 2,963 feet (250–903m) above sea level, and, from several peaks, you can see clear down to the south coast and Ponce. The forest, with frequent rain and high humidity, is covered with Caribbean pine and has several ponds and streams. Some of the forest's most interesting sites are near the northern entrance by Guavate. On one peak is Nuestra Madre, a Catholic spiritual meditation center that permits visitors to stroll the grounds. The large natural pond, called Charco Azul, is a favorite spot for a swim. It is surrounded by a picnic area and campground. There are over 50 species of birds in the forest.

Guavate is just the start of Cayey, which is a beautiful town through which to take a drive. Another mountain road with fine restaurants is found in its **Jájome** sector. This is probably a better choice for visitors wanting a more refined dining experience than the raucous pig roasts in Guavate. To get here, take the main exit to Cayey, turn left on Rte. 1, and then exit on to Rte. 15 on the left and follow signs to the community. From some spots, you can see all the way down to the south coast. Two of these are the **El Mesón de Melquiades ★** (Rte. 741, Cayey; ✆ **787/738-4083;** www.elmesonde melquiades.com) and **The Sand and the Sea Restaurant and Country Lodging ★** (Rte. 715, Km 5.2, Cayey; ✆ **787/738-9086**). The veteran Mesón de Melquiades makes the most of its envious cliffside location with fine Puerto Rican and continental classics. A drive through the Puerto Rican mountainside is the perfect prelude for a country lunch, which makes this spot a choice locale for many. It's open Thursday through Saturday 11am to 8pm and Sunday 11am to 7pm. The Sand and the Sea, open Friday through Sunday noon to 9pm, serves upscale Puerto Rican dishes (the mussels, squid, and shrimp a la criolla, for example) with an incredible view. A preferred spot for a weekend lunch for *sanjuaneros* looking for a respite from the city since 1974, when Broadway songwriter Hal Hester and Broadway artist Julio Guasp brought their Old San Juan restaurant o Cayey.

Farther up into the mountains is **Aibonito,** a pretty town overlooking the island's gorgeous green valleys. From Rte. 15, take the exit to Rte. 14 and follow signs for Aibonito. A good time to visit is during the annual Fiesta de las Flores at the end of June and beginning of July, a festival stretching across 2 weeks where local growers present some of the most beautiful flowers grown on the island, including the most regal of orchids. However this mountain town, with its cool, crisp air, is worth a trip any time of the year.

PONCE & THE SOUTHWEST

For those who want to see a less urban side of Puerto Rico, head south to Ponce and the breathtaking southwest, for great beaches, dramatic coastal bluffs, and green flatlands unfolding across the horizon to the foothills of the Cordillera Central mountain range. Ponce is a great center for sightseeing, and you can take a side trip to the bonsai-like Guánica State Forest; visit Puerto Rico's second-oldest city and site of the oldest church in the New World, San Germán; and venture north through the island's central mountains to the lush Toro Negro rainforest. Both nature reserves are hits with hikers and bird-watchers.

Founded in 1692, Ponce is Puerto Rico's second-largest city, and its historic sectors have been beautifully restored. San Germán and Ponce are home to some of the finest historic architecture in the hemisphere.

Ponce also attracts beach lovers. No, there's no real beach in town, but to the west are the coastal towns of Guánica, La Parguera, and Boquerón, where the best swimming beaches on the island are located. The southwest is where Puerto Ricans go for holidays by the sea. This is the real Puerto Rico, which hasn't been taken over by high-rise resorts and posh restaurants.

Puerto Rico's west coast mimics the U.S. southwest; cacti pop up from sunbaked rock crevices, while cattle graze in the rolling Lajas Valley in the shadow of the majestic central mountains. All across the region, a beautiful western sunset settles over its charming beach towns, with their white sands and aquamarine waters, a quintessential corner of the Caribbean.

PONCE ★★

75 miles (121km) SW of San Juan

"The Pearl of the South," Ponce was named after Loíza Ponce de León, great-grandson of Juan Ponce de León. Founded in 1692, Ponce is today Puerto Rico's principal shipping port on the Caribbean. The city is well kept and attractive, with an air of being stuck in the past, a provincial colonial town. On weekday afternoons, men dressed in starched *guayaberas* and hats play dominoes while uniformed school girls run along the large walkways.

Its historic district underwent a $440-million restoration for 1992's 500th anniversary celebration of Christopher Columbus's voyage to the New World, and improvements have continued so that it is just as stunning more than 20 years later. The streets are lit with gas lamps and lined with neoclassical buildings, just as they were a century ago. Horse-drawn carriages roll by, and strollers walk along sidewalks edged with pink marble.

Contemporary Ponce has been restored to its former splendor, the city as it was at the turn of the 20th century, when it rivaled San Juan as a wealthy business and cultural center.

Sitting in its sun-bleached plaza on a sunny afternoon, visitors may be struck by Ponce's heat, and the nearly always-dry weather conditions. Threats of rain are most often held at bay by the Central Mountains; you can see the potential humidity condensing into a violet haze over them in the distance as the late afternoon finally begins to fade.

Essentials

If you're driving, take Las Américas Expressway south to the Luis A. Ferré Expressway (Hwy. 52), then continue south. Once you pass over the central mountain range and reach the south coast, you will continue west until Ponce. The trip takes about 1½ hours.

GETTING AROUND   The town's inner core is small enough that everything can be visited on foot. Taxis provide the second-best alternative.

VISITOR INFORMATION   Maps and information can be found at the **tourist office,** Paseo del Sur Plaza, Ste. 3 (📞 **787/841-8044**). It's open daily from 8am to noon, and 1 to 4pm.

Where to Stay
EXPENSIVE

Hilton Ponce Golf & Casino ★★   The only full-scale resort in the Ponce region, the Hilton spreads across 74 acres of Caribbean coast with a very good golf course, a pool that kids love (it has a slide), gardens, a playground, and other family-friendly amenities. As you might expect, it also houses boutiques, a health and fitness facility and other services. The casino, bars and nightclubs are the most expansive (and fun) along the south coast, the restaurants are among the city's best. So why two rather than three stars? While the tropical guest rooms are comfortable and clean, with nice amenities and extras like terraces or balconies, some could use a refresh (many of the bathrooms, in particular, are quite dated). But considering the resort's other allures, most take these flaws in stride.

Av. Caribe 1150, Ponce. 📞 **800/445-8667** or 787/259-7676. www.hilton.com. 153 units. $169–$199 double; $469–$529 suite. 14 percent resort fee. Valet parking $18; self-parking $10. **Amenities:** 2 restaurants; 2 bars; bikes; casino; children's program; fitness center; 27-hole golf course; playground; pool; room service; 2 tennis courts; rooms for those w/limited mobility, Wi-Fi with resort fee.

MODERATE

Holiday Inn Ponce ★   There are trade-offs with most every hotel and with this one they are the drives you'll have to take, both to the nearby beach (which is not within walking distance) and to the historic core of Ponce, as the hotel is located outside of town. Still, this Holiday Inn has its allures from a lovely, big pool to swell views to comfortable, well-maintained, spacious rooms. We also think the staff here is among the most gracious and helpful in the area. And heck, the price is often right (surf the Internet) and though you'll be spending a lot of time in your car, at least the parking here is free. There's also an often hopping casino on-site.

3315 Ponce By Pass, Exit 221, El Tuque, Ponce. 📞 **800/465-4329** or 787/844-1200. www.holiday inn.com. 116 units. $115 double. Free parking. **Amenities:** Restaurant; bar with live music; gym; pool; room service; whirlpool; Free Wi-Fi.

Ponce

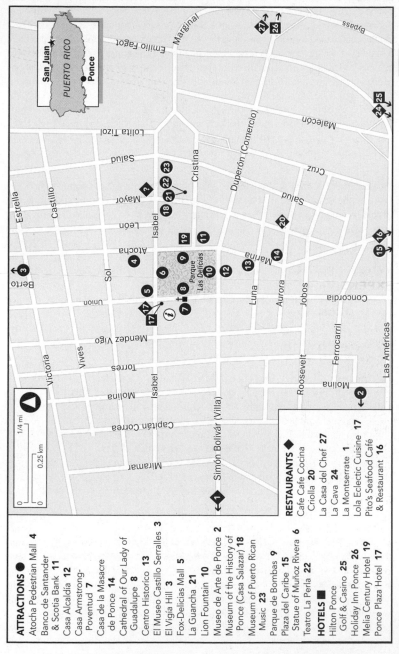

7

PONCE & THE SOUTHWEST | Ponce

ATTRACTIONS ●

Atocha Pedestrian Mall **4**
Banco de Santander
  & Scotia Bank **11**
Casa Alcaldía **12**
Casa Armstrong-
  Poventud **7**
Casa de la Masacre
  de Ponce **14**
Cathedral of Our Lady of
  Guadalupe **8**
Centro Histórico **13**
El Museo Castillo Serrallés **3**
El Vigía Hill **3**
Fox-Delicias Mall **5**
La Guancha **21**
Lion Fountain **10**
Museo de Arte de Ponce **2**
Museum of the History of
  Ponce (Casa Salazar) **18**
Museum of Puerto Rican
  Music **23**
Parque de Bombas **9**
Plaza del Caribe **15**
Statue of Muñoz Rivera **6**
Teatro La Perla **22**

HOTELS ■

Hilton Ponce
  Golf & Casino **25**
Holiday Inn Ponce **26**
Melia Century Hotel **19**
Ponce Plaza Hotel **17**

RESTAURANTS ◆

Cafe Cafe Cocina
  Criolla **20**
La Casa del Chef **27**
La Cava **24**
La Montserrate **1**
Lola Eclectic Cuisine **17**
Pito's Seafood Café
  & Restaurant **16**

147

Meliá Century Hotel ★★   This architectural jewel had its luster restored in a 2013 renovation that completely remade the property's guest rooms and spruced up public areas. First opened in 1895, the hotel remains Puerto Rico's oldest in continuous operation and lures guests with its marble floors, beautiful woodwork, high decorative ceilings and distinctive doors and balconies. The recent renovations boosted the comfort-level of the guest rooms (with new and antique furnishings), and now each has a balcony overlooking Ponce's historic core. The Meliá also added new restaurants: Mocha Coffee Bar and Bistro and Panorama Sky Lounge on the hotel roof (that rooftop also holds the wonderfully chic pool area; it's a real scene). *Historic note:* The hotel was expanded by three architectural masters in three different eras: Alfredo Wiechers Pierett in 1915, Francisco Porrata-Dori in 1940, and Enrique Soler in 1960.

Calle Cristina 2, Ponce. ℂ 787/813-5050. www.meliacenturyhotel.com. 73 units (shower only). $104–$150 double. Parking $6. **Amenities:** Restaurant; bar; outdoor pool; room service; rooms for those w/limited mobility, free Wi-Fi.

Ponce Plaza Hotel & Casino ★   Another convenient option, right on Plaza Las Delicias, the beautiful heart of historic Ponce. If you want Old World charm, however, make sure you reserve one of seven colonial suites located in the historic part of the hotel; most of the guest rooms are in a modern addition and lack character. And don't book here if you want to swim laps in the pool: It's just barely big enough to get wet in! The hotel is blessed with great views of the plaza and city, but gets noisy on weekend nights. The restaurant, Lola Eclectic Cuisine, is among the best in Ponce.

Calle Riena, Ponce. ℂ **787/813-5050.** www.ramadaponce.com. 70 units. $99–$129 double; $109–$140 suite. Parking $11 per day. East of Ponce on Hwy. 52, opposite the Interamerican University. **Amenities:** Restaurant; bar; fitness center; outdoor pool; room service; rooms for those w/limited mobility; Wi-Fi in public areas.

Where to Eat
EXPENSIVE

La Casa del Chef ★ PUERTO RICAN/SPANISH   Consistently good, traditional Puerto Rican, Spanish and French cuisine is served in the attractive, semi-formal dining room here by warm and efficient waitstaff. Old boleros and Spanish loves songs play in the background, and there are wonderful local paintings adorning the walls…so most don't really mind the lackluster view of a mall parking lot. The menu takes in old-style classics like an excellent Steak Diane and chicken cordon bleu, as well as beef tenderloin stuffed with lobster and shrimp, a host of fish dishes, and *super fino* renditions of local hits like seafood *asopao* and *mofongo* and fried red snapper, served atop a fresh avocado, tomato, onion, and herb *mojo*. A flan is a perfect ending to the meal.

23 Callejón Fagot, Cuartro Calles, adjacent to Plaza del Sur Mall. ℂ **787/843-1298.** Dinner $16–$40. Sun–Thurs noon–9pm, Fri–Sat noon–11pm.

La Cava ★ INTERNATIONAL   This is one of the finer dining spots in Ponce, a not particularly trendy place but one that serves a good meal. It specializes in steaks, seafood and fine wines and delivers on all three. Our picks include the glorious chateaubriand, pistachio-crusted lamb chops, and the very fine risottos (including some based on island staples like pigeon pea and pumpkin). There appetizers are a bit more unusual, including a scallop mango ceviche and langoustines over root vegetable mash.

In the Ponce Hilton, Av. Caribe 1150. ℂ **787/813-5050.** Reservations recommended. Main courses $18–$36. Mon–Sat 6:30–10:30pm.

Lola Eclectic Cuisine ★★ CARIBBEAN A recent menu update here has made a very good restaurant even better. Today Lola serves classic steaks, a beef Wellington and a filet mignon demi-glaze with mushroom risotto; and mouthwatering fish plates, such as codfish filet in a sweet Spanish pepper sauce, and a sea bass in creamy tarragon sauce. Starter are just as good: really fresh salads and a long, adventurous appetizer menu with items like sweet plantain balls stuffed with chorizo and guava, risotto croquettes with an Alfredo sauce, and mahi mahi tempura in spicy aioli. The dining room and bar are bright and Bohemian, and are adjacent to a beautiful Spanish colonial courtyard. Live music happy hours on Friday and Saturday nights, are quite popular with the city's young professionals.

Esq. Calle Reina y Calle Union, Ponce. © **787/813-5050.** Reservations recommended. Main courses $17–$32. Mon–Fri 11:30am–11pm, Sat–Sun noon–11:30pm.

MODERATE

Casa de Las Tias ★ PUERTO RICAN Thursday night is burger and deli night (surprisingly good burgers and sandwiches). The rest of the time, Casa de Las Tias serves up tasty Puerto Rican cuisine like pork tenderloin, cod fish, and *ropa vieja,* slow cooked stewed beef, as well as ratatouille and fricassee. The beautifully restored residence housing the restaurant is adorned with the work of local master artist Antonio Martorell. For dessert, try the almond flan or the "drunken cake," a homemade rum, red wine, and brandy soaked sponge cake with fruit syrup. Run by media personalities, the place always has a hip crowd.

Calle Isabel 46. © **787/840-7185.** $9–$29. Thurs–Fri 6–10pm, Sat noon–10pm, Sun noon–6pm.

La Montserrate Sea Port Restaurant ★★ SEAFOOD One step above a seafood shack, this no frills restaurant has nothing fancy about it, but is tremendously appealing nonetheless, thanks to its killer sea view and a fresh fish menu. Sit on the back dining terrace that overlooks the water and make sure to try some of the *empanadas* (fried seafood turnovers), the house specialty; they're filled with either lobster, conch, shrimp, or the fresh catch of the day. The octopus and conch ceviche entrees are outstanding, as is the snapper in creole sauce, fresh lobster and other fish, all of which come with island sides (tostones, rice and beans, and so forth) and salad. Sometimes less is more.

Sector Las Cucharas, Rte. 2, Km 218.2. © **787/841-2740.** Main courses $10–30. Daily 11am–10pm.

Pito's Seafood Café & Restaurant ★★ SEAFOOD Delicious fresh fish and other seafood are served in basic island style from this restaurant hanging out over the Caribbean Sea. The views stretch for miles and you can almost see your fish being pulled from the waters below. There's sweet Caribbean lobster, a mixed grilled seafood platter, Puerto Rican classics like *mofongo* stuffed with seafood, and fried whole red snapper. Primo desserts include a variety of flans and a rich chocolate mousse. The guava and cheese is also a good choice if there's still wine left. Pito's is the best of a string of restaurants that line Highway 2 where it hugs the Caribbean Sea in a gentle curve in sector Las Cucharas.

Hwy. 2, Las Cucharas, Ponce. © **787/841-4977.** Reservations recommended. Main courses $12–$39. Sun–Thurs 11am–10pm, Fri–Sat 11am–midnight.

INEXPENSIVE

Café Café Cocina Criolla Espresso Bar ★★ PUERTO RICAN/CAFE A top bargain in downtown Ponce, both the coffee and *cocina criolla* menu are hyper local, and super flavorful (there's also great sangria). It's something fried to start, probably white cheese and yucca balls, but then the possibilities broaden substantially: mahi mahi in roasted garlic and cilantro, an island take on chicken saltimbocca, grilled churrasco, and a bunch of the usual suspects, including stuffed *mofongo*. You're not allowed to leave before trying coffee flan!

Calle Aurora 2638, corner Calle Mayor. ℭ **787/840-7185.** Lunch $9–$16. Mon–Fri 11am–3pm.

Seeing the Sights
ATTRACTIONS IN PONCE

Most visitors go to Ponce to see the city's historic section, with its whimsical architectural style. While the city dates back to 1692, its unique "Ponce Creole" architecture, mixing Spanish colonial, Caribbean, and contemporary influences, was mostly created from the 1850s through the 1930s. The style is marked by the use of wide balconies, distinctive masonry work, and neoclassical touches: plaster garlands, punched tin ceilings, and stained glass panels. Other architectural motifs such as metal grill work are present within specific geographic areas of the city. The style takes European concepts but adapts them to the city's tropical climate by using pastel colors on building facades and adding high ceilings that help keep houses cool.

The city's unique look was created during the years of Ponce's heyday, in the 19th century, when it trumped San Juan as the island's most important city and rose as a regional trading power. Cut off from San Juan by geographic barriers, Ponce's trade brought foreign influences and style, not only in architecture but in music and cuisine.

In addition to the attractions listed below, the **weekday marketplace,** open Monday through Friday from 8am to 5pm, at calles Atocha and Castillo, is colorful. Perhaps you'll want to simply sit in the plaza, watching the Ponceños at one of their favorite pastimes—strolling about town.

Museo de la Masacre de Ponce ★★★ MUSEUM   On Palm Sunday, March 21, 1937, a pro-independence, Nationalist Party march, intended to protest the incarceration of party founder and independence icon Pedro Albizu Campos, turned deadly. Police set up a blockade to stop the march after a permit was cancelled and ended up killing 19 people, including women and children, and wounding 100 more. The confrontation took place right outside the former shoemaker's shop that houses this facility. The museum provides a concise, unvarnished history of the modern independence movement and the official repression brought against it. The event is still marked with a ceremony each year.

At calles Aurora and Marina, Plaza Las Delicias. ℭ **787/844-9722.** Free admission. Tues–Sun 8:30am–4:20pm.

Cathedral of Our Lady of Guadalupe ★★ CATHEDRAL   In 1660, a rustic chapel was built on this spot on the western edge of the Plaza Las Delicias, and since then fires and earthquakes have razed the church repeatedly. In 1919, a team of priests collected funds from local parishioners to construct the Doric- and Gothic-inspired building that stands here today. Designed by architects Francisco Porrata Doría and Francisco Trublard in 1931, and featuring an impressive pipe organ installed in 1934, it remains the spiritual center of the city. The cathedral, named after a famous holy shrine in Mexico, is the best-known church in southern Puerto Rico.

At calles Concordia and Union. ℭ **787/842-0134.** Free admission. Mon–Fri 6am–12:30pm; Sat–Sun 6am–noon and 3–8pm.

El Museo Castillo Serrallés ★★★ HISTORIC HOME   An Andalusian-style castle, built during the 1930s by the rum-making Serrallés family, this Spanish Revival beaut is built atop the most iconic hilltop along the southern coast. Architect Pedro Adolfo de Castro, also an accomplished poet and musician, designed the residence as well as some 100 other mansions. Walk through the huge courtyards and enjoy the panoramic views from its breathtaking parlors and terraces. The dining room is entirely carved from wood, with a ceiling cut into exquisite figures and scenes; the handmade furniture follows this same intricate, artisanal design. There's a compelling documentary on the family and its rum tradition in the theater as well as photographic and historical exhibits, plus a small cafe and souvenir shop. Outdoors are terraced gardens and a butterfly area, a beautiful spot to take in views of the city. You'll need to take a taxi here if you don't have a car.

El Vigía 17. ⓒ **787/259-1774.** http://castilloserralles.org. Admission $13 adults, $6.50 seniors, $5.50 children & students (includes all attractions on El Vigía Hill). Thurs–Sun 9:30am–5:30pm.

El Vigía Hill ★★   The city's tallest geologic feature, El Vigía Hill (300 ft./91m), dominates Ponce's northern skyline. Its base and steep slopes are covered with a maze of 19th- and early-20th-century development. In addition to the castle (see above), the soaring Cruz del Vigía (Virgin's Cross) is also located here. Built in 1984 of reinforced concrete to replace a 19th-century wooden cross in poor repair, this modern 100-foot (30m) structure bears lateral arms measuring 70 feet (21m) long and an observation tower (accessible by elevator), from which you can see all of the natural beauty surrounding Ponce. The cross commemorates Vigía Hill's colonial role as a deterrent to contraband smuggling. In 1801, on orders from Spain, a garrison was established atop the hill to detect any ships that might try to unload their cargo tax-free along Puerto Rico's southern coastline.

At the north end of Ponce. See admission information above.

Museo de Arte de Ponce ★★★ ART MUSEUM   This superb art museum, the largest in the Caribbean, holds 4,500 works encompassing the finest collections of European and Latin American art in the region, with works dating back 500 years, and a growing collection of contemporary art. Iconic pieces include Fredrick Lord Leighton's gorgeous "Flaming June" and "Brushstrokes in Flight," a 28-foot high painted metal sculpture by Roy Lichtenstein that marks the main entrance. A 2010, $30 million renovation breathed new life into this cultural institution, expanding exhibition and theatre space, and renovating public areas.

Av. de Las Américas 23–25. ⓒ **787/848-0505.** www.museoarteponce.org. Follow Calle Concordia from Plaza Las Delicias miles (2.4km) south to Av. de Las Américas. Admission $9 adults, $6 seniors, students, and children.

Museum of the History of Ponce (Casa Salazar) ★ MUSEUM   Opened to commemorate the 500th anniversary of the city's founding, this museum traces the history of Ponce back to its roots in the days of the Taíno. There are exhibits on ecology, architecture, the economy, medicine, politics, and the people of Ponce. It's housed in the Casa Salazar, an eye-poppingly lovely example of the city's turn-of-the-20th-century style, which mixed neoclassic and Moorish details such as pressed-tin, mosaic tile, and stained glass.

Calle Isabel 51–53 (at Calle Mayor). ⓒ **787/844-7071.** Free admission. Tues–Sun 8am–4:30pm.

Museum of Puerto Rican Music ★ MUSEUM   A quaint museum housed in a dazzling restored turn-of-the-20th-century mansion designed by Alfredo Wiechers, it showcases historic Spanish, African, and Taíno musical instruments, some of which can be played; the guitar collection is a highlight. There are also exhibits on the foundations of Puerto Rican music, like the *bomba* and *plena,* which traces their roots back to Africa and are a major influence in modern *salsa.*

Calle Isabel 50. ℂ **787/848-7016.** Free admission. Wed–Sun 8:30am–4pm.

Parque de Bombas ★★ LANDMARK   The black-and-red Parque de Bombas, an 1882 wooden Victorian firehouse whose facade is synonymous with the city itself, houses an excellent city tourist-information office kiosk. The intricate wooden structure was built in 1882 for an agricultural fair, but became the first headquarters of the city's volunteer fire brigade. It's located right on Plaza Las Delicias at the heart of the historic district.

Plaza Las Delicias. ℂ **787/284-3338.** Free admission. Daily 9:30am–6pm.

Teatro la Perla ★ THEATER   This theater, built in the neoclassical style in 1864, remains one of the most visible symbols of the economic prosperity of Ponce during the mid–19th century. Designed by Juan Bertoli, an Italian-born resident of Puerto Rico who studied in Europe, it was destroyed by an earthquake in 1918 and rebuilt in 1940 according to the original plans; it reopened to the public in 1941. It is noted for acoustics so clear that microphones are unnecessary. The theater is the largest and most historic in the Spanish-speaking Caribbean. Everything from plays to concerts to beauty pageants takes place here.

At calles Mayor and Christina. ℂ **787/843-4322.** Prices and hours vary.

NEARBY ATTRACTIONS

Hacienda Buena Vista ★ HISTORIC SITE   Built in 1833, this was once one of the most successful plantations on Puerto Rico, producing coffee, corn, and citrus. It was a working coffee plantation until the 1950s, and 86 of the original 500 acres (35 of 202 hectares) are still part of the estate. Today, the hacienda preserves an old way of life, with its whirring water wheels, artifacts of 19th-century farm production and rooms furnished with authentic pieces from the 1850s. Visitors tour the hacienda first and then the shade-grown coffee plantation, sprinkled with fruit and wood trees; it's carved from lush tropical forest along the Canas River. From Av. de Las Américas, go west until Rte. 500, which you will take to Rte. 123 (Calle La Poncena), and turn left. At Km 16.8 you will find the Hacienda.

Rte. 123, Barrio Magüeyes Km 16.8. ℂ **787/722-5882** (weekdays), 284-7020 (weekends). Tours $10 adults, $7 children and seniors. Reservations required. 2-hr. tours Wed–Sun at 8:30am, 10:30am, 1:30pm, and 3:30pm (in English only at 1:30pm). A 30-min. drive north of Ponce, in the small town of Barrio Magüeyes, btw. Ponce and Adjuntas.

Ponce's Tastiest Ice Cream

Stop for an ice cream or drink at **King's Ice Cream** ★★ (ℂ **787/843-8520),** right across the street from the Parque de Bombas on the city's main square, open from 9am to 11pm. This institution has been scooping up delicious ice cream for decades. The almond is wonderful, as are tropical fruit flavors passion fruit or tamarind. It's closer to Italian gelato than U.S. ice cream and is perfect for the city's steamy afternoons. Enjoy your creamy scoop on a beautiful stone bench at Plaza Las Delicias under a shade tree.

Tibes Indian Ceremonial Center ★ RUINS   Bordered by the Río Portuguéz and excavated in 1975, this is the oldest cemetery in the Antilles. It contains some 186 skeletons, dating from A.D. 300, as well as pre-Taíno plazas from A.D. 700. The site also includes a re-created Taíno village, seven rectangular ball courts, and two dance grounds. The arrangement of stone points on the dance grounds, in line with the solstices and equinoxes, suggests a pre-Columbian Stonehenge. On-site are a museum, an exhibition hall that presents a documentary about Tibes, a cafeteria, and a souvenir shop. Go east along Av. de Las Américas until Av. De Hostos, which turns immediately into Calle Salud. Take a left at Calle Trioche and a right at Calle Mayor Cantera, which leads into the Carretera Tibes. Go right on Rte. 503, then bear left to stay on the road.

Rte. 503, Tibes, at Km 2.2. © **787/840-2255.** Admission $3 adults, $2 children, $1.50 seniors. Guided tours in English and Spanish are conducted through the grounds. Tues–Sun 8am–4:20pm. 2 miles (3.2km) north of Ponce.

Beaches & Outdoor Activities

Ponce is a city—not a beach resort—and should be visited mainly for its sights. There are no beaches within the city, but an offshore cay ringed with white sand and aquamarine waters filled with marine life is just a ferry ride away.

About 30 minutes to the west, however, are some of Puerto Rico's best beaches. They ring the coast from Guánica through Cabo Rojo.

Because the northern shore of Puerto Rico fronts the often-turbulent Atlantic, many snorkelers prefer the more tranquil southern coast, especially the waters off the coast of **La Parguera.** Throughout the southwest coast, water lovers can go snorkeling right off the beach, and it isn't necessary to take a boat trip. Waters here are not polluted, and visibility is usually good, unless there are heavy winds and choppy seas.

La Guancha is a sprawling boardwalk around Ponce's bayside harbor area near the Ponce Hilton. Several eateries are located here, and it is the scene of free concerts and other events at night. There's no beach, but during weekend afternoons children and their families come here to fly kites or ride bicycles. Hundreds of yachts and pleasure craft tie up here, which is also home to the Ponce Yacht Club. La Guancha is a relatively wholesome version of Coney Island, with a strong Hispanic accent and vague hints of New England. On hot weekends, the place is mobbed with families who listen to merengue and salsa. Lining the boardwalk are small establishments selling beer, party drinks, fried beach snacks, and souvenirs. There is also a lookout tower here, which is worth a climb.

A ferry runs from La Guancha to **Caja de Muertos,** or **Coffin Island** ★★, an uninhabited cay that's covered with mangrove swamps and ringed with worthwhile beaches. It's some of the best snorkeling in the southwest. A 125-passenger ferry run by **Island Venture** (© **787/842-8546** or 866-7827; www.islandventurepr.com) provides transportation to and from the island. It leaves at 8:30am and returns at 3:30pm. Roundtrip fare is $25 for adults and $20 for children. Bring lunch and snorkeling gear, or you can sign up for a deluxe package ($54 for adults, $33 for children), which includes beer and soft drinks, hot dogs, and chicken kebabs.

Other private outfits will take passengers to the island, with some providing snorkeling equipment and even lunch to guests. There are hiking trails, gazebos, and basic bathrooms, but no running water. The island has a lighthouse and a nice beach. Make sure to visit Almeida Cave. Legend says it was named after a pirate who buried his bride there following a fatal attack, visiting her every year to adorn her coffin with stolen gold, silver and emeralds.

The city has a municipal-run **tennis** facility at sports complex **Polideportivo Frankie Colón Alers** (✆ 787/432-7500). There are also private facilities at **Club Deportivo de Ponce,** or Ponce Sports Club (✆ 787/383-4066 or 787/842-1260) and **Centro de Tenis La Rambla,** or La Rambla Tennis Center (✆ 787/642-1545). All the courts are open daily and have lights for night play.

One of the south coast's best golf courses is the **Costa Caribe Golf & Country Club ★** (✆ 787/812-2650), on the site of the Hilton Ponce & Casino (see below). This 27-hole course has beautifully landscaped holes—with commanding views of the ocean and mountain—are laid out in former sugar-cane fields. The no. 12 hole, one of the most dramatic, calls for a 188-yard carry over water from the back tees. Trade winds add to the challenge. The three 9's can be played in 18-hole combinations, as conceived by golf architect Bruce Besse. The greens are undulating and moderate in speed, averaging 6,000 square feet (557 sq. m). Greens fees are $74 Friday to Sunday and holidays, and $63 Monday to Thursday; golf carts are included in the greens fees. There is also tennis available.

Another course, **Club Deportivo del Oeste,** Hwy. 102, Km 15.4, Barrio Joyuda, Cabo Rojo (✆ 787/851-8880 or 787/254-3748), lies 30 miles (48km) west of Ponce. This course is an 18-holer, open daily from 7am to 5pm. Greens fees are $37 ($26 twilight) weekdays and $48 ($37 twilight) weekends, and include a golf cart.

Ponce also has several nice parks, which may be especially attractive if you are travelling with children. The **Julio Enrique Monagas Park** (✆ 939/247-9336) is a sprawling oasis with two ponds with paddle boats, several splash parks, beach volleyball courts, an exotic bird aviary, a skate park and a miniature train. There are a number of picnic gazebos across the park and a children's playground. The **Luis A. Wito Morales Park** (✆ 787/812-0076) is another green dream with amenities, located in the middle of the Cerrillos State Forest Reserve next to the large Lake Cerrillos. Four miles into the highlands north of the city, the lush park has barbecue areas, picnic gazebos, basketball, baseball and beach volleyball facilities and a splash park and play area for the kids.

Shopping

Ponce's historic downtown has a small but vibrant shopping district that radiates from its central Plaza Las Delicias. **The Atocha Pedestrian Mall ★**, which runs north of the plaza along a single block, is a decidedly local affair, with sidewalk merchants hawking homemade sweets and cheap colorful jewelry in front of electronics and clothing shops. Follow it to the end to reach the city's Plaza de Mercado, the recently renovated traditional farmers market selling fresh fruit, vegetables, herbs, flowers and much more. The area has been a commercial district for centuries.

The historic district has many shops attuned to the cultural wonder that surrounds them, with beautiful handmade crafts and high quality works of art for sale. Many stores are a throwback to a simpler time

For artisans' work, **Mi Coquí ★★**, Calle Marina 9227 (✆ 787/812-0216), right on the plaza near the ice cream shop, is much more than a souvenir shop. They do sell many of the higher quality souvenirs you have seen before, but there are also real works of art, quality *santos, vejigantes* carnival masks, and original prints and paintings. The staff is knowledgeable and helpful, informative and friendly. Prices are quite good for many pieces when the quality is considered.

Utopía ★, Calle Isabel 78 (✆ 787/848-8742), also right on Plaza Las Delicias, is another fine shop dedicated to high quality crafts and works of art, including the colorful carnival masks for which the city is famous. Gourmet items, handmade jewelry, and more are on offer. The store also carries indigenous arts and crafts from elsewhere in Latin America.

El Candil ★, Plaza Vilariño, Corner Calles Unión and Sol (*C* **787/242-6693**), has a fine book and music selection and an excellent cafe, with gourmet coffee and tea as well as wine and tapas. There are more than 500 titles available; selections are weighted towards Spanish titles, but there are several fine editions regarding Puerto Rico and the arts that visitors will find interesting.

Plaza del Caribe ★, Hwy. 2 (*C* **787/848-5566** or 848-1229), is the biggest mall in the south, with many of the same stores that are found in your local mall back home (Sears, JCPenny's, and American Eagle Outfitters, among others), you may for a moment forget where you are. But with local surf and clothing shops, Caribbean cuisine in the food court, and Spanish titles dominating music and print choices, this is not quite home. Like other big malls in Puerto Rico, there is always some festival or other event taking place in the mall's wide passageways, be it fresh Puerto Rican coffee, or a boat show, that expands on the shopping possibilities.

THE SOUTHWEST COAST

The southwest corner of the island is where the locals go to kick back and chill out. The area is a favored vacation spot for San Juan and Ponce residents, as well as a weekend getaway destination. In fact, for many travelers the area will be too crowded during Easter week and the month of July, the height of the Puerto Rico tourism season. Here are some of Puerto Rico's great beaches, notably **Guánica** and **Boquerón Beach ★★**, and a lot of mom-and-pop operations that offer nightly rentals and good seafood dinners.

Southern Puerto Rico is increasingly gaining a reputation among **scuba divers,** although the outfitters are a bit lean here and not as well organized or plentiful as in the Cayman Islands. The attraction is the continental shelf that drops off a few miles off the southern coast. Within this watery range is a towering wall that is some 20 miles (32km) long and filled with one of the best assortments of marine life in the West Indies. Diving is possible from the town of La Parguera in the west all the way to Ponce in the east. The wall drops from 60 to 120 feet (18–37m) before it "vanishes" into 1,500 feet (457m) of sea. With a visibility of around 100 feet (30m), divers experience the beautiful formations of some of Puerto Rico's most dramatic coral gardens.

Bird-watchers should head to the **Guánica State Forest ★★★**, which is the sanctuary that has the greatest number of birds on the island. For beachcombers, there are many hidden places, such as Gilligan's Island off the coast of the little village of Guánica. For snorkelers, there are miles of coral reefs, awash with tropical fish, coral, and marine life. The Cabo Rojo Lighthouse, south of Boquerón, offers views of the rocky coastline and a panoramic sweep of the Caribbean.

Guánica ★★★

Guánica, on the Caribbean Sea, lies 73 miles (118km) southwest of San Juan and 21 miles (34km) west of the city of Ponce. The Guánica Dry Forest and adjacent area is a UNESCO-designated world biosphere reserve. The rare bonsai-like forest is home to more than 100 species of migratory and resident birds, the largest number in Puerto Rico. The beach at Guánica is pristine, and the crystal-clear water is ideal for swimming, snorkeling, and diving. Directly offshore is the famed Gilligan's Island, plus six of Puerto Rico's best sites for night or day dives. The area was once known for its leaping bullfrogs but Spanish conquerors virtually wiped out this species. Happily, the bullfrogs have come back and live in the rolling, scrub-covered hills that surround the 18-acre (7.3-hectare) site of the Copamarina Beach Resort, the area's major hotel (see below).

Guánica is adjacent to the unique Dry Forest and experiences very little rainfall. Nearby mountains get an annual rainfall of 15 feet (4.6m), but Guánica receives only about 15 inches (38cm). This is the world's largest dry coastal forest region. The upper hills are ideal for hiking. Guánica was once the haunt of the Taíno Indians, and it was the place where Ponce de León first explored Puerto Rico in 1508. One of his descendants later founded the nearby city of Ponce in 1692.

It is also the site of the landing of the Americans in 1898 during the Spanish-American war that began Puerto Rico's century-long relationship with the United States. You reach the harbor by taking the main exit to Guánica from Rte. 116 to Calle 25 de Julio. A large rock monument on the town's *malecón,* or harbor, commemorates the landing. The Williams family, descendants of a doctor who arrived with the troops and settled here after marrying a local girl, still live in one of the historic wooden homes along the waterfront. The area has lots of seafood restaurants and bars, as well as snack vendors along a bayside promenade. It is festive on weekend evenings.

HIKING & BIRD-WATCHING IN GUÁNICA STATE FOREST ★★

Heading directly west from Ponce, along Rte. 2, you reach **Guánica State Forest ★** (© 787/821-5706), a setting that evokes Arizona or New Mexico. Here you will find the best-preserved subtropical ecosystem on the planet. UNESCO has named Guánica a World Biosphere Reserve. Some 750 plants and tree species grow in the area.

The Cordillera Central cuts off the rain coming in from the heavily showered northeast, making this a dry region of cacti and bedrock, a perfect film location for old-fashioned western movies. It's also ideal country for birders. Some 50 percent of all of the island's terrestrial bird species can be seen in this dry and dusty forest. You might even spot the Puerto Rican emerald-breasted hummingbird. A number of migratory birds often stop here. The most serious ornithologists seek out the Puerto Rican nightjar, a local bird that was believed to be extinct. Now it's estimated that there are nearly a thousand of them.

To reach the forest, take Rte. 334 northeast of Guánica, to the heart of the forest. There's a ranger station here that will give you information about hiking trails. The booklet provided by the ranger station outlines 36 miles (58km) of trails through the four forest types. The most interesting is the mile-long (1.6km) **Cueva Trail,** which gives you the most scenic look at the various types of vegetation. You might even encounter the endangered bufo lemur toad, once declared extinct but found, thankfully, still jumping in this area.

SCUBA DIVING, SNORKELING & OTHER OUTDOOR PURSUITS

The best dive operation in Guánica is **Island Scuba** (© 787/309-6556), the closest to famed southwest diving sites like The Wall, a 22-mile-long undersea formation, cut with crevices and canyons that is a diver's delight. Many of the sites, rife with coral, schools of tropical fish and big game fish, lie within 2 miles of the óutfitter, which is on the water in Playa Santa. There are some 40 dive sites along the Wall, including The Canyons, The Parthenon and The Trench. Run by a husband and wife team whose enthusiasm for diving is infectious, there are trips every day. The warm blue water make this a perfect spot to try the sport, and beginners will see rainbow corral gardens and tropical fish glittering all around, and probably a slumbering nurse sharks and barracuda as well. But the quantity and quality of area dive sites make this a winner with diving aficionados as well. A two-tank dive costs $100, plus $20 for full diving equipment, including snacks and drinks, and a beginner's discovery course is $150 Full PADI diving courses and a scuba course.

At one of the local beaches, **Playa Santa ★★**, west of town, **Pino's Boat & Water Fun** (*(C)* **787/821-6864** or 484-8083) will meet all your water sports needs and make sure you have tons of fun in the process. They rent paddleboats, kayaks, and standup paddle boards at prices ranging from $15 to $25 an hour. A banana-boat ride costs $8 per person, while water scooters cost $60 per person for an hour. It operates from a beach shack that has beach chairs and umbrellas and sells beach supplies.

One of the most visited sites in the area is **Gilligan's Island ★**, one of a number of mangrove and sand cays near the Caña Gorda peninsula. Part of the dry forest reserve, it is set aside for recreational use. A small ferry departs from in front of **Restaurant San Jacinto** (*(C)* **787/821-4941**), just past Copamarina Beach Resort, periodically from 10am to 5pm, weather permitting; round-trips cost under $8 per person. Alternately, you can rent kayaks and paddle boards from Mary Lee's guesthouse and a few other spots in the San Jacinto sector. **Ballena Beach ★★★** is farther down Rte. 333, in the coastal border of the Dry Forest. This is a beautiful beach, with huge palm trees and golden sand. During winter storms, surfers flock here for rare, tubular waves.

WHERE TO STAY

Copamarina Beach Resort ★★★   Surrounded by the Guánica Dry Forest and its undeveloped coastline, this two-story, low-slung resort is perhaps the island's most quintessentially Caribbean property, right down to its red roofing and the verandas and terraces surrounding the property. It's popular with locals and European travelers looking for a true nature experience, and it's one of my favorite resorts in Puerto Rico. It's among the most laid back properties on the island, yet, there's lots to do: visiting off-shore cays and deserted beaches, diving, bird-watching, or simply enjoying the large pool and lush grounds filled with towering palms, flaming flamboyant trees, and tumbles of violet and burnt orange bougainvillea. Standup paddleboards, kayaks, and snorkel gear are available at the on-site water sports center that can also arrange diving, fishing, and sailing trips. Beginners can experience the tropical splendor beneath the water through "snuba," which offers shallow diving with lighter weight equipment more akin to snorkeling. The large simple rooms have subtle tropical interiors, with double door openings to terraces or balconies, modern oversized bathrooms, and comfortable beds and furnishings. With a spa, health club, tennis, and fine restaurant, there's little reason to leave.

Rte. 333, Km 6.5, Caña Gorda, Guánica. *(C)* **888/881-6233** or 787/821-0505. www.copamarina.com. 106 units. $155–$195 double; $350–$400 suite; $850–$1,000 villa. 20 percent resort fee. Free parking. From Ponce, drive west along Rte. 2 to Rte. 116 and go south to Rte. 333, then head east. **Amenities:** 2 restaurants; bar; babysitting; health club; 2 outdoor pools; room service; spa; tennis courts; rooms for those w/limited mobility; computer; free Wi-Fi, computer access.

Mary Lee's by the Sea ★★   This jumble of cottages, homes and apartments cling to a seaside cliff along a dramatically beautiful stretch of Caribbean coastline. A narrow pathway cuts through the blooming plants and trees and connects the units in the main compound as it crisscrosses downhill to a dock and small beach, a break in the mangrove chocked coastline. Other larger units are spread across the San Jacinto area, a hilltop full of residences in the midst of the protected and pristine Guánica dry forest. The California style units are whimsical, extremely colorful, and comfortable; some have kitchenettes, and they vary in size, with some appropriate for families, and others for couples. Most have tremendous views. Barbecue facilities, kayaks, and paddleboards are all available for guest use. This is a low-key spot for vacationers looking to relax, and at night the symphony of the forest, and the gentle beating of the coastline, takes over. If you want to party, stay closer to town; the winding road to get here from the nearest bar is too dangerous at night.

Rte. 333, Km 6.7, Guánica. *C* **787/821-3600.** www.maryleesbythesea.com. 11 units. $130 studio; $150 1-bedroom apt; $180-225 2-bedroom apt; $185-$300 3-bedroom.1 percent resort fee. From Ponce, take Rte. 2. When you reach Rte. 116, head south toward Guánica. The hotel is signposted from the road. **Amenities:** Laundry service; barbeque; kitchenettes; free Wi-Fi in common areas.

Parador Guánica 1929 ★ Parador Guánica 1929, a former plantation residence, sits in the midst of the ruins of an old sugar mill, with huge shade trees and plantation homes dotting the surrounding hillside. A lovely wraparound verandah on both of its two levels leads to the modern, simple but colorfully decorated rooms. The staff is young and eager to please, and the hotel is a great value, especially for families (who will appreciate the large pool area). Breakfast and other meals are served on the downstairs side veranda, with the rest given over to the glories of just hanging out. A really charming property in a pretty part of Puerto Rico that still feels part of a lost era.

Rte. 3116, Km 2.5, Av. Los Veteranos, Ensenada, Guánica. *C* **787/821-0099** or 787/893-4423. www. tropicalinnspr.com. 21 units. $84 double. **Amenities:** Pool; gym; playground w/basketball court; free Wi-Fi.

WHERE TO EAT

Alexandra ★★★ INTERNATIONAL Ever since Nuevo Latino cooking pioneer Alfredo Ayala took over, this has been one of the finest restaurants in Puerto Rico. Ayala drove the gourmet *nueva criolla* cuisine movement in the 1980s and 1990s with San Juan restaurants like Ali-Oli and Chayote, after training under Eric Ripert of Le Bernardin in New York. These days he is blissfully dishing out more subdued hallelujahs to the glories of island cuisine from this beautiful corner of the Puerto Rico. Guests are served right-out-of-the-ocean fresh seafood, and dishes based on locally grown herbs, fruits, and vegetables. Seafood linguine, in a tomato saffron sauce, and a mahi-mahi with local herbs and vegetables are world class. We also recommend conch carpaccio in a fennel arugula salad with mango and avocado, and sweet onion in a balsamic and lemon vinaigrette. There are changing vegetarian specials, a delicious crabmeat and pumpkin risotto, and Caribbean seafood paella. The dining room looks out over the pool area and coastline. Reservations recommended.

In the Copamarina Beach Resort, Rte. 333, Km 6.5, Caña Gorda. Guánica. *C* **787/821-0505.** Main courses $19–$40. Daily 6–10pm.

Bodegas Andreu Solé ★★ WINERY/TAPAS This bohemian bistro-bar spills out of a restored plantation home on Ensenada Bay, serving up locally produced wine from a nearby vineyard along with, frankly, better imported wines and a short but tasty Spanish tapas menu. There's jazz, Spanish ballad singers, and other excellent music acts most weekend nights. Located on one of the prettiest roads in Puerto Rico, which ribbons along the mangrove-choked coast and the overgrown ruins of an old sugar mill just getting here is spectacular. You can also tour their nearby vineyard.

PUERTO RICO'S SECRET beaches

Some of Puerto Rico's most beautiful and isolated beaches lie on the island's southwestern coast, on the Caribbean Sea, far from major highways. Stretching between Ponce in the east and Cabo Rojo on Puerto Rico's extreme southwestern tip, these beaches flank some of the least densely populated parts of the island. And because the boundaries between them are relatively fluid, only a local resident (or perhaps a professional geographer) could say for sure where one ends and the other begins.

If you consider yourself an aficionado of isolated beaches, it's worth renting a car and striking out for these remote locales. Drive westward from Ponce along Hwy. 2, branching south along Rte. 116 to **Guánica,** the self-anointed gateway and capital of this string of "secret beaches."

By far the most accessible and appealing beach is **Caña Gorda ★**. Set about a quarter mile (.4km) south of Guánica, at the edge of a legally protected marsh that's known for its rich bird life and thick reeds, Caña Gorda is a sprawling expanse of pale beige sand that's dotted with picnic areas and a beach refreshment stand/bar, showers, bathrooms, and other facilities. Just beyond the public beach is the well-recommended **Copamarina Beach Resort** (© 787/821-0505); see p. 157. You can check in for a night or two of sun-flooded R&R. Even if you're not staying at the hotel, consider dropping in for a Cuba Libre, a margarita, or a meal.

Farther along is **Ballena Beach,** which stretches for a mile or more along a deserted beachfront, protected by rocky bluffs and a grove of towering palm trees. There are several other smaller beaches as Rte. 333 cuts farther into the dry forest and ends at an undeveloped parking area, adjacent to a foundation built right on the coast, with the sandy

Tamarindo Beach beyond it. Hills surround the area, covered by the dwarfed pines at the outskirts of the reserve.

Another beautiful beach in town is **Playa Santa,** which also lies off Rte. 116 (the exit to Rte. 325 is signposted). The white-sand beach has incredibly tranquil salty water, and there is a string of eateries serving snacks and cold drinks around a harbor beside it. **La Jungla** and **Manglillo** are two other beautiful, undeveloped beaches bordering here, with great snorkeling because of coral reefs just offshore and interesting mangrove canals. The road to Playa Santa first cuts through a section of undeveloped dry forest before ending at the beach town. An unmarked dirt road on the left-hand side leads to another breathtakingly beautiful sand beach.

In the very southwest sector of Puerto Rico are some relatively hidden and very secluded beaches, although getting to them is a bit difficult along some pot-holed roads. Head west on Rte. 101, cutting south at the junction with Rte. 301, which will carry you to one of the most westerly beaches in Puerto Rico, **Playa Sucia.** The beach opens onto **Bahía Sucia ★**, whose name rather unappetizingly translates as "Dirty Bay." Actually it isn't dirty; it's a lovely spot. Hikers willing to walk a while will also be rewarded for their efforts from the **Boquerón public beach** and over the bluffs bordering it.

All these beaches might be hard to reach, but persevere and you'll be met with warm water and long, uncrowded stretches of sand, where towering king palms and salt-tolerant sea grapes provide an idyllic tropical backdrop for sun and surf. Keep in mind that most of the beaches mentioned here have virtually no services or public utilities. Pack what you'll need for the day—food, water, sunscreen, and so forth.

Rte. 3116, Km 2.5, Av. Los Veteranos, Ensenada, 00647. ✆ **787/951-9622.** Tapas $5–$10. Fri–Sat 8pm–midnight, Sun 12:30–4:30pm.

Jibarito en Playa ★ SEAFOOD/PUERTO RICAN The only game in town these days on Guánica's town harbor, this spot is known for its weekend parties (with karaoke or live music) and its fried red snapper and mixed seafood salad, steaks, and delish seafood *empanadillas*. It's far more serene during the week, when you can take a quiet meal, and chat with the locals (it's a convivial place), in the simple, wooden dining room. A second floor offers great views, pool tables, and a dance floor.

Ave. Esperanza Idrach, in front of the *malecón* (waterfront), Guánica. ✆ **787/674-8892.** Main courses $8–$29. Wed–Sun 11am–9pm.

La Parguera ★

This charming fishing village lies 78 miles (126km) southwest of San Juan and 26 miles (42km) west of Ponce, just south of San Germán. From San Germán, take Rte. 320 directly south and follow the signposts. Note that this route changes its name several times along the way, becoming Rte. 101, 116, 315, 305, and then 304 before reaching La Parguera—even though it's all the same highway.

The name of the village comes from *pargos,* meaning snapper. Its main attraction, other than its coast and diving, is **Phosphorescent Bay** ★, which contains millions of luminescent dinoflagellates (microscopic plankton). A disturbance causes them to light up the dark waters. For dramatic effect, they are best seen on a moonless night. The **Fondo de Cristal III** (✆ **787/899-5891**) is a glass-bottomed boat that trolls the bay nightly from 7:30pm to 12:30am from La Parguera pier, depending on demand. The trip costs $8 per person. There are also smaller boats (**Johnny's Boats** and **Torres Boats**) that will take you out and let you swim at night. **Paradise Scuba & Snorkeling Center** (see below) also runs a kayak trip to the bay for $30. The bay here is not as shiny as those in Fajardo and Vieques.

Offshore are some 12 to 15 reefs with a variety of depths. The Beril reef goes down to 60 feet (18m), then drops to 2,000 feet (610m). This wall is famous among divers, and visibility ranges from 100 to 120 feet (30–37m). These reefs also provide some of the best snorkeling possibilities in Puerto Rico. Marine life is both abundant and diverse, including big morays, sea turtles, barracudas, nurse sharks, and manatees. **Paradise Scuba & Snorkeling Center,** Paguera Shopping Center, at La Parguera (✆ **787/899-7611**), offers the best diving and snorkeling. A two-tank dive costs $120; a sunset snorkel and Bio-Bay combo trip costs $60 per person, with equipment and food and drinks included. Lessons and a variety of trips like the 2 hour Bio-Bay trip for $30 (including snacks and beverages) are available. The town has no natural beach, but its **Playa Rosada** is a swimming area with wooden docks, bathrooms, showers and picnic areas.

La Parguera takes on a carnival atmosphere on weekend evenings when families and young couples come into town for drinks and snacks and to blow off some steam. Most of the action is around the cluster of bars and food stands near the main dock. There is often live music at the bars by the waterfront, and children play games on the town plaza on the water. Make sure to go into **Sangria Coño** ★★ to try a glass of the fine Caribbean sangria made here, as well as the empanadillas. The interior is well air-conditioned, with photos of Puerto Rican patriots, local art, and independence slogans on the walls. There is a backroom game arcade for the kids. Grabbing a slice at **Tony's Pizza** ★ (thin crispy crust and super cheesy) is a ritual for most families.

WHERE TO STAY

Parador Villa Parguera ★   For years, this had been La Parguera's best property and it still has its charms. But we have to start out with a warning: Nearby is a night-club that has been blasting music until 3am (this was a new development in 2014). So if you stay on the wrong night of the week, you may not sleep much. That being said, the management has been forthright with its customers about which nights are prob-lematic and, if you can avoid those, know you'll get comfortable, well-kept rooms, a pool, a central location, and an excellent full-service restaurant that has live shows on weekend evenings. There is a dock at the hotel, where boats tie up. Hire a small *yola* to bring you to one of the beautiful small islands for the day, or rent it for the whole day and explore. The area is excellent for snorkeling, diving, and sailing.

Main St. 304, Carretera 304, Km 303, La Parguera, Lajas. ✆ **787/899-7777.** www.villaparguera.net. 74 units (all with either shower or tub). $96–$107 double. 2 children 9 or under stay free in parent's room. Drive west along Rte. 2 until the junction with Rte. 116; then head south along Rte. 116 and Rte. 304. **Amenities:** Restaurant; bar; pool; rooms for those w/limited mobility, free Wi-Fi in com-mon areas.

WHERE TO EAT

Besides the following recommendations, the formal dining room at **Parador Villa Parguera** (see "Where to Stay," above) also is a solid dinner option.

Moon's Bar & Tapas ★★ TAPAS   This wooden, open air spot at the entrance to town has surprisingly sophisticated tapas, employing fresh seafood and fine cuts of meat, an adequate wine selection, and really great sangria. Try the fresh grouper and mahi mahi tacos, mushrooms stuffed with chorizo and cheese, or tempura shrimp in a sweet Thai sauce. The churassco and chicken kebabs here are also first rate. The place is small and often crowded, and there is always good music and conversation (the staff is super friendly). This is the "in" spot in La Parguera.

Calle Principal, Hwy. 304, Km 3.2. ✆ **787/362-0935.** Tapas $5–$19. Thurs–Fri 3–11pm, Sat–Sun 1–11pm.

La Casita ★ SEAFOOD   This simple, inexpensive family restaurant has been the most reliable meal in town for decades. There's nothing fancy about the place; its unvarnished wooden dining room has the feel of a summer camp cafeteria to it, but it knows what it is doing when it comes to preparing fresh fish, Caribbean lobster, and the *comida criolla* standards served here. Fish is grilled, baked, or sautéed and there are a choice of sauces, including garlic and sweet tomato. It also has the best flan in town.

Calle Principal 304. ✆ **787/899-1681.** Main courses $12–$25 Fri–Sat 4–9:30pm, Sun noon–8pm.

Boquerón ★★

Lying 85 miles (137km) southwest of San Juan and 33 miles (53km) west of Ponce is the little beach town of Boquerón. It is just south of Cabo Rojo, west of the historic city of San Germán, and near the western edge of the Boquerón Forest Preserve.

What puts sleepy Boquerón on the tourist map is its lovely public beach, one of the island's finest for swimming. It is also known for the shellfish found offshore. The beach has facilities, including lockers and changing places, plus kiosks that rent water-sports equipment. Parking costs $3. On weekends, the resort tends to be crowded with families driving down from San Juan.

The outfitter that offers the best scuba diving in the area is **Mona Aquatics,** on Calle José de Diego, directly west of the heart of town (✆ **787/851-2185**) near the town

A Wildlife Refuge for Bird Fanciers

The area around Cabo Rojo, the **Refugio Nacional Cabo Rojo (Red Cape National Refuge; ℰ 787/851-7297),** attracts serious bird-watchers to its government-protected sector. The refuge, run by the U.S. Fish & Wildlife Service, is on Rte. 301 at Km 5.1, 1 mile (1.6km) north of the turnoff to El Combate. At the entrance to the refuge is a visitor center. The only time you can visit the refuge is from 9am to 4pm Monday to Saturday; admission is free. Migratory birds, especially ducks and herons as well as several species of songbirds, inhabit this refuge. Birders have reported seeing at least 130 species. Trails for bird-watchers have been cut through the reserve. The best time to observe the birds is during the winter months, when they have fled from their cold homelands in the north.

marina and Hotel Boquemar. A two-tank dive off the coast's famed diving area costs $75 per person (equipment rental $51).

From Boquerón, you can head directly south to **El Faro de Cabo Rojo** at the island's southernmost corner. The century-old Cabo Rojo Lighthouse lies on Rte. 301, along a spit of land between Bahía Sucia and Bahía Salinas. Looking down from the lighthouse, you'll see a 2,000-foot (610m) drop along jagged limestone cliffs. The lighthouse dates from 1881, when it was constructed under Spanish rule. The famous pirate Roberto Cofresi used to terrorize the coast along here in the 19th century and was said to have hidden out in a cave nearby.

WHERE TO STAY

Grand Bahia Ocean View Hotel ★   Located on a remote stretch of coast near the Cabo Rojo Lighthouse within a 2,800 acre nature reserve, the Grand Bahia Ocean View is beloved of bird watchers and other nature enthusiasts. This sunbaked region has salt flats and a lush mangrove reserve—a haven for many birds, both migratory and native. On property, the most popular areas are the handsome infinity pools. Unfortunately, the beach is choked with mangroves and therefore, not appropriate for swimming, though it's a lovely place to stroll and tan. Oversized guest rooms have distinctive decor; most have four-poster beds and Spanish colonial furnishings, and all are comfortable and tasteful. The hotel's **Agua al Cuello** restaurant is one of the finest in the area, worth a visit even if you are not staying here. The property went through a recent reorganization and name change and is offering special package rates including meals (in addition to the standard rates listed below) to entice would-be guests.

Rd. 301, Km 11.5, Sector El Faro, Cabo Rojo. ℰ **787/254-1212.** www.bahiasalina.com. 22 units. $150–$240 double. Children 11 and under stay free in parent's room. **Amenities:** Restaurant; bar; high-speed Internet access; 2 outdoor pools; room service; rooms for those w/limited mobility, A/C, TV.

Cofresi Beach Hotel ★   On the road into Boquerón Village, this spot rents fully equipped 1 to 3 bedroom apartments at reasonable rates. These are basic, somewhat dated lodgings, with only a small pool and minimal service levels, but having a kitchens allows guest to cut food bills significantly. An 8-minute walk to a lovely, serene beach and a 10 minute walk to town, the location is also a winner. The small staff is friendly but don't speak much English so is a decidedly do–it–yourself type of facility.

Calle Muñoz Rivera 57, P.O. Box 1209, Boquerón. © **787/254-3000.** www.cofresibeach.com. 12 units. $129 1-bedroom; $165 2-bedroom; $219 3-bedroom. **Amenities:** Pool.

Parador Boquemar ★   Located near the heart of Boquerón Village, its location remains Boquemar's biggest attribute. Public areas and the pool space are cramped, but the place is well-kept if not particularly attractive (think dim lighting in rooms that don't have a single picture on the walls). It's recommended because it is clean, comfortable, and right in town, which has its appeal, since you can walk to bars and restaurants, as well as the public beach and all water sports and boat outfitters. Also, it's a bit removed from the center of action and noise and crowds of weekend and holiday evenings that is a problem with other village guest houses.

Carretera 101, Poblado de Boquerón, Cabo Rojo. © **787/851-2158.** www.boquemar.com. 75 units (shower only). $107–$128 double; $133 junior suite, free parking. **Amenities:** Restaurant; bar; outside pool; rooms for that w/limited mobility; Wi-Fi in lobby;

WHERE TO EAT

Boquerón has great roadside food stands. You can get everything from fresh oysters to hand-rolled burritos from vendors set up along the beach village's main drag. Open air bars and restaurants also sell turnovers stuffed with fresh fish, lobster, or conch, as well as seafood ceviche salad in plastic cups.

Galloway's ★★★ SEAFOOD   There are few better spots to see the day fall into night than at this rustic seaside restaurant, which sits on the water at the southwestern corner of the island. I love the fresh mahi mahi and red snapper, the grilled lobster, and the *mofongo* stuffed with shrimp. There is a front bar, where televised sports and good natured gossip are on tap along with burgers, nachos, and pasta. The service is always well-intentioned, but sometimes slow. But with the sun fading over the western horizon, and the water lapping at the dock beside your table, you won't be in a hurry anyway.

12 Calle José de Diego, Poblado de Boquerón, Cabo Rojo. © **787/254-3302.** Main courses $11–$29. Thurs–Tues noon–midnight.

La Cascada ★ CREOLE/CONTINENTAL   The hardest working restaurant in Boquerón, wakes early with American style breakfast, moves into sandwiches and burgers for lunch, and then into Puerto Rican and continental classics for dinner. A waterfall runs down a large interior tiled wall of the restaurant, creating the illusion of stream running over rocks, and tropical printed table clothes cover the rattan tables. Try the *mofongo*, which uses yucca instead of plantain. The house specialty, Arroz Cascada, is fried rice with fresh seafood and is excellent. La Cascada is a *meson gastronómico*, which carries the Puerto Rico Tourism Company seal of approval.

In the Parador Boquemar, Carretera 101, Poblado de Boquerón, Cabo Rojo. © **787/851-2158.** Breakfast $5–$10; main courses $12–$29. Daily 7:30–10:30am; Thurs–Tues 5–9pm.

SAN GERMÁN ★★

104 miles (167km) SW of San Juan, 34 miles (55km) W of Ponce

Only an hour's drive from Ponce and right near the beaches of the southwest coast, and just over 2 hours from San Juan, San Germán, Puerto Rico's second-oldest town, is a little museum piece. It was founded in 1512 and destroyed by the French in 1528. Rebuilt in 1570, it was named after Germain de Foix, the second wife of King

Ferdinand of Spain. Once the rival of San Juan, San Germán harbored many pirates who pillaged the ships that sailed off the nearby coastline. Indeed, many of today's residents are descended from the smugglers, poets, priests, and politicians who once lived here.

The pirates and sugar plantations are long gone, but the city retains colorful reminders of its Spanish colonial past. Flowers brighten some of the patios here as they do in Seville. Also like in a small Spanish town, many of the inhabitants stroll through the historic zone in the early evening. Nicknamed *Ciudad de las Lomas* (City of the Hills), San Germán boasts verdant scenery that provides a pleasant backdrop to a variety of architectural styles—Spanish colonial (1850s), *criolla* (1880s), neoclassical (1910s), Art Deco (1930s), and international (1960s)—depicted in the gracious old-world buildings lining the streets. So significant are these buildings that San Germán is included in the National Register of Historic Places.

The city's 249 historical treasures are within easy walking distance of one another. Regrettably, you must view most of them from the outside. If some of them are actually open, count yourself fortunate, as they have no phones, keep no regular hours, and are staffed by volunteers who rarely show up. Also, be aware that the signage for the historic buildings can be confusing, and many of the streets in the old town tend to run one-way. Most of the city's architectural treasures lie uphill from the congested main thoroughfare (Calle Luna). We usually try to park on the town's main street (Carretera 102, which changes its name within the borders of San Germán to Calle Luna), and then proceed on foot through the city's commercial core before reaching the architectural highlights described below.

One of the most noteworthy churches in Puerto Rico is **Iglesia Porta Coeli (Gate of Heaven) ★★★** (© 787/892-0160), which sits atop a knoll at the eastern end of a cobble-covered square, the Parque de Santo Domingo. Dating from 1606 and built in a style inspired by the Romanesque architecture of northern Spain, this is the oldest church in the New World. Restored by the Institute of Puerto Rican Culture, and sheathed in a layer of salmon-colored stucco, it contains a museum of religious art with a collection of ancient *santos,* the carved figures of saints that have long been a major part of Puerto Rican folk art. Look for the 17th-century portrait of St. Nicholas de Bari, the French Santa Claus. Inside, the original palm-wood ceiling and tough ausubo-wood beams draw the eye upward. Other treasures include early choral books from Santo Domingo, a primitive carving of Jesus, and 19th-century Señora de la Monserrate Black Madonna and Child statues. Admission is $3 for adults, $2 for seniors and children over 12, free for children 12 and under. The church is open Wednesday through Sunday from 8:30am to noon and 1 to 4:30pm.

Less than 100 feet (30m) downhill from Iglesia Porta Coeli, at the bottom of the steps that lead from its front door down to the plaza below, is the **Casa Morales** (also known as the **Tomás Vivoni House,** after its architect), San Germán's most photographed and widely recognized house. Designed in the Edwardian style, with wraparound porches, elaborate gables, and elements that might remind you of a Swiss chalet, it was built in 1913, reflecting the region's turn-of-the-20th-century agrarian prosperity. (Note that it is a private residence and can be admired only from the outside.)

The long and narrow, gently sloping plaza that fronts Iglesia Porta Coeli is the Parque de Santo Domingo, one of San Germán's two main plazas. Street signs also identify the plaza as the Calle Ruiz Belvis. Originally a marketplace, the plaza is paved with red and black cobblestones. It is bordered with cast-iron benches and portrait busts of prominent figures in the town's history. This plaza merges gracefully with a second plaza, which street signs and maps identify as the Plaza Francisco Mariano Quiñones, the Calle José Julian Acosta, and the Plaza Principal. Separating the two plazas is the unused (and closed to the public) **Viejo Alcaldía (Old Town Hall)** ★. Built late in the 19th century, it's awaiting a new vision, perhaps as a museum or public building.

San Germán's most impressive church—and the most monumental building in the region—is **San Germán de Auxerre** ★ (*C* 787/892-1027), which rises majestically above the western end of the Plaza Francisco Mariano Quiñones. Designed in the Spanish baroque style, it was built in 1573 in the form of a simple chapel with a low-slung thatch roof. Its present grandeur is the result of at least five subsequent enlargements and renovations. Much of what you see today is the result of a rebuilding in 1688 and a restoration in 1737 that followed a disastrous earthquake. Inside are three naves, 10 altars, three chapels, and a belfry that was rebuilt in 1939, following an earthquake in 1918. The central chandelier, made from rock crystal and imported from Barcelona in 1866, is the largest in the Caribbean. The pride of the church is the *trompe l'oeil* ceiling, which was elaborately restored in 1993. A series of stained-glass windows with contemporary designs was inserted during a 1999 restoration. The church can be visited daily from 8 to 11am and 1 to 3pm.

A few lesser sights are located near the town's two main squares. **Farmacia Martin,** a modern pharmacy, is incongruously set within the shell of a graceful but battered Art Deco building at the edge of the Parque Santo Domingo (Calle Ruiz Belvis 22; *C* 787/892-1122). A cluster of battered and dilapidated clapboard-sided houses line the southern side of the Calle Dr. Ueve, which rambles downhill from its origin at the base of the Iglesia Porta Coeli. The most important house is no. 66, the **Casa Acosta y Fores.** Also noteworthy is **Casa Juán Perichi,** a substantial-looking structure at the corner of Calle Dr. Ueve and Parque Santo Domingo, nearly adjacent to the Iglesia Porta Coeli. Both houses were built around 1917, of traditional wood construction, and are viewed as fine examples of Puerto Rican adaptations of Victorian architecture. Regrettably, both are seriously dilapidated, although that might change as San Germán continues the slow course of its historic renovations.

To the side of the Auxerre church is the modern, cement-sided **Public Library,** Calle José Julia Acosta, where you might be tempted to duck into the air-conditioned interior for a glance through the stacks and periodicals collection. It's open Monday through Thursday from 8am to 8:30pm, Friday from 8am to 6pm, and Saturday from 8am to 1pm and 2 to 4:30pm. Behind the Auxerre church is at least one masonry-fronted town house whose design might remind you of southern Spain (Andalusia), especially when the flowers in the window boxes add splashes of color.

Where to Eat

Tapas Café ★   You can stop for drinks and a bite or a full meal at this white and blue Andalucian-style restaurant, with a high ceiling and sandstone and mosaic facades. The garlic shrimp, Serrano ham and manchego cheese, excellent *paella,* and *caldo gallego* are all worthwhile. Wash it all back with the fine house sangria; both the red and white are excellent. Tapas Café is located in San Germán's beautiful historic heart, amid centuries-old cathedrals and public buildings.

Calle Dr. Santiago Veve 50, San Germán. *C* **787/264-0610.** Tapas $2–$15. Wed–Thurs 5–10pm; Fri–Sat 5–11pm; Sun 11am–9pm.

THE SOUTHERN MOUNTAINS

The mountain towns surrounding the gorgeous Toro Negro Forest Reserve straddle Puerto Rico's highest peaks that run along the center of the island. The area is included here because it is most accessible from the south, from Ponce and surrounding towns. The mountain towns include Villalba, Orocovis, Adjuntas, and Jayuya, as well as parts of Utuado, Coamo, and Juana Díaz. Even from Ponce, the best route to this region is to head east first along the coastal Hwy. 2 to neighboring Juana Díaz. Then take Rte. 149 north through town and into the lush mountains of Villalba. Continue straight until the intersection of Rte. 143 west to get to **Toro Negro Forest Reserve** (there's an entrance at Km 32.4).

Toro Negro Forest Reserve ★ & Lake Guineo ★

North of Ponce, **Toro Negro Forest Reserve ★★★** (𝒞 787/867-3040) lies along the Cordillera Central, the cloud-shrouded, lush central mountain chain that spans Puerto Rico's spine from the southeast town of Yabucoa all the way to outside Mayagüez on the west coast. This 7,000-acre (2,833-hectare) park, ideal for hikers, straddles the highest peak of the Cordillera Central at the very heart of Puerto Rico, quite near the midway point between east and west coasts. A forest of lush trees, the reserve also contains the headwaters of several main rivers and lakes, and has several crashing waterfalls. The reserve lies at the borders of four mountain towns: Villalba, Jayuya, Adjuntas, and Orocovis.

The lowest temperatures recorded on the island—some 40°F (4°C)—were measured at **Lake Guineo ★**, the island's highest lake, which lies within the reserve. The best trail to take here is a short, paved, and wickedly steep path on the north side of Rte. 143, going up to the south side of **Cerro de Punta,** which at 4,390 feet (1,338m) is the highest peak on Puerto Rico. Allow about half an hour for an ascent. Once at the top, you'll be rewarded with Puerto Rico's grandest view, sweeping across the lush interior from the Atlantic to the Caribbean coasts. Other mountains in the reserve also offer hiking possibilities. The reserve spans several distinct types, including a sierra palm forest, which, in places, forms a complete canopy from the sun, and a mountainous cloud forest, with dwarfed, but vibrantly green plants and trees.

The main entrance to the forest is at the Doña Juana recreational area, which has a swimming pool filled with cold water from the mountain streams, a picnic area, and a rustic campground. An adjacent restaurant serves up Puerto Rican barbecued chicken and pork and other local delicacies. Many hiking trails originate from this area. One of the best is a 2-mile (3.2km) trek to an observation post and the impressive 200-foot (61m) Doña Juana Falls.

Jayuya lies north of the reserve, but to access it, you must return east along Rte. 143 to Rte. 149, and take that north, farther into the central mountains to Rte. 144, which you'll take back west to access the town. This is a beautiful area, filled with old coffee estates and lush mountain forest. The local *parador* is a country inn built on the grounds of an old coffee plantation (**Parador Hacienda Gripiñas;** see below), which is one of the best places to stay in Puerto Rico's interior. There's also a fine restaurant on the grounds. Built by a Spanish coffee baron more than 150 years ago, the restored plantation home is surrounded by gardens and coffee fields.

Jayuya is also known for the relics found here from Puerto Rico's Taíno past. Off Rte. 144 is La Piedra Escrita, the Written Rock, a huge boulder beside a stream, with Taíno petroglyphs carved into the stone. It's a wonderful picnic spot. Jayuya also hosts an annual Indigenous Festival in November, which combines native crafts with music and food. The **Cemi Museum** ★, Rte. 144, Km 9.3 (𝄯 **787/828-1241**), in town has a collection of Taíno pottery and *cemís,* amulets sacred to the island's indigenous peoples. The adjacent **Casa Museo Canales** ★, Rte. 144, Km 9.4 (𝄯 **787/828-1241**), is a restored 19th-century coffee plantation home with interesting exhibits. Both museums charge $1.50 for adults and 75¢ for children and are open from 9am to 3pm every day.

Where to Stay & Eat

Hacienda Gripiñas ★ This 150-year old plantation home is surrounded by lush green mountains and coffee fields, with the property dotted with palms and tropical gardens and in the distance patches of rainforest clinging to the mountainside. The wooden residence has plenty of porches and balconies to take in the view and offers myriad ways to relax, with hammocks and wooden sling chairs spread throughout. Built by a Spanish nobleman in 1853, it has unfortunately fallen a bit from its royal past and suffers from a general lack of maintenance. On paper, the restaurant is fine if uninspired. A trail leads to Cerro Punta, the island's highest point. It's always peaceful and relaxed.

Rte. 527, Km 2.5, Jayuya. 𝄯 **787/828-1717.** www.haciendagripinas.net. 18 units. Mon–Thurs $90, Sat–Sun $105 double. **Amenities:** Restaurant; library; 2 pools, Wi-Fi in common areas.

MAYAGÜEZ & THE NORTHWEST

Mayagüez lies in the middle of Puerto Rico's west coast, a major fun-in-the-sun zone, but it lacks its own quality beach. Yet Puerto Rico's third largest city is close enough to several world-class beaches in Rincón, Aguadilla, and Isabela to make it a great jumping off point for a unique Caribbean vacation.

To the north, along the northwest coast that stems from Rincón to Isabella, lie the Caribbean's best surfing beaches, which compare favorably to those of California and the East Coast. These are the beaches we'll focus on in this chapter. And to the south are equally attractive beaches with among the calmest waters in the Caribbean, offering excellent snorkeling, scuba, and sailing opportunities.

The city is not as renowned for its historic sites, architecture, and attractions as San Juan or Ponce, but it has all three.

Mayagüez is also close to the western mountains, especially Maricao, perhaps the prettiest of the mountain towns in Puerto Rico. You can rent a cabin at the Monte del Estado national park, or just spend the day in its swimming pool fed by mountain streams.

Throughout the northwest beach towns, there are a few top-level properties, several modestly priced and attractive hotels and guesthouses, and a few noteworthy *paradores,* privately operated country inns approved by the Puerto Rico Tourism Company that choose to participate in its joint promotion program.

This western part of Puerto Rico contains the greatest concentration of *paradores,* along the coast and in the cool mountainous interior of the west. They're a wonderful escape from pollution and traffic on a hot day.

Mona Island can also be explored from the coast near Mayagüez. It's one of the island's biggest adventure jaunts in Puerto Rico, and shouldn't be missed.

MAYAGÜEZ ★

98 miles (158km) W of San Juan; 15 miles (24km) S of Aguadilla

Approaching from the north, where Hwy. 2 swoops down along beautiful coastal overpasses, it's easy to dismiss Mayagüez at first glimpse as a rather drab commercial port city, but the so-called "Sultan of the West" tends to win over visitors who give it a chance to show off its charms.

Despite outward appearances as a city, Mayagüez makes for a convenient stopover for those exploring the west coast.

Mayagüez

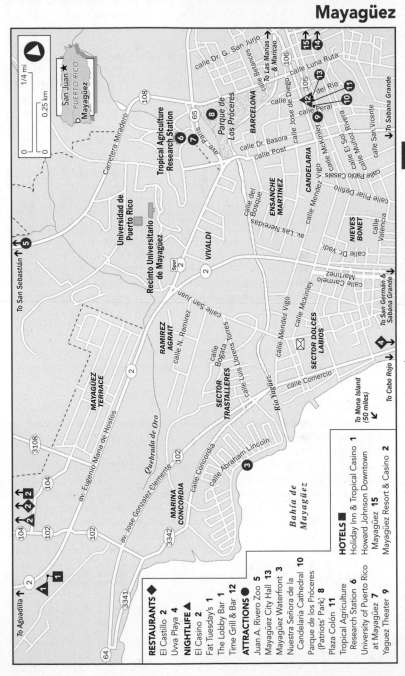

San Juan ★
PUERTO RICO
Mayagüez ●

1/4 mi
0.25 km

calle Dr. G. San Jurio
calle Betances
BARCELONA
To Las Marías
& Maricao
calle Luna Ruta
15
14
106
105
del Rio
13
11
calle Jose de Diego
calle Peral
calle Dr. Basora
calle Post
CANDELARIA
calle El Sol
calle Munõz Rivera
calle San Vicente
To Sabana Grande
10
9
12
calle Sabana Grande
To San Sebastián
5
Carretera Miradero
Tropical Agriculture
Research Station
ave. París
65
Parque de
Los Próceres
8
7
6
Universidad de
Puerto Rico
ENSANCHE
MARTINEZ
calle del
Bosque
calle Mendez Vigo
calle Pablo Casals
calle Pilar Defilio
NIEVES
BONET
calle
Valencia
Recinto Universitario
de Mayagüez
Spur
2
VIVALDI
2
av. Las Nereidas
calle Dr. Vadi
calle
San Juan
calle Carmelo
Martínez
To San Germán &
Sabana Grande
RAMIREZ
AGRAIT
calle N. Ramirez
calle
Bogota
calle McKinley
SECTOR DOLCES
LABIOS
4
To Cabo Rojo
MAYAGÜEZ
TERRACE
2
av. Eugenio María de Hostos
Quebrada de Oro
SECTOR
TRASTALLERES
calle Luis Llorens Torres
calle Mendez Vigo
Rio Yagüez
calle Comercio
3
3108
104
102
102
102
102
3342
MARINA
CONCORDIA
calle Concordia
calle Abraham Lincoln
av. José Gonzalez Clemente
To Mona Island
(50 miles)
Bahía de
Mayagüez
To Aguadilla
2
1
3341
64

RESTAURANTS ◆
El Castillo **2**
Uvva Playa **4**

NIGHTLIFE ▲
El Casino **2**
Fat Tuesday's **1**
The Lobby Bar **1**
Time Grill & Bar **12**

ATTRACTIONS ●
Juan A. Rivero Zoo **5**
Mayagüez City Hall **13**
Mayagüez Waterfront **3**
Nuestra Señora de la
Candelaria Cathedral **10**
Parque de los Próceres
(Patriots' Park) **8**
Plaza Colón **11**
Tropical Agriculture
Research Station **6**
University of Puerto Rico
at Mayagüez **15**
Yaguez Theater **9**

HOTELS ■
Holiday Inn & Tropical Casino **1**
Howard Johnson Downtown
Mayagüez **15**
Mayagüez Resort & Casino **2**

If you want a big-wave beach with dramatic coastal cliffs, you can head north to Rincón, Aguadilla, and Isabella (see Rincón, later). And if you want white sand and palms, with tranquil aquamarine water, head south to Cabo Rojo, Lajas, and Guánica (see chapter 7).

Famed for the size and depth of its **harbor** (the second largest on the island, after San Juan's harbor), Mayagüez was built to control the **Mona Passage,** a route essential to the Spanish Empire when Puerto Rico and the nearby Dominican Republic were vital trade and defensive jewels in the Spanish crown. Today this waterway is notorious for the destructiveness of its currents, the ferocity of its sharks, and the thousands of boat people who arrive illegally from either Haiti or the Dominican Republic, both on the island of Hispaniola.

Queen Isabel II of Spain recognized Mayagüez's status as a town in 1836. Her son, Alfonso XII, granted it a city charter in 1877. Permanently isolated from the major commercial developments of San Juan, Mayagüez, like Ponce, has always retained its own distinct identity.

Today the town has been hit by the closure of its tuna packing industry (which once packed 60 percent of the tuna consumed in the United States) and its manufacturing plants, victims to the exodus of jobs to countries where labor can be bought at a cheaper price.

But the town has a future in tourism and in some of the life science and high-tech manufacturing springing up around the fine University of Puerto Rico Mayagüez campus, which specializes in engineering and the sciences. The university community adds much to the city's cultural life.

Puerto Rico invested some $400-million on public-works projects surrounding the hosting in the city of 2010 Caribbean and Central American Games, and an outdoor natatorium on the UPR campus, an overhauled sports stadium and coliseum, and a pedestrian park unfolding along the city's west coast, are among the attractions that still stand today and add to the appeal of Mayaguez.

Essentials

GETTING THERE   **Cape Air** (© **800/227-3247;** www.capeair.com) flies from San Juan to Mayagüez four times daily (flying time: 30 min.). Round-trip passage starts at $106 per person, and can run as high as $246.

If you rent a car at the San Juan airport and want to drive to Mayagüez, it's fastest to take the northern route that combines sections of the newly expanded De Diego Expressway, Rte. 22, with the older Rte. 2. Estimated driving time for a local resident is about 120 minutes, although newcomers usually take about 30 minutes longer. The southern route, which combines the modern Luis A Ferré Expressway, Rte. 52 with transit across the outskirts of historic Ponce, and final access into Mayagüez via the southern section of Rte. 2, requires a total of about 3 hours and affords some worthwhile scenery across the island's mountainous interior.

GETTING AROUND   **Taxis** meet arriving planes. If you take one, negotiate the fare with the driver first, because cabs are unmetered here.

There are branches of **Avis** (© **787/832-0406**), **Budget** (© **787/832-4570**), and **Hertz** (© **787/832-3314**) at the Mayagüez airport.

VISITOR INFORMATION   The **Mayagüez Municipal Tourism Development Office** (© **787/832-5882**) can help orient visitors. In Aguadilla's Rafael Hernández Airport, there is also a **Puerto Rico Tourism Company** office (© **787/890-3315**). If you're starting out in San Juan, you can inquire there before you set out (see "Visitor Information," under "Orientation," in chapter 5).

Exploring the Area
MAYAGÜEZ ATTRACTIONS

The area surrounding the city's elegant central Plaza Colón is among the prettiest in the city, with several restored historic buildings. A bronze monument of Christopher Columbus atop a globe surrounded by 16 female statues dominates the plaza, which is also marked by mosaic tiled walkways and gurgling fountains, blooming tropical gardens, and squat leafy trees.

The neo-Corinthian **Mayagüez City Hall** and the **Nuestra Señora de la Candelaria,** which has gone through several incarnations since the first building went up in 1780, are noteworthy buildings right off the plaza.

Make sure to stroll down nearby **Calle McKinley,** home to the fabulous, recently restored **Yaguez Theater.** The neoclassical jewel served as both an opera and a silent movie house and is still in active use today. Originally inaugurated in 1909, a fire destroyed the structure in 1919, but it was rebuilt. The city's smashing Art Deco post office is also located here.

Mayagüez's historic waterfront district, with a restored 1920s Custom House and rows of neat warehouses, is also worth a look. The century-old **University of Puerto Rico Mayagüez** campus is also beautiful.

To soak in the magical sunsets of the Puerto Rican west coast, either head to the hills surrounding the city or down to the lineal coastal park that was built as part of multiple capital works projects for the city's hosting of the 2010 Caribbean and Central American Games.

Juan A. Rivero Zoo ★ ZOO   As the only zoo in Puerto Rico, this 14-acre (5.7-hectare) attraction is worth a stop if you're traveling with kids. The birdhouse has a nifty elevated walkway allowing visitors to look down on colorful tropical birds (there are also nonlocal species, such as eagles, hawks, and owls). Surprisingly, the Zoo features an "African safari" exhibit (giraffe, lions, elephants, zebras, and rhinos) along with areas devoted to Puerto Rico's animals (including the jaguar). You can see the entire zoo in 2 hours.

Rte. 108, Barrio Miradero, Mayagüez Union. www2.pr.gov/agencias/cdpn/zoologico/Pages/default.aspx. ⓒ **787/834-8110.** Admission $13 adults, $8 children and seniors, free children 4 and under and seniors 75 or older. Parking $3. Wed–Sun and holidays 8:30am–4pm.

The Tropical Agricultural Research Station ★★ PARK/GARDEN   Not a botanical garden per se, this is a working research facility of the U.S. Department of Agriculture that just happens to be a gorgeous, and wonderfully serene, arboretum. At the administration office, ask for a free map of the complex, which encompasses a huge collection of tropical plant species intended for practical use, including cacao, fruit trees, spices, bamboo, timbers, and ornamentals from across the globe. Tree huggers will be in seventh heaven. It's located on Rte. 65, between Post Street and Rte. 108, adjacent to the University of Puerto Rico Mayagüez campus and across the street from the **Parque de los Próceres (Patriots' Park).**

2200 Av. Pedro Albizu Campos. ⓒ **787/831-3435.** Free admission. Mon–Fri 9am–5pm.

BEACHES & WATERSPORTS

Nearly the entire west coast has great beaches except for Mayagüez, but beach lovers might consider staying here if they want to explore several different beaches. That's because the city perhaps alone puts visitors in such easy reach of the tranquil Caribbean waters to its south, or the rough surfing paradise to its north.

Trips to either area, which can be combined with, say, a day of sailing and snorkeling or windsurfing lessons, can be arranged through either of the large hotels. Or refer to the destination location either below (for the north) or chapter 10 for the south.

Where to Stay

Holiday Inn & Tropical Casino ★
A frill-free but comfortable, full-service hotel, the Holiday Inn is an affordable option that's conveniently located in the center of Mayagüez. The interior, which attempts a modern tropical look, strikes me as a bit cold, but public areas, and guestrooms, especially bathrooms and beds, pass muster. The lobby bar, hotel restaurants, and casino are all appealing and usually draw crowds, especially on weekends when live music is played.

2701 Rte. 2, Km 149.9, Mayagüez. © **800/465-4329** or 787/833-1100. www.hidpr.com. 142 units. $112–$120 double; $145 suite. Free parking. **Amenities:** Restaurant; 2 bars; casino; gym; outdoor pool; room service; rooms for those w/limited mobility; free Wi-Fi.

Howard Johnson Downtown Mayagüez ★
Don't let the HoJo name fool you; this Spanish colonial charmer on Plaza Colón is the most authentic lodging in town and has the most character. The former monastery is right in the heart of the historic part of the city, with the superb Ricomini Café across the street (guests get a free continental breakfast there). A tiny pool is in the courtyard and the large rooms are very clean and comfortable, if a bit dark (but that may be good for sleeping).

Calle Mendez Vigo Este 57, Mayagüez. © **787/832-9191.** www.hojo.com. 35 units. $110–$130 double, $165 suite, 2 percent resort fee. Rates include continental breakfast at neighboring bakery. Free parking. **Amenities:** Pool; 1 room for those w/limited mobility, free Wi-Fi.

Mayagüez Resort & Casino ★
The outdoor areas are the lure here: Set on a hill, in the midst of 20 lush acres of colorful tropical plants and trees (including rare species, such as a Sri Lankan cinnamon tree), this resort has a swell river pool, with slides, that unfolds beneath towering palms and between giant boulders. Indoors, well—rooms and public areas are clean but in sore need of renovation and the Wi-Fi is iffy. That being said the on-site El Castillo restaurant has good food, which gets even better at night. The property is located close to the University of Puerto Rico local campus, the zoo, and the downtown historic district.

Rte. 104, Km 0.3 Mayagüez. © **888/689-3030** or 787/832-3030. www.mayaguezresort.com. 140 units. $215–$290 double; $365 suite. Resort fee $20 per night. Parking $5. **Amenities:** 2 restaurants; 3 bars; casino; babysitting; small fitness room; Jacuzzi; playground; children's pool; Olympic-size pool; room service; steam room; 3 tennis courts; rooms for those w/limited mobility; Wi-Fi.

Where to Eat

Gonzalez Seafood Restaurant ★★★
SEAFOOD
The owner (yes, his last name is Gonzalez) is a smiling but serious presence here, as he roams this shorefront restaurant, making sure that both the food and the service impress. They usually do, whether you order the excellent grilled red snapper or what we consider to be one of the best paellas in Puerto Rico. Both the outdoor tables, and those in the glassed–in terrace over the water, get wonderful sunset views, so time your meal accordingly.

Carr 102 Km 6.6 Bo Guanajibo, Mayagüez. © **787/265-7497.** $10–$30. Daily 8am–10pm.

Uva Playa Restaurante ★
INTERNATIONAL
A stylish but relaxed spot, Uva Playa brings waterfront dining to the city with large windows that look out over the sea

MONA ISLAND: THE galápagos OF PUERTO RICO

Located off of Mayagüez, about halfway between Puerto Rico and the Dominican Republic, **Isla Mona** ★★★ is an Edeni, totally undeveloped island, teeming with giant iguanas, three species of endangered sea turtles, red-footed boobies, and countless other seabirds. It features a tabletop plateau with mangrove forests and cacti, giving way to dramatic 200-foot-high (61m) limestone cliffs that rise above the water and encircle much of Mona.

Snorkelers, spelunkers, biologists, and eco-tourists find much to fascinate them in Mona's wildlife, mangrove forests, coral reefs, and complex honeycomb, which is the largest marine-originated cave in the world. The island is also blessed with miles of secluded white-sand beaches and palm trees.

Uninhabited today, Mona was for centuries the scene of considerable human activity. The pre-Columbian Taíno Indians were the first to establish themselves here. Later, pirates used it as a base for their raids, followed by guano miners, who removed the rich crop fertilizer from Mona's caves. Columbus landed on Mona during his 1494 voyage, and Ponce de León spent several days here en route to becoming governor of Puerto Rico in 1508. The notorious pirate Captain Kidd used Mona as a temporary hideout.

Mona can be reached by organized tour from Mayagüez, and only 100 visitors are allowed on the island at a time. Camping is available for $10 per night. Everything needed, including water, must be brought in, and everything, including garbage, must be taken out.

For more information, call the **Puerto Rico Department of Natural and Environmental Resources** at ℂ **787/ 999-2200.**

To reach the island, it's best to go with a tour operator who can secure permits and provide overnight supplies. **Adventures Tourmarine,** Rte. 102, Km 14.1, Playa Joyuda, Cabo Rojo (ℂ **787/ 255-2525;** www.tourmarinepr.com). Captain Elick Hernández operates boat charters to Mona with a minimum of 10 passengers, each paying about $150 for a round-trip day adventure. **Acampa Nature Adventures,** Av. Piñero 1221, San Juan (ℂ **787/706-0659;** www. acampapr.com), runs a 4-day, 3-night trip to Mona, which includes all equipment, meals, and guides. The trips are run in groups with a 10-person limit. Price depends on how many people are in the group. San Juan dive shops, such as **Ocean Sports,** Av. Isla Verde 77 (ℂ **787/ 268-2329**), will also run dive trips off Mona Island. However you plan to get there, make your reservations well in advance.

Warning: The passage over is extremely rough, and many passengers prone to seasickness take Dramamine the night before the boat ride. There is no bottled water on the island, so bring your own. Also bring food, mosquito repellent, and even toilet paper. Alcoholic drinks are forbidden. While Mona's uninhabited landscape and surrounding turquoise water are beautiful, this can also be a dangerous, unforgiving place. In 2001, a Boy Scout got lost and died from hypothermia; in 2005, a psychologist suffered the same fate.

and an outdoor terrace with tables right at the edge of the beach. The food and service match the lovely locale with a menu that's heavy on seafood, including a *cazuela* of Caribbean lobster, fresh catch of the day, and a wide array of shellfish. For land lovers there's roast chicken with *guayaba* sauce and pork loin. Uva also offers a long list of appetizers (try the beer-marinated ribs or smoked salmon cakes) and tasty pizzettas and burgers. Wash it all down with one of their famed mojitos.

Guanajibo Blvd 552, Mayagüez. ☎ **787/652-3266.** $10–$30. Thurs–Sat 5–11pm, Sun 11am–8pm.

Mayagüez Nightlife

Time Grill & Bar ★   Right off Plaza Colon, this sports bar and restaurant offers well-priced drinks and basic pub grub in a relaxed atmosphere. There is frequent live music on weekends, pool, sports on TV, and fab views from the balconies. It's a favorite of the city's university students. Open Monday to Saturday 7pm to 2am. Calle Méndez Vigo Este 11, behind Plaza Colón, Mayagüez. ☎ **787/652-4757.**

El Casino ★   Saturday evening is the best night to hit the Mayagüez Resort's casino, which mixes entertainment with its games of chance. There is always something happening at its Player's Bar, making this as much a social scene as a gambling haven. Open 24 hours. At the Mayagüez Resort & Casino, Rte. 104. ☎ **787/832-3030.**

Fat Tuesday's ★   A fun spot in this west coast town, which embraces the Mardi Gras philosophy with frozen daiquiris and good times. Open daily 5pm to 2am. At the Holiday Inn & Tropical Casino Mayagüez, Rte. 104. ☎ **787/833-1100.**

The Lobby Bar ★   The Holiday Inn's main lobby bar has a convivial happy hour and frequent live music, which attracts local professionals as well as tourists. There's also an entrance to the Tropical Casino. Open daily 5pm to 2am. At the Holiday Inn & Tropical Casino Mayagüez, Rte. 104. ☎ **787/833-1100.**

RINCÓN

100 miles (161km) W of San Juan; 6 miles (9.7km) N of Mayagüez

North of Mayagüez lies the resort town of Rincón, the first of a string of beach destinations you'll encounter as you head north, but not the closest, as the town lies at the western end of a piece of land jutting off the coast.

I always lose my bearings driving to and around Rincón, and any GPS system you are relying on will surely go haywire (basically giving a different direction each time you punch in the locations). That's probably as it should be as you drive a jumble of circuitous country roads over the verdant spine of La Cadena Hills to reach the town, the center of which eludes most visitors, who head to the guesthouses and hotels along the coast. Rincón sits on a flattened peninsula of land jutting off Puerto Rico's western coast, so there's water on three sides, which also has a confusing effect.

Rincón long ago stopped being that sleepy coastal village attracting surfers and bohemian travelers from around the world. They, of course, are still coming, but a building boom has brought a wave of new condos, hotels, and luxury vacation residence projects, which has attracted more and more visitors here over the last decade. In fact, the town is beginning to worry about the pace of development and its effect on the beautiful natural resources here.

There's still a lot of space to get lost in, though, with the surrounding hills on one side, and water on the town's other three borders. Rincón dates from the 16th century, when a landowner allowed poor families to set down roots on his land. It was a sleepy agricultural town for centuries afterwards. It eventually gained fame as the Caribbean's best surfing spot, a fact reinforced by its hosting the World Surfing Championship in 1968. It remains the surfing capital of the Caribbean, a center for expat North Americans, and a tourist magnet.

Western Puerto Rico & the Northwest Coast

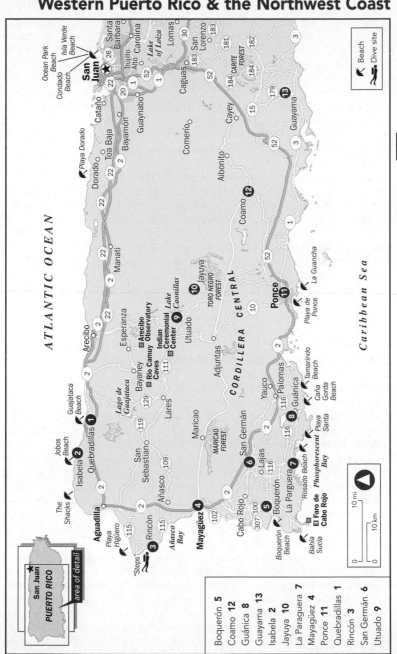

Boquerón **5**
Coamo **12**
Guánica **8**
Guayama **13**
Isabela **2**
Jayuya **10**
La Parguera **7**
Mayagüez **4**
Ponce **11**
Quebradillas **1**
Rincón **3**
San Germán **6**
Utuado **9**

With over a dozen beaches in town, great surfing, sailing, and snorkeling, and an ever better nightlife and cultural scene, it's not hard to see why. It continues evolving as a destination, reinforcing the fact it's one of the best stops to make in Puerto Rico.

There was a time when nonsurfers visited Rincón for only one reason: the Horned Dorset Primavera Hotel, not only one of the finest hotels in Puerto Rico, but one of the best in the entire Caribbean. Now there are several reasons for them to come.

Surfing & Other Outdoor Pursuits

There are 8 miles (13km) of beachfront in Rincón, and each little spot seems to have its own name: **Las Maria's, Indicator, Domes, the Point, Steps/Tres Palmas, Dog Man's.** The reasons behind the names are also varied. One stems from the hulk of an abandoned nuclear power plant just off the beach, another for an old man who lived nearby.

Part of the town's appeal is that it has both rough surfing beaches and tranquil Caribbean coastal areas. Along the north side of Rincón, the Atlantic coast gets large, powerful waves, while other beaches are tranquil, perfect for snorkeling. Yet many beaches provide both, depending on the time of year.

During winter, uninterrupted swells from the North Atlantic form perfect waves, averaging 5 to 6 feet (1.5–1.8m) in height, with rideable rollers sometimes reaching 15 to 20 feet (4.6–6.1m). In 2008, a rare winter storm created 25- to 30-foot (7.6–9.1m) waves here that had local surfers musing whether it was the biggest surf ever. On the southern side of Rincón, the ocean is calm, and long, wide sand beaches unfold with swaying palm trees along them.

The best surfing beaches include **Las Maria's, Spanish Wall,** and **Domes** near the town lighthouse on the north side. **Córcega** is probably the best of the Caribbean beaches. Some beaches, meanwhile, can show different faces at different times of the year. For instance, **Steps,** which is also named **Tres Palmas,** is a great surfing beach in winter, but in summer is calm and one of the best spots for snorkeling. It was recently named a natural marine reserve.

Visitors need to proceed with caution during winter when venturing into the surf off Rincón, which can be particularly strong, with powerful riptides and undertows that routinely cause drownings. This should not stop visitors from coming here, however. The town has beaches with both tranquil and strong surf. Just proceed with caution and ask locals about surf conditions.

Windsurfing, and, increasingly, kite-boarding are also extremely popular here, with **Sandy Beach** a favored site because it does not have the rocks found on the ocean floor that some of the other beaches in the area have. Also, from December to February, it gets almost constant winds every day. Windsurfers wait on the terrace of Tamboo Tavern (see "Where to Eat," later in this chapter) for the right wind conditions before hitting the beach.

Excellent scuba, snorkeling, parasailing, and sailing are also available in Rincón, making it one of the most active of Caribbean destinations.

Endangered humpback whales winter here, attracting a growing number of whale-watchers from December to March. The lighthouse at El Faro Park is a great place to spot these mammoth mammals.

Rincón remains a mecca for surfing aficionados, but it's also a great place to learn the sport. Learn from the best, local surfing expert Ramses Morales, through his **Surf Lessons Puerto Rico & Adventure Co.** (© 787/617-4731; www.surflessonspuerto rico.com). Rates start at $75 for 2-hours, $100 for half-day, and $175 for a full day.

Private lessons start at $90. Ramses is among the most respected local surfers, and he knows where the best spot from among the multitude of surf breaks on any given day, depending on the particular expectations of his clients. He's great with beginners, but can also help kick up the game of the most experienced surfers. He's a serious teacher, who places an emphasis on safety, and has certifications as a surf instructor and in first aid and rescue.

The **Rincón Surf School** (P.O. Box 1333, Rincón; © 787/823-0610) offers beginners lessons or can teach surfers how to improve their performance. One lesson costs $95, and there are also 2-day ($180), 3-day ($260), and 5-day ($390) packages. A private 2-hour lesson is $150, $75 each for two people. The school also arranges surf vacation packages in conjunction with the Casa Verde Guesthouse. **Puntas Surf School** (P.O. Box 4319, HC-01 Calle Vista del Mar; © 787/366-1689 or 939/697-8040) is another great option. Melissa Taylor, and a group of surf professionals whose love of the sport is infectious, they say they can teach would-be surfers of any age, from 5 to 105. Private lessons cost $50 per hour, $85 for 2 hours. Group rates are $40 per person per hour, and package deals are also available. Board rentals are $25 per day, $60 for 3 days, $100 for a week. A professional photographer takes pictures, which you can purchase after your lesson.

You can't get closer to walking on water than on the 2-hour paddleboard tour run out of the **Mar Azul Surf Shop,** Rte. 413, Km 4.5, Bo Puntas (© 787/823-5692). When conditions are right, you can stare into the colorful world of coral reefs and tropical fish shimmering beneath the clear Caribbean Sea that your board gently cuts through. The **West Coast Surf Shop,** Muñoz Rivera 2E, Rincón (© 787/823-3935), is another of the more established of the many surfing outfitters in town. Both are open daily 9am to 6pm. The shops rent surfing equipment and give lessons. **Hot Wavz Surf Shop,** Maria's Beach (© 787/823-3942), also rents long boards, as well as boogie boards. Prices for board rentals start at around $25 daily. Snorkeling gear can also be rented at these shops.

Good snorkeling can be found just off the beach. When conditions are right, **Steps/ Tres Palmas** is a great spot. Scuba divers and snorkeling enthusiasts will also want to head out to **Desecheo Island,** the large mass of land seen offshore from Rincón looking west. A quick half-hour boat trip, the small island is a nature reserve with great coral formations and large reef fish. Visibility is 100-plus feet (30m), and average water temperature is between 80° and 86°F (27°–30°C).

One of the most popular local scuba outfitters is **Taíno Divers,** Calle Black Eagle 564, Black Eagle Marina at Rincón (© 787/823-6429; www.tainodivers.com), which offers local boat charters along with scuba and snorkeling trips. A 6-hour snorkeling trip to Desecheo Island is $95; a 2-tank dive is $129, plus $25 for equipment rental; a beginner scuba course is $170. Prices include gourmet sandwiches and drinks. Trips depart at 8am and return at 2pm. They also offer sunset cruises for $50.

Makaira Fishing Charters (© 787/823-4391 or 787/299-7374; www.fishrinconpr. com) offers fishing charters from a no-frills, tournament-rigged, 35-foot Contender. Half-day rates for up to four people are $575, full-day $850; for up to six, $629 or $925. **Moondog Charters** (© 787/823-3059) also runs fishing excursions and dive charters aboard a 32-foot Albermarle Express Sport Fisherman.

Katarina Sail Charters (© 787/823-7245; www.sailrinconpuertorico.com) has daily sailing trips aboard a 32-foot catamaran. The day sail (from around 10:20am–2:30pm) consists of some fine cruising, a stop for a swim and snorkel, and then lunch. It costs $75, $38 for children 12 and under. The sunset sail ($55 for adults and $28 for kids) leaves at 4:30pm and returns after sunset about 2 hours later. Watching the western sun set while sailing and listening to great music is wonderful, with rum punch, beer, and nonalcoholic drinks included in the price.

Most hotels on the beach have good watersports rentals, but we like **Coconut Water Sports** (℃ 787/309-9328; www.villacofresi.com/havefun.php), over at Corcega Beach, on the town's southern Caribbean shore. You can do it all, whether you want to jet ski ($60 for a half hour), or paddle board or kayak ($15–$20 per hour). The banana boat ride ($12 per person) is 20 minutes of fun. **Flying Fish Parasail** (℃ 787/823-2359;** www.parasailpr.com) runs parasailing trips ($75 per person) and snorkeling adventures out of the Black Eagle Marina. **Capital Water Sports Xtreme Rentals** (℃ 787/823-2789) at Sunset Village by the public beach also rents watersports equipment, including jet skis and small boats, and gives banana boat tow rides and runs water skiing trips.

The most visible and sought-after whale-watching panorama in Rincón is **Parque El Faro de Rincón** (Rincón Lighthouse Park), which lies on El Faro Point peninsula at the extreme western tip of town. Within its fenced-in perimeter are pavilions that sell souvenirs and snack items, rows of binoculars offering 25¢ views, and a stately looking lighthouse built in 1921. The park is at its most popular from December to March for whale-watching, and in January and February for surfer gazing. The park is locked every evening between midnight and 7am. Otherwise, you're free to promenade with the locals any time you like.

The park's snack bar is called **Restaurant El Faro,** Barrio Puntas, Carretera (Rte.) 413, Km 3.3 (no phone), which serves basic Puerto Rican fare and burgers. Best for a drink or ice cream.

Julie, at **Pintos "R" Us** (℃ 787/516-7090), is Rincón's resident cowgirl, and she gives a 2-hour ride along beautiful beaches and coastal headland. Julie and her gentle horses also ride through forest and along country roads that wind past cattle grazing on oceanfront plantation fields, as well as such local landmarks as the town's lighthouse and shuttered nuclear plant that today houses a museum. The standard tour is 2 hours, but there are also half-day, full-day, and full-moon rides. Prices range from $55 to $185. Julie is a great tour guide, and because she knows everyone in town, you will meet a lot of them along the way. Julie also runs a nonprofit to care for animals, including horses, who have been rescued from abusive situations. Riders meet at the Black Eagle Marina for tours.

The Rincón Town Skate Park (℃ 787/823-2899) is an indoor skate park downtown that charges $5 per session and rents all needed equipment for $15.

Work out at **La Paz Pilates and Yoga Studio** (℃ 787/823-2885), a downtown studio offering both affordable group workouts and private lessons. They also give and teach massage. A great, well-run spot where everybody knows what they are doing. It's located in the heart of downtown, next to the Post Office. Classes are given in the morning and the early evening. Drop-in rate for a class is $10, 3-pack $25, private lesson $45 per hour. A massage is $50 for 30 minutes, or $75 for an hour.

Where to Stay
EXPENSIVE

Horned Dorset Primavera ★★★   Set in a dreamscape of 8 acres of coastline and lush gardens, this Relais & Châteaux hotel is a luxury compound of incredible style and natural beauty. Built on the ruins of a century-old coastal railroad, the property encompasses a main plantation home, Spanish villas, and seafront terraces overlooking the coastline and lush grounds. The large residences have private oceanfront plunge pools and verandas, and weave a beautiful tapestry of Moroccan, Asian, and European influences throughout the stylish rooms with antique four-poster beds and sofas, marble bathrooms, Persian rugs, and fine linens. The pool is set in a sunken garden and there is a yoga studio that looks like a rarified treehouse. This is one of Puerto Rico's most stunning properties, perfect for a romantic getaway. Even if you don't stay here, consider dinner or lunch at either of its two exceptional restaurants (see below), just to experience a bit of the splendor.

Apt 1132, Rincón. ⓒ **800/633-1857** or 787/823-4030. www.horneddorset.com. 55 units. Winter $770 suites, $1,185 residences; holidays $1,170 suites, $1,685 residences; off-season $470 suites, $880 residences. 15 percent hotel fee. Free parking. No children 11 and under. **Amenities:** 2 restaurants; bar; fitness center; kayaking (free); library; massage; 3 outdoor pools (1 infinity); room service; Wi-Fi.

Rincón Beach Resort ★★
The open air lobby of this secluded resort looks out on a turquoise infinity pool that stretches across the private stretch of Almirante Beach that fronts the hotel, with gentle lapping surf and the chatter of birds and *coquís* filling the air. And in the first minutes of your stay, you can see why you've picked this place. It's certainly not for the rooms, which are spacious (especially the one- and two-bedroom apartments), but sparsely decorated in a manner that can only be charitably described as dated. That being said, all are close to the beach and pool, which is why you're here. The restaurant, Brisas (see below) draws locals as well as visitors, especially for its $20 steak nights every Monday through Wednesday. The resort is a bit removed from the center of Rincón, so you'll need a car to explore the area.

Rte. 115, Km 5.8, Añasco. ⓒ **866/598-0009** or 787/589-9000. www.rinconbeach.com. 118 units. Double $181–$215, Suites $365–$525. Free parking. **Amenities:** Restaurant; bar; gym; outdoor pool; meeting rooms; rooms for those w/limited mobility, free Wi-Fi in common areas.

Rincón of the Seas Grand Caribbean Hotel ★
Another beachfront property, with lush grounds and a mix of Caribbean and Art Deco style, the hotel is set on one of the area's nicest beaches. The poolside bar is a lot of fun, and the property attracts a diverse crowd of locals along with visitors, which adds to the appeal. The Art Deco areas are the nicest, but also the most expensive; beach cabanas are more private and have better views than the standard guestrooms, which frankly, could use a bit of TLC (they're not dirty, just well worn). The hotel's public areas and grounds have fabulous tropical flora throughout and towering palms.

Rte. 115, Km 12.2, Rincón. ⓒ **866/274-6266** or 787/823-7500. www.rinconoftheseas.com. 112 units. $165–$175 double; $295 Art Deco suite. Free parking. **Amenities:** 2 restaurants; 2 bars; outdoor pool; meeting rooms and ballroom; rooms for those w/limited mobility; free Wi-Fi.

MODERATE

Casa Isleña Inn ★★★
This cozy, lovingly maintained inn is among my favorite spots in Puerto Rico. The service is warm and personal, the inn is right on the beach and the rooms, housed in a hacienda-style residence with mosaic patios and terraces, feature tropical colors, and fine woodwork. They're not overly fancy, but large and very comfortable. With just nine rooms, there's always plenty of space to splash around in the pool or swim serious laps, and plenty of lounge chairs available, whether you're looking for sun or shade. On property is a small bar and tapas restaurant with tables under a veranda, which is also where breakfast is served. Try for one of the second-floor rooms, which have better breezes and views. The best rooms are 203 and 254 and only cost an additional $20 per night.

Barrio Puntas Carretera Interior 413, Km 4, Rincón. ℂ **888/289-7750** or 787/823-1525. www. casaislena.com. 9 units (shower only). Winter $165–$205 double, off-season $125–$165 double. Extra person $25. Free parking. **Amenities:** Beach; pool; restaurant; bar; 1 room for those w/limited mobility; free Wi-Fi.

La Rosa Inglesa ★★   You'll be longing for this English beauty long after you have left Rincón, and your relationship with breakfast will never be the same again. This charming bed-and-breakfast, run by an expat British couple, has three plush units (a double, a suite, and a larger apartment) with a pool and attractive grounds. The view from the property is awe-inspiring as is the gourmet breakfast (see restaurant review, below) that is included with your stay. The only downside to staying here? The B&B is on top of a steep hill, which can be scary to drive at night.

Barrio Puntas, Carretera Interior 413, Km 2, Rincón. ℂ **787/823-4032.** $112 double; $145 suite; $210 apt. Rates include breakfast. Free parking. **Amenities:** Restaurant serving breakfast; bar; babysitting; pool; kitchenettes; room service; free Wi-Fi.

Lemontree Waterfront Cottages ★★   At these colorful, good-value seaside suites, you fall asleep with the sound and smell of the surf and wake up easily with its gentle murmuring. Yes, that's how close to the water you'll be. All the units have big terraces, kitchenettes, comfortable beds and colorful if simple furnishings, along with hotel amenities like cable TV, DVDs, and air conditioning. The Mango, Piña, and Papaya are the nicest units, all one-bedroom oceanfront suites. The Papaya can be combined with the most economic suite, the "Quenepa," to make a three-bedroom unit. The staff here are a wonderfully friendly and helpful bunch.

Rte. 4290, Rincón. ℂ **888/418-8733** or 787/823-6452. www.lemontreepr.com. 6 units. Winter $199–$215; summer $119–$149. Special rates for longer stays. Free parking. **Amenities:** Free Wi-Fi, kitchenettes.

Tres Sirenas Beach Inn ★★★   The "Three Mermaids" is named for the owner's three daughters, and this family-run B&B, is certainly a loving tribute. Tasteful West Indian and Spanish decor (teak furnishings, fresh flowers in conch shells, terra cotta tiles) make each of the five units feel special, as do their gorgeous sea views. The industrious staff can arrange anything you want to do, whether it's learning to surf or taking a yoga class by the pool. A hearty breakfast is served overlooking the ocean.

Sea Beach Dr. 26, Rincón. ℂ **787/823-0558.** www.tressirenas.com. 5 units. Winter $185–$290. Off-season $170–$260 Resort fee 7 percent. Free parking. **Amenities:** Hot tub, outdoor pool, room service, included breakfast, smoke-free rooms, free Wi-Fi.

INEXPENSIVE

The Lazy Parrot ★★   No, it doesn't look like much from the front, and it's not on the beach, but guests tend to fall in love with "The Parrot" nonetheless. The pool area and sun terrace is lovely and expansive, rooms are spacious, comfortable and rigorously well-maintained, and the service is very friendly. Add the fact that you have the wonderful Mi Familias restaurant (see below) right on site, a popular bar, and boutique and you get a property that is easily one of Rincón's best spots to stay. *Tip:* Pay a little extra for one of the upstairs "panoramic" rooms with a view of the Cadena Hills and the coast.

Rte. 413, Km 4.1, Barrio Puntas, Rincón. ℂ **800/294-1752** or 787/823-5654. www.lazyparrot.com. 21 units. $135 double value rooms; $175 double panoramic rooms. Resort fee 5 percent. Rates include continental breakfast. Parking available across the street. **Amenities:** 2 restaurants; bar; babysitting; pool; room service; free Wi-Fi common areas.

Villa Cofresi ★★   A family-run hotel right on a beautiful beach, Villa Cofresi is refreshingly down to earth, fun, and the most Puerto Rican experience in Rincón. The management and staff are friendly and helpful, and there are a pool and terrace overlooking the coast, with a vivacious bar and two nice restaurants. Rooms are not elegant, but they are clean, airy, and comfortable. There is a game room for kids, all sorts of watersports equipment for rent, sunset happy hours, and really tasty food.

Rte. 115, Km 12, Rincón. ℂ **787/823-2450.** www.villacofresi.com. 80 units. Double $145 high season, $101 low season. Suites $175 high season, $145 low season. Free parking. **Amenities:** Restaurant; bar; outdoor pool; room service; rooms for those w/limited mobility; free Wi-Fi.

Where to Dine
EXPENSIVE

Restaurant Aaron ★★★ FRENCH/CARIBBEAN   Tucked into the exceptional Horned Dorset Primavera Hotel, this beautiful restaurant overlooking the sea may be the most romantic spot for a meal in all of Puerto Rico. To reach the dining room, you walk through blooming tropical gardens and up a curving staircase that leads to the second floor where French doors and windows overlook the beachfront along the west coast's plushest hideaway. The menu changes often, but recent outstanding entrees have included *beurre rouge* Caribbean lobster tail, pistachio crusted rack of lamb, steak *au poivre,* and seared tuna with gnocchi. Appetizers are a must, including the pan-seared mango foie gras and beef tartare with white truffle oil. The restaurant also offers an expensive ($125 per person) but delicious tasting menu. **The Blue Room** is the more casual bistro on the first floor, but it's still a beauty, with dining areas open to the sea or the hypnotic gardens. It serves French, Puerto Rican, and light American fare, including everything from lamb Provençal to four seasons pizza.

In the Horned Dorset Primavera Hotel. ℂ **787/823-4030.** Reservations recommended. Entrees $29–$36; fixed-price tasting menu $125 for 13 courses. Wed–Sun 7–9:30pm.

Brasas Restaurant ★★ INTERNATIONAL   One of Rincón's finer dining experiences, the menu here has both classic and contemporary dishes served in a large and comfortable Spanish-style dining. There's an emphasis on Spanish and Puerto Rican flavors, and an excellent selection of steak and fresh seafood, plus a wine list with more than 300 titles. Start out with the Cioppino A La Brasas, a mix of sautéed shrimp, mussels, calamari, and fresh fish. The restaurant has a delicious pork chop in a guava rum sauces and grilled mahi-mahi in fresh tropical fruit sauce, or try one of the delicious pastas, like the grilled chicken fettuccine in a rosemary garlic cream sauce. Genuinely friendly service and a relaxed atmosphere add to the enjoyment.

Rte. 115, Km 5.8, Añasco. ℂ **787/589-9000.** Reservations recommended. Main courses $16–$30; breakfast buffet $15. Daily 7–10:30am and 5:30–10:30pm.

Francisco's Caribbean Local Cuisine ★★ PUERTO RICAN   The menu at the Lazy Parrot's main restaurant has a pan Caribbean focus that is heavily rooted in local cooking thanks to a new, and very impressive, chef in the kitchen. With fresh local herbs and produce driving the selections, the menu changes frequently, but you may find seared shrimp in a coconut-spice rum glaze with green rice, tuna in a mango salsa and garlic mashed potatoes, or grilled chicken with shallots and white wine on the menu. Some think the mofongo served here is the best on the island. The second floor restaurant also serves up panoramic views of the hotel's blooming grounds and the green hillsides surrounding the town.

Rte. 413, Km 4.1, Barrio Puntas, Rincón. ℂ **787/823-0101.** Main courses $13–$25. Daily 5:30–10pm.

La Copa Llena at Black Eagle ★★★ INTERNATIONAL An oceanfront spot with out-of-this-world food and some of the best views in town for sunset dining from the rustic bar fronted by an outdoor wooden terrace overlooking the ocean. You can make a meal off the creative small plates such as grilled octopus in a papaya salad, or Vietnamese grilled pork or quinoa fritters. Or go all in with such impressive entrees as coconut steamed mussels, lamb chops in salsa verde, and the incredible T-bone. Deserts like lava chocolate cake and mango sorbet ensure a strong finish. Weekend brunches (duck hash, crepes, and scrambled eggs with green chiles and tomatillos on corn tortillas) are also noteworthy, and there are daily happy hours from 3pm to sunset. This scene is quintessential Rincón.

At the Black Eagle Marina, off Rte. 413, Rincón. ℂ **787/823-0896.** Tapas $3–$16, main courses $16–$36, brunch $6–$14. Tues–Sun 3pm–midnight, brunch Sat–Sun 10am–2pm.

MODERATE

La Ana de Cofresi ★★ INTERNATIONAL Is there a better place to watch the sunset in Rincón? It certainly doesn't seem like there could be when you have a Coco Pirata ("Pirate Cocktail") in your hand. The atmosphere's always festive at this long-established favorite, especially at the bar. But you can get delish seafood, steaks, Puerto Rican food, and continental standards at good prices here, too, in the more formal dining room (the house special is a scrumptious plantain-crusted mahi mahi in cilantro cream sauce). The whole enterprise is a family-run affair, with a lot of heart.

At the Villa de Cofresi Hotel, Rd. 115, Km 12.0, Rincón. ℂ **787/823-2450.** Main courses $14–$43. Daily noon–10pm.

Tamboo Seaside Grill ★★ AMERICAN/CARIBBEAN There are few dining spots on the island as close to the sand as this one, and hip Tamboo takes full advantage of its unique location on a popular surfing beach with an expansive two-level deck set amidst the sand dunes and palm trees. It's a prime spot for both surfers and beach goers, and a great location for whale watching (not to mention people-watching). You can find just about everything on the menu, but those in the know stick to fresh seafood liked grilled Caribbean lobster and mahi mahi in caper sauce. Stand out starters include crispy calamari in a coconut chile sauce and plantain-crusted shrimp with chipotle-lime aioli. There are also inexpensive wraps, sandwiches, and salads. The friendly and professional owners also run the attached inn, **Beside the Pointe** (www.besidethe pointe.com/lodging.html), which offers clean, modern rooms within steps of all the surfing, beach, and bar action.

Rte. 413, Km 4, Sandy Beach, Rincón. ℂ **888/823-8550** or 787/823-8550. Reservations not accepted. Main courses $15–$44; wraps and sandwiches $7–$12. Bar daily noon–2am; restaurant Thurs–Tues noon–9:30pm.

INEXPENSIVE

BD Café ★★ CAFE Although it recently changed owners, and names, this spot still brings the sophistication of a big city cafe to the tropical paradise of Rincón. Expert hands make the rich gourmet coffee and pack the fresh herb tea. Smoothies, a specialty, mix everything from bananas to acai to agave. Throw in the delicious baked goods, and no wonder this is *the* spot to come after surfing the waves or diving in the sea. It's also a real great community center, with free Wi-Fi, newspapers and magazines; and locals willing to answer any question that might occur to a visitor.

Rte. 413, Km 4.1 (2 doors away from Lazy Parrot), Barrio Puntas, Rincón. ℂ **787/823-0963.** Smoothies from $4, coffee and tea from $3, baked goods and panini $3–$8. Wed–Mon 7am–4pm.

La Rosa Inglesa ★★★ BREAKFAST   La Rosa Ingles serves the best breakfast I can ever remember eating. Everything from the bread to the sausage to the tea and fruit preserves are handcrafted by the expat British owners, from the "Full Monty" (a classic Brit meal of eggs, stewed tomatoes, and mushrooms) to the "Dead Elvis" (French toast with caramelized bananas, cinnamon, and syrup). The turkey and sweet potato hash, with pancetta and rosemary, is another house favorites. You have to drive up an insanely steep road to get here, but that also means that the views from the dining room and terrace (breakfast is served in both spots) are awe-inspiring. Get here early as it does get crowded.

Barrio Puntas, Carretera Interior 413, Km 2, Rincón. ℂ **787/823-4032.** Breakfast $7–$12. Daily 8am–noon; closed Sept-Nov.

Mi Familias Pizzeria ★★ PIZZA/BAR   Truly gourmet pizza, as well as paninis and delicious burgers, are served in this delightful outdoor cafe set poolside at the Lazy Parrot Inn on a beautiful stone terrace. Baked in an authentic Italian-style brick oven, the pies are incredibly light and crisp. The bar makes wonderful sangria, mojitos, and other cocktails, and has a good stock of craft beer and wine options.

Lazy Parrot Inn, Rte. 413, Km 4.1, Barrio Puntas, Rincón. ℂ **787/823-0101.** Main course $9–$16. Daily 11:30am–10pm.

Rincón Nightlife

Happy hour starts in the late afternoon in Rincón, which is filled with great places to watch the sunset. Join the surfers for a "sundowner" at **Calypso's Tropical Bar,** Maria's Beach (ℂ 787/823-1626), which lies on the road to the lighthouse. Happy-hour specials are daily 5 to 7pm, and the bar stays open until the last customer leaves (usually long after midnight), but the party gets started early as the bar sits right behind the town's best beach.

Surfers flock to **Big Kahuna Burger Bar & Grill** at Casa Verde Guest House along Sandy Beach Road (ℂ 787/823-3756), which has delicious and economically priced burgers, jerk chicken, fresh fish sandwiches, and a variety of wings. There's a young crowd, really friendly staff, and live music several nights a week.

Tamboo Tavern (ℂ 787/823-8550) on Sandy Beach attracts young sun worshippers and surfers with the best mojitos and margaritas in town. It was named one of the best beach bars in America by both "Travel + Leisure" and "Esquire" magazines, as much for its laid back vibe as for its spectacular surf and sunset views. During the day it's the perfect spot for a break from the sun, and at night DJs, live bands, and popular music keep the crowds happy. The **Rum Shack** (ℂ 787/823-0101), at the Lazy Parrot, also draws a sizeable crowd of locals and travelers.

Bohio Beach Bar (ℂ 787/823-2450), which is located on the seaside deck of Villa Cofresi, is the spot for happy hour weekend fun, when the party gets going even before the sun goes down. One "pirate special," a rum and coconut drink, is enough to get you in the mood and you'll quickly merge into the fun-loving crowd. Friendly bartenders and wait staff, great music, and outdoor pool tables add to the experience.

AGUADILLA & THE NORTHWEST

Aguadilla is the biggest town on Puerto Rico's northwest corner, which is filled with great beaches and other natural blessings for an active vacation experience. And it makes a good base from which to explore the area, with lots of hotels, restaurants,

BEACH chic: SHOPPING IN RINCÓN

Nothing heralds Rincón's arrival as a real tourism destination more than the fact that it has developed a shopping culture. It's a west coast beach town, so surf shops still rule, but they're now as much about fashion as function. Nothing shows that more than **Natty Surf Boutique & Gallery** (✆ 787/823-7000, at Sunset Village), which has a large beach-fashion collection for women, an art gallery, and surfboards. **Sunset Village,** on Calle Cambija next to Rincón public beach, where Natty Surf is located, is a modern beachfront structure that's home to shops and restaurants and is near the town's public beach.

Perhaps nowhere is the upgrading of the Rincón retail scene more evident than at its traditional town square, which recently underwent a renovation. New restaurants and chic boutiques have opened alongside the Catholic Church, local bakery, and simple bars and cafe. There is also free Wi-Fi, surf, and tourist shops.

Several properties, from higher-end guest houses to the larger hotels, have upgraded their shops and are stocking fashionable clothes, island fine art, gourmet foods, and coffee, jewelry, and much more beyond basic necessities.

For anything from a sarong to a pair of sandals, head to the **Mango Beach Shop** (✆ 787/823-2100) in Puntas. The **Red Door Boutique** (✆ 720/289-5079), also in Puntas, is an inspired gift shop.

A number of galleries have also sprung up in town, some of single artists, some serious fine-art ventures, and others a mix of original art and jewelry and fashion items. One that stands out, The **Playa Oeste Tropical Surf Art Gallery & Gift Shop** Carretera (Rte.) 413, Km 0.5 (✆ 787/823-4424), has fine art, photography, jewelry, and other crafts.

If you want to really shop till you drop, head to Barceloneta where you'll find the **Prime Outlets,** 1 Prime Outlets Blvd. (✆ 787/846-5300), with more than 90 stores, including Coach, Adidas, Kenneth Cole, and Ralph Lauren, offer factory outlet prices at a beautiful outdoor mall that feels like a downtown village. It's open Monday through Saturday 9am to 9pm and Sunday 11am to 7pm. To get there, take PR 2 (Hwy. 2) north to Arecibo, and then take the De Diego Expressway 22 towards San Juan. Take the exit (salida) 55 in Barceloneta for the Prime Outlets.

good infrastructure, a fairly large mall, and lots of attractions, such as a water park and golf course.

Several airlines now run direct flights to the town's **Rafael Hernández Airport,** especially during the high season. It's the island's second largest international airport after Luis Muñoz Marín in San Juan; visitors who want to spend their whole vacation in the west don't need to go through San Juan. Puerto Rico's best surfing spots run from Rincón south of here, around the northwest corner to Isabela, and points east along the north coast.

The region also is near such major attractions as the **Arecibo Observatory** and the **Río Camuy Cave Park** (see chapter 6). In addition to its coast, there are mountain forests and lakes nearby. Aguadilla has an ice-skating rink, water park, and a very reasonably priced golf course, adding to its family appeal.

Crash Boat beach is popular, and gets crowded on weekends, but during the week it's usually quiet and picturesque. There are a few beach shacks and stands selling seafood, snacks, and cold drinks, and brightly colored wooden fishing boats are often parked on the beach. There's a former Navy fueling pier on the beach, where aquamarine water kisses the white sand. In winter, the northern end of the beach faces open water and is much rougher. Waves at Aguadilla's beaches are among the fiercest in the island, carrying in them the full force of the Atlantic. There are several fine surf breaks and beautiful beaches in town.

Aguadilla is more than its beaches. It's coming into its own in other ways. With an international airport, several offshore companies with operations here, and a large U.S. Coast Guard presence, it's one of the island's more prosperous areas. You can see this in the renovations taking place in Aguadilla's historic downtown waterfront district, and the continual growth in new hotels, restaurants, shops, and services for tourists each year.

The **Isabela** coastline is also beautiful. Narrow country roads weave between cliffs and white beaches, set off by dramatic rock formations and submerged coral reefs that send surf crashing skyward. This is an area of salt-water wells and blowholes, through which dramatic eruptions of saltwater spew from submerged sea caves. Several are found in the area known as **La Princesa,** and **Jobos Beach** is home to the most famous, **El Pozo de Jacinto,** which is located on a huge rock formation at the eastern end of Jobos Beach. There is a local legend surrounding the sinkhole, where the strong ocean currents blast through the huge opening, so that it has become something of a tourist attraction. Visitors should be warned, climbing out to see El Pozo can be very dangerous, as the rocks are slippery. They also must respect the power of the sea, as local riptides have caused the drowning deaths of many area swimmers.

Jobos Beach, the heart and soul of the Isabela-Aguadilla coastline, is a large beach with a famed surf break, which cuts from its eastern to western end, but swimmers can frolic along more protected areas along this mammoth shore. There are also guest-houses and restaurants here, and on summer and holiday weekends it's got a party atmosphere.

For many reasons, the eastern end of Jobos is the place to be. An area at the base of the rock formation is partially sheltered from the strong ocean currents and is the best place for casual bathing. Even if you want to surf, you can walk out to the end of the rock formation, as it's a point break here. Surfers catch waves that crash at an angle towards the coastline, so the waves stretch across Jobos Beach as they make their way to shore. There are a number of bars, beach shacks and street stands along the shore that serve cold beer, tasty fresh fish turnovers, and chicken kebabs. It's a fine town and can enjoyably rambunctious on holiday weekends.

Further east, **Montones Beach** has rock outcroppings and reefs that make a beguiling seascape and also protect the water from the raging surf in this area. You won't find the restaurants and bars here that you will in Jobos, but you can find your own secluded spot on the beach.

Area development, however, appears to be accelerating, and newly built condominiums and other properties have marred access to some beaches. There are still miles of open beachfront though, and most development is confined to small hotels and low-slung villas.

The good surfing, and increasingly the burgeoning northwest beach culture, extends east beyond Arecibo to Barceloneta and Manatí. East of Isabela, steep cliffs drop in flat jagged lines to the rough surf along the rugged Atlantic coastline of **Quebradillas. Guajataca Beach,** named after a powerful Taíno Indian chief, is a great spot, but think twice about swimming here. The currents are extremely powerful and dangerous, and while surfers love it, casual swimmers should proceed with caution. The white sand is as smooth as silk though, so it's a great spot for sunbathing and watching the surfers risking all and loving every minute of it. It's also a great spot for seashell collecting. The beach is also called **El Tunel** because there's a large abandoned railroad tunnel carved out of a mountain at the entrance to the beach. It was once part of a railroad that ran all around the Puerto Rico coast to haul sugar cane. There is a parking area here and a no-frills, open-air restaurant and bar. It's a nice shady spot, a cool respite from the sun-bleached beach.

Essentials

GETTING THERE & GETTING AROUND   Both JetBlue and Spirit airlines have nonstop flights from East Coast destinations, particularly from New York and Florida, direct to the **Rafael Hernández Airport** (Antigua Base Ramey, Hangar 405, Aguadilla; ✆ 787/891-2226). Many other flights offer connections from San Juan onto Aguadilla.

There are branches of **Avis** (✆ 787/890-3311), **Budget** (✆ 787/890-1110), and **Hertz** (✆ 787/833-3170) at the Aguadilla airport.

If you're driving from San Juan, travel west on the De Diego Expressway, Rte. 22, then Rte. 2 (trip time: 2 hr.).

VISITOR INFORMATION   There is a Puerto Rico Tourism Company office in Aguadilla for the whole northwest region, from Mayagüez in the south through Isabela on the north coast (✆ 787/890-3315).

Watersports & Other Outdoor Pursuits

While Rincón has wider name recognition, Aguadilla and Isabela have equally good surf spots. In fact, the Puerto Rican Pipeline is actually composed of beaches in the three towns. **Gas Chambers, Crash Boat, Surfer's,** and **Wilderness** rule in Aguadilla, while the preferred spots in **Isabela** include **Jobos, Middles,** and **Shacks.** The best time to surf is from November through March, but summer storms can also kick up the surf. In the summer season, however, when the waves diminish, these northwest beaches double as perfect spots for windsurfing and snorkeling, with calm waters filled with coral reefs and marine life. The towns are quite close together, and the string of beaches through both really forms a single destination.

Shacks draws snorkelers and scuba divers, who all converge on one section of the large beach filled with reefs and coral caverns that teem with rainbow-hued fish. It's also the best spot in the area for kite-boarding and windsurfing.

The good surfing extends east from Isabela to Arecibo, and beyond out to Barceloneta and Manatí, and really all the way into San Juan.

Aquatic Dive and Surf (Rte. 110, Km 10, outside gate 5 of Rafael Hernández Airport; ✆ 787/890-6071; www.aquaticapr.com) is a full-service dive and surf shop that also rents equipment and gives lessons in scuba and surfing. The outfit also runs mountain-bike excursions to the Guajataca Forest. Prices depend on season and group size, but surf lessons cost from $50 to $65 for 1½ hours, and a two-tank scuba dive is from $75 to $125. Bicycle tours cost around $65 per person and last up to 3 hours. Surf and scuba equipment rentals run from $20 to $45 per day, while bicycles are $25 per day.

The Hang Loose Surf Shop (Rte. 4466, Km 1.2, Jobos Beach, Isabela; ✆ 787/872-2490; Tues–Sun 10am–5pm) is well stocked with equipment. It gives surf lessons ($60 per hour for a private lesson) and rents boards for $25 daily. The shop is owned by Werner Vega, a great big-wave rider, who is one of Puerto Rico's premier board shapers.

Tropical Trail Rides (Rte. 4466, Km 1.9, Isabela; © 787/872-9256; www.tropical trailrides.com) has excellent horseback riding tours along the undeveloped Isabela coast. The basic 2-hour tour ($50 per person) brings you through an almond forest, along deserted beaches, and explores an area of coastal caves. This is the place to fulfill that horseback-riding-on-the-beach fantasy.

The Northwest has more going for it than its beaches, however. That's especially so with **Aguadilla,** which has converted many of the old facilities of the former Ramey Air Force Base and put them to good public use (such as developing an international airport on a portion of it). **Punta Borinquén Golf Club,** Rte. 107 (© 787/890-2987), 2 miles (3.2km) north of Aquadilla's center, across the highway from the city's airport, was originally built by the U.S. government as part of Ramey Air Force Base. Today it is a public 18-hole golf course, with coastal views, open daily from 7am to 7pm. Greens fees are a bargain at $20 to $22 per round; golf carts rent for $34; clubs for $15. The clubhouse has a bar and a simple restaurant. **Parque Aquatico las Cascadas** (Hwy. 2, Km 126.5, Aguadilla; © 787/819-0950 or 819-1030) is a water park run by the municipality that kids love. There are giant slides and tubes and the Río Loco rapids pool. From May through September, it's open 10am to 5pm daily. It opens again in winter on weekends from 10am to 5pm. Tickets are $25 for adults, $23 for kids ages 4 to 12, free for 3 and under. Parking is $3 and lockers $5.

You probably did not come to Puerto Rico to go ice skating, but you can do it at the **Aguadilla Ice Skating Rink** (Hwy. 442; © 787/819-5555, ext. 221). This is another city-run facility open from 10am to 6:30pm, and then from 7 to 11:30pm. It's popular with kids and is a training facility for island figure skaters. Cost is $13 per hour including skate rentals. The rink runs 1-hour sessions spread out across the day from 10am to 10pm.

Isabela enjoys a reputation for horse breeding. This activity is centered on Arenales, south of the town, where a number of horse stables are located.

WHERE TO STAY

Marriott Courtyard Aguadilla ★ Though not on the beach (it's minutes from one of the finest ones in this region), the Marriott boasts a large pool area that kids love. Onsite are a bar, popular casino, restaurant, and a cafe. On weekend evenings, there is live music and dancing. Built on the former Air Force Base in what was a hospital, the place is super clean and well-maintained, if somewhat sterile, but with comfortable and bright guest rooms. The staff is friendly and helpful.

West Parade/Belt Road Antigua Base Ramey, Aguadilla. © 800/321-2211 or 787/658-8000. www. marriott.com. 152 units. $139–$174 double; $189–$209 suite. Parking $8 daily. **Amenities:** 2 restaurants; 2 bars; babysitting; fitness center; 2 pools; room service; free Wi-Fi.

Ocean Front Hotel and Restaurant ★ Right on Jobos Beach, this friendly little guesthouse has a sweeping sundeck and terrace, along with a nice bar and seafood restaurant. The rooms are basic, but they are clean and comfortable and open up right on a fantastic beach. It can be a little loud on weekends, especially holiday weekends, but is quite the rest of the time. This is a bargain for a room on a great beach. You'll be satisfied if you're not looking for luxury.

Carretera 4466, Km 0.1, Jobos Beach, Isabela. © 787/872-0444. www.oceanfrontpr.com. 25 units (shower only). $85–$125 double; $125–$150 quad. Free parking. **Amenities:** Restaurant; bar; Wi-Fi.

Royal Isabela ★★★ "Islands Magazine" called the Royal Isabela the "best resort in Puerto Rico" and we'd agree it's in the top five. A lush tropical enclave, The Royal Isabela meshes Old World charm with the area's natural beauty to create a first class experience for guests. Built atop a coastal headland offering inspiring views, the property spreads across 426 acres, from coastal cliffs to lush tropical forest and rivers. The 20 *casitas,* small houses for guests, surround the stone and wood La Casa, main house, which has a restaurant and library and functions as a guest clubhouse. Each of the expansive casitas have 1,500 square feet of space, including separate living rooms and bedrooms with four-poster canopied beds and luxurious private decks with plunge pools. The golf course, one of the best in the Caribbean, has won accolades for its beauty and difficulty. It cuts across 3 miles of coastal cliffs, which loom up to 300 feet above the sea, and slithers through lush tropical forest and pastoral farmland marked by native grass, natural sand dunes, and deep canyons. *Note:* Breakfast and most drinks (beer, soda, water) are included in the room rates.

Av. Noel Estrada 396, Isabela. ℂ **855/609-5888** or 787/609-5888. www.royalisabela.com. 20 units. Double $649–$849 high season, $499–$699 low season, 10 percent hotel fee. Continental breakfast included. Free parking. **Amenities:** Restaurant; golf; clubhouse; pool; tennis; croquet; horseback riding; gym; water sports; yoga; hot tub; free Wi-Fi.

Villa Montana Beach Resort ★★★ A honeymoon-worthy spot, this resort is made up of lovely, Caribbean-style plantation villas—with cathedral ceilings, peaked tin roofs, courtyards, and verandas—spread along a 35-acre (14-hectare) beachfront plot with two pools, a 3-mile (4.8km) beach, and surrounding tropical forests. Villas are boutique chic, with a muted color palette enlivened by pops of color, terra cotta tile, and luxe hacienda–style furnishings. The grounds are covered with towering trees, explosions of tropical flora, and endangered Puerto Rican parrots and other exotic birds. The resort's **Eclipse Restaurant** is one of the best in all Puerto Rico, with an open dining room overlooking the beach and forged from wood, stone, and other natural materials. It serves excellent wood-fired Neapolitan pizza, juicy steaks, and delectable seafood risotto, among other gourmet offerings. For those who don't want to just tan (or head to the lovely spa), the resort offers a full roster of activities from horseback riding to biking to every watersport you can imagine, with a surf break on site. Guests also hike through tropical forests or use the climbing wall on the property.

Carretera 4466, Km 1.9, Barrio Bajuras. ℂ **888/780-9195** or 787/872-9554. www.villamontana.com. 60 units. High season $275–$300 double; $600–$600 villas, low season $150–$228 double, $520–$625 villas, 9 percent resort fee. Free parking. **Amenities:** 2 restaurants; bar; babysitting; basketball, climbing wall; 2 pools; spa; tennis court; volleyball court, free Wi-Fi.

Villas del Mar Hau ★ A collection of brightly painted Puerto Rican country villas, right on the beach at Playa Montones, Villa del Mar Hau is quite popular with families. That's likely because the compound has a lovely private beach, a game room, sports courts, good restaurant, market, and even a laundry, making it easy to stay put. Huge reefs protect the beach and making it an ideal spot for kids to swim. The villas are basic in their decor, but are right on the beach, and the parador's main building is fronted by a huge wooden sundeck overlooking the surf.

Carretera 4466, Km 8.3, Playa Montones, Isabela. ℂ **787/830-8315.** www.hauhotelvillas.com. 42 units (shower only). Double $176–$223, cottages $281, 6 percent hotel fee. Free parking. From the center of Isabella, take Rte. 466 toward Aguadilla. **Amenities:** Restaurant; bar; babysitting; barbecue area; horseback riding; pool w/snack bar; tennis; watersports/equipment rentals; free Wi-Fi.

WHERE TO EAT

La Spezie Resto-Pub ★★ Most of the food here is cooked either over an open, wood-fired grilled or in a brick oven which produces perfectly seared South American style grilled steaks and artisanal pizza that have a wonderful smokiness to them. (The food is meant to evoke the cuisine of La Plata River, which runs between Argentina and Uruguay.) The fare is complimented by the impressive wine and beer selection, though we always go for the primo house sangria. All of this is served in a pleasant brick and dark wooden bar and dining room by friendly, professional staff.

Circulo E 326B, Ramey Base, Aguadilla. © **787/658-6226.** Main courses $12–$30. Mon–Thurs 4–10pm, Fri–Sat 4–11pm, Sun 2–9pm.

One-Ten Thai ★★ THAI   Incredibly delicious Thai food at rock bottom prices, all washed down with a wide selection of craft beers from around the world—what could be better? You pick a protein (shrimp, chicken, beef, pork, or tofu) and then choose whether to have it as a red and green curry, pad gra prow, lime peanut stir fry, or set in "drunken noodles." *Be careful:* They *will* make if fiery if you request spice. Though there's often a wait for a table (reservations aren't accepted), there's a bar where you can wait and live music on many nights.

Carretera 110, Km 0.1, Aguadilla. © **787/890-0113.** Main course $10–$14. Wed–Sun 5–10pm.

THE WESTERN MOUNTAINS

The west is also a good area to head up into the mountains, and Maricao, west of Mayagüez, is one of the prettiest of Puerto Rico's mountain towns. You can reach Maricao from Mayagüez, but you'll have to take a number of routes heading east. First take Rte. 106 east to Rte. 119. Turn right onto Rte. 119. Take this until the community of Las Vegas, then turn left on Rte. 357 toward Maricao, which you will reach when you intersect with Rte. 105. The scenery is beautiful, but the roads are narrow and the going is slow. It's quicker to head south along Hwy. 2 to Sabana Grande, and then take Hwy. 120 directly to Maricao.

One of the nicest spots is the **Monte del Estado National Park** (Rte. 120, Km 13.2; © 787/873-5632), a picnic area and campground in the Maricao Forest, with wonderful pools fed by mountain streams. The stone observation tower, 2,600 feet (792m) above sea level, provides a panoramic view across the green mountains up to the coastal plains, and you can see clear out to Mona Island. Nearly 50 species of birds live in this forest, including the Lesser Antillean pewee and the scaly-naped pigeon. Nature watchers will delight to know that there are some 280 tree species in this reserve, 38 of which are found only here. The area has about 18 rivers and creeks running through the forest.

Maricao is coffee country, and there are several plantations and historic plantation houses in the town.

Nearby is **Lares,** which has a lovely central plaza with shady trees and scattered tropical gardens. The plaza, La Plaza de la Revolucíon, is named after one of the few nationalist uprisings in Puerto Rican history. El Grito de Lares ("The Cry of Lares") took place when hundreds of Puerto Rican patriots seized the town from the Spanish on September 28, 1868. While a republic of Puerto Rico was declared, the Spanish quickly resumed control. Today, thousands of independence supporters come here to commemorate the event each year on its September 28 anniversary. Surrounded by mountains and green valleys, it is one of the island's prettiest towns, though it lacks hotels and attractions for tourists.

From Isabela, you can visit **Lago de Guajataca** and the **Guajataca Forest Reserve,** which are located in the mountains south of town.

Before heading into **Bosque Estatal de Guajataca (Guajataca Forest) ★★**, you can stop in at the **Departamento de Recursos Naturales y Ambienta Oficina,** Rte. 446, Km 9, Barrio Llanadas (© **787/872-1045** or 787/999-2000), which is open daily

7am to 3:30pm. The office has a stock of detailed hiking routes through the forest reserve. Guajataca Forest sprawls across nearly 2,400 acres (971 hectares) of forestland, rising and falling at various elevations, ranging from 500 to 1,000 feet (152–305m) or more. The woodland in the forest is punctuated by *mogotes* (tropical cone and tower karsts) and covered with 25 miles (40km) of hiking trails. It is also home to the endangered Puerto Rico boa (you are unlikely to encounter one) and is the habitat of nearly 50 different species of birds. The highlight of the forest is the *Cueva del Viento,* the "Cave of the Wind." The hiking trails have been well marked by park rangers.

Reaching the lake from the forest can be difficult. Take Rte. 446 south until you reach Rte. 119. The **Lago de Guajatac** ★, one of the most majestic bodies of water on Puerto Rico, is our favorite lake for some R&R on the island. It is both a 4-mile-long (6.4km) body of water and a wildlife refuge. For a scenic look at the lake, drive along its north shore, a haven for island freshwater anglers. You can go fishing here, but you have to bring your own equipment. The most sought-after fish is *tucunare,* with which the lake is stocked. At the dam here, you can gaze upon an evocative "lost valley" of conical peaks.

Where to Stay & Eat

Centro Vacacional Monte del Estado ★ Basic cabins here sleep up to six and are outfitted with full kitchens, beds, barbecue pits, and picnic tables. The forest and views are beautiful, and there are thermal baths in the reserve near the cabins. It's a great spot for bird watching and hiking.

Carretera 120, Km 13.2, Maricao. ℂ **787/873-5632.** 24 units. $65–$72 cabins (4–6 people). Parking $3. **Amenities:** Basketball court; game room with ping pong and billiards; 2 pools; kitchen in room.

Café Rustica ★ PUERTO RICAN A, yes, rustic restaurant on the foothills of the Cordillera Central outside Mayagüez, the cafe serves delicious Puerto Rican food, steaks, and seafood. The specialty of the house is a chicken breast stuffed with lobster and shrimp, wrapped in bacon, and served with garlic cream sauce—it's worth the calories.

Rte. 105, Km 9.1, Barrio Limón, Mayagüez. ℂ **787/834-5653.** Main course $8–$24. Tues–Thurs 11am–2pm, Fri–Sat 11am–9pm, Sun 10:30am–9pm.

EASTERN PUERTO RICO

The northeast corner of the island, less than an hour from San Juan, contains the island's major attractions: El Yunque rainforest, two of the world's rare bioluminescent bays whose waters glow at night, and several great beaches, including Luquillo Beach (also see chapter 6). There are a variety of landscapes, ranging from miles of forest to palm groves and beachside settlements. Here, you will find one of the best resorts on the island, El Conquistador Resort, which literally sits on the northeast corner of Puerto Rico, where the Atlantic Ocean and the Caribbean Sea meet.

At Fajardo, a preeminent sailor's haven, you can catch ferries to the nearby island municipalities of Vieques and Culebra (see chapter 10). The east coast city is actually the start of a chain of islands, moving onwards to the island towns and weaving along the neighboring U.S. and British Virgin Islands and beyond. The area forms perhaps the greatest pleasure-boating area in the world.

The Navy completed its exodus from Roosevelt Roads base south of Fajardo in 2004, and the government is proposing a massive tourism development, but for the moment Ceiba and Naguabo are sleepy, quaint towns that are worth a look.

Halfway down the coast is Humacao, home to **Palmas del Mar Resort,** an ever-growing resort and upscale vacation-home community on a wildly gorgeous beachfront, with a Wyndham Garden Hotel. Visitors can also rent private vacation homes and villas throughout the resort, which sprawls across 2,700 acres (1,093 hectares) and has a yacht club, equestrian center, the Caribbean's largest tennis center, a beach and country clubs, great beaches, and lush tropical grounds. Plenty of watersports activities are available. Luxury residences, used as both vacation properties and year-round homes, are divided into distinct communities. Palmas also has its own school and post office.

The José Celso Barbosa Expressway 53 heads south from Humacao and then joins Rte. 3, and turns the southeast corner of Puerto Rico towards Guayama and Puerto Rico's long Caribbean coast, which is at its prettiest at its eastern and western extremes.

At Yabucoa, take the coastal Rte. 901, which switches back and forth along oceanfront cliffs and sleepy coastal villages, to experience one of the most breathtaking series of views on the island. The road continues to hug the coast as it reconnects with Hwy. 3 and rounds the southeast corner of Puerto Rico to Guayama. There are several nice beaches along the way.

This once important sugar town has long since been converted into an industrial and commercial center, but time stands still at its downtown plaza, which has beautiful Spanish colonial architecture, restored buildings, and a provincial air.

ATLANTIC OCEAN

Condado Beach | Ocean Park Beach | Isla Verde Beach

165 | 26

San Juan

Cataño | Loiza | Coco Beach | Luquillo Beach | Las Croabas | Cabezas de San Juan Nature Reserve

22 | 36 | 26

Santa Barbara

Bayamón | 20

Guaynabo | 1 | 18 | 66 | Carolina | Río Grande | 3 | 194 | Fajardo | Fajardo Beach

Trujillo Alto | *Lake of Loiza* | 66 | 186 | 191 | 53

El Yunque | Ceiba | To Culebra

Lomas

Comerío | Caguas | 30 | Juncos | Rio Blanco | Daguao

San Lorenzo | 183 | La Permina | 31 | 192 | Naguabo | Naguabo Beach

52 | 183 | 30 | Punta Santiago | Cayo Santiago

Cayey | 184 | *Carite Forest* | 181 | Humacao | Playa de Humacao

15 | 179 | 184 | 182 | To Vieques

179 | Yabucoa | 3

Guayama | 3 | 3

Pasaje de Vieques

0 — 10 mi
0 — 10 km

Caribbean Sea

El Yunque **1**
Fajardo **5**
Humacao **2**
Las Cabezas de San Juan Nature Reserve **7**
Las Croabas **6**
Luquillo Beach **8**
Naguabo **4**
Palmas del Mar **3**

FAJARDO

35 miles (56km) E of San Juan

A huge submerged coral reef off Fajardo's coast protects its southeastern waters, which are also blessed by trade winds—a sailors' delight. The Caribbean waters here are run through with coral and marine life, from barracudas and nurse sharks to shimmering schools of tropical fish, making this area a diving and snorkeling paradise.

There are dozens of small islands off the coast of this eastern town. Fajardo itself has untrammeled beaches surrounded by wilderness, with great snorkeling and scuba opportunities right offshore. It also has a bioluminescent bay and other natural wonders. Its unvarnished town center has atmospheric bars and *cafetíns* serving up cold drinks and tasty Creole cooking at bargain prices.

There are seven marinas in town, and with reason: Fajardo is the first of a string of ports extending to Vieques and Culebra, the U.S. and British Virgin Islands, and the Windward island chain, the pleasure-boating capital of the Caribbean. There are also gorgeous beaches, snorkeling spots, and untamed forest.

Las Croabas, a seafront village within the municipality, is the site of the El Conquistador Resort & Golden Door Spa, a leader in luxury since its casino was used as the setting for

TO THE lighthouse: EXPLORING LAS CABEZAS DE SAN JUAN NATURE RESERVE

Las Cabezas de San Juan Nature Reserve is better known as El Faro, or "the Lighthouse." Located in the northeastern corner of the island, it is one of the most beautiful and important areas in Puerto Rico. Here you'll find seven ecological systems and a restored 19th-century Spanish colonial lighthouse. From the lighthouse observation deck, majestic views extend to islands as far off as St. Thomas in the U.S. Virgin Islands.

Surrounded on three sides by the Atlantic Ocean, the 316-acre (128-hectare) site encompasses forestland, mangroves, lagoons, beaches, cliffs, offshore cays, and coral reefs. Boardwalk trails wind through the fascinating topography. Ospreys, sea turtles, and an occasional manatee are seen from the windswept promontories and rocky beach.

The nature reserve is open Wednesday through Sunday. Reservations are required; for reservations during the week, call (☏ **787/722-5882;** during the weekend, reserve by calling (☏ **787/860-2560** (weekend reservations must be made on the day of your visit), or visit www.paralanaturaleza.org, which gives detailed information on this and other nature tours. Owned by the nonprofit Conservation Trust of Puerto Rico, it is run by Trust tour and educational arm m Para la Naturaleza. Admission is $10 for adults, $7 for children 13 and under, and $5 for seniors. Guided 2½-hour tours are conducted at 9:30, 10, and 10:30am, and 2pm (in English at 2pm).

Laguna Grande, within the reserve, is one of the world's best bioluminescent bays, along with one on the neighboring island of Vieques. The presence of multitudes of tiny organisms, called dinoflagellates, in the protected bay is responsible for the nocturnal glow of its waters. They feed off the red mangroves surrounding the water. Kayaking through the bay at night should be on your bucket list. We highly recommend veteran tour company **Las Tortugas Adventures,** P.O. Box 1637, Canóvanas 00729 (☏ **787/636-8356** or 787/809-0253; http://kayak-pr.com). It was founded by Gary Horne, one of the most experienced guides in Puerto Rico; he's a certified dive master and coast guard veteran. There are two nightly tours of the bay at 6 and 8pm Monday through Saturday, which cost $45 per person—or daytime kayak and snorkel adventures for $75, which we highly recommend as well. For $100, you can tour the rainforest and the beach and take the biobay tour at night. Offseason rates can fall by more than 20 percent. Another option is a kayak adventure along the Río Espiritu Santo, a beautiful river that cuts through El Yunque rainforest. **Kayaking Puerto Rico,** Fajardo (☏ **787/435-1665** or 787/245-4545; www.kayakingpr.com), is another reputable kayak tour operator, with good guides and equipment. **Yokahu Kayak Trips,** Fajardo (☏ **787/604-7375;** www.yokahukayaks.com), and **Enchanted Island Eco Tours,** Rte. 191, Km 1.7, Laguna Grande, Fajardo (☏ **787/888-2887**), also run similar snorkeling and biobay tours. It also rents motorized inflatable boats if you want to cruise around on your own.

pivotal scenes in the 1964 James Bond classic film "Goldfinger." Today, the Mediterranean-inspired fantasy resort has its own funicular, waterpark, a marina, and a private ferry to bring guests to its private beach island. The resort is divided into a main hotel, an upscale Mediterranean village (Las Casitas), and two modern resort communities, all tied together with lush landscaping. It also has full sports, spa, health, and beauty facilities.

Las Croabas is a charming fishing village, with boats tied up at harbor and open-air seafood restaurants. Many are clustered along Rte. 987 at the entrances of the Seven Seas public beach and Las Cabezas de San Juan Nature Reserve, over 300 acres (121 hectares) of dry forest, virgin coast, and mangrove swamp. It also borders the exquisite bioluminescent bay, with glowing nocturnal waters. The restored 19th-century light-house still functions. The road ends in a circle, which wraps around a park at the village harbor. Several operators rent kayaks for daytime snorkeling trips or evening trips to the bio bay at the adjacent nature reserve. You can paddle across the bay and through mangrove canals to make it to the bio bay.

Getting There

If you're staying at El Conquistador, staff members greet guests at the San Juan airport and transport them to the resort. Guests can also take a taxi to the resort for $80, but that's more than the roundtrip fare aboard the plush resort shuttle from Luis Muñoz Marín Airport ($74 adults, $54 for children 12 and under—for hotel guests only). If you're driving from San Juan, head east along the new Rte. 66 Corridor Noreste highway and then Rte. 3 toward Fajardo. At the intersection, cut northeast on Rte. 195 and continue to the intersection with Rte. 987, at which point you turn north. To fully enjoy all El Conquistador's offerings, you'll probably want to stay there for several days. You might want to rent a car from Fajardo for only part of your stay, and take the shuttle to and from the airport.

Outdoor Activities

In addition to the lovely beach and the many recreational facilities that are part of **El Conquistador** (p. 195), there are other notable places to play in the vicinity.

Some of the best snorkeling in Puerto Rico is in and around Fajardo. Its public beach, **Playa Seven Seas,** is an attractive and sheltered strip of sand. The beach lies on the southwestern shoreline of Las Cabezas peninsula and is crowded on weekends, but the snorkeling is fine, especially on its western and eastern extremities.

At the western end of this beach and along a half-mile dirt path cutting though a wooded mount, you'll come to another path through shrub forest heading to **Playa Escondido** (Hidden Beach), a small white-sand cover with coral reefs in aquamarine waters right off this beach.

If you continue straight for another mile, you will come to the gorgeous **El Convento Beach,** stretching out along the miles-long undeveloped coastline between Fajardo and Luquillo. *Note:* Swimming is prohibited here.

The area has managed to ward off development despite the building craze taking place across much of the rest of Puerto Rico, with only a few unmarked dirt roads providing access, and paths such as the one from Seven Seas. The area is a nesting ground for endangered sea turtles, and its waters teem with reefs and fish. A small forest runs along much of the beach, and behind it stands the imposing El Yunque rainforest, looming over the white-sand beach and pristine blue waters. About a mile down the beach is the governor's official beach house, El Convento, a rustic wooden cottage. Just beyond the cottage is a great spot to snorkel. The water plunges steeply just offshore and is pocked with large reefs, which draw even large fish close to shore.

Environmentalists have pushed to protect this area from development, while developers want to build two large resorts. The administration is currently drawing up boundaries of a proposed nature reserve, which is to allow some "low-impact" tourism back from the coast.

To get here, you can hike from Fajardo's Seven Seas Public Beach, outside the resort just before Las Croabas village. It's a 2-mile (3km) hike through a trail in the shrub forest on its eastern end to El Convento Beach, a miles-long stretch of largely untouched beachfront, home to sea turtles and reef-studded waters with great snorkeling. The official vacation home of Puerto Rico's governor is the only development to speak of. The dirt road leading to it is the only road near the beach, one of the reasons it has been able to escape the stampede of development that has remade most of Puerto Rico over the last several decades.

TENNIS   The seven Har-Tru courts at **El Conquistador** (see below) are among the best tennis courts in Puerto Rico, rivaling those at Palmas del Mar. The staff at the pro shop are extremely helpful to beginning players. Courts are the least crowed during the hottest part of the day, around lunch hour.

WATERSPORTS   Several operators offer day sailing trips, usually from 10am to 3pm, from Fajardo marinas, which include sailing, snorkeling, swimming, and a stop at one of the island beaches where lunch is usually served. It's the easiest way to experience the Caribbean marine world while in Puerto Rico. Prices, including lunch and equipment, start from $69 per person. The trips are aboard luxury catamarans, with plush seating, a sound system, and other comforts, such as a bar. Captains know the best spots, where reefs attract schools of feeding fish. These are among the most gin-clear and tranquil waters in Puerto Rico. They are teeming with wildlife, including several species of fish such as grouper, but also lobster, moray eels, and sea turtles. Among the local operators are **Traveler Sailing Catamaran** (© **787/863-2821;** www.travelerpr.com), **East Island Excursions** (© **787/860-3434;** www.eastislandpr.com), **Salty Dog Catamarans** (© **787/717-6378**), and **Catamaran Spread Eagle** (© **787/887-8821;** www.snorkelingpr.com). **Erin Go Bragh Charters** (© **787/860-4401**) offers similar day trips aboard a 50-foot sailing ketch.

For scuba divers, **La Casa del Mar** (at the marina; © **787/863-3483** or 787/863-1000, ext. 7919) is one good option operating out of El Conquistador. You can go for ocean dives on the outfitter's boats; a two-tank dive goes for $99 or $125 if you go further out to sites off Vieques and Culebra. Equipment is extra but is often included in dive packages. A PADI snorkel program, at $60 per person, is also available or take a trip to Culebra for $95. **Sea Ventures Dive Center** (Rte. 3, Km 51.4, Puerto del Rey; © **787/863-3483;** www.divepuertorico.com) has a $109 offer for a two-tank dive $119 with equipment, a $150 discover package for beginners and a $60 snorkel tour.

Fajardo's seven marinas are proof that it is a sailor's paradise. The most renowned is the **Puerto del Rey Marina** (Rte. 3, Km 51.4; © **787/860-1000** or 787/801-3010; www.puertodelrey.com). The swankiest marina in Fajardo, it's a beautiful 1,100-slip facility south of town, the largest in the Caribbean. It's like a city unto itself with restaurants, bars, and a host of other services. **Villa Marina Yacht Harbour** (Rte. 987, Km 1.3; © **787/863-5131** or 787/863-5011; www.villamarinapr.com) is the other main marina in town, and is the shortest ride to the offshore cays and isolated white-sand beaches on the mainland. Charters operate out of both. There's a private 35-slip marina at the lowest level of the El Conquistador (© **787/863-1000**).

Where to Stay
EXPENSIVE
El Conquistador Resort: The Waldorf Astoria Collection ★★★   Few
resorts in the Caribbean, let alone Puerto Rico, measure up to El Conquistador. It operates almost like a self-contained city, with a top-notch spa, 18-hole championship golf

course, a number of outstanding restaurants, and a glitzy casino, not to mention a range of activities for children including Camp Coquí. You may never want to leave, and frankly you can have a great vacation without doing so: The resort sprawls across 500 acres of dramatic cliffs and down along a harbor area, overlooking the coast with an infinite view of water stretching out from all sides. The lush garden terraces share the view, as do the numerous pools that stretch across the bluff where the heart of the resort is nestled. A funicular takes guests down to sea level and the resort marina, where there's a small kid-pleasing waterpark (waterslides, lazy river), and a ferry that whisks guests to the resort's private island. On Palomino (the island's name) guests can explore caverns and nature trails; engage in horseback riding or watersports; or just unwind on the beautiful beaches.

When making reservations, note that the resort is divided into a main hotel, marina rooms near the dock, cliff top rooms (Las Vistas), golf course rooms (Las Brisas), plus the plush villas of Las Casitas Village, a resort within a resort, with its own private pools and dining areas, so be sure to check all the options before you book. All the buildings have elegant Mediterranean motifs, from blooming Spanish courtyards to neoclassical facades and fountains. Furnishings inside are similarly luxurious and ultra-comfortable.

Av. Conquistador 1000, Las Croabas, Fajardo. ⓒ **888/543-1282** or 787/863-1000. www.elconresort.com. 918 units. Winter $229–$359 double, $739–$1,547 suites, $778–$1,478 Las Casitas villas; off-season $189–$339 double, $699–$899 suites, $379–$859 Las Casitas villas. 18 percent resort fee. MAP (breakfast and dinner) packages are available. Children ages 16 and under stay free in parent's room. Valet parking $21; self-parking $16. **Amenities:** 12 restaurants; 8 bars; casino; nightclub; children's programs; dive shop; fishing; golf course; health club; 35-slip marina; 7 pools; room service; sailing; spa; 7 Har-Tru tennis courts; smoke-free rooms; rooms for those w/limited mobility; free Wi-Fi.

MODERATE

The Fajardo Inn ★ More than an affordable base to explore Puerto Rico's awesome northeast corner, the Fajardo Inn is an entertaining getaway, with good food, a fun jungle–themed pool area and miniature golf and tennis. Both the upscale Creole Star Fish restaurant and the casual Blue Iguana Mexican Grill & Bar get high marks. Throw in the handsome Mediterranean villa architecture and comfortable, if simple, rooms, and this is a solid choice. Plus, you think about the bill at all, you will sleep much more soundly here than at the nearby El Conquistador.

Parcela Beltrán 52, Fajardo. ⓒ **787/860-6000.** www.fajardoinn.com. 105 units (shower only). $125–$175 double; $175–$300 suite. 9 percent resort fee. 15-min. walk east of the center of Fajardo. Free parking. **Amenities:** 2 restaurants; 2 bars; pool; room service; snorkeling and diving arranged; 1 room for those w/limited mobility; free Wi-Fi.

Where to Eat

EXPENSIVE

Blossoms ★★ CHINESE/JAPANESE Take a culinary tour of Asia, with sushi, Teppanyaki, and Hunan and Szechwan specialties in a dining space that has the subdued elegance of the Orient Express, with views out over the coast, the open air kitchen, and expansive fish tanks. The Teppanyaki show of cooking on a hot table is popular with families and groups. Away from the "chop chop" is top-flight Chinese fare like the Szechwan spicy lobster and roast Peking duck. The sushi bar is quiet, refined and also quite good. The whole experience is a notch above what you'd expect at a resort this size.

Rte. 987, Km 3.4, in the El Conquistador Resort. ⓒ **787/863-1000.** Main courses $17–$49. Daily 6–11:30pm.

La Picolla Fontana ★ NORTHERN ITALIAN   The marble accented Italian restaurant in the El Conquistador is luxurious and romantic, the perfect fit for the elegantly prepared northern Italian classics. The clams Alfonso; baked mushrooms stuffed with ricotta, basil, and sundried tomatoes; and the asparagus with prosciutto and tomatoes are all stand out appetizers. But it's dishes like the filet mignon sorrentina with prosciutto, eggplant, marinara sauce, and mozzarella, that make me love this place. Dreamy risottos such as Maine lobster and champagne and beef tenderloin with Chianti only increase the passion, as does the sheer Roman hedonism of the desserts. Note that the portions are extra-large here, as are the prices, so don't be shy about sharing.

Rte. 987, Km 3.4, in the El Conquistador Resort. ℂ **787/863-1000.** Reservations recommended. Main courses $23–$65. Daily 6–10:30pm.

MODERATE

El Bohio ★★ SEAFOOD/PUERTO RICAN   One of several fine open air seafood and *comida criolla* family restaurants in Fajardo, El Bohio is a local favorite because of its flawless execution of authentic island seafood dishes, as well as the steak, chicken, and pork staples of Puerto Rican cuisine. You can't go wrong with delicate coconut arepas stuffed with shrimp in sweet tomato sauce, the huge platter of conch salad, or scrumptious Caribbean lobster tacos. There's also mainstream options from fried red snapper to kingfish *escabeche.* End the meal with a creamy flan.

Rte. 987, Las Croabas, Fajardo. ℂ **787/863-0865.** Main courses $10–$30. Mon–Wed 5pm–midnight, Fri–Sun 3–10pm, Fri–Sat 5–11pm.

La Estación ★★ BARBECUE   This is down home *nuyorican* barbecue, island Puerto Rican flavor cured in the Bronx, and the results are tasty indeed. That goes for all the barbecued fare (beef, pork, fresh fish, shellfish, and vegetables) as well as such delish sides as green papaya salad. If you're not up for a big meal, come for the bar scene and the live music. La Estacion—a former gas station—is the local hipster haunt and a very fun place to hang out (especially if you can nab one of the outdoor tables).

Rte. 987, Km. 4, Las Croabas, Fajardo. ℂ **787/863-4481.** Main courses $10–$30. Mon–Wed 5pm–midnight, Fri–Sun 3–10pm, Fri–Sat 5–11pm.

Costa Linda ★★ SEAFOOD/PUERTO RICAN   For over 40 years this family run restaurant has been wowing both visitors and locals alike with super-fresh seafood at very reasonable prices. Try the mofongo stuffed with fresh seafood, or *arepas rellenas,* a delicate pastry filled with conch escabeche or red snapper. It's not a fancy spot, but it's breezy and colorful, with warm service and good prices.

Rte. 987, Las Croabas, Fajardo. ℂ **787/645-2867.** Main courses $6.50-$23. Mon–Wed 10am–7:30pm, Thurs–Sun 10am–9pm.

CEIBA & NAGUABO

South of Fajardo is Ceiba, the site of the former Roosevelt Roads Navy base, and the seaside fishing town of Naguabo. Once dominated by the presence of the Navy, which set sail in 2004, the two towns are now sleepy places, waiting for government plans to transform the former military base into a new "Caribbean Riviera." For now, you can come here to enjoy a nice seafood lunch at the town harbors or visit the south side of El Yunque rainforest.

The local Ports Authority has taken over the former navy airport; visitors can now catch flights to San Juan, Vieques, Culebra, and other Caribbean islands from here.

Naguabo's town harbor is fronted by modest seafood restaurants and is a great place to stop for a lunch on a sunny afternoon. Towards the southern end of town, there are a number of casual, open-air seafood restaurants, clustered together beneath tin roofs, serving tasty, economically priced seafood and other local specialties. Towards the northern end of town there are a number of casual, sit down, full-service restaurants. Your best bet is a seat overlooking the sea at El Makito.

Naguabo is also home to a charming guest house, Casa Flamboyant, nestled in the lush south side of El Yunque rainforest, about a half-hour drive along country roads from the town harbor.

Getting Around

The Ceiba International Airport (☎ **787/863-1011** or 787/534-4100) has replaced the Fajardo and Humacao airports. The Ceiba airport hosts several small airlines serving Vieques and Culebra and other destinations. All the small airlines—Vieques Air Link, Isla Nena, Air Flamenco—that served the islands from Fajardo now serve them from Ceiba. To get here from Fajardo, take Expressway 53 south to exit 2 (the Puerto del Rey Marina exit) and pick up Hwy. 3 south. Follow signs to the Ceiba airport until you exit on Tarawa Drive. You'll pass a guardhouse at the entrance to the former base and proceed along the main road for the airport. Secure parking runs about $8 daily.

Where to Stay

Casa Flamboyant ★★★   The name is apt, if you're a nature lover: Surrounded by rainforests with stunning views of Puerto Rico's east coast, it's hard to have a more over-the-top experience of the beauties of nature than here (and we mean that in a good way; heck, you can walk to the entrance of El Yunque just down the road, or take hikes from the property). The rooms, for once, live up to the natural surroundings. Filled with art and freshly cut flowers, they're downright sumptuous; two are located in the main house and one is set apart (if privacy is a premium for you, book the latter, called the Rainbow Room). Those who want to cool off, head to the infinity pool, or, since the property is right in the rainforest, take a plunge in a mountain pool beneath waterfalls. A superb breakfast is included in the room rate. No children are allowed.

Off Rte. 191. Naguabo. ☎ **787/559-9800.** www.rainforestsafari.com/flamboy.html. 3 units. $200 double; $250 private suite. Breakfast included. Free parking. **Amenities:** Pool; free Wi-Fi, included breakfast.

Where to Eat

Restaurant El Makito ★★   If you're looking for a picturesque seafood spot, you can't do better than this lovely family restaurant on a picture perfect piece of coast that remains off the beaten path for many tourists. There are fantastic views of the ocean from its terrace and the comfortable dining room has glass doors and windows that overlook the sea. The menu is built around several daily fresh fish options served a la *criolla,* fried, or in garlic butter sauce, to name a few options. There's also seafood *mofongo* and Puerto Rican seafood *asopaos,* or stews, not to mention grilled lobster tails and stuffed fish and seafood platters. Portions are huge and flavorful.

Malecón, Playa Húcares, Carrertera 3, Naguabo, Puerto Rico. ☎ **787/874-7192.** Main courses $10–$65. Mon–Thurs 11am–8:30pm, Fri–Sun 11am–10:30pm.

PALMAS DEL MAR

46 miles (74km) SE of San Juan

Halfway down the east coast, south from Fajardo, lies the resort and luxury residential community of Palmas del Mar in the municipality of Humacao. Here you'll find one of the most action-packed sports programs in the Caribbean, offering golf, tennis, scuba diving, sailing, deep-sea fishing, and horseback riding. Palmas del Mar's location is one of its greatest assets. The pleasing Caribbean trade winds steadily blow across this section of the island, stabilizing the weather and making Palmas del Mar ideal for many outdoor sports.

Palmas del Mar sprawls across 2,700 acres (1,092 hectares) of beautifully landscaped coast, a self-contained resort and residential community with several different luxury neighborhoods, ranging from Mediterranean-style villas to modern marina town houses. On the grounds are six pools, two golf courses, 20 tennis courts, a fitness center, and a dive shop. Fishing, bike or car rentals, babysitting, and horseback riding can be arranged.

It's a town unto itself with a school, hospital, and post office, several restaurants, shops, and other facilities that any town center would have. There's one existing hotel and two luxury properties under construction. Several of the residences are available for rent through a vacation club or real estate office.

Getting There

You'll want a rental car to get around (unless you are content with a golf cart and staying within the resort). If you're driving from San Juan, take Hwy. 52 south to Caguas, then Hwy. 30 east to Humacao. Follow the signs from there to Palmas del Mar.

A van ride to the San Juan international airport is $25 per person for up to four people; the price drops to $20 the five passengers or more. For reservations, call **Palmas del Mar Transportation and Tours** (℗ 787/285-4323). Service is available 24/7 every day.

The Ceiba International Airport north of Humacao is the closest airport. It's located at the old Roosevelt Roads Naval Base in Ceiba (see above).

Beaches & Outdoor Activities

BEACHES   Palmas del Mar Resort has 3 exceptional miles (4.8km) of white-sand beaches (all open to the public). Nonguests must park at the hotel parking ($2 per hour), and there are showers and bathrooms near the beach. The waters here can get rough in winter but are generally calm, and there's a watersports center and marina. (see "Scuba Diving & Snorkeling," below). The **Rancho Buena Vista Equestrian Center** is one of the largest and best equipped in the Caribbean, catering to the expert but also luring newcomers with tantalizing tours and "resort courses." Trails through tropical forest, beachfront and other coastline are held throughout the day.

FISHING   Some of the best year-round fishing in the Caribbean is found in the waters just off Palmas del Mar. **Capt. Bill Burleson,** based in Humacao (℗ 787/850-7442), operates charters on his customized, 46-foot sport-fisherman, *Karolette,* which is electronically equipped for successful fishing. Burleson prefers to take fishing groups to Grappler Banks, 18 nautical miles (33m) away, which lie in the migratory paths of wahoo, tuna, and marlin. A maximum of six people are taken out, costing $750 for 4½ hours, $940 for 6 hours, or $1,280 for 8 hours. Burleson also offers snorkeling charter expeditions starting at $750 for up to six people for 4½ hours.

GOLF   Few other real-estate developments in the Caribbean devote as much attention and publicity to their golf facilities as the **Palmas del Mar Athletic Club** (✆ 787/656-3000; www.palmaspac.com). Both the older Gary Player–designed Palm course, and the newer Reese Jones–designed Flamboyant course, have pars of 72 and layouts of around 2,250 yards (2,057m). Crack golfers consider holes 11 to 15 of the Palm course among the toughest five successive holes in the Caribbean. The pro shop services both courses and is open daily from 6:30am to 6pm. Course rates are $75 weekdays and $85 on weekends and holidays. Call the Golf Club (✆ 787/656-3015) for reservations.

HIKING   Palmas del Mar's land is an attraction in its own right. Here you'll find more than 6 miles (9.7km) of Caribbean ocean frontage—3½ miles (5.6km) of sandy beach amid rocky cliffs and promontories. Large tracts of the 2,700-acre (1,093-hectare) property have harbored sugar and coconut plantations over the years, and a wet tropical forest preserve with giant ferns, orchids, and hanging vines covers about 70 acres (28 hectares) near the resort's geographic center.

SCUBA DIVING & SNORKELING   Some of the best dives in Puerto Rico are right off the eastern coast. Two dozen dive sites south of Fajardo are within a 5-mile (8km) radius offshore. See "The Best Scuba Diving" section, in chapter 1.

Set adjacent to a collection of boutiques, bars, and restaurants at the edge of Palmas del Mar's harbor, **Palmas Sea Ventures Dive Center,** Palmas Del Mar Marina, 110 Harbor Dr. (✆ 787/863-3483 or 800/739-DIVE; www.divepuertorico.com), owns a 44-foot-long dive boat with a 16-foot (4.9m) beam to make it stable in rough seas. They offer both morning and afternoon sessions of two-tank dives (for experienced and certified divers only), priced at $119 each (equipment included). Half-day snorkeling trips, $60 per person, depart both morning and afternoons on demand to the fauna-rich reefs that encircle Monkey Island, an offshore-uninhabited cay. A discover scuba course for beginners is $150.

TENNIS   The **Tennis Center at Palmas del Mar** (✆ 787/656-3025 or 656-9043), the largest in Puerto Rico, features 14 hard courts, two artificial turf Omni courts, and four Har-Tru clay courts. Fees for guests are $10 per hour during the day and $10 extra per court at night. Fees for nonguests are $20 per hour during the day and $10 extra per court at night.

Where to Stay

Some of the nicest lodging options are the privately owned villas and vacation homes spread throughout the several luxury communities that comprise Palmas del Mar. Prices start as low as $175 nightly but can range all the way up to $1,000. Weekly rates range from $1,375 to $5,000, with a typical resort and cleaning fee of $75 per stay. The studios and villas at **Oceana Beach Resort at Palmas del Mar** (✆ 787/850-0042; http://palmasdelmarvacations.com/beach-village-palmas-del-mar), have long been favorites of vacationers with their resort-level accommodations. But other equally attractive rentals are available at the Marbella Club, Los Lagos, Aquabella, Costa Verde, and The Views and can be arranged through **Palmas del Mar Properties** (✆ 800/285-2700; www.palmasdelmar.com).

Wyndham Garden Palmas Del Mar ★   In the heart of Palmas del Mar, steps from the beach, is this fine resort set within a larger vacation paradise. The rooms upstairs have balconies and views, but there is no elevator at this three-flight hotel, meaning you will have to walk up the stairs. There's a lot to do here with pools for both children and adults, a 24-hour fitness area, and casino gaming, plus guest privileges at nearby Palmas Del Mar beach where you can try out the exceptional tennis and golf club facilities, restaurants, bars, and clubs.

Candelero Dr. 170, Humacao. © **787/850-6000.** www.starwoodhotels.com. 107 units. $139–$235 double; $189-$335 suite. 14 percent resort fee. Valet parking $16; self-parking $13. **Amenities:** Restaurant; 2 bars; casino; fitness center; golf; kids' pool; outdoor pool; room service; scuba diving; tennis; smoke-free rooms; rooms for those w/limited mobility; free Wi-Fi.

Where to Eat

Thanks to the kitchens that are built into virtually every unit in Palmas del Mar, many guests prepare at least some of their meals at home. This is made relatively easy thanks to the on-site supermarket at the Palmanova Plaza, which has well-stocked fresh produce and meats, a wide variety of goods, and excellent wine selection.

Blue Hawaii ★ PAN ASIAN   A super friendly staff keeps this Polynesian-looking, but Asian-food serving, lounge-restaurant bright and bouncy, and the long menu has something for everyone. We're particularly fond of the Szechuan hot and sour soup and the fried dumplings as starters; either sushi or blackened shrimp, make nice entrees, as does the oddly named "Seafood Convention Chinese Style" (lobster, shrimp, scallops, and vegetables).

In the Palmanova Shopping Center. © **787/285-6644.** Reservations recommended. Main courses $15–$50. Daily noon–10:30pm.

Chez Daniel ★★ FRENCH   Normandy native Daniel Vasse serves classic French cuisine here—bouillabaisse, onion soup, duck confit, rack of lamb—but he uses local ingredients and what he calls "controlled creativity" to keep it interesting. The restaurant, one of Puerto Rico's finest since opening in 1985, is quite romantic and set in a choice location at the Palmas marina. The brunch is outrageously good.

Marina de Palmas del Mar. © **787/850-3838.** Reservations required. Main courses $26–$34 at dinner; $8–$19 at lunch; $45 Sun brunch (includes 1 drink). Wed–Mon 6:30–10pm, Sun noon–3pm. Closed June.

Tapas Bar@Chez Daniel ★★ FRENCH   More unbuttoned than Chez Daniel, but still stylish, Chef Vasse's casual bistro and tapas menu offers up selections ranging from sangria and paella to French wine and grouper in *beurre blanc* sauce. Or make a meal of tapas such as rabbit fritters, sautéed mushrooms, or grilled asparagus with

Where the Locals Go for Soul Food

Need to escape the confines of the resort for the evening? Drive out to one of the simple seafront restaurants and seafood shacks along the east coast. Several such restaurants can be found in the **Punta Santiago** sector just off Hwy. 3, where you can find memorable renditions of *mofongo* stuffed with seafood and hearty seafood stews, grilled fresh fish, baked lobster, and a wide variety of fish and shellfish served in tasty garlic, Creole, and citrus sauces. Many of these basic restaurants have enviable coastal locations. Good options in Humacao include **Daniel Seafood Restaurant** Calle Marina 7, Punta Santiago (© **787/852-1784**), **Frentemar Seafood,** Hwy. 3, Km 79.1, Punta Santiago (© **787/364-7396**), and **La Nueva Casa del Mofongo,** Hwy. 3, Km 70.9 Punta Santiago (© **787/852-1232**).

manchego cheese. There's live jazz and other music performances most nights, and brunch is fantastic. It's adjacent to Chez Daniel.

Marina at Palmas del Mar, Harbour Dr. 110. ✆ **787/850-3838.** Reservations recommended. Tapas $6–$18; paellas $14–$20; lunch menu $7–$22. Wed–Sun noon–10pm.

THE SOUTHEAST

More and more visitors are discovering the bewitching allure of Puerto Rico's wild and wooly southeast coast, with deep sand beaches, powerful waves, and cliffs cutting across the landscape straight down to the coast. There are still empty beaches with lighthouses, but now there are more restaurants and lodging options than just a few years ago.

In Yabucoa, you can also catch the start of the Panoramic Route, a tangle of narrow country roads crisscrossing Puerto Rico's mountainous interior from the east to west coasts (see chapter 4). The coastal Rte. 901 cuts along steep oceanfront cliffs and descends into such sleepy coastal villages as Maunabo and Patillas. Along the way is El Horizonte, where the food is as satisfying as the views. At Punta Tuna, along this road in town, there is a beautiful lighthouse built in 1892 and a wide public beach beside it with restaurants, bathroom facilities, and an outdoor picnic area. A better place to go swimming is Playa Emajaguas, a rare, wide, sandy beach in the area. It does not get as crowded as Playa Lucía, farther down the road, right next door to a larger hotel.

Beyond Maunabo, the main coastal road merges with Hwy. 3 as it passes through the pretty town of Patillas, which has one of the nicest resorts in the area. Arroyo has the fine Centro Vacacional Punta Guiliarte, a National Parks Company public beach and vacation center.

Off Rte. 3, Rte. 901 climbs steep oceanfront cliffs, cutting back and forth in switchbacks that afford outstanding views of the Caribbean and the islands in the distance. The road again descends into Maunabo, a sleepy coastal village that, despite its charms, remains off the beaten path for most visitors to Puerto Rico. At Punta Tuna, there is a beautiful lighthouse built in 1892 and a nice public beach beside it, with restaurants, bathroom facilities, and an outdoor picnic area. The wide sand beach here is among the nicest in the region. Elsewhere in town, the beaches are mostly deserted, used more by fishermen than beachgoers. The sand is heavier, darker, and deeper than elsewhere in Puerto Rico, and the currents can be strong. The beaches, protected by palm trees and bluffs, are beautiful, however.

Where to Stay & Eat
MODERATE
Caribe Playa Resort ★ A sleepy beachfront inn that lies on a wonderful stretch of coast, the Caribe features rooms close enough to the beach that you can hear the waves and go to sleep smelling the sea. This is not the Ritz; amenities are minimal, and while we found it to be clean and comfortable, the place lacks the style that could make it a very special place. There is, however, a nice pool area with all the beach chairs and hammocks you could need. The beach itself is tops for surfing, and when calm snorkeling, but there is a dangerous undertow which keeps a lot of vacationers out of the waves here. Food is basic international and Puerto Rican fare, served on a terrace overlooking the ocean.

Hwy. 3, Km 112.1, Patillas. ✆ **787/839-7717.** www.caribeplaya.com. 34 units (shower only). $130–$150 double. **Amenities:** Restaurant; bar; pool; free Wi-Fi.

Hotel Parador Palmas de Lucía ★   At the eastern end of the scenic winding roads that encompass the Ruta Panorámica, right near a pretty beach called Lucía, is this clean, family friendly find with lots of amenities. It's part of the family-run Tropical Inns Puerto Rico Company, which has become synonymous with affordable, well-maintained accommodations, which is exactly what you'll find here. With game rooms, basketball and volleyball courts, children have a lot to do, and there are laundry facilities and other practical features that will please parents. All inclusive meal plan options also help keep expenses down.

Palmas de Lucía, rtes. 901 and 9911, Camino Nuevo, Yabucoa. © **787/893-4423.** www.palmasde lucia.com. 34 units (shower only). $102 double. From Humacao, take Rte. 53 south to Yabucoa, to the end of the hwy., where you connect with Rte. 901 to Maunabo. After a 2-min. drive, turn left at the signposted Carretera 9911, which leads to Playa Lucía. **Amenities:** Restaurant; bar; basketball court; pool; free Wi-Fi in public areas.

El Nuevo Horizonte ★★ PUERTO RICAN/SEAFOOD   Perched atop Yabucoa's rocky coastline, El Nuevo Horizonte offers delicious seafood dishes which are consumed while diners enjoy one of the best views on the island. You can see Vieques, Culebra, and the U.S. Virgin Islands on clear days. Paella Rey, with juicy lobster, clams, shrimp, and mussels on velvety saffron rice, is a house specialty, but the stuffed *mofongo* and fresh fish sautéed in *criolla* sauce are also fabulous. If you are driving in the area and want to stop to enjoy a meal, this is your spot.

Rte. 901, Km 8.8, Yabucoa. © **787/893-5492.** Main courses $12–$45. Thurs–Sat 11am–10pm; Sun 11am–8pm.

VIEQUES & CULEBRA

Just a short boat or airplane ride away from the main island of Puerto Rico are Vieques and Culebra, the two island municipalities that round out the Puerto Rico archipelago. Their pristine white-sand beaches, breathtaking coastal views, and lush hillsides have earned these two small jewels their status as the Spanish Virgin Islands. Still blissfully underdeveloped (without a fast-food restaurant or traffic light between them), Vieques and Culebra have been able to avoid the hustle and bustle of the main island, making them a haven for those looking to get away from it all.

BEACHES   Vieques is visited mainly for its 40-odd white-sand beaches, which provide the perfect backdrop for every kind of watersports activity under the sun. **Sun Bay,** a government-run, panoramic crescent of sand, is the beach to visit if you have only 1 day to spend on the island.

Culebra's draw is undoubtedly its horseshoe-shaped **Flamenco Beach,** with silky white sand and sapphire waters that make it one of the most photographed and sought-after beaches in the Caribbean. **Zoni Beach,** on the island's northeastern edge, is a snorkeler's paradise for its beautiful reefs just offshore.

THINGS TO DO   Vieques, the larger of the two islands, offers more tourist facilities and options to eat, stay, and play than its smaller sister Culebra. Vieques's two main towns, **Isabel Segunda** on the northern shore and **Esperanza** on the south, are where most of the action is. The **Fort Conde de Mirasol Museum** and the **Punta Mula lighthouse** on the north are not only worth visiting for their historic value, but for the breathtaking views they offer as well.

Culebra, on the other hand, has a more laid-back attitude, but compensates for what may seem like a lack of excitement with the spectacular quality of its turquoise beaches. **Dewey,** Culebra's only town, is where you may head for a fresh seafood meal or cap off a day of taking in the sun with a cocktail.

EATING & DRINKING   Just because Vieques and Culebra are surrounded by water doesn't mean eating is limited to seafood, which by the way, is as fresh as it can get. To the delight of visiting foodies, the islands have quickly become a magnet for some of the tastiest cuisines, from *criollo* to fusion, at mostly reasonable prices. In Vieques, the **Next Course** and **El Quenepo** are favorites, while in Culebra, **Mamacita's** and **Susie's** are the go-to places for a good meal and drink.

NATURE   Despite being small, Vieques and Culebra both host expansive nature reserves that are open to the public. The **Vieques National Wildlife**

Refuge comprises 15,500 acres of mostly beachfront property that is home to a variety of tropical vegetation and the habitat of some endangered species such as the sea turtle, the manatee, and the brown pelican. Another of Vieques' major attractions is **Mosquito Bay,** also called **Phosphorescent Bay,** which on cloudy or moonless nights takes on a unique glow created by tiny bioluminescent creatures.

In Culebra, the **Culebra Wildlife Refuge** is one of the most important turtle-nesting sites in the Caribbean; it also houses large seabird colonies, notably terns and boobies.

A deterioration in the government-run ferry service to both islands during 2014 has all but eliminated it as a transportation option for most travelers, meaning you'll have to fly from either San Juan (a 20-min. flight) or Ceiba (a 5-min. flight) to visit the so-called Spanish Virgin Islands. The ferry is usually significantly late, cancelled trips are common and buying advanced ferry tickets is difficult if not impossible. Mechanical failures have also prompted on occasion the employment of the dreaded "triangle," which is a single ferry serving both islands on one long trip. Only travelers without any discernable time constraints or schedule should consider the ferry. The situation makes it difficult to travel by land or sea on crowded holidays, as the limited number of airplane seats sell out because everyone who can avoid taking the ferry does so. That goes for rental cars too.

VIEQUES ★

41 miles (66km) E of San Juan, 7 miles (11km) SE of Fajardo

About 7 miles (11km) east of the big island of Puerto Rico lies Vieques (Bee-*ay*-kase), an island about twice as large as Manhattan, with about 10,000 inhabitants and some 40 palm-lined white-sand beaches.

From World War II until 2004, about two-thirds of the 21-mile-long (34km) island was controlled by U.S. military forces, both its western and eastern ends. In the west, there was a base and munitions storage facility. In the east, vast swaths of the wilderness and pasture land were leased for grazing to local cattle farmers, which created a buffer zone between the civilian population and the war games and bombing range farther out to the east.

Unlike the U.S. military, the Spanish conquistadores didn't think much of Vieques. They came here in the 16th century but didn't stay long, reporting that the island and neighboring bits of land held no gold and were, therefore, *las islas inútiles* (the useless islands). The name Vieques comes from the native Amerindian word *bieques,* meaning "small island."

The Spaniards later changed their minds and founded the main town, **Isabel Segunda,** on the northern shore. Construction on the last Spanish fort built in the New World began here around 1843, during the reign of Queen Isabella II, for whom the town was named. The fort, never completed, is not of any special interest. The island's fishermen and farmers conduct much of their business here. The **Punta Mula lighthouse,** north of Isabel Segunda, provides panoramic views of the land and sea.

On the south coast, **Esperanza,** once a center for the island's sugar-cane industry and now a pretty little fishing village, lies near **Sun Bay (Sombe) public beach ★.** Sun Bay, a government-run, panoramic crescent of sand, is the beach to visit if you have only 1 day to spend on the island. It's a beautiful beach that tumbles endlessly along a graceful arc, blessed by palm trees and patches of scrub forest. The ruins of the Playa Grande sugar plantation, once the center of life in Vieques, lie on former Navy lands near the southwest coast. Playa Grande's former boulevard, once lined with stylish wooden mansions, continued to cut a swath through the dense dry tropical forest as a kind of civilized stronghold during the 6 decades of navy occupation. Today you can visit the ruins, which have undergone some restoration work since the navy left. Nearby **Playa Grande** beach is a long, palm lined, white sand beach, but the sea here can be rough and unpredictable, with killer rip tides.

With 40 beaches, all sorts of watersports adventures are possible. The island's varied terrain also offers plenty of land adventures. Kicking back, however, continues to be the number-one pastime in Vieques.

Essentials

GETTING THERE   Unless you're on a budget, skip the ferry and fly to Vieques, especially if your time is limited. The extra money you'll spend will buy you another day on one of its beautiful beaches. With the steep decline in the government-run ferry service during 2014, the ferry is no longer a convenient option for most travelers. Flights to Vieques leave from Isla Grande Airport near the heart of San Juan as well as the main Luis Muñoz Marín International Airport near Isla Verde. Your best hassle-free option if you are leaving from San Juan is Isla Grande. **Vieques Air Link** (✆ **888/901-9247** or 787/741-8331; www.viequesairlink.com) has the most flights and among the best prices. It operates six flights from the smaller and more convenient Isla Grande Airport and three daily flights from LMM International. The VAL flight from Isla Grande, about $144 round-trip, is the most reliable and convenient travel option to Vieques. It's about half the rate from LMM International, which is $242. This makes sense only if you are flying direct through to Vieques and are not visiting San Juan or other places in Puerto Rico. **Seaborne Airlines** (✆ **866/359-8784** or 787/946-7800; www.seaborneairlines.com) also serves Vieques from LMM International with a daily flight starting at about $198 roundtrip. **Air Flamenco** (✆ **787/724-1105** or 724-1818; www.airflamenco.net) is another option, with regular daily flights from Isla Grande for $140, including tax. There are also flights from **Ceiba,** which are more economical if you can get there. VAL charges $68 roundtrip, while Air Flamenco charges $60. Secure parking at the airport costs $8 per night.

The **Puerto Rico Maritime Transportation Authority** has four scheduled **ferry** trips for passengers a day to Vieques from the eastern port of Fajardo (9:30am, 1pm, 4:30pm, and 8pm), but the agency has had trouble sticking to a schedule with its aging fleet and myriad other issues. The trip takes about an hour, but the whole experience can take the better part of a day. The round-trip fare is $4.50 for adults, $2 for children. Tickets for the morning ferry that leaves Saturday and Sunday sell out quickly, so you should be in line early at the ticket window in Fajardo to be certain of a seat on the 9am boat. Otherwise, you'll have to wait until the 1pm ferry. For more information about these sea links: (http://vieques.com/passenger-cargo-ferry-guide; ✆ **787/497-7740**). Ferries return from Vieques to Fajardo at 6:30 and 11am, and 3 and 6pm every day. Departures are subject to big delays, however, and outright cancellations of scheduled trips have become increasingly common. Only the most laissez faire of travelers can consider it as an option, and it only makes sense for the extreme budget minded. The downturn was sparked by the cancellation of the contract with a private ferry operator hired to provide supplemental service to the government-run ferry line precisely because of its chronic deficiencies and lapses. If a similar initiative takes place, service could improve quickly and dramatically.

10

ATLANTIC OCEAN

Pasaje de la Vírgen

Cayo Norte

Culebrita

Cabeza de Perro

Canal de Cayo Norte

Zoni Beach

CULEBRA

Fulladosa Bay

Flamenco Beach

250

Dewey (Puebla)

Ensenada Honda

Playa Carlos Rosario

Culebra Airport

251

The Wall

Cayo de Luis Peña

Sonda de Vieques

To Vieques

Sonda de Vieques

Cayo Lobo

Cayo Lobito

To Fajardo

Vieques & Culebra

CULEBRA

VIEQUES

Fajardo

PUERTO RICO

Laguna Anones

Yallis

Punta Jalova

Caribbean Sea

Punta Conejo

VIEQUES NATIONAL WILDLIFE REFUGE

200

Chiva

Punta Ferro

Forte Conde de Mirasol Museum

Santa Maria

Isabel Segunda

Barriada Monte Santo

Colonia Lujan

997

Punta Mula Lighthouse

To Culebra

To Fajardo

Puerto de Vieques

Proyecto Barracon

Colonia Puerto Real

Esperanza

Cayo de Afuera

Playa Sun Bay

Sun Bay

Punta Negra

Playa Esperanza

996

995

996

Vieques Airport

Mosquito

200

Pasaje de Vieques

Mosquito Bay

Laguna Kiana

VIEQUES NATIONAL WILDLIFE REFUGE

Punta Arenas

Punta Boca Quebrada

Punta Goleta

Airport
Beach
Dive Site
Ferry Route
Lightouse

VIEQUES HOTELS
Bananas Guesthouse **5**
Bravo Beach Hotel **16**
Casa de Amistad **13**
Casa Flamboyan **7**
Crow's Nest **14**
Hacienda Tamarindo **4**
Hix House **1**
Inn on the Blue Horizon **3**
La Finca Caribe Rustic Villa & Cottages **8**
Lazy Jack's **19**
Malecon House **20**
Trade Winds Guesthouse **6**
W Retreat & Spa **2**

VIEQUES RESTAURANTS
Bananas Restaurant **5**
Buen Provecho **10**
Carambola **3**
Duffy's **7**
El Patio/Bieke's Bistro **12**
El Quenepo **18**
El Yate **12**
Next Course **17**
Noche/Tin Box **9**
Taverna **11**
Trade Winds Restaurant **6**

CULEBRA HOTELS
Bahia Marina **21**
Casa Ensenada **21**
Club Seabourne **21**
Casa Yaboa **21**
Posada La Hamaca **21**
Tamarindo Estates **22**

CULEBRA RESTAURANTS
Dinghy Dock **24**
Heather's Pizza **24**
Mamacita's **21**
Susie's **24**
Zaco's Tacos **23**

207

GETTING AROUND Public cabs or vans called *públicos* transport people around the island. To fully experience Vieques, however, you should rent a jeep. The mountainous interior, more than a dozen beaches, and the nature reserves on former military bases absolutely require it. *Públicos* are economical, however, and can be used to and from the airport and ferry on the days you arrive and leave Vieques if you plan to veg at the hotel pool and beach those days, and you can cut down on car expenses.

Most island rental companies offer small SUV and Jeeps, as well as standard autos, which are fine if that's all that's available. A recreational vehicle will ensure you can make it to any beach, even those accessible by rutty dirt roads. Prices generally range from $50 to $110 daily.

Maritza Car Rentals (*📞* **787/741-0078;** www.martizascarrental.com) is a Vieques veteran with a fleet of Jeep Wranglers ($70–$80) and scooters ($50) and a few other models ($50–$110). **Island Car Rental** (*📞* **800/981-5181** or 787/741-8822; www.islandcarrental.com) has Jeep Wranglers ($85) and Dodge Grand Caravans ($100), while **Vieques Car Rental** (*📞* **787/741-1037** or 787/435-1323; www.viequescarrental.com) has a wide variety of models from $65 to $95 daily. You can prearrange pickup at the airport, ferry terminal, or hotel.

Where to Stay
EXPENSIVE

Malecón House ★★ Warm, attentive service and a great location (within walking distance of the shops and restaurants of Esperanza, but still quiet) keeps Malecón House filled with repeat guests. Yes, its high season rates approach what you'd expect to pay at a full-scale resort, but most who stay here feel that the personal attention each guest receives makes it worth the price. Rooms feature a clean, handsome minimalist interior; and the house boasts an attractive pool area and a large rooftop terrace. A handful of rooms have ocean views, while others offer extra space and foldout couches. Rates include a breakfast of fresh baked goods and fruit.

Calle Flamboyán 105. *📞* **787/741-0663.** www.maleconhouse.com. 10 units. Double $160–250 low season, $210–$300 high season. Rates include continental breakfast. **Amenities:** Pool; rooftop terrace with tables and seating; smoke-free rooms; Wi-Fi (free, in common areas); free breakfast.

Hix Island House ★★★ No glass windows separate guests from the elements at this zen, innovative, eco-lodge. Designed by award-winning architect John Hix entirely of poured concrete, mosquito netting and retractable doors are used in the rooms when the elements get fierce. But that's a rare occurrence, and most find staying here, using the private outdoor showers, sitting on their terraces and communing with nature to be a remarkably serene experience. In fact, that's just about all you can do at Hix Island House: The remote, 12-acre complex has a swimming pool and a daily yoga class, and that's it. Guests are provided with food and a kitchen, but must travel if they want entertainment or a restaurant meal. Still, those who stay here often find it a tremendously joyous, rejuvenating experience. Book early, as Hix House gets many repeat guests.

Rte. 995, Km 1.5. *📞* **787/741-2302.** www.hixislandhouse.com. 19 units. Winter $175–$450 double; off-season $135–$345 double. Resort fee 7 percent. **Amenities:** Outdoor pool; yoga classes; beach chairs, coolers, snorkeling gear, boogie boards; free Wi-Fi at front desk.

Inn on the Blue Horizon ★★ Spread across a bluff outside Esperanza that overlooks a pristine swath of the southern coast, this resort's top selling points are its lush grounds and the serenity it affords guests. TV, in-room phones and children under

16 are all forbidden here. As well, a Mediterranean spirit runs through the property, evident in the mosaic path that cuts through tropical vegetation, its soaring lobby, and the regal infinity pool (one of the best on the island; there are also tennis courts and a gym). Lodgings are in the main building and scattered in a handful of cottages, and are all decorated with antiques and eclectic furnishings, though some could use a bit of TLC (they're not dirty, just a bit old, with scuff marks and chipped furniture here and there). Still, the location near Esperanza is convenient and the grounds are lovely.

Rte. 996, Km 4.3. ℭ **787/741-3318.** www.innonthebluehorizon.com. 10 units (some with shower only). Winter $180–$440 double; off-season $162–$399 double; holidays $200–$400 double. 5 percent resort fee plus $8 per day. **Amenities:** Restaurant; cafe/bar; gym; outdoor pool; tennis courts; free Wi-Fi.

W Vieques Retreat & Spa ★ Though it doesn't have much of an island vibe, the W offers high style, a cosmopolitan social scene and very cushy rooms to its guests. The main building is quite handsome, with a chic bar and formal restaurant, plus the Living Room lounge with plush furnishings, bar service, books and board games, and a fabulous ocean view terrace. The black pool is a beauty, though the pool area as a whole is a bit small. The beach also looks nice, but it's not one of the island's best, so consider renting a car to better explore the island. This is nonetheless a worthy spot, and it's conveniently located near town and the airport.

Rte. 200, Km 3.2. ℭ **787/741-4100.** www.wvieques.com. 156 units. Winter from $388–$1,112 double; off-season $265–$545 double. $66 resort fee. Pets allowed. **Amenities:** 3 restaurants; 3 bars; free airport transfers; bicycle rental; concierge; 24-hour health club; 2 infinity-edge pools; 24-hour room service; spa; tennis courts; watersports equipment; free Wi-Fi.

MODERATE

Bravo Beach Hotel ★★ Forgot your snorkel gear or floaties? That's not a problem at this gracious, family-run property. The staff keep a stash of everything you'd need for the beach and loan it out for free, just the first hint that the friendly, resourceful people who work here go beyond the usual to keep guests happy. Bravo Beach Hotel sits on the narrow coastal road north of Isabela Segunda, on a lushly landscaped beachfront property. The ocean's too rough for swimming, but most don't mind as Bravo has two uncrowded, lovely pools. As for the digs, they consist of crisply contemporary rooms, suites and standalone villas, all of which are wonderfully spacious, practical (villas and suites come with usable kitchens and all have fridges) and pretty, with such niceties as Frette linens on the beds and quality shampoos and soaps in the bathrooms.

North Shore Rd. 1. ℭ **787/741-1128.** www.bravobeachhotel.com. 12 units. Double $105–$155 low season, $130–$225 high season; suites $200 low season, $275 high season; $118–$380 villas (depending on high or low season). Rates include continental breakfast. Free parking. **Amenities:** 2 outdoor pools; smoke-free rooms; free Wi-Fi common areas.

Crow's Nest ★ On the road to Isabel Segunda from Esperanza, this cozy inn offers unpretentious, comfortably furnished doubles and suites with kitchenettes. The beautiful pool area and flourishing grounds are set on 5 lush acres (you'll see wild horses roaming nearby). There is good value here if you want to cook your own meals to hold down costs; Continental breakfast is included.

Rte. 201, Km 1.6, Barrio Florida. ℭ **787/741-0033.** www.crowsnestvqs.com. 17 units (shower only). Doubles: $153; Suites $261–$283. Continental breakfast included. **Amenities:** Bar; pool; free Wi-Fi.

Hacienda Tamarindo ★★ This exquisite, artfully decorated inn is set around a huge tamarind tree, from which the property takes its name. The decor (lovely, with mosaic tiles and dark wood furnishings) is by the original owner, a well-respected interior designer, and the maintenance is topnotch. The only thing that keeps this inn from getting three stars is its location, which is, alas, not on the beach (it's a 5-min. walk to the beach down a sand path and a 10-min. walk to Esperanza). However, most guests don't seem to mind, renting jeeps to beach hop and using the property's large pool. A delicious cooked-to-order breakfast is included with rates. No children under 17 allowed during high season (13 during low season).

Rte. 996, Km 4.5, Barrio Puerto Real. ℂ **787/741-0420.** www.haciendatamarindo.com. 17 units (some with shower only, some with tub only). Winter $199–$265 double, $250–$375 suite; off-season $155–$210 double, $189–$275 suite. 10 percent resort fee. **Amenities:** Bar; pool; free Wi-Fi.

INEXPENSIVE

Bananas Guesthouse ★ This congenial little place is right in the midst of the action, and has waterfront rooms, to boot. Yes, digs tend to be tiny and Spartan (basic wood-frame furniture, ceiling fans, screened-in porches), but they're meticulously well kept. Spend extra to get a room with air-conditioning, as much to block out the noise as for the heat.

Barrio Esperanza, 142 Calle Flamboyan. ℂ **787/741-8700.** 7 units. $70–$100 double. **Amenities:** Restaurant; bar.

Casa de Amistad (House of Friendship) ★★★ This adorable guesthouse is decorated with flare and care (the mattresses are superb), with a staff that make guests feel like family. To that end they'll lend you, free of charge, beach chairs, coolers and other beach gear and maintain an honor bar for beers and bottled water. The walled-in compound has a small pool and lovely courtyard garden (with barbecue area), a communal kitchen, and a lounge with books, computer, and television. Minimum stays of 3 nights are required during the high season (up to 5 nights during certain holidays) and 2 nights in the off season.

Calle Benitez Castaño 27. ℂ **787/741-3758.** www.casadeamistad.com. 7 units. Winter $95–$125 double; summer $75–$110 double. **Amenities:** Small outdoor pool; courtyard garden/sun terrace; communal kitchen; TV room; small boutique; free Wi-Fi.

Casa Flamboyán ★★ A true bargain in the heart of Esperanza, Casa Flamboyán rents four colorful, attractive and meticulously clean rooms; each has a private terrace with knockout ocean views. You're right above Duffy's restaurant and walking distance to everything in the village, but with its efficient air-conditioning and modern and well-maintained windows and doors, you can still shut off the world and fall into a sound sleep. Your hostess Donna is a gem: She knows everything about the island and offers valuable tips to her guests.

Calle Flamboyán, northwest of Esperanza. ℂ **787/741-9090.** www.caribbeangreatescape.com. 4 units. $90 double. Rate includes Continental breakfast. **Amenities:** Free Wi-Fi.

La Finca Caribe Guest House & Cottages ★★★ Although it's located in the middle of the island, just a short ride to the island's beaches and restaurants, La Finca has the feeling of being on a remote lush hillside, deep in the wilds of a far-off paradise. Guests can look over all that nature from the huge terrace in the main plantation house, which also houses the communal kitchen and living area. Like the other buildings, this handsome wooden structure is enhanced by a homey decor of vibrantly colorful country fabrics and furnishings. The main house, Casa Grande, has three bedrooms that sleep up to six (book them separately or rent the whole house). On property are also three villas (sleeping two, five, and six people each), for those who want more privacy. The management can arrange activities throughout Vieques, but most guests spend at least one day just hanging out at the resort, picking fruit from the trees, swimming in the saltwater pool, and lounging in the hammocks.

Rte. 995, Km 1.2. ℂ **787/741-0495.** www.lafinca.com. 10 units, 4 cottages. Winter $107 double, $135–$185 cottage double, weekly cottages $325–$1,450; off-season $97 double, $125–$1850 cottage double, weekly cottages $325–$1,450. One-time "short-stay" fee of $30 for 3 days or less during off-season and 4 days or less during the high season. Charge of $30 per person per additional guest in double-occupancy rooms. **Amenities:** Communal kitchen; salt water pool; beach chairs, toys, coolers, snorkeling gear, boogie boards, books and board games; laundry; Wi-Fi $5.

Trade Winds Guesthouse ★ Trade Winds is a triple-C property: cheap, comfortable, and clean. And that's about it, though rooms do have air-conditioning, ceiling fans, and small fridges. The hotel also rents a 1-bedroom apartment and 2-bedroom house nearby. Two other plusses: an excellent breakfast at the on-site restaurant and friendly, helpful staff. *Note:* This is a favorite with divers and is often booked up during holiday weeks.

Calle Flamboyan 107, Barrio Esperanza. ℂ **787/741-8666.** www.tradewindsvieques.com. 11 units (shower only). Year-round $80–$115 double, $220–$260 suite. Continental breakfast included. **Amenities:** Restaurant; bar; free Wi-Fi.

Where to Dine
EXPENSIVE
Carambola ★★ INTERNATIONAL This restaurant is one of the finer sports in Vieques to dine, with cuisine worthy of the fabulous setting (it's in the Inn on the Blue Horizon's main building, and looks over its gorgeous grounds). The French cut pork chop and herb curry shrimp are excellent, as is the rosemary passion fruit lamb chop. We also found a lot to like in appetizers such as mussels in white wine coconut sauce and ginger tamarind ribs. Perched on a seaside bluff outside Esperanza, the open sided—and very popular—onsite bar offers panoramic coastal views.

In the Inn on the Blue Horizon, Rte. 996, Km 4.3 (1 mile/1.6km west of Esperanza). ℂ **787/741-3318.** Reservations required. Main courses $23–$39. Daily 6–10:30pm.

El Quenepo ★★ CONTINENTAL Dine by candlelight at Esperanza's most romantic restaurant, which is blessed by sea breezes and a view of the bay. The spiny lobster and ahi tuna are impressive plates as are the *amarillo* wrapped tenderloin in an almond baklava crust and dorado wrapped in pancetta. If you spend more than a few days in Vieques, you'll probably want to eat here more than once…if your wallet is deep enough: Portions aren't large, but prices are.

Calle Flamboyan 148, Barrio Esperanza. ℂ **787/741-1215.** Reservations recommended. Dinner $27–$34. Dec-May Tues–Sun 5:30pm–10pm. June-Sept Wed–Sun 5:30pm–9:30pm.

Sorcé ★ VIEQUENSE/COMIDA CRIOLLA The W's marquee restaurant is named after an archaeological dig in south Vieques that uncovered artifacts from La Hueca indigenous peoples dating back to 160 B.C. One could say the chef here is "archeological" in his approach, too, concentrating on local recipes passed down through the generations and using island herbs and other ingredients. The food that emerges is similar to Puerto Rican cuisine, but like the Sorcé ceramics (which were marked by the styles of other Caribbean cultures), it reflects other influences, as well. We've been disappointed by breakfasts here, but the lunch, especially the fish tacos, is good, and the dinners are largely delicious (if pricey for what you get). The red snapper filet in white wine, capers, peppers, olives and tomatoes is a stand-out dish; the beef tender-loin in rum peppercorn sauce is another hit.

In the W Vieques Retreat & Spa, Rte. 200, Km 3.2, Vieques. ℂ **787/741-7022.** Reservations recom-mended. Breakfast and lunch $10–$18; dinner $22–$36. Daily 7:30am–11am, 1–3pm, and 6–10pm.

Next Course ★★ CARIBBEAN   The presence of Next Course on the country road linking Isabela Segunda, on the north coast, with the village of Esperanza on the south, has given birth to a nascent but growing culinary scene along the very pretty, winding Route 201. The restaurant offers diners global cuisine, a mélange of Asian, European and Puerto Rican influences, the food matched in the eclectic decor. Among the offerings is a surf and turf (poached lobster and exquisite dry aged steak) that's as good as any you would find in New York City. Guests dine in the handsome interior dining room or out on the terrace under the stars.

Rte. 201, Km 3.2 ℂ **787/741-10288.** Reservations essential. Main courses $22–$30. Fri–Wed 5:30–10pm. Closed August through mid-October.

NOCHE/TIN BOX ★★ INTERNATIONAL   Located in the bucolic heart of Vieques, these two separate restaurants, run by the same owner and management team, share a lot backed by tropical jungle. They also boast the same rustic chic vibe, great music, and inventive cuisine, which uses fresh herbs and produce grown on site. Tin Box specializes in upscale BBQ and raw bar specialties; the smoked chicken and ribs are primo as is the velvety rich mac 'n cheese and jicama salad. Noche is more upscale and has the best filet mignon on the island as well as a superb seafood stew. Both restaurants are small so reservations are a good idea; either dining room is a fine bet.

Intersection of Routes 996 and 201. ℂ **787/741-7700.** Reservations recommended. Main courses $14–$60. Dec–Apr Thurs–Mon 6pm–10pm.

MODERATE

Bieke's Bistro ★ PUERTO RICAN   A favorite with locals and visitors alike, this spot serves flavorful *comida criolla* in a homey, friendly atmosphere. The menu is short, the selections straightforward, but the delivery dead on. Red snapper, breaded chicken, *churrasco:* These are the type of expertly done, simple dishes on offer. The Bistro's specialty bar and coffee and tea menu also makes this a top stop for a drink and a snack.

Calle Antonio G. Mellado 340 (Rte. 200, in Isabel Segunda). ℂ **787/741-6381.** Main courses $6–$28. Mon–Sat 10:30am–10:30pm.

Duffy's ★   Duffy's is a pleasant pub in Esperanza, with great bay views, solid food, fine music and a friendly staff. The burgers, daily specials and catch of the day are usually the best choices, but some of the sandwiches and other pub faves do rise to their level. Swell house specialty drinks and a lively bar area round out the experience.

Calle Flamboyán (El Malecón) Esperanza, Vieques. ℂ **787/741-7000.** Main courses $6–$29. Daily 11am–11pm.

Trade Winds Restaurant ★ BREAKFAST/SEAFOOD   We love this place for breakfast, when it offers a mouthwatering range of omelets, French toast and pancakes, and other specialties (like the breakfast burrito and vegetarian egg white frittata). Beyond the meal quality, the view of Esperanza's quaint waterfront is at its most sub-lime in the morning. Dinners have gotten better in recent years, and focus on seafood, with dishes such as fresh Caribbean lobster in spiced rum butter sauce or the catch of the day in a pineapple salsa. For lunch, we can recommend the appetizers (conch fritters and Caribbean fishcakes) and salad selection, especially the Greek salad with grilled shrimp, feta, tomatoes, cucumbers, and red onions.

In Trade Winds Guesthouse, Calle Flamboyan, Barrio Esperanza. ℂ **787/741-8666.** Reservations recommended. Breakfast $7–$13; lunch $9–$16; main courses $14–$30. Thurs–Mon 8am–2pm; daily 5:30–9:30pm.

INEXPENSIVE

Bananas Restaurant ★ INTERNATIONAL   This may be the only restaurant in Vieques to offers a gluten free menu, but we think it's the laid back vibe and great views across the bay that bring in the crowds. As for the food, it consists of tasty burgers, sandwiches, and salads, as well as more sophisticated fare like coconut snapper, lobster risotto, and stuffed *mofongo*. There's a big bar, airy indoor and outdoor dining areas, friendly staff, and good service.

Calle Flamboyan (El Malecón), in Esperanza. ℂ **787/741-8700.** Salads and sandwiches $11–$14; main courses $14–$20. Daily 8am–6pm (kitchen). Bar is open later.

Buen Provecho ★ DELI CAFÉ   This upscale deli/cafe/market, run by amiable hipster ex-pats from the East Coast of the U.S., is *the* spot for a quick breakfast (eggs to crepes and burritos); you can also grab a light meal to go for later at the beach. There's a fine coffee and tea selection, plus soups and sandwiches.

C. Munoz Rivera 123, Isabela Segunda. ℂ **787/529-7316.** Salads, sandwiches, and breakfasts $3–$15. Tues–Sat 8am–6pm.

Taverna ★★ MEDITERANNEAN   Authentic Italian fare with a light touch, right in Isabela Segunda. On offer here: shrimp scampi, fresh fish picatta, veal marsala, and an incredible linguini with clams in a white wine sauce. Raves extend to the homemade pastas and delicious thin crust brick oven pizza. Taverna's only open for dinner weeknights and has great prices, so it's always crowded.

Calle Carlos Lebrum 453, right off the plaza Isabel Segunda. ℂ **787/741-7760.** Reservations recommended. Main courses $9–$26. Mon–Fri 5:30–9pm. Closed May–Dec.

El Yate Bar & Restaurant ★★ PUERTO RICAN   It's easy to overlook El Yate, with its old-school bar in front, and modest dining room out back. But we think the local food served here (and always sided by ice cold beers) is topnotch, especially the tasty, fresh seafood turnovers. Plus, the prices are easy on the wallet and the staff is super friendly. What could be better?

Calle Rieckehoff (next to the Ferry Dock, in Isabel Segunda). ℂ **787/297-9722.** Appetizers $5–$9; sandwiches $9–$12; main courses $8–$25. Cash only. Daily 8am–10pm.

Lazy Jack's ★★   Surprisingly good pizza and pub fare—fish 'n chips, burgers, and pulled pork sandwiches—in a colorful casual spot right on Esperanza's breezy *malecon* are what keeps Lazy Jack's bustling. The hand-rolled, thin crust pizza is light and crispy, and the homemade sauce flavorful. All in all, a fun spot for a meal.

Calle Flamboyán (El Malecón) Esperanza, Vieques. ℂ **787/741-1864.** Pub fare $9–$12; pizza $8–$23. Cash only. Daily noon–11pm (weekends 11:30pm).

Nature Reserve

The **Vieques National Wildlife Refuge** ★★★ comprises 15,500 acres (6,273 hectares)—much of it idyllic beachfront property—relinquished by the U.S. Navy to the U.S. Fish & Wildlife Service when the navy abandoned its Vieques training ground in 2003. This is now the largest landmass of its kind in the Caribbean. Refuge lands lie on both the eastern and western ends of Vieques. In 2001, 3,100 acres (1,255 hectares) on the western end were already turned over to the refuge. These tracts of virgin land-scape contain several ecologically distinct habitats, including the island's best white-sand beaches along with upland forests and mangrove wetlands, the latter the habitat of some endangered species such as the sea turtle, the manatee, and the brown pelican. Binocular-bearing bird-watchers also flock to the site. The coastal area of the refuge is characterized by coral reef and sea-grass beds, and there are scores of beautiful beaches. The refuge is open to the public and also contains a **Visitor Center** at Vieques Office Park, Rd. 200, Km 0.4 (℅ **787/741-2138**). The refuge is open daily during daylight hours.

Aficionados of Vieques praise the island for its wide profusion of sandy beaches. Since the pullout of the U.S. Navy, some of the sites that were formerly off-limits have been made accessible to hikers, cyclists, bird-watchers, beachcombers, and other members of the public. There are 40 beaches on this small island—that's a whole lot of endless afternoons of exploring.

Beaches

Along the eastern end, inside the former Camp Garcia base, the best beaches are **Red Beach** (Bahia Corcha), **Blue Beach** (Bahia de la Chiva), and **Playa Plata.** To reach these, take the tarmac-covered road that juts eastward from a point near the southern third of Rte. 997. Entrance to this part of the island, formerly occupied by the Navy, will be identified as **Refugio Nacional de Vida Silvestre de Vieques,** with warnings near its entrance that camping and littering are not allowed. Drive for about a mile (1.6km) along this road, turning right at the sign pointing to Red Beach (Bahia Cor-cha). En route, you'll have one of the few opportunities in the world to gun your rented car along the battered tarmac of what used to be a landing strip (a very long one). Pretend, if you like, however briefly, that you're on a test track for the Indianapolis 500, naturally exercising all due caution. The Fish & Wildlife Service has been doing improvement work and environmental testing at many of the beaches within the reserve and periodically closes off public access while work is ongoing.

The crescent-shaped Red Beach, with wide-open views of the ocean, and Blue Beach, protected by mangroves and scrub trees, are two of the more beautiful east-end beaches. There are signs, within the park, to minor beaches **Playa Caracas, Caya Melones,** and even **Playuela,** but the access roads are blocked off by the Park Service.

Myriad coves, such as **Playa Chiva,** pepper the coastline between Blue Beach and the end of the line, Playa Plata, which is covered with sea grapes, scrub trees, and palmettos.

Also near the border of the former eastern navy holdings is **Sun Bay Beach,** or *Balneario Público Sun Bay.* Its entrance lies off the southern stretch of Rte. 997. You'll recognize it by a metal sign. Just beyond, you'll see a park dotted with trees, an absurdly large number of parking spaces (which no one uses), and a formal entryway to the park, which virtually everybody ignores. Locals, as a means of getting closer to the water and the sands, drive along the access road stretching to the left. It parallels a ¾-mile (1.2km) stretch of tree-dotted beachfront, and they park wherever they find a spot that appeals to them. If you continue to drive past the very last parking spot along Sun Bay Beach, a rutted and winding and very hilly road will lead, after a right-hand fork, to **Media Luna Beach** and **Navio Beach,** two beautiful and isolated beaches, perfect for snorkeling and evening barbecues. The beaches can get rough, with waves good for surfers but not so much swimmers. A left-hand fork leads to the muddy and rutted parking lot that services Mosquito Bay (or Phosphorescent Bay). Right beside Esperanza village is **Playa Esperanza,** which is a great place for snorkeling.

Take a drive to the west end of the island to visit more beaches. The former Navy base and ammunition storage post has two fine beaches: **Green Beach,** in the northwest corner of the island beside a nature reserve, which is the best spot for swimming and snorkeling. On the south coast, another pretty beach lies beside the ruins of the Playa Grande sugar plantation. You'll have to pass the eerie **navy radar facility,** a field of antennas, to get there, and the surf is generally rougher here, and more exposed to open ocean and sharks. You are better off swimming at Green Beach.

The beaches are beautiful, but the western end is more physically haunted by the island's military past. Most of the eastern end remains off limits to people, as decades of bombardment from aircraft and offshore carriers have left it littered with unexploded ordnance.

Adventure Tours

For a small island, Vieques offers a surprisingly large number of opportunities for diving, snorkeling, sailing, and other watersports. Natural conditions are superb, and prices remain a bargain. More and more operators are popping up each year, which should only improve the offerings and the value for customers. **Blue Caribe Kayaks,** Calle Flamboyan 149 (El Malecón; ✆ 787/741-2522), have been in business for more than a decade. Kayak rentals are $15 an hour, $25 for a half-day, and $35 for a full day. Snorkeling equipment (fins, mask, and snorkel) rent for $10 daily. Guided snorkeling tours by kayak transport you for $45 through gin-clear waters, with stunning coral and brilliantly colored tropical fish, en route to an offshore cay with great beaches.

If you want to go diving, the Vieques veteran is **Nan-Sea Charters,** Calle Flamboyan 149, Vieques (✆ 787/741-2390), which brings an insider's knowledge to your dive experience.

Abe's Snorkeling & Bio-Bay Tours (✆ 787/741-2134; www.abessnorkeling.com) also offers competitive rates, hands-on inspection of marine critters, and some amusing storytelling, at least if you're with Abe. The company offers several tours lasting between 2 and 6 hours, ranging in price from $40 to $150. Children 4 and under go for free, while older kids up to 11 years old pay half-price for the expeditions. Ask about full-day island tours, 6 whole hours of fun.

Black Beard Sports, Calle Muñoz Rivera 101, Isabela Segunda, Vieques (✆ 787/741-1892; www.blackbeardsports.com), is a PADI dive center offering introductory dive trips and half-day open-water dives with equipment included for $150. If you have your gear, the open-water dive is $120, $150 with rental gear. They also have class programs ranging from $130 to $400, and varying in skill level and duration. Its downtown location in a restored Puerto Rican casita has a great sporting goods and sportswear shop. They rent dive equipment, snorkels and fins, mountain bikes, kayaks, fishing gear and other stuff, even tents.

A well-rehearsed outfit that's good at leading newcomers into the island's most savage landscapes is **Vieques Adventure Company** (✆ 787/692-9162; www.bike vieques.com). Gary Lowe and members of his staff lead mountain bikers on half-day ($150 per person) tours of obscure trails that are noteworthy for their panoramas and technical difficulties. Use of a mountain bike, usually an aluminum-framed, 28-speed, state-of-the-art model, is included in the price. You can rent one of these bikes, without the services of a trail guide, for $25 per day. The company also rents sea kayaks ($45 daily). Anglers will want to try a kayak fly-fishing tour at a price of $175 per person for a truly unique experience. The company also runs glass bottomed canoe tours of the biobay at night ($50).

Taxi Horses (℗ **787/206-0122;** www.blackbeardsports.com), gives 2-hour group tours that leave at 10am and 4pm daily (riders must arrive 30 min. before each departure). The guides are engaging and the coastal route breathtakingly beautiful. $75 per person when two or more riders form a group.

Fin Time Adventures (℗ **787/981-4109;** www.fintimeadventures.com) and **SeaVieques** (℗ **787/435-0256;** www.seavieques.com) offer daylong snorkel and sail trips on beautiful sailing vessels, and indulge with nice lunches and open bars.

Natural Attraction

One of the major attractions on the island is **Mosquito Bay ★**, also called **Phosphorescent Bay,** with its glowing waters produced by tiny bioluminescent organisms. These organisms dart away from boats, leaving eerie blue-white trails of phosphorescence. "The Vieques Times" wrote: "By any name, the bay can be a magical, psychedelic experience, and few places in the world can even come close to the intensity of concentration of the dinoflagellates called pyrodiniums (whirling fire). They are tiny (1/500-in.) swimming creatures that light up like fireflies when disturbed, but nowhere are there so many fireflies. Here a gallon of bay water may contain almost three-quarters of a million." The ideal time to tour is on a cloudy, moonless night. If the moon is shining on a cloudless night, you can save your money, as you'll see almost nothing. Some boats go, full moon or not. While it is no longer possible to swim in these glowing waters, boat operators usually stop in the middle of the bay to let visitors dip their feet to activate the organisms. Periodic weather events involving tides can dim the bay. In 2014, the Puerto Rico Department of Natural & Environmental Resources put restrictions in place to limit tours to Friday through Sunday and also placed a limit on the number of visitors who can experience the bay each night over fears the traffic could be harming the delicate natural balance.

Island Adventures (℗ **787/741-0720;** www.biobay.com) operates trips in Phosphorescent Bay aboard *Luminosa.* These 2-hour trips are not offered around the time of the full moon. Similar tours are also offered on kayaks by **Blue Caribe Kayak** (℗ **787/ 741-2522**), **Abe's Snorkeling & Bio-Bay Tours** (℗ **787/741-2134;** www.abes snorkeling.com), and **Blackbeard Sports** (℗ **787/741-1892;** www.blackbeardsports. com). Prices range from $45 to $65.

Historic Site

Fort Conde de Mirasol Museum ★★, Barriada Fuerte at Magnolia 471 (http:// enchanted-isle.com/elfortin; ℗ **787/741-1717**), is more than just an impressive historic fortress with amazing grounds and views; it's also an engaging museum that helps visitors embrace Vieques' history. The last of Spain's fortresses to be built in the world, it takes its name from the count who convinced the crown to build the fort in the 1840s. The carefully restored fortress is perched on a hill above Isabel Segunda. The archeology collection of Taíno finds is wonderful, as are exhibits about the "great liberator" Simón Bolívar who visited here, and about the town's 60-year long struggle against the Navy presence. Tropical gardens bloom on the grounds surrounding the fortress, and there are stunning views of the coast and town every way from every direction. The museum and fort are open Wednesday through Sunday 10am to 4pm. Admission is $3 suggested donation for adults.

Shopping

Exciting new shopping opportunities on Vieques have mushroomed in recent years in the wake of the navy exit and the ensuing tourist influx. For the first time in years, the clothing stores in Isabel Segunda and Esperanza are actually in fashion.

The Malecón House Boutique (Calle Flamboyán 105, Esperanza, ✆ 787/741-0663) has stylish clothing, jewelry, and swimwear for women. Forward-looking fashion, jewelry, and gifts are on offer at **Funky Beehive** (Calle Antonio G. Mellado 359, corner Calle Muñoz Rivera, Isabel Segunda; ✆ 787/741-3192). **Vieques Flowers & Gifts** (Calle Flamboyán 134, Esperanza; ✆ 787/741-4197) also offers swimwear, beach supplies, and summery fashion for visitors as well arts and crafts and gourmet items. **Lucky 1** (✆ 720/366-1337; www.1upcycledfurniture.com) has wooden pallet furniture by designer-builder Lenni Calipo in a showroom outside Esperanza. **Placita Reyes** (Rte. 200, 201) is a farmer's market with fresh fruits and vegetables from 7am to 4pm on Tuesday, Wednesday, and Friday.

Art Galleries

Nowhere is Vieques' burst of creativity greater than in the growth of island art galleries. A number of international artists have settled here, and together with the sizeable number of fine island artists, there is a particularly vibrant arts community. Because the island is such an obvious influence on the artists, their work tends to reflect the beauty of Vieques. A pioneer on the local art scene, **Siddhia Hutchinson Fine Art Studio & Gallery,** at the Hotel Carmen, Calle Muñoz Rivera, Isabel Segunda (✆ 787/741-1343), features not only Hutchinson's work, but also the work of artists inspired by the Caribbean. The gallery has original paintings, sculpture, ceramics, photographs, prints, and jewelry. The **Vieques Historical & Conversation Trust,** Calle Flamboyán 138 (✆ 787/741-8850; www.vcthg.org), is a nonprofit dedicated to preserving Vieques culture has a fascinating gift shop and gallery, along with museum exhibits. **Ileana Jové's Glass Art,** at Birdsnest Studios vacation rentals outside Isabel Segunda, Rte. 997, Km 1.5 (✆ 787/741-4694) has great jewelry and mosaic works. **Caribbean Walk Gallery,** Calle Antonio Mellado 357, Isabel Segunda (✆ 787/741-7770), is another local gift shop that is worth a peek.

Vieques Nightlife

This is still a relatively quiet place, but there are more places to party, and the parties are getting more festive every year. In general, there is still no place better than the Esperanza *malecón* on a Friday night, drinking cheap, cold, beer and listening to some great music and conversation.

Bar Plaza ★   Cool off in the hot afternoon and step into the past in this storied bar near the town plaza, with its high ceilings and doors that swing wide open to the outside street. There's a pool table and a jukebox with mostly old classic salsa and bolero music. Open daily 9am to 9pm. Plaza del Recreo, in Isabel Segunda. ✆ 787/741-2176.

Lazy Jack's ★★   Whether it's karaoke, live music, fiestas around sporting events or a house DJ, there's always something going on at Lazy Jack's. And there's always a crowd since it's the house pub and cafe for a hostel in back. The solidly good food, frozen drinks, and beer also wins it a core following among locals and visitors. The kitchen is the latest operating in town. It's open Sunday through Thursday 11am to midnight, Friday and Saturday 11am to 2am. On the Waterfront, adjacent to the ferryboat piers, in Isabel Segunda. ✆ 787/741-3400.

La Nasa ★   This wooden beach shack is the only establishment on the waterfront side of the street in Vieques. It serves cold beer and rum drinks and blares brash salsa and other tropical music at night. There's often live music on weekends and holidays. Grab a cheap plastic seat and have a cold one. The place isn't fancy, but the conversation is animated and the view over the water is worth a million dollars. Open daily until 10pm, later on weekends. Calle Flamboyán, in Isabel Segunda. No phone.

El Guayacán ★   Up front there's flavorful Puerto Rican food at affordable prices, in back there's a happening hangout bar, often with live music jams during the evening. It's a great place to party and meet people. Open daily until 10pm, later on weekends. At Plaza Guayacán, Calle Flamboyán 134, Esperanza. No phone.

CULEBRA ★

52 miles (84km) E of San Juan; 18 miles (29km) E of Fajardo

Sun-bleached Culebra, 18 miles (29km) east of Puerto Rico's main island and halfway to St. Thomas in the U.S. Virgin Islands, is just 7 miles (11km) long and 3 miles (5km) wide and has only 2,000 residents. The island is blessed by the persistent enchantment of the tropical weather, and the landscape is dotted with everything from scrub and cacti to Poinciana, frangipanis, and coconut palms. It has stunning beaches and emerald waters, and some of the finest diving, snorkeling, and sailing in the region, not to mention a gorgeous countryside.

This small island is all about having fun in the surf and the sun, but after a hard day at the beach, you can kick it back several notches and relax. There are a growing number of chic vacation homes and upscale inns, and places to get a good meal. But most visitors will want to save their energy for Culebra's white-sand beaches, clear waters, and long coral reefs.

Culebra was settled as a Spanish colony in 1886. Like Puerto Rico and Vieques, it became part of the United States after the Spanish-American War in 1898. In fact, Culebra's only town, a fishing village called **Dewey,** was named for Admiral George Dewey, a U.S. hero of that war, although the locals defiantly call it **Puebla.**

From 1909 to 1975, the U.S. Navy used Culebra as a gunnery range and as a practice bomb site in World War II. Today the four tracts of the **Culebra Wildlife Refuge,** plus 23 other offshore islands, are managed by the U.S. Fish & Wildlife Service. The refuge is one of the most important turtle-nesting sites in the Caribbean, and it also houses large seabird colonies, notably terns and boobies.

Culebrita, a mile-long (1.6km) coral-isle satellite of Culebra, has a hilltop lighthouse and crescent beaches. There are nearly two dozen other cays surrounding the island in the midst of stunning Caribbean waters.

Essentials

GETTING THERE   **Vieques Air-Link** (✆ **787/741-8331;** www.viequesairlink.com) flies to Culebra twice a day from San Juan's Isla Grande Airport. Round-trip is $148. Flying from Ceiba is cheaper at $88 roundtrip. Another option is **Air Flamenco** (https://airflamenco.net/Newsite; ✆ **787/724-1818** or 721-7332), which charges $140 roundtrip from San Juan's Isla Grande and $60 roundtrip from Ceiba.

The **Puerto Rico Port Authority** operates four **ferries** per day from the mainland port of Fajardo to Culebra; the trip takes about 90 minutes. The round-trip fare is $4.50 for adults, $2.25 for children 3 to 12 (free for 2 and under). Ferry service has really faltered during 2014, making it recommendable to fly here instead.

GETTING AROUND   With no public transportation, the only way to get to Culebra's beaches is by bike or rental car.

There are a number of small **car-rental** agencies on the island, mostly renting jeeps or similar vehicles. Prices range from $45 to $85 daily. **Carlos Jeep Rental,** Parcela 2, Barriada Clark, Dewey (✆ **787/742-3514;** www.carlosjeeprental.com), is 3 minutes from the airport. The outfitter rents jeeps and golf carts, and with advance notice, will meet you at the airport. When you drop off your rental, the staff will also drive you back to the airport. **Jerry's Jeeps** (✆ **787/742-0526;** www.jerrysjeeprental.com) is located in front of the airport and offers jeeps and golf carts as does **Willie's Jeep Rental,** Calle Escudero, Barriada Clark (✆ **787/742-3537**), which is a 5-minute walk from the airport.

Bike riding is a popular means of getting around the island's hills, dirt trails, and bad roads. **Culebra Bike Shop & Kayak Rental,** at Hotel Kokomo, across from ferry, Dewey (http://culebrabikeshop.com; ✆ **787/742-0589**), rents bikes for $15 a day in addition to kayaks, beach chairs and umbrellas, and snorkeling gear. You can rent mountain bikes at **Dick and Cathy** (✆ **787/742-0062**) as well. Just call to reserve, and they will deliver to your hotel. You can also rent scooters from rental car companies and **JM Rentals** (✆ **787/717-7583**).

Where to Stay
MODERATE
Bahia Marina ★★★   Want to feel at home quickly on Culebra? Bunk down at these amenity-laden, attractive two-bedroom, two-bath villas. Set on a ridge overlooking Fulladoza Bay and backed by a tropical nature reserve, all units come with full kitchens and view-blessed balconies. On-site are terrific restaurants and bars, a pool with a swim up bar, and the dock for the Pez Vela catamaran.

Rte. 250, Km 2.5, Fulladoza Bay. ✆ **787/742-0535.** www.bahiamarina.net. 18 units. $295. From Dewey (Puebla), follow Rte. 250 (also called Fulladoza Rd.) along the south side of the bay for 1¾ miles (2.8km). **Amenities:** Restaurants; bars; DVD library; 3 pools; free Wi-Fi in common areas.

Casa Yaboa ★   This eco-lodge is located on a secluded 5-acre coastal plot, a sun-drenched shallow beach perfect for snorkeling and sunbathing. It comprises three cedar cottages with kitchens and great views, numerous areas to relax in hammocks and lounge chairs, terraces and barbecue areas, and gardens and walking paths. The grounds are filled with riotous tropical foliage and huge shade trees.

Rte. 250, Culebra. ✆ **787/340-7058** or 413-0310. www.casayaboaculebra.com. 3 cottages (shower only). Tree Nest $150, Bubi House $190, and Casa Guayacán $240. **Amenities:** 10 percent discount at Susie's Restaurant; watersports/equipment rentals.

Club Seabourne ★★★   Perhaps the best lodging on the island, Club Seabourne is located on the winding country road from town to Fulladoza Bay and offers expansive views over the coastline. To give guests real privacy, the contemporary, light-filled and comfortable guest rooms are spread out in tropical villas across the elevated property; you may feel like you're totally on your own, except at meal times when guests crowd the excellent restaurant (Gio Gastro Bar) and the convivial bar. The cherry on top of it all? A staff that bends over backwards to coddle each and every guest.

Fulladoza Rd. ✆ **787/742-3169.** www.clubseabourne.com. 12 units (shower only). Winter $185 double, $279–$339 villas; off-season $169 double, $249–$309 villas. Rates include breakfast, 1 hour kayak and bike rental, 2 drinks. From Dewey (Puebla), follow Rte. 250 (also called Fulladoza Rd.) along the south side of the bay. It's 1½ miles/2.4km from town. **Amenities:** Restaurant; bar; pool; 1 room for those w/limited mobility; dock; free Wi-Fi.

Tamarindo Estates ★★ Quiet, low-key rooms located inside a dozen cottages scattered across 60 acres of lush coastline: That's what you get at Tamarindo Estates. It's not the be-all and end-all for luxury, but with glorious views and all the comforts of home (usable kitchens and seating areas, quality beds), who's complaining? Plus, the pool is gorgeous, fronting the coastline, and there's a secluded bay with clear still water that is perfect for snorkeling. Only 10 minutes from downtown Dewey, it feels a universe away.

Tamarindo Beach Rd. ℭ **787/742-3343.** www.tamarindoestates.com. 12 cottages (shower only). Winter $169 double; off-season $149 double. **Amenities:** Pool; beach house; in room kitchens; free Wi-Fi.

INEXPENSIVE
Casa Ensenada Waterfront Guesthouse ★ Don't expect bend-over-backwards treatment here; in fact, you're pretty much left to your own devices with a minimum of staff interruption. To some this is a bother; to others bliss. That being said, the staff do a good job of keeping the simple units here quite clean (some have kitchenettes, a real plus); and they lend out kayaks free. The location, which is in walking distance of everywhere in town you'd want to go, but still quiet, is another key perk.

Calle Escudero 142. ℭ **787/241-4441** or 866/210-0709. www.casaensenada.com. 3 units (shower only). Winter $125 double, $150–$175 up to five people; spring and summer $85 double, $85–$150 for up to six (taxes included in rates). **Amenities:** Bikes; library; BBQ; watersports/equipment rentals; free Wi-Fi.

Posada la Hamaca ★ Bright and quite appealing, this guesthouse provides basic comforts in a great location on the Dewey channel. Rooms are clean and comfortable and some have kitchenettes; you get a lot of bang for your buck here. A great dock/terrace area and barbecues are available for guests to use.

Calle Castelar 68. ℭ **787/742-3516.** www.posada.com. 10 units. Winter $90–$103 double, $123–$160 suites with kitchens; off-season $81–$96, $114–$142 suites with kitchens. Plus $3 per reservation nightly resort fee. **Amenities:** Free Wi-Fi.

Where to Dine
EXPENSIVE
Susie's ★★ TROPICAL FUSION This casual, homey spot serves up surprisingly creative and sophisticated food. Since the menu relies on locally grown herbs and produce, it changes frequently, but it often features grouper bites with Asian slaw and sweet soy sauce; filet mignon with a wild mushroom and truffle sauce; an excellent curried lamb chops; and grilled kingfish *escabeche*, a Puerto Rican favorite. It's a really fine dining experience, worth the price. *One warning:* Wear bug spray, as you're sitting outdoors and the mosquitos can be fierce.

Calle Sardinas 2, Dewey. ℭ **787/742-0574.** Reservations recommended. Main courses $10–30. Tues–Sun 6–9:30pm.

MODERATE
Dinghy Dock ★★ AMERICAN/CARIBBEAN/PUERTO RICAN An ownership change has made this place literally bigger and better, and that includes both the quality of the food and the physical space. The menu consists seafood classics, great brunch and lunch fare, and late night snacks. A new bar has made this place more of a hangout, but there's still a special feel to dining directly on the waterfront dock. Kids love throwing their leftover food over the side and watching the giant tarpin fight over

it. As for what to order: You won't go wrong with the succulent BBQ chicken and ribs or the fresh Caribbean lobster. Service is friendly and efficient.

Punta del Soldado Rd., outside Dewey. © **787/742-0233** or 742-0581. Breakfast $5–$12; lunch $6–$18; main courses $12–$30. Daily 8am–9pm.

Homeless Dog Café ★★ TROPICAL SOUL FOOD Not quite a restaurant, this culinary wonder delivers food to your doorstep anywhere on Culebra from 4pm to 1am. The wife and husband team behind the venture (Peri heats up the kitchen, while Hector takes all the good lovin' to your doorstep) delivers food as soulful as it is flavorful, with a daily changing menu. Delicious dishes are rooted in Peri's native U.S. Southern cooking and the tropical flavors of her Caribbean home. Recent specials have included chicken and dumplings, sweet fish and green onions, and smothered pork chops with delicious coleslaw and potato salad, plus daily desserts such as coconut crème cupcakes and chocolate ice bucket cake.

Rte. 250, Km 0.1. © **939/452-9563.** www.facebook.com/pages/The-Homeless-Dog-Cafe/130849730283213. Entrees $8–$20. Wed–Mon 4pm–1am.

Mamàcita's ★★ PUERTO RICAN This tropical bar and restaurant on the Dewey Canal combines friendly and fun service, a friendly clientele, and a choice locale to make this one of the best spots on the island for the last 20 years. Quality food and drinks make this a must stop from brunch to nighttime. Start out with a tropical bruschetta or the chicken taquitos. Maine courses range from excellent pastas to a standout mango chutney pork chop and a swordfish with tamarind citrus sauce.

Calle Castelar 64–66. © **787/742-0090.** Lunch $7–$20; main courses $14–$30. Fri–Wed 11am–3pm and 6–9:30pm; weekend breakfast buffet 8am–11am.

INEXPENSIVE

Heather's Pizzeria ★★★ PIZZA Serving superb pizza, pastas, salads and sandwiches, this place has a rocking sound system and a staff that's super friendly and knowledgeable about the island. It's a gathering spot for local ex-pats who appreciate the high quality and economical Italian/American food.

Calle Marquez 14, Dewey. © **787/742-3175.** Pizzas, sandwiches, and platters $9–$25. Thurs–Tues 5–10pm, bar open till 11pm. Closed 1–2 weeks in Oct.

Zaco's Tacos ★★ MEXICAN It's back to basics at this island taqueria, where bright primary colors meet fresh and flavorful tacos. The prices are affordable and the service super friendly. There are fab drinks, too, from margaritas to fruit smoothies.

Calle Marquez 21. © **787/742-0243.** www.zacostacos.com. Appetizers and main courses $2–$9. Wed–Sun noon–8pm.

Beaches

The island's most popular beach is **Flamenco Beach ★★★**, a mile-long (1.6km) horseshoe-shaped cove on the northwestern edge. It's a mile-long arc of the silkiest, lightest white sand you will ever see, fronting a sapphire covered sea. It's one of the most photographed beaches on the Caribbean, and with reason.

Walk over the hill beside the beach to **Playa Carlos Rosario ★★**. The sands here aren't quite as good as those at Flamenco, but the snorkeling is even better in these clear waters. A barrier reef protects this beach, so you are almost guaranteed tranquil waters. Snorkelers can also walk south from Playa Carlos Rosario for a quarter-mile (.4km) to a place called **"the Wall" ★**. There are 40-foot (12m) drop-offs into the water where you are likely to see schools of fish gliding by.

The isolated **Zoni Beach** ★★★ is a 1-mile (1.6km) strip of sand flanked by large boulders and scrub. Located on the island's northeastern edge, about 7 miles (11km) from Dewey (Puebla), it's one of the most beautiful beaches on the island. Snorkelers, but not scuba divers, find it particularly intriguing; there are beautiful reefs just off-shore, but the surf sometimes makes underwater visibility a bit murky during rough weather.

Adventure Tours

Known for its unspoiled underwater vistas, and absence of other divers, Culebra is what the Caribbean used to be before crowds of divers began exploring the sea. At least 50 dive sites, all around the island, are worthwhile. **Culebra Divers,** Calle Pedro Marquez 138 (© **787/742-0803;** www.culebradivers.com), offers a resort course for novice divers, including training in a sheltered cove, and a tank dive in 15 to 20 feet (4.6–6.1m) of water ($125). Full PADI certification costs $395 and includes five open-water dives. You'll have to arrange to study the material before arrival, and you'll do the real practice once you are here. Certified divers pay $98 for a two-tank open-water dive. The outfitter rents equipment for $15 daily. It's rare that more than six divers go out in one of these boats on any day. Snorkeling tours are also given for $60 per person. Captain Bill Penfield gives tours on his *Pez-Vela* (© **787/215-3809**), a 33-foot sailing catamaran with room for six passengers. Go on a snorkel/picnic, deep-sea fishing, or simply take a leisure sail to nearby islands, coves, and deserted beaches. Bill is an excellent and professional captain who will provide you with a quintessential Caribbean experience. Lunch, drinks, and snacks are included in a $125 per person rate. Tours are given daily, and group rates are available. **Snorkel SVI-Culebra** (http://sites. google.com/site/culebraislandsnorkel; © **787/930-2111**) offers kayak snorkel and fishing trips for $95 full day, $65 half-day from the island that traverse waters choked with tropical fish and reefs and venture on to deserted cays.

PLANNING YOUR TRIP TO PUERTO RICO

P uerto Rico's unique political situation makes it a hassle-free destination for U.S. travelers, who will basically be subject to the same guidelines as interstate travel. All you need is a government-issued identification. You won't face any of the hassles of foreign government entry requirements and processes you would at many other Caribbean destinations. Also, several major airlines offer direct flights to airports in San Juan and Aguadilla from major cities throughout the United States, especially from the East Coast, and beachfront guesthouses or big scale hotels are minutes from the airports. Being part of the U.S. also means there are no currency exchange hoops to jump through and your bank card will work as easily here as it will at home.

GETTING THERE

It's a 3½-hour flight from New York City, and it's quick for carry-on passengers, who can be at their destinations minutes after touchdown. San Juan's Luis Muñoz Marín International Airport has improved dramatically since private management took over its administration in 2013, with a quicker baggage process, well-maintained facilities, and better services. It's the only large passenger airport under private management within the United States.

Getting to your destination fast is a big reason to visit Puerto Rico. The country's ease of entry makes it a good alternative to not only Aruba or Cancun for that winter getaway, but a viable option to Vermont or New Hampshire for a long weekend getaway in October. This chapter discusses the where, when, and how of your trip to Puerto Rico—everything required to plan your trip and get it on the road. It's what you need to do *before* you go to make this largely hassle-free destination even more manageable.

By Plane

Puerto Rico is by far the most accessible of the Caribbean islands, with frequent airline service. It's also the major airline hub of the Caribbean Basin. Because it's part of the United States, there are no hassles for U.S. travelers related to border entry, currency exchange, and so forth.

Puerto Rico has more than 130 daily flights to and from 16 destinations in the continental U.S., the most in the Caribbean. Fourteen regional airlines provide more than 100 daily flights to 29 Caribbean destinations. Eighteen airlines provide 317 weekly flights to international destinations.

Airlines traveling to Puerto Rico include: **American Airlines** (✆ 800/433-7300 in the U.S. and Canada; www.aa.com); **Avianca** (✆ 800/284-2622; www.avianca.com); **Delta** (✆ 800/221-1212 in the U.S. and Canada; www.delta.com); **JetBlue** (✆ 800/538-2583 in the U.S. and Canada; www.jetblue.com); **Spirit Air** (✆ 801/401-2200 in the U.S. and Canada; www.spiritair.com); **United Airlines** (✆ 800/231-0856, or 800/864-8331 in the U.S. and Canada; www.united.com); **US Airways** (✆ 800/622-1015 in the U.S. and Canada; www.usairways.com); **Air Canada** (✆ 888/247-2262; www.aircanada.com); **Copa Airlines** (✆ 800/772-4642; www.copaair.com); **Condor** (✆ 866/960-7915 in the U.S. and Canada, or 490 180 57/0-7202 in Germany; www.condor.com); **LIAT** (✆ 866/549-5428 from Puerto Rico and the U.S. Virgin Islands, 888/844-5428 from elsewhere in the Caribbean, or 268/480-5601 from elsewhere, including the U.S.; www.liatairline.com); **Seaborne Airlines** (✆ 888/359-8687; www.seaborneairlines.com); **Southwest Airlines** (✆ 800/435-9792; www.southwest.com); and **WestJet** (✆ 855/547-2451 in the U.S., or 888/937-8538; www.westjet.com).

GETTING AROUND

By Plane

Seaborne moved its home base to San Juan, Puerto Rico from St. Croix in 2014 as it began an expansion of services throughout the Caribbean, serving 16 airports and expanding its aircraft fleet to 21, including 16 34-seat Saab 340Bs, including the Dominican Republic, Dominica, Guadeloupe, St. Kitts & Nevis, Tortola, Martinique, Virgin Gorda, St. Maarten and the U.S. Virgin Islands. It's filling the void left by the exit of American Eagle from the Caribbean market. **Cape Air** (✆ **800/CAPE-AIR [227-3247];** www.flycapeair.com) flies from Luis Muñoz Marín International Airport to Culebra, Mayagüez, and Vieques several times a day. They also offer many flights daily to St. Thomas, St. Croix, Tortola, Virgin Gorda, Nevis and Anguilla. **Vieques Air Link** (✆ **888/901-9247** or 787/741-8331; www.viequesairlink.com) and **Air Flamenco** (✆ **787/724-1818,** 724-1105, or 721-0332; www.airflamenco.net) offer several daily flights between San Juan, Ceiba and the island towns of Viequs and Culebra. They also provide service to nearby U.S. Virgin Islands.

By Car

There is good news and bad news about driving in Puerto Rico. First, the good news: Puerto Rico offers some of the most scenic drives in all the Caribbean.

Of course, if you want to stay only in San Juan, having a car is not necessary. You can get around San Juan on foot or by bus, taxi, and in some cases, hotel minivan. It will probably cost you more just to park your car at your hotel, then grabbing a cab or two a day.

Now the bad news: Renting a car and driving in Puerto Rico, depending on the routes you take, can lead to a number of frustrating experiences, as our readers relate to us year after year. These readers point out that local drivers are often reckless, as evidenced by the number of fenders with bashed-in sides. The older coastal highways provide the most scenic routes but are often congested. Some of the roads, especially in the mountainous interior, are just too narrow for automobiles. If you do rent a car, proceed with caution along these poorly paved and maintained roads, which most often follow circuitous routes. Avoid driving during heavy rains, when cliffslides or landslides are not uncommon.

Two reputable local agencies are **Charlie Car Rental** and **Target Rent a Car.** Watch out for small local agencies that may tempt you with special reduced prices. If you're planning to tour the island by car, you won't find any local branches that will help you if you experience trouble. And some of the agencies widely advertising low-cost deals won't take credit cards and want cash in advance. Also, watch out for hidden extra costs, which sometimes proliferate among the smaller and not very well-known firms, and difficulties connected with resolving insurance claims.

Avis, Budget, and **Hertz** are some of the big companies operating in Puerto Rico, providing pickup and drop off service from hotels and major locations like the airport and cruise ship docs. Be alert to the minimum-age requirements for car rentals in Puerto Rico. Both Avis and Hertz require that renters be 25 or older; at Budget, renters must be 21 or older, but those between the ages of 21 and 24 pay a $10 to $25 daily surcharge to the agreed-upon rental fee.

Added security comes from an antitheft double-locking mechanism that has been installed in most of the rental cars available in Puerto Rico. Car theft is common in Puerto Rico, so extra precautions are always needed.

Distances are often posted in kilometers rather than miles (1km = 0.62 mile), but speed limits are displayed in miles per hour.

International visitors should note that insurance and taxes are almost never included in quoted rental-car rates in the U.S. Be sure to ask your rental agency about additional fees for these. They can add a significant cost to your car rental. *Note:* In Puerto Rico, gasoline is sold by the liter, not by the gallon. The cost of gasoline is about the same as in the United States. Current prices are hovering around 98¢ a liter (3.78 of which make up a gallon). Taxes are already included in the printed price. One U.S. gallon equals 3.8 liters or .85 imperial gallons.

By Public Transportation

Cars and minibuses, known as *públicos,* provide low-cost transportation around the island. Their license plates have the letters "P" or "PD" following the numbers. They serve all the main towns of Puerto Rico; passengers are let off and picked up along the way, both at designated stops and when someone flags them down. Rates are set by the Public Service Commission. *Públicos* usually operate during daylight hours, departing from the main plaza (central square) of a town.

Information about *público* routes between San Juan and Mayagüez is available at **Lineas Sultana,** Calle Esteban González 898, Urbanización Santa Rita, Río Piedras (② 787/765-9377). Information about *público* routes between San Juan and Ponce is available from **Choferes Unidos de Ponce,** Terminal de Carros Públicos, Calle Vive in Ponce (② 787/764-0540). There are several operators listed under Lineas de Carros in the local Yellow Pages.

Fares vary according to whether the *público* will make a detour to pick up or drop off a passenger at a specific locale. (If you want to deviate from the predetermined routes, you'll pay more than if you wait for a *público* beside the main highway.) Fares from San Juan to Mayagüez and from San Juan to Ponce range from $20 to $40. Be warned that although prices of *públicos* are low, the routes are slow, with frequent stops, often erratic routing, and lots of inconvenience.

Getting around San Juan is getting easier all the time. You have two local bus lines, a *público* system that covers the entire metro area, and the Tren Urbano, a light urban rail system connecting Santurce with the Hato Rey financial district, the university and medical center districts, and important suburban locations in Bayamón and Guaynabo. Tren Urbano riders can transfer free to city buses and vice versa.

So if you are staying in San Juan, having a car is not necessary. You can get around San Juan on foot or by bus, taxi, and in some cases, hotel minivan. The Tren Urban, a light rail system connecting Santurce to the financial, university, and medical districts, and important suburban destinations in Bayamón and Guaynabo, is a great ride. Prices are 75¢, on par with public buses, and riders can transfer into the bus system free of charge, but officials were in the process of doubling the fare to $1.50. There are also ferries from Old San Juan to Catano and the Hato Rey financial district are also being integrated into the system.

The train and accompanying buses cover virtually all of San Juan. They keep special expanded schedules during big events, such as a festival in Old San Juan, and also for when big acts play at the Puerto Rico Coliseum, or the Tourism Company throws a New Year's Eve party at the convention center. For more information, call ℂ **866/900-1284,** or log onto www.ati.gobierno.pr.

Taxis are also reasonably priced and work late into the evening in the city's major districts. So they are your go-to option for a night of clubbing or to get home after a late night.

TIPS ON WHERE TO STAY
Hotels & Resorts

There is no rigid classification of Puerto Rican hotels. The word "deluxe" is often used—or misused—when "first class" might be a more appropriate term. We've presented fairly detailed descriptions of the hotels in this book, so you'll get an idea of what to expect once you're there.

You'll find Puerto Rico is way over its bum rap for bad service unless you are expecting Swiss efficiency. Sure this is still the tropical life, and there is something called "island time," but both the speed and quality of service, whether it's your evening meal or hotel check-in, has improved dramatically in recent years. And Puerto Rico's hotel and hospitality workers more than make up for any lack with genuinely friendly service that will make you feel welcome.

Ask detailed questions when booking a room. Entertainment in Puerto Rico is often alfresco, so light sleepers obviously won't want a room directly over a band. In general, back rooms cost less than oceanfront rooms, and lower rooms cost less than upper-floor units. Always ascertain whether transfers (which can be expensive) are included. And make sure that you know exactly what is free and what costs money. Some resorts seem to charge every time you breathe and might end up costing more than a deluxe hotel that includes most everything in the price.

The most important question to ask is if the property charges a hotel or resort fee, which can be hefty, as much as 18 percent of the cost of your entire stay. Once the provenance of the biggest properties, the fee is also being employed by your better guest houses these days. Knowing such fees is essential information when deciding where to stay, as it could make what seemed a good deal look suddenly otherwise. The practice is largely confined to San Juan and resort properties out on the island, but make sure to verify (we've included the fee after the room rates in this guide).

Puerto Rican Guesthouses

A unique type of accommodation is the guesthouse, where Puerto Ricans themselves usually stay when they travel. Ranging in size from 7 to 25 rooms, they offer a familial atmosphere. Many are on or near the beach; some have pools or sundecks, and a number serve meals.

In Puerto Rico, however, the term "guesthouse" has many meanings. Some guesthouses are like simple motels built around pools. Others have small individual cottages with their own kitchenettes, constructed around a main building in which you'll often find a bar and a restaurant serving local food. Some are surprisingly comfortable, often with private bathrooms and swimming pools. You may or may not have air-conditioning. The rooms are sometimes cooled by ceiling fans or by the trade winds blowing through open windows at night.

For value, the guesthouse can't be topped. If you stay at a guesthouse, you can journey over to a big beach resort and use its seaside facilities for only a small fee. Although bereft of frills, the guesthouses we've recommended are clean and safe for families or single women. However, the cheapest ones are not places where you'd want to spend a lot of time because of their modest furnishings.

For further information on guesthouses, contact the **Puerto Rico Tourism Company,** La Princesa Building, Paseo La Princesa 2, Old San Juan (✆ **800/866-7827** or 787/721-2400).

Paradores

In an effort to lure travelers beyond the hotels and casinos of San Juan's historic district to the tranquil natural beauty of the island's countryside, the Puerto Rico Tourism Company offers *paradores puertoriqueños* (charming country inns), which are comfortable bases for exploring the island's varied attractions. Vacationers seeking a peaceful idyll can also choose from several privately owned and operated guesthouses.

Using Spain's *parador* system as a model, the Puerto Rico Tourism Company established the *paradores* in 1973 to encourage tourism across the island. Each of the *paradores* is situated in a historic place or site of unusual scenic beauty and must meet high standards of service and cleanliness. Some of the *paradores* are located in the mountains and others by the sea. Most have pools, and all offer excellent Puerto Rican cuisine. Many are within easy driving distance of San Juan.

Properties must meet certain benchmark standards of quality to be admitted to the program, so tourists feel comfortable staying at the property. One complaint about the program is that variances in quality still range widely from one property to the next. For more information, call ✆ **800/866-7827** or check out www.gotoparadores.com.

Some of the best *paradores* are in western Puerto Rico (see chapter 9). The Tourism Company also operates a similar program which promotes worthy local restaurants called **Mesones Gastronómicos** (✆ 800/981-7575).

Villas & Vacation Homes

There are also excellent vacation homes in resort communities such as Rincón and Vieques. For luxurious Old San Juan apartment rentals, check **Vida Urbana,** Calle Cruz 255, Old San Juan (✆ **787/587-3031;** www.vidaurbanapr.com). Two short-term specialists in Condado and Isla Verde are **San Juan Vacations,** Cond. Marbella del Caribe, Ste. S-5, Isla Verde (✆ **800/266-3639** or 787/727-1591; www.sanjuanvacations.com), and **Ronnie's Properties,** Calle Marseilles 14, Ritz Condominium, Ste. 11-F, San Juan (www.ronniesproperties.com). Puerto Rico villas and vacation homes are also available through popular online worldwide accommodation rentals such as **Airbnb** (www.airbnb.com), **Homeaway** (www.homeaway.com), and **Flipkey** (www.flipkey.com).

Private apartments are rented either with or without maid service. This is more of a no-frills option than the villas and condos. An apartment might not be in a building with a swimming pool, and it might not have a front desk to help you. Among the major categories of vacation homes, cottages offer the most freewheeling way to live. Most cottages are fairly simple, many opening in an ideal fashion onto a beach, whereas others may be clustered around a communal pool. Many contain no more than a simple bedroom together with a small kitchen and bathroom. For the peak winter season, reservations should be made at least 5 or 6 months in advance.

Rental Agencies

Agencies specializing in renting properties in Puerto Rico include:

- **VHR, Worldwide,** 235 Kensington Ave., Norwood, NJ 07648 (✆ **800/633-3284** or 201/767-9393; www.vhrww.com), offers the most comprehensive portfolio of luxury villas, condominiums, resort suites, and apartments for rent in the Caribbean, including complete packages for airfare and car rentals.

- **Hideaways Aficionado,** 767 Islington St., Portsmouth, NH 03801 (✆ **800/843-4433** or 603/430-4433; www.hideaways.com), provides a 144-page guide with illustrations of its accommodations, so that you can get an idea of what you're renting. Most villas come with maid service. You can also ask this travel club about discounts on plane fares and car rentals.

The Active Vacation Planner

There are watersports opportunities throughout Puerto Rico, from San Juan's waterfront hotels to eastern resorts and the offshore islands of Vieques and Culebra all the way to the Rincón on the west coast and Cabo Rojo in the south.

Boating & Sailing

The waters off Puerto Rico provide excellent boating in all seasons. Winds average 10 to 15 knots virtually year-round. Marinas provide facilities and services on par with any others in the Caribbean, and many have powerboats or sailboats for rent, either crewed or bareboat charter.

Puerto Rico is ringed by marinas. In San Juan alone, there are three large ones. The upscale **Club Nautico de San Juan** (✆ **787/722-0177**) and neighboring **San Juan Bay Marina** (✆ **787/721-8062**) are adjacent to the Condado bridge and the Convention Center district in Miramar. The other marina, the **Cangrejos Yacht Club** (Rte. 187, Piñones; ✆ **787/791-1015**), is near the airport, outside Isla Verde at the entrance to Piñones.

All three have several sailing charters and dive and fishing operators.

Fajardo, on Puerto Rico's northeast corner, boasts seven marinas, including the Caribbean's largest, the **Puerto del Rey Marina** (Rte. 3, Km 51.4; ✆ **787/860-1000** or 801-3010), and the popular **Villa Marina Yacht Harbour** (Rte. 987, Km 1.3; ✆ **787/863-5131** or 863-5011), offering the shortest ride to the best snorkeling grounds and offshore beaches. Other town marinas include **Puerto Chico** (Rte. 987, Km 2.4; ✆ **787/863-0834**) and **Puerto Real** (Playa Puerto Real; ✆ **787/863-2188**).

Along the south coast, one of the most established and charming marinas is the **Ponce Yacht & Fishing Club** (La Guancha, Ponce; ✆ **787/842-9003**).

But marinas, both small and large, can be found throughout island coasts. Check local listings for a "Club Nautico." Those with pleasure crafts, sailing, and watersports offerings catering to tourists include **Club Nautico de Boquerón** (✆ **787/851-1336**) and **Club Nautico de La Parguera** (✆ **787/899-5590**), which are each located just outside their respective village centers.

Several sailing and ocean racing regattas are held in Puerto Rico annually. The east of Puerto Rico and the southwest are particularly attractive for sailors. Fajardo is the start of a series of ports, extending from Puerto Rico's own offshore islands through the U.S. and British Virgin Islands to the east, which is probably the Caribbean's top sailing destination.

The easiest way to experience the joys of sailing is to go out on a day trip leaving from one of the Fajardo marinas (with transportation from San Juan hotels often included). The trips usually take place on large luxury catamarans or sailing yachts, with a bar serving drinks and refreshments, a sound system, and other creature comforts. Typically, after a nice sail, the vessel weighs anchor at a good snorkeling spot, then makes a stop on one of the beautiful sand beaches on the small islands off the Fajardo coast. Operators include **Traveler** (© **787/863-2821**), **East Island Excursions** (© **787/860-3434**), **Catamaran Spread Eagle II** (© **787/887-8821**). **Erin Go Bragh Charters** (© **787/860-4401**).

Also on the east coast is **Karolette Charter,** Palmas del Mar, Calle AB-12, Rte. 3, Km 86.4, Humacao (© **787/637-7992** or 850-7442), which offers snorkeling trips for $107 per person, or charters for $640 for 4½ hours or $840 for 6 hours.

Out west, **Katarina Sail Charters** (© **787/823-SAIL** [7245]) in Rincón gives daily sailing trips aboard a 32-foot (9.8m) catamaran; there are both a day sail and a sunset sail on offer.

For the typical visitor interested in watersports—not the serious yachter—our favorite place for fun in the surf is the aptly named **San Juan Water Fun** on Isla Verde Beach in back of the Wyndham El San Juan Hotel & Casino, Avenida Isla Verde in Isla Verde, San Juan (© **787/644-2585** or 643-4510). Here you can rent everything from a two-seater kayak for $30 per hour to a banana boat that holds eight passengers and costs $15 per person for a 20-minute ride. Fly high on a parasail trip, $70 per person for 10 minutes of heavenly glory.

If you're staying in eastern Puerto Rico, the best place for watersports rentals is the **watersports center** at Rio Mar Beach Resort, 6000 Rio Mar Blvd., Rio Grande (© **787/888-6000**), with scuba and snorkeling trips, and a great selection of small boats. WaveRunners cost about $100 per hour, and two-seat kayaks go for $35 per hour. There are complimentary sailing lessons for beginners with sailboat rental.

In the southwest, **Pino's Boat & Water Fun** (© **787/821-6864** or 484-8083) at Guánica's Playa Santa has everything from paddleboats or kayaks to water scooters for rent.

Camping

Puerto Rico abounds in remote sandy beaches, lush tropical forests, and mountain lakesides that make for fine camping.

Although it has been technically illegal to camp on beaches (except in designated areas) for the last decade, it is commonly done in off-the-beaten path coastal areas, especially in Guánica, Isabela, Fajardo, and the offshore islands of Vieques and Culebra.

Also, there are more than enough campgrounds available in coastal areas, as well as in the mountains and local state forests and nature reserves.

Some of the nicest campgrounds, as well as the best equipped and safest, are those run by the government **Compañia de Parques Nacionales** (Av. Fernández Juncos 1611, Santurce; © **787/622-5200;** www.parquesnacionalespr.com).

Six of the seven campsites it operates are located on the coast—at Luquillo, Fajardo, Vieques, Arroyo, Añasco, and Vega Baja. It also runs a fine campground in the mountain town of Maricao, in the middle of a lush forest with a view.

Some of these are simple places where you erect your own tent, although they are outfitted with electricity and running water; some are simple cabins, sometimes with fireplaces. Showers and bathrooms are communal. To stay at a campsite costs between $15 and $25 per night per tent.

Many sites offer very basic cabins for rent. Each cabin is equipped with a full bathroom, a stove, a refrigerator, two beds, and a table and chairs. However, most of your cooking will probably be tastier if you do it outside at one of the on-site barbecues. In nearly all cases, you must provide your own sheets and towels.

The agency, the National Parks Company, in English, also operates more upscale "vacation centers," which feature rustic cabins and more tourist-ready "villas," on par with many island inns.

State forests run by the **Departamento de Recursos Naturales y Ambientales** also allow camping with permits. Except for cabins at Monte Guilarte State Forest, which cost $20 per night, camping sites are available at $5 per person. For further information about permits, contact the DRNA (Rte. 8838, Km 6.3, Sector El Cinco, Río Piedras; ✆ **787/999-2200**).

There are seven major on-island camping sites in the following state forests: **Cambalache State Forest,** near Barceloneta; **Carite State Forest,** near Patillas; **Guajataca State Forest,** near Quebradillas; **Monte Guilarte State Forest,** near Adjuntas; **Susua State Forest,** near Yauco; **Río Abajo State Forest,** near Arecibo; and our favorite, **Toro Negro Forest Reserve,** near Villaba, where you can camp in the shadow of Puerto Rico's highest peaks.

It's also possible to camp at either of two wildlife refuges, **Isla de Mona Wildlife Refuge,** lying some 50 miles (80km) off the west coast of Puerto Rico surrounded by the rough seas of Mona Passage, and at **Lago Lucchetti Wildlife Refuge,** a beautiful mountain reservoir between Yauco and Ponce.

Meanwhile, visitors can also camp at **El Yunque National Forest** (✆ **787/888-1810**), which is under the jurisdiction of the U.S. Forest Service. There is no cost, but permits are required. They can be obtained in person at the Catalina Service Center (Rte. 191, Km 4.3) daily from 8am to 4:30pm, and weekends at the Palo Colorado Visitor Center (Rte. 191, Km 11.9) from 9:30am to 4pm. It's primitive camping within the rainforest.

Deep-Sea Fishing

While fishing is good year round, the winter season from October to early March is among the best. Blue marlin can be caught all summer and into the fall, and renowned big-game fishing tournaments take place in August and September.

Charters are available at marinas in major cities and tourism areas. Most boats range between 32 and 50 feet; fit six passengers; can be chartered for half- or full-day; and usually include bait, crew, and equipment.

Big game fish are found close to shore across Puerto Rico, so you won't waste time traveling to fishing spots. A mile off the San Juan coast, the ocean floor drops 600 feet (183m), and the awesome Puerto Rico Trench, a 500-mile-long (805km) fault that plunges to a depth of 28,000 feet (8,354m), lies about 75 miles (121km) directly north. It's a 20-minute ride to where the big game fish are biting, so it's possible to leave in the morning, make the catch of the day, and be back at the marina in the early afternoon.

Deep-sea fishing is top-notch throughout the island. Allison tuna, white and blue marlin, sailfish, wahoo, dolphinfish (mahi mahi), mackerel, and tarpon are some of the fish that can be caught in Puerto Rican waters, where 30 world records have been broken. Charter arrangements can be made through most major hotels and resorts and at most marinas. The big game fishing grounds are very close offshore from San Juan, making the capital an excellent place to hire a charter. A half-day of deep-sea fishing

(4 hr.) starts at around $550, while full-day charters begin at around $900. Most charters hold six passengers in addition to the crew.

In San Juan, experienced operators include **Sea Born Fishing Charters** (℃ 787/723-2292), as well as **Castillo Fishing Charters** (℃ 787/726-5752), and **Caribbean Outfitters** (℃ 787/396-8346).

Rincón also has a number of deep-sea fishing charters, such as **Makaira Fishing Charters** (℃ 787/823-4391 or 299-7374) and **Moondog Charters** (℃ 787/823-3059).

In Palmas del Mar, which has some of the best year-round fishing in the Caribbean, you'll find **Capt. Bill Burleson** (see "Palmas del Mar," in chapter 10).

Golf

With nearly 30 golf courses, including several championship links, Puerto Rico is rightly called the "Scotland," or the "golf capital," of the Caribbean, especially because they have been designed by the likes of Robert Trent Jones, Sr., his son Rees Jones, Greg Norman, George and Tom Fazio, Jack Nicklaus, Arthur Hills, and Puerto Rico's own Chi Chi Rodriguez.

Many of the courses are jewels of landscape architecture, running through verdant tropical forest and former coconut groves, or winding in dramatic switchbacks aside a breathtaking stretch of coast. Year-round summer weather and mostly gentle breezes add to the joy of playing here.

See Best Places to Golf in Chapter 1.

Hiking

The mountainous interior of Puerto Rico provides ample opportunities for hill climbing and nature treks. These are especially appealing because panoramas open at the least-expected moments, often revealing spectacular views of the distant sea.

The most popular, most beautiful, and most spectacular trekking spot is **El Yunque,** the sprawling "jungle" maintained by the U.S. Forest Service and the only rainforest on U.S. soil.

El Yunque is part of the **Caribbean National Forest,** which lies a 45-minute drive east of San Juan. More than 250 species of trees and some 200 types of ferns have been identified here. Some 60 species of birds inhabit El Yunque, including the increasingly rare Puerto Rican parrot. Such rare birds as the elfin woods warbler, the green mango hummingbird, and the Puerto Rican lizard-cuckoo live here.

Park rangers have clearly marked the trails that are ideal for walking. See "El Yunque," in chapter 6, for more details.

A lesser forest, but one that is still intriguing to visit, is the **Maricao State Forest,** near the coffee town of Maricao. This forest is in western Puerto Rico, east of the town of Mayagüez. For more details, see "Mayagüez," in chapter 8.

Ponce is the best center for exploring some of the greatest forest reserves in the Caribbean Basin, notably **Toro Negro Forest Reserve** with its **Lake Guineo** (the lake at the highest elevation on the island); the **Guánica State Forest,** ideal for hiking and bird-watching; and the **Carite Forest Reserve,** a 6,000-acre (2,428-hectare) park known for its dwarf forest. For more details, see "Ponce," in chapter 7.

Equally suitable for hiking are the protected lands (especially the **Río Camuy Cave Park**) whose topography is characterized as "karst"—that is, limestone riddled with caves, underground rivers, and natural crevasses and fissures. Although these regions pose additional risks and technical problems for trekkers, some people prefer the opportunities they provide for exploring the territory both above and below its surface. See "Arecibo & Camuy," in chapter 6, for details about the Río Camuy Caves.

Outdoor Adventure

If you'd like to experience Puerto Rico on horseback, there are several options, with tours generally running from $50 to $75 per person for around a 2-hour trip. **Hacienda Caribalí** (© 787/889-5829 or 690-3781; www.haciendacaribalipuertorico.com) offers 2-hour tours on majestic Paso Fino horses that take riders along the Mamayes River in the shadow of El Yunque rainforest. The 600-acre (243-hectare) ranch also offers four-wheelers and mountain bike tours, and has a go-kart track. If you are way out west, check out **Pintos 'R' Us** (© 787/516-7090) in Rincón. The 2-hour horseback ride tour is a fabulous ride through gorgeous beach and coastal headlands, winding country roads, and forested mountain paths. **Tropical Trail Rides** (© 787/872-9256; www.tropicaltrailrides.com) gives beach tours on Paso Fino horses at a beautiful locale in Isabela, which also has cavernous cliffs and tropical forests, as well as at the 2,200 acre Hacienda Campo Rico in Carolina, in the San Juan metropolitan area.

Several other tour operators cater to special tastes, including **Castillo Tours & Travel Service,** 2413 Laurel St., Punta Las Marias, Santurce (© 787/791-6195; www.castillotours.com), which is known for some of the best deep-sea fishing, rainforest, and catamaran tours.

AdvenTours, Luquillo (© 787/530-8311; www.adventourspr.com), features customized private tours that include such activities as bird-watching, hiking, camping, visits to coffee plantations, and kayaking.

Enchanted Island Eco Tours, Rte. 191, Km 1.7, Laguna Grande, Fajardo (© 787/888-2887), offers some of the best rainforest hikes, kayak trips and mountain-bike tours, both for individuals and groups. They also offer kayak tours to one of several **Bioluminescent Bays** in Fajardo, where you enter the water at dusk and paddle through calm water teeming with small marine organisms that respond to the slightest touch by glowing an eerie greenish yellow. The top-notch **Las Tortugas Adventures** (© 787/809-0253 or 637-8356; www.kayak-pr.com) also runs tours to Fajardo's bio bay, as well as river tours of the rainforest and kayaking/snorkeling trips to deserted beaches, rimmed with reefs and teeming schools of tropical fish. **Kayaking Puerto Rico,** Fajardo (© 787/435-1665 or 787/245-4545; www.kayakingpr.com), is another reputable kayak and water sports tour operator. It also rents motorized inflatable boats if you want to cruise around on your own.

Scuba Diving & Snorkeling

SCUBA DIVING   The continental shelf, which surrounds Puerto Rico on three sides, is responsible for an abundance of coral reefs, caves, sea walls, and trenches for scuba diving and snorkeling.

Open-water reefs off the southeastern coast near **Humacao** are visited by migrating whales and manatees. Many caves are located near Isabela on the west coast. A large canyon off the island's south coast is ideal for experienced open-water divers. Caves and the sea wall at **La Parguera** are also favorites. **Vieques** and **Culebra islands** have coral formations. **Mona Island** offers unspoiled reefs at depths averaging 80 feet (24m), with an amazing array of sea life. Uninhabited islands, such as **Icacos,** off the northeastern coast near Fajardo, are also popular with snorkelers and divers alike.

These sites are now within reach, because many of Puerto Rico's dive operators and resorts offer packages that include daily or twice-daily dives, scuba equipment, instruction, and excursions to Puerto Rico's popular attractions.

Introductory courses for beginners start at $125, and two-tank dives for experienced divers begin at around $95, but most cost at least $125.

In San Juan, try **Caribe Aquatic Adventures,** Calle 19 1062, Villa Nevarez (✆ 787/281-8858), or **Ocean Sports** (Av. Isla Verde 77; ✆ 787/268-2329).

Diving off the east, southwest, or northwest coasts is more rewarding, however.

In Rincón, there's **Taíno Divers,** Black Eagle Marina at Rincón (✆ 787/823-6429), which offers trips to the waters surrounding Desecheo Island natural reserve.

The ocean wall in the southwest is famous, with visibility ranging from 100 to 120 feet (30–37m) and reefs filled with abundant sea life. **Paradise Scuba Center,** Hotel Casa Blanca Building, at La Parguera (✆ 787/899-7611), and **Mona Aquatics,** Calle José de Diego, Boquerón (✆ 787/851-2185), are two good operators in the area.

In Guánica, **Island Scuba** (✆ 787/309-6556) is the closest operator to many of the area's famed dive sites. Excellent guides and teachers and there are dive trips every day.

The **Dive Center** at the Wyndham Rio Mar Beach Resort (✆ 787/888-6000) is one of the largest in Puerto Rico.

(See "Diving, Fishing, Tennis & Other Outdoor Pursuits," in chapter 5, for more details.)

Elsewhere on the island, several other companies offer scuba and snorkeling instruction. We provide details in each chapter.

SNORKELING   Because of its overpopulation, the waters around San Juan aren't the most ideal for snorkeling. In fact, the entire north shore of Puerto Rico fronts the Atlantic, where the waters are often turbulent.

Yet there are some protected areas along the north coast that make for fine snorkeling, even in surf capitals such as Rincón and Aguadilla. Many of the best surfing beaches in winter turn into a snorkeler's paradise in summer when the waves calm down.

The most ideal conditions for snorkeling in Puerto Rico are along the shores of the remote islands of **Vieques** and **Culebra** (see chapter 10).

The best snorkeling on the main island is found near the town of **Fajardo,** to the east of San Juan and along the tranquil eastern coast (see chapter 9).

The calm, glasslike quality of the clear Caribbean along the south shore is also ideal for snorkeling. The most developed tourist mecca here is the city of Ponce. Few rivers empty their muddy waters into the sea along the south coast, resulting in gin-clear waters offshore. You can snorkel off the coast without having to go on a boat trip. One good place is at **Playa La Parguera,** where you can rent snorkeling equipment from kiosks along the beach. This beach lies east of the town of Guánica, to the east of Ponce. Here tropical fish add to the brightness of the water, which is generally turquoise. The addition of mangrove cays in the area also makes La Parguera more alluring for snorkelers. Another good spot for snorkelers is **Caja de Muertos** off the coast of Ponce. Here a lagoon coral reef boasts a large number of fish species.

Surfing

Puerto Rico's northwest beaches attract surfers from around the world. Called the "Hawaii of the East," Puerto Rico has hosted a number of international competitions. October through February are the best surfing months, but the sport is enjoyed in Puerto Rico from August through April. The most popular areas are from Isabela to Rincón—at beaches such as Wilderness, Middles, Jobos, Crashboat, Las Marías, and the Spanish Wall.

There are surf spots across the entire north coast from San Juan to the northwest, including Los Tubos in Vega Baja.

San Juan itself has great surfing spots, including La 8, just outside of Old San Juan in Puerta de Tierra, near Escambrón Beach, which has some of the largest waves. Pine Grove in Isla Verde is a great spot to learn, because of the small, steady, well-formed waves there.

International competitions held in Puerto Rico have included the 1968 and 1988 World Amateur Surfing Championships and the annual Caribbean Cup Surfing Championship. Currently, Corona sponsors an annual competition circuit taking place in Isabela and Rincón.

If you want to learn to surf, or perfect your technique while in Puerto Rico, it's quite easy to find experienced teachers and organized lessons.

Operating right near the Ritz-Carlton and Courtyard Marriott hotels in Isla Verde, the best surf lessons are given by professional surfer William Sue-A-Quan at his **Walking on Water Surfing School** (© 787/955-6059; www.gosurfpr.com). He and a few associates work on the beach at Pine Grove and also offer lessons through the Ritz-Carlton. They've taught students as young as 5 and as old as 75.

Rincón also has many surf schools, some of which book packages that include lodging. You can't do better than Ramses Morales at **Surf Lessons and Adventure Co.** (© 787/617-4731; www.surflessonspuertorico.com), a local pro who is a naturally gifted teacher, for beginners or more advanced surfers. **The Rincón Surf School** (P.O. Box 1333, Rincón; © 787/823-0610) offers beginner lessons and weeklong packages. **Puntas Surf School** (P.O. Box 4319, HC-01 Calle Vista del Mar; © 787/366-1689 or 207/251-1154) is another good option, run by Melissa Taylor and a group of seasoned instructors. Group lessons (for four) start at $60 for 90 minutes; private $50 per hour.

Board rentals are available at many island surf shops, with prices starting at $25 a day. We list them in subsequent chapters.

Standup paddle boards are widely available for rent, with prices around $20 per hour. The Condado Lagoon is perhaps the most popular spot to rent a board, and there is even a SUP yoga class given on a nightly basis.

Kiteboarding & Windsurfing

Kiteboarding has far surpassed windsurfing in popularity off Puerto Rico's beaches. The best spot for either sport is found at the Ocean Park-Punta Las Marias areas in the Greater San Juan metropolitan area. Other spots on the island for windsurfing and kiteboarding include Santa Isabel, Guánica, and La Parguera in the south; Jobos and Shacks in the northwest; and the island of Culebra off the eastern coast.

15 Knots Kiteboarding School, Av. Isla Verde 4851, Isla Verde (© 787/362-7228), has a wide range of classes, including a tandem kiteboard ride with an instructor, and also rents equipment.

Guided Tours

An escorted tour is a structured group tour with a group leader. The price usually includes everything from airfare to hotel, meals, tours, admission costs, and local transportation.

Puerto Rico Tours (© 787/504-4422; www.puertoricotours.com), provides transportation and sightseeing tours to Old San Juan, the Barcardi Rum Distillery, El Yunque rainforest, kayaking and snorkeling trips, Ponce historical tours and much more. Prices range from $40 to $95 per person. Other leading escorted tour operators include **Sunshine Tours** (© 866/785-3636; www.puerto-rico-sunshinetours.com), which helps you take in all the major sites of the island from Ponce to El Yunque. **Legends of Puerto Rico** (© 787/605-9060; www.legendsofpr.com) hosts personalized tours, specializing in entertaining cultural and nature adventure tours.

Volunteer & Working Trips

Rico Suntours (© 787/722-2080; www.rstpuertorico.com) and **Travel Services, Inc.** (© 787/982-1200; www.destinationpuertorico.com) are full service destination management companies arranging tours, transportation and specially arranged events and itineraries. Among their specialties is organizing volunteer and philanthropic tours and other activities for groups and individuals. Options include participating in a community project in the coastal town of Piñones and then taking a kayak or bicycle tour run by community-based outfits. Other tours include working with a facility that provides food and services to San Juan's homeless populations and local organizations helping stray cats and dogs. Animal lovers take note: Puerto Rican *satos* (mutts) are the loyalist, friendliest dogs known to man. You can adopt a dog through the **Save A Sato Foundation** (www.saveasato.org). If you are visiting in spring and want to help guard nesting sites of rare leatherback and other sea turtles, contact the local **Sierra Club** chapter (www.puertorico.sierraclub.org) or Culebra-based **Coralations** (www.coralations.org).

Walking Tours

Legends of Puerto Rico (℗ **787/605-9060;** www.legendsofpr.com) offers day and evening walking tours of Old San Juan.

[FastFACTS] PUERTO RICO

Area Codes Puerto Rico has two area codes: 787 and 939. The codes are not geographically specific. For all calls on the island, the area code must be used.

Business Hours Offices are generally open 9am to 5pm Monday through Friday, but most institutions are open Saturday for at least a half day. Stores are generally open from 9am to either 7pm or 9pm Monday through Saturday and Sunday 11am through 6pm. Most malls and big box retailers are open 9am to 9pm Monday to Saturday, 11am to 7pm on Sundays. Normal banking hours are 8am to 4pm or 9am-5pm Monday through Friday and 8:30am to noon on Saturday. Most banks have some branches with extended hours, open all day Saturday and on Sundays from 11 to 4pm, as well as extended evening hours to 6pm.

Car Rental See "Getting There by Car," earlier in this chapter.

Cellphones See "Mobile Phones," later in this section.

Crime See "Safety," later in this section.

Customs U.S. citizens do not need to clear Puerto Rican Customs upon arrival by plane or ship from the U.S. mainland. Every visitor 21 years of age or older may bring in, free of duty, the following: (1) 1 U.S. quart of alcohol; (2) 200 cigarettes, 50 cigars (but not from Cuba), or 3 pounds of smoking tobacco; and (3) $100 worth of gifts. These exemptions are offered to travelers who spend at least 72 hours in the United States and who have not claimed them within the preceding 6 months. It is forbidden to bring into the country almost any meat products (including canned, fresh, and dried meat products, such as bouillon, soup mixes, and so on). Generally, condiments including vinegars, oils, pickled goods, spices, coffee, tea, and some cheeses and baked goods are permitted. Avoid rice products, as rice can often harbor insects. Bringing fruits and vegetables is prohibited, as they may harbor pests or disease. International visitors may carry in or out up to $10,000 in U.S. or foreign currency with no formalities; larger sums must be declared to U.S. Customs on entering or leaving, which includes filing form CM 4790. On departure, U.S.-bound travelers must have their luggage inspected by the U.S. Department of Agriculture, because laws prohibit bringing fruits and plants to the U.S. mainland. Fruits and vegetables are not allowed, but otherwise, you can bring back as many purchased goods as you want without paying duty.

For details regarding U.S. Customs and Border Protection, consult your nearest U.S. embassy or consulate, or **U.S. Customs** (www. customs.gov).

For more information on what you can bring home:

U.S. Citizens: U.S. Customs & Border Protection (CBP), 1300 Pennsylvania Ave., NW, Washington, DC 20229 (✆ **877/287-8667;** www.cbp.gov).

Canadian Citizens: Canada Border Services Agency, Ottawa, Ontario, K1A 0L8 (✆ **800/461-9999** in Canada, or 204/983-3500; www.cbsa-asfc.gc.ca).

U.K. Citizens: HM Customs & Excise, Crownhill Court, Tailyour Road, Plymouth, PL6 5BZ (✆ **0845/010-9000;** from outside the U.K., 020/8929-0152; www. hmce.gov.uk). For information on importation of plants or animals, see the Department for Food, Environment, and Rural Affairs (DEFRA) website (www. defra.gov.uk/foodfarm/ food/personal-import/ topics/faq.htm).

Australian Citizens: Australian Customs Service, Customs House, 5 Constitution Ave., Canberra City, ACT 2601 (✆ **1300/363-263;** from outside Australia, 612/6275-6666; www. customs.gov.au).

New Zealand Citizens: New Zealand Customs, The Customhouse, 17–21 Whitmore St., P.O. Box 2218, Wellington, 6140 (✆ **04/ 473-6099** or 0800/428-786; www.customs.govt.nz).

Disabled Travelers

Most disabilities shouldn't stop anyone from traveling. There are more options and resources out there today than ever before.

The Americans with Disabilities Act is enforced as strictly in Puerto Rico as it is on the U.S. mainland—in fact, a telling example of the act's enforcement can be found in Ponce, where the sightseeing trolleys are equipped with ramps and extra balustrades to accommodate travelers with disabilities. Unfortunately, hotels rarely give much publicity to the facilities they offer persons with disabilities, so it's always wise to contact the hotel directly, in advance, if you need special facilities. Tourist offices usually have little data about such matters.

You can obtain a free copy of **"Air Transportation of Handicapped Persons,"** published by the U.S. Department of Transportation. Write for "Free Advisory Circular No. AC12032," Distribution Unit, U.S. Department of Transportation, Publications Division, 3341Q 75 Ave., Landover, MD 20785. No phone requests are accepted, but you can write for a copy of the publication or download it for free at http://isddc.dot.gov.

The U.S. National Park Service offers a Golden Access Passport that gives free lifetime entrance to U.S. national parks, including those in Puerto Rico, for persons who are blind or have permanent disabilities, regardless of age. You can pick up a Golden Access Passport at any NPS entrance-fee area by showing proof of medically determined disability and eligibility for receiving benefits under federal law. Besides free entry, the Golden Access Passport also offers a 50 percent discount on federal-use fees charged for such facilities as camping, swimming, parking, boat launching, and tours. For more information, go to www.nps.gov/fees_ passes.htm, or call ✆ **888/467-2757.**

Many travel agencies offer customized tours and itineraries for travelers with disabilities. **Flying Wheels Travel** (✆ **507/451-5005;** www.flyingwheelstravel. com) offers escorted tours and cruises that emphasize sports and private tours in minivans with lifts. **Access-Able Travel Source** (✆ **303/232-2979;** www. access-able.com) offers extensive access information and advice for traveling around the world with disabilities. **Accessible Journeys** (✆ **800/846-4537** or 610/521-0339; www.disability travel.com) caters specifically to slow walkers and wheelchair travelers and their families and friends.

Organizations that offer assistance to travelers with disabilities include **Moss Rehab** (✆ **800/CALL-MOSS** [800/225-5667]; www.moss resourcenet.org), which provides a library of accessible-travel resources online; the **American Foundation for the Blind (AFB;** ✆ **800/ 232-5463** or 212/502-7600; www.afb.org), a referral resource for the blind or visually impaired that includes information on traveling with Seeing Eye dogs; and **SATH** (Society for Accessible Travel & Hospitality; ℂ **212/447-7284;** www.sath.org; annual membership fees: $45 adults, $30 seniors and students), which offers a wealth of travel resources for all types of disabilities and informed recommendations on destinations, access guides, travel agents, tour operators, vehicle rentals, and companion services. **AirAmbulanceCard.com** is now partnered with SATH and allows you to preselect topnotch hospitals, in case of an emergency, for $195 a year ($295 per family), among other benefits.

For more information specifically targeted to travelers with disabilities, the community website **iCan** (www.icanonline.net) has destination guides and several regular columns on accessible travel. Also check out the quarterly magazine **"Emerging Horizons"** (www.emerginghorizons. com; $15 per year, $20 outside the U.S.); and **"Open World"** magazine, published by SATH (see above; subscription: $13 per year, $21 outside the U.S.).

A tip for British travelers: The **Royal Association for Disability and Rehabilitation (RADAR),** Unit 12, City Forum, 250 City Rd., London, EC1V 8AF (ℂ **020/ 7250-3222;** www.radar.org. uk), publishes information for travelers with disabilities.

Doctors Hotels will be able to recommend a good doctor, which are listed under "medicos" in the telephone directory. There are also several hospitals and other healthcare facilities in San Juan that have medical staff on site around the clock. Also see "Hospitals," later in this section.

Drinking Laws The legal age for purchase and consumption of alcoholic beverages is 18; proof of age is required and often requested at bars, nightclubs, and restaurants, so it's always a good idea to bring ID when you go out. Do not carry open containers of alcohol in your car or any public area that isn't zoned for alcohol consumption. The police can fine you on the spot. Don't even think about driving while intoxicated.

Driving Rules See "Getting Around," earlier in this chapter.

Drugstores It's a good idea to carry enough prescription medications with you to last the duration of your stay. If you're going into the hinterlands, take along the medicines you'll need. If you need any additional medications, you'll find many drugstores in San Juan and other leading cities. One of the most centrally located pharmacies is **Walgreens,** 1130 Ashford Ave., Condado (ℂ **787/ 725-1510**), open 24 hours. There is at least one 24-hour Walgreens in every tourist district (Condado, Old San Juan, and Isla Verde), and they are linked with the U.S. chain for prescriptions. There are also locations throughout the island in major cities and shopping malls. Another option is the **Puerto Rico Drug Co.,** Calle San Francisco 157 (ℂ **787/725-2202**), in Old San Juan, which is open daily from 7:30am to 9:30pm. A wellstocked **CVS Pharmacy,** Paseo Gilberto Concepcion de Gracia 105 (ℂ **787/725-2500**), is located near the cruise ship docks in Old San Juan and is open 7am to midnight daily. The chain's newest branch is a megastore at the San Juan Marriott Resort & Stellaris Casino.

Electricity Like Canada, the United States uses 110–120 volts AC (60 cycles), compared to 220–240 volts AC (50 cycles) in most of Europe, Australia, and New Zealand. Downward converters that change 220–240 volts to 110–120 volts are difficult to find in the United States, so bring one with you.

Embassies & Consulates All embassies are in the nation's capital, Washington, D.C. Some consulates are in major U.S. cities, and most nations have a mission to the United Nations in New York City. If your country isn't listed below, call for directory information in Washington, D.C. (ℂ **202/555-1212**), or check **www.embassy.org/ embassies**.

The embassy of **Australia** is at 1601 Massachusetts Ave. NW, Washington, DC 20036 (ℂ **202/797-3000;** www.usa.embassy.gov.au). Consulates are in New York, Honolulu, Houston, Los Angeles, and San Francisco.

The embassy of **Canada** is at 501 Pennsylvania Ave. NW, Washington, DC 20001 (📞 **202/682-1740;** www.canadainternational.gc.ca/washington). Other Canadian consulates are in Buffalo (New York), Detroit, Los Angeles, New York City, and Seattle.

The embassy of **Ireland** is at 2234 Massachusetts Ave. NW, Washington, DC 20008 (📞 **202/462-3939;** www.embassyofireland.org). Irish consulates are in Boston, Chicago, New York City, San Francisco, and other cities. See website for complete listing.

The embassy of **New Zealand** is at 37 Observatory Circle NW, Washington, DC 20008 (📞 **202/328-4800;** www.nzembassy.com). New Zealand consulates are in Los Angeles, Salt Lake City, San Francisco, and Seattle.

The embassy of the **United Kingdom** is at 3100 Massachusetts Ave. NW, Washington, DC 20008 (📞 **202/588-6500;** http://ukinusa.fco.gov.uk). Other British consulates are in Atlanta, Boston, Chicago, Cleveland, Houston, Los Angeles, New York City, San Francisco, and Seattle.

Emergencies In an emergency, dial 📞 **911.** Or call the local police (📞 **787/343-2020**), fire department (📞 **787/722-1120**), or emergency medical corps (📞 **787/775-0550**).

Gasoline Please see "Getting Around by Car," earlier in this chapter.

Health Puerto Rico poses no major health problem for most travelers. If you have a chronic condition, however, you should check with your doctor before visiting the islands. For conditions such as epilepsy, diabetes, or heart problems, wear a **MedicAlert Identification Tag** (📞 **800/825-3785;** www.medicalert.org), which will immediately alert doctors to your condition and give them access to your records through MediCAlert's 24-hour hot line.

Finding a good doctor in Puerto Rico is easy, and most speak English. See "Hospitals," on p. 239, for the locations of hospitals.

If you worry about getting sick away from home, consider purchasing **medical travel insurance** and carry your ID card in your purse or wallet. In most cases, your existing health plan will provide the coverage you need. See "Insurance," on p. 239, for more information.

Pack **prescription medications** in your carry-on luggage, and carry prescription medications in their original containers. Also bring along copies of your prescriptions, in case you lose your medication or run out. Carry the generic name of prescription medicines, in case a local pharmacist is unfamiliar with the brand name.

And don't forget sunglasses and an extra pair of contact lenses or prescription glasses.

Contact the **International Association for Medical Assistance to Travelers (IAMAT;** 📞 **716/754-4883,** or 416/652-0137 in Canada; www.iamat.org) for tips on travel and health concerns in the countries you're visiting, and for lists of local, English-speaking doctors. The United States **Centers for Disease Control and Prevention** (📞 **800/311-3435;** www.cdc.gov) provides up-to-date information on health hazards by region or country and offers tips on food safety. The website **www.tripprep.com**, sponsored by a consortium of travel medicine practitioners, may also offer helpful advice on traveling abroad. You can find listings of reliable clinics overseas at the **International Society of Travel Medicine** (www.istm.org).

It's best to stick to **bottled water** here. Although tap water is said to be safe to drink, many visitors experience diarrhea, even if they follow the usual precautions. The illness usually passes quickly without medication, if you eat simply prepared food and drink only bottled water until you recover. If symptoms persist, consult a doctor.

The **sun** can be brutal, especially if you haven't been exposed to it in some time. Experts advise that you limit your time on the beach the first day. If you do overexpose yourself, stay out of the sun until you recover. If your exposure is followed by fever or chills, a headache, or a feeling of nausea or dizziness, see a doctor.

Sandflies (or "no-see-ums") can still be a problem in Puerto Rico but are not the menace they are in other Caribbean destinations. They appear mainly in the early evening, and even if you can't see these tiny bugs, you sure can "feel-um." Your favorite insect repellent will protect you from them, should they become a problem.

Mosquitoes are a nuisance, and while they do not carry malaria in Puerto Rico, they do carry the dreaded **dengue fever.** Transmitted by Aedes mosquitos, its symptoms include fever, headaches, pain in the muscles and joints, skin blisters, and in severe cases hemorrhaging. It usually is gone after a week but the strongest cases are fatal, and the illness is painful, giving rise to its popular nickname "breakbone" fever. The similar mosquito-borne chikungunya virus also made an appearance in Puerto Rico as it marched across the Caribbean. First identified in Africa in 1953, it causes a high fever and severe pain in the joints, but is rarely fatal. There is no vaccine for either disease although dengue vaccines are in the development stage. Treatment entails pain relief as well as hydration and nutritional IV treatments.

Hookworm and other **intestinal parasites** are relatively common in the Caribbean, though you are less likely to be affected in Puerto Rico than on other islands. Hookworm can be contracted by just walking barefoot on an infected beach. *Schistosomiasis* (also

called *bilharzia*), caused by a parasitic fluke, can be contracted by submerging your feet in rivers and lakes infested with a certain species of snail.

Like major urban areas along the East Coast, Puerto Rico has been hard hit by **AIDS** and other sexually transmitted diseases. Exercise *at least* the same caution in choosing your sexual partners and practicing safe sex as you would at home.

Hospitals   In a medical emergency, call ✆ **911. Ashford Presbyterian Community Hospital,** Av. Ashford 1451, San Juan (✆ **787/721-2160**), maintains 24-hour emergency service and is the most convenient to the major tourism districts. Another option is **Pavia Hospital,** 1462 C. Asia, Santurce (✆ **787/727-6060**). Service is also provided at **Clinica Las Americas,** Franklin Delano Roosevelt Ave. 400, Hato Rey (✆ **787/765-1919**), and at **Puerto Rico Medical Center,** Av. Americo Miranda, Río Piedras (✆ **787/777-3535**). **San Jorge Children's Hospital**, Calle San Jorge 25, Santurce (✆ **787/268-3610**), is Puerto Rico's finest children's hospital and one of the premiere institutions in the entire Caribbean and is also minutes from San Juan's tourism districts.

Insurance   Most health insurance policies cover you if you get sick away from home, but they are not likely to provide for medical evacuation in case

of life-threatening injury or illness. It's a good idea to buy a travel insurance policy that provides for **emergency medical evacuation.** If you have to buy a one-way same-day ticket home and forfeit your nonrefundable round-trip ticket, you might be out big bucks. And the cost of a flying ambulance could wipe out your life's savings.

Check with your insurer, particularly if you're insured by an HMO, about the extent of its coverage while you're overseas. With the exception of certain HMOs and Medicare/Medicaid, your medical insurance should cover medical treatment—even hospital care—overseas. However, most out-of-country hospitals make you pay your bills up front, and they send you a refund after you've returned home and filed the necessary paperwork.

If you require additional insurance, try one of the following companies:

- **MEDEX International** (✆ **888/MEDEX-00** [633-3900] or 410/453-6300; www.medexassist. com).

- **Travel Assistance International** (✆ **800/821-2828;** www. travelassistance.com); for general information on services, call the company's Worldwide Assistance Services, Inc. at ✆ **800/777-8710.**

- **The Divers Alert Network** (DAN; ✆ **800/446-2671** or 919/684-2948; www.diversalert network.org).

On domestic flights, checked baggage is covered up to $3,300 per ticketed passenger. On international flights (including U.S. portions of international trips), baggage coverage is limited to approximately $9.07 per pound, up to approximately $635 per checked bag. If you plan to check items more valuable than what's covered by the standard liability, see if your homeowner's policy covers your valuables, or get baggage insurance as part of your comprehensive travel-insurance package. Don't buy insurance at the airport, where it's usually overpriced. Be sure to take any valuables or irreplaceable items with you in your carry-on luggage, because many valuables (including books, money, and electronics) aren't covered by airline policies.

If your luggage is lost, immediately file a lost-luggage claim at the airport, detailing the luggage contents. Most airlines require that you report delayed, damaged, or lost baggage within 4 hours of arrival. The airlines are required to deliver luggage, once found, directly to your house or destination free of charge.

For information on traveler's insurance, trip cancellation insurance, and medical insurance while traveling, please visit www.frommers.com/planning.

Internet & Wi-Fi Free Wi-Fi connections are widely available, from Old San Juan's Plaza de Armas to Starbucks to local Burger King and McDonald's outlets throughout the island. Many hotels and guesthouses also have Wi-Fi connections for guests (many free) and public computers for use by guests. Many public plazas have Wi-Fi service, and public libraries also have Internet areas. Free Wi-Fi spots abound at shopping centers, hotels, and restaurants.

Language English is understood at the big resorts and in most of San Juan. Out in the island, Spanish is still *numero uno*, but many residents will know at least some English.

Legal Aid While driving, if you are pulled over for a minor infraction (such as speeding), never attempt to pay the fine directly to a police officer; this could be construed as attempted bribery, a much more serious crime. Pay fines by mail, or directly into the hands of the clerk of the court. If accused of a more serious offense, say and do nothing before consulting a lawyer. In the U.S., the burden is on the state to prove a person's guilt beyond a reasonable doubt, and everyone has the right to remain silent, whether he or she is suspected of a crime or actually arrested. Once arrested, a person can make one telephone call to a party of his or her choice. The international visitor should call his or her embassy or consulate.

LGBT Travelers Puerto Rico is the most gay-friendly destination in the Caribbean, with lots of accommodations, restaurants, clubs, and bars that actively cater to a gay clientele.

A good source is www.orgulloboricua.net, which is a Web portal for the island's gay and lesbian community; it has an introduction for visitors in English. In Spanish is the radio show/Web blog www.saliendodelcloset.org, which involves leading figures in the gay community and has links to several points of interest.

The **International Gay & Lesbian Travel Association (IGLTA;** ✆ 800/448-8550 or 954/776-2626; www.iglta.org) links travelers up with gay-friendly hoteliers, tour operators, and airline and cruise-line representatives. It offers monthly newsletters, marketing mailings, and a membership directory that's updated once a year. Membership is $225 yearly, plus a $100 administration fee for new members.

Above and Beyond Tours (✆ 800/397-2681; www.abovebeyondtours.com) offers gay and lesbian tours worldwide and is the exclusive gay and lesbian tour operator for United Airlines.

Now, Voyager (✆ 800/255-6951; www.nowvoyager.com) is a San Francisco–based gay-owned and -operated travel service.

Olivia Cruises & Resorts (✆ 800/631-6277; www.olivia.com) charters entire resorts and ships for exclusive lesbian vacations and offers smaller group experiences for both gay and lesbian travelers. (In 2005, tennis great Martina Navratilova was named Olivia's official spokesperson.)

Gay.com Travel (✆ 800/929-2268 or 415/644-8044; www.gay.com/travel or www.outandabout.com) is an excellent online successor to the popular **"Out & About"** print magazine.

The following travel guides are available at many bookstores, or you can order them from any online bookseller: **"Spartacus International Gay Guide"** (Bruno Gmünder Verlag; www.spartacusworld.com/gayguide) and **"Odysseus: The International Gay Travel Planner"** (Odysseus Enterprises Ltd.), both good, annual, English-language guidebooks focused on gay men; and the **"Damron"** guides (www.damron.com), with separate, annual books for gay men and lesbians.

Mail At press time, domestic postage rates are 49¢ for a letter. For international mail, a first-class letter of up to 1 ounce starts at $1.15 (the rate for both Canada and Mexico); a first-class postcard costs the same as a letter. For more information, go to **www.usps.com**.

If you aren't sure what your address will be in the United States, mail can be sent to you, in your name, c/o General Delivery at the main post office of the city or region where you expect to be. (Call ✆ **800/275-8777** for information on the nearest post office.) The addressee must pick up mail in person and must produce proof of identity (driver's license, passport, and so forth). Most post offices will hold mail for up to 1 month, and are open Monday to Friday from 8am to 6pm, and Saturday from 9am to 3pm.

Medical Requirements Unless you're arriving from an area known to be suffering from an epidemic (particularly cholera or yellow fever), inoculations or vaccinations are not required for entry into the United States.

Mobile Phones Major carriers with a presence in the U.S., market, such as AT&T, Sprint, and T-Mobile, also battle it out in the island's competitive wireless market. Prices are low, and coverage is very good, even out at sea. Each carrier maintains a network and all are investing in network upgrades, with AT&T out front in the race for a 4-G network, and all are GSM networks.

Check with your carrier to see if Puerto Rico is included in national calling plans, which usually offer unlimited calling and roaming. Most do. Puerto Rico subscribers of all major carriers have the option of enrolling in a national calling plan that includes calls and free roaming to the United States mainland.

Calls can also be placed through Skype and other VoIP services via the Internet.

Cellular telephones can be purchased at RadioShack, Walgreens, and other stores listed throughout the guide. They come loaded with minutes and can be used on the spot and cost as little as $35. Refill cards are sold everywhere, from major grocery stores to gas stations. Internet access, such as widespread, high-powered Wi-Fi service, is so great that Web-based options like Skype can be used to stay in touch, especially if your smart phone has that Wi-Fi option.

Money & Costs Frommer's lists exact prices in the local currency. The currency conversions quoted above were correct at press time. However, rates fluctuate, so before departing consult a currency exchange website such as **www.oanda.com/currency/converter** to check up-to-the-minute rates.

ATMs The U.S. banking presence has markedly diminished on the island in recent years, but island banks, led by Banco Popular, are hooked into the U.S. banking system, use the

THE VALUE OF U.S. DOLLAR VS. OTHER POPULAR CURRENCIES

US$	Aus$	Can$	Euro€	NZ$	UK£
1	A$0.93	C$0.93	€1.35	NZ$0.86	£1.70

same ATM networks, and have the same fee structures. Many have a presence on the U.S. mainland. Spanish and Canadian banks also have a presence.

ATMs are linked to a network that most likely includes your bank at home. Cirrus (☏ **800/424-7787;** www.mastercard.com) and PLUS (☏ **800/843-7587;** www.visa.com) are the two most popular networks in the U.S.; call or check online for ATM locations at your destination.

Credit Cards   Credit cards are invaluable when you're traveling. They are a safe way to carry money and provide a convenient record of all your expenses. You can also withdraw cash advances from your credit cards at any bank (though you'll start paying hefty interest on the advance the moment you receive the cash). At most banks, you don't even need to go to a teller; you can get a cash advance at the ATM if you know your PIN. If you've forgotten yours, or didn't even know you had one, call the number on the back of your credit card and ask the card issuer to send it to you. It usually takes 5 to 7 business days, though some banks will provide the number over the phone if you tell them your mother's maiden name or pass some other security clearance test.

In San Juan and at all the big resorts on the island, even some of the smaller inns, credit cards are commonly accepted. Moreover, an incredible array

of establishments accept payment with ATM cards. However, as you tour through rural areas and if you intend to patronize small, out-of-the-way establishments, it's still wise to carry sufficient greenbacks for emergencies. Visa and MasterCard are accepted most widely throughout Puerto Rico.

Beware of hidden credit-card fees while traveling. Check with your credit or debit card issuer to see what fees, if any, will be charged for overseas transactions. Recent reform legislation in the U.S., for example, has curbed some exploitative lending practices. But many banks have responded by increasing fees in other areas, including fees for customers who use credit and debit cards while out of the country—even if those charges were made in U.S. dollars. Fees can amount to 3 percent or more of the purchase price. Check with your bank before departing to avoid any surprise charges on your statement.

Currency   The U.S. dollar is the coin of the realm. Keep in mind that once you leave Ponce or San Juan, you might have difficulty finding a place to exchange foreign money (unless you're staying at a large resort), so it's wise to handle your exchange needs before you head off into rural parts of Puerto Rico.

Currency Exchange   There is a currency exchange at Luis Muñoz Marín International Airport and at large

bank branches such as Banco Popular.

Traveler's Checks   Traveler's checks are something of an anachronism from the days before the ATM made cash accessible at any time. Even given the fees you'll pay for ATM use at banks other than your own, it is still probably a better bet than traveler's checks.

You can get traveler's checks at almost any bank. **American Express** offers denominations of $20, $50, $100, $500, and (for cardholders only) $1,000. You'll pay a service charge ranging from 1 to 4 percent. You can also get American Express traveler's checks over the phone by calling ☏ **800/221-7282;** Amex gold and platinum cardholders who use this number are exempt from the 1 percent fee.

Visa offers traveler's checks at Citibank locations nationwide, as well as at several other banks. The service charge ranges between 1 and 2 percent; checks come in denominations of $20, $50, $100, $500, and $1,000. Call ☏ **800/732-1322** for information. AAA members can obtain Visa checks for a $9.95 fee (for checks, minimum of $300 up to $1,500) at most AAA offices or by calling ☏ **866/339-3378.**

MasterCard also offers traveler's checks. Call ☏ **800/223-9920** for a location near you.

Newspapers & Magazines   "Caribbean Business" (www.caribbean businesspr.com) is a weekly

business newspaper that has the most up-to-date news on Puerto Rico in English. There is a weekly print edition but its website, with a mobile telephone version, is a constantly updated general news. If you read Spanish, you might enjoy **"El Nuevo Día,"** the most popular local tabloid. There is also **"El Vocero"** and **"Primera Hora."** Few significant magazines are published on Puerto Rico, but **"Time"** and **"Newsweek"** are available at most newsstands.

Packing   Puerto Ricans love to dress up and some restaurants and clubs have dress codes, so you should bring at least one outfit that can meet formal dress codes. Also, while the weather is warm year-round, it is advisable to bring a light jacket of sweater for air-conditioned restaurants and theaters. For more helpful information on packing for your trip, download our convenient Travel Tools app for your mobile device. Go to www.frommers.com/go/mobile and click on the Travel Tools icon.

Passports   Because Puerto Rico is a United States Commonwealth, **U.S. citizens** coming from mainland destinations do not need passports to enter Puerto Rico.

That said, **it still is best to carry plenty of documentation.** Be sure that your ID is up to date: An expired driver's license or passport, for example, might keep you from boarding a plane.

Visitors from other countries, including Canada, need a valid passport to land in Puerto Rico. For those from countries requiring a visa to enter the U.S., the same visa is necessary to enter Puerto Rico.

Petrol   Please see "Getting Around by Car," earlier in this chapter.

Police   In an emergency, dial *(C)* **911** or 787/343-2020.

Safety   The U.S. Department of State issues no special travel advisories for the Commonwealth of Puerto Rico, the way it might for, say, the more troubled island of Jamaica. However, there are crime problems in Puerto Rico, and violent crime fueled by drug trafficking has been on the rise. Still, crime rarely surfaces along San Juan's Condado and Isla Verde beaches and Old San Juan. Caution is required at night, as muggings do happen, and isolated areas should be avoided.

Burglary, including vandalizing of automobiles, is another problem, so don't leave valuables in cars, even when the doors are locked.

Take precautions about leaving valuables on the beach, and exercise extreme care if you're searching for a remote beach where there's no one in sight. The only person lurking nearby might be someone not interested in surf and sand but a robber waiting to make off with your possessions.

Avoid wandering around the darkened alleys and

small streets of San Juan's Old City at night, especially those off the oceanside Norzagaray Boulevard, which is relatively deserted at night.

If you are traveling out on the island, plan to do your driving during the daylight hours, both for road-safety and crime-precaution reasons. A wrong turn at midnight could lead to a whole lot of trouble of all stripes.

In short, crime exists here as it does everywhere. Use common sense and take precautions. Theft and occasional muggings do occur on the Condado and Isla Verde beaches at night, so you might want to confine your moonlit beach nights to the fenced-in and guarded areas around some of the major hotels. The countryside of Puerto Rico is safer than San Juan, but caution is always in order. Avoid narrow country roads and isolated beaches at night and exercise caution on them during the day.

Senior Travel   Members of **AARP,** 601 E St. NW, Washington, DC 20049 (*(C)* **888/687-2277** or 202/434-2277; www.aarp.org), get discounts on hotels, airfares, and car rentals. AARP offers members a wide range of benefits, including "AARP The Magazine" and a monthly newsletter. Anyone 50 or older can join.

The **U.S. National Park Service** offers a **Golden Age Passport** that gives seniors 62 years or older lifetime entrance to U.S.

national parks for a one-time processing fee of $10. The pass must be purchased in person at any NPS facility that charges an entrance fee. Besides free entry, a Golden Age Passport also offers a 50 percent discount on federal-use fees charged for such facilities as camping, swimming, parking, boat launching, and tours. For more information, visit www.nps.gov, or call © **888/467-2757.**

Grand Circle Travel (© **800/221-2610** or 617/350-7500; www.gct.com) offers package deals for the 50-plus market, mostly of the tour-bus variety, with free trips thrown in for those who organize groups of 10 or more.

SAGA Holidays (© **800/ 343-0273;** http://travel.saga.co.uk/holidays.aspx) offers tours and cruises for those 50 and older. SAGA also offers a number of single-traveler tours.

Recommended publications offering travel resources and discounts for seniors include: the quarterly magazine **"Travel 50 & Beyond"** (www.travel50 andbeyond.com); **"Travel Unlimited: Uncommon Adventures for the Mature Traveler"** (Avalon); **"101 Tips for Mature Travelers,"** available from Grand Circle Travel (© **800/221- 2610** or 800/959-0405; www.gct.com); and **"Unbelievably Good Deals and Great Adventures That You Absolutely Can't Get Unless You're Over 50"** (McGraw-Hill), by Joan Rattner Heilman.

Smoking Stringent anti-smoking regulations have been passed banning smoking in all public areas including restaurants, bars, casinos, and hotel rooms. Enforcement, however, is less strict than other areas in the United States. Smoking is even banned at outdoor cafes that are serviced by waiters or waitresses, but this prohibition is often overlooked.

Taxes The United States has no value-added tax (VAT) or other indirect tax at the national level. Every state, county, and city may levy its own local tax on all purchases, including hotel and restaurant checks and airline tickets. These taxes will not appear on price tags. Puerto Rico levies a 7 percent sales and use tax on most major goods and services. All hotel rooms on Puerto Rico are subject to a 9 to 11 percent tax (*paradores* carry a 7 percent levy).

Telephones Many convenience, grocery, and retail postal service stores sell **prepaid calling cards** in denominations up to $50. Many public pay phones at airports now accept American Express, MasterCard, and Visa. **Local calls** made from most pay phones cost 75¢. Most long-distance and international calls can be dialed directly from any phone. **To make calls within the United States and to Canada,** dial 1 followed by the area code and the seven-digit number. **For other international calls,** dial 011 followed by the country code, city code, and the number you are calling.

Calls to area codes **800, 888, 877,** and **866** are toll-free. However, calls to area codes **700** and **900** (chat lines, bulletin boards, "dating" services, and so on) can be expensive—charges of 95¢ to $3 or more per minute. Some numbers have minimum charges that can run $15 or more.

For **reversed-charge or collect calls,** and for person-to-person calls, dial the number 0 then the area code and number; an operator will come on the line, and you should specify whether you are calling collect, person-to-person, or both. If your operator-assisted call is international, ask for the overseas operator.

For **directory assistance** (Information), dial 411 for local numbers and national numbers in the U.S. and Canada. For dedicated long-distance information, dial 1, then the appropriate area code plus 555-1212.

Time Puerto Rico is in the Atlantic Time Zone, which is 1 hour ahead of Eastern Standard Time. However, because the island does not recognize Daylight Savings Time, it actually shares the same time as the U.S. East Coast when it celebrates DST, which is now 8 months, most of the year. The continental United States is divided into **four time zones:** Eastern Standard Time (EST), Central Standard Time (CST), Mountain Standard Time (MST), and

Pacific Standard Time (PST). Alaska and Hawaii have their own zones. For example, when it's 9am in Los Angeles (PST), it's 7am in Honolulu (HST),10am in Denver (MST), 11am in Chicago (CST), noon in New York City (EST), 5pm in London (GMT), and 2am the next day in Sydney.

Daylight saving time (summer time) is in effect from 1am on the second Sunday in March to 1am on the first Sunday in November, except in Arizona, Hawaii, the U.S. Virgin Islands, and Puerto Rico. Daylight saving time moves the clock 1 hour ahead of standard time.

Tipping In hotels, tip **bellhops** at least $1 per bag ($2–$3 if you have a lot of luggage) and tip the **chamber staff** $1 to $2 per day (more if you've left a big mess for him or her to clean up). Tip the **doorman** or **concierge** only if he or she has provided you with some specific service (for example, calling a cab for you or obtaining difficult-to-get theater tickets). Tip the **valet-parking attendant** $1 every time you get your car.

In restaurants, bars, and nightclubs, tip **service staff** and **bartenders** 15 to 20 percent of the check, tip **checkroom attendants** $2 per garment, and tip **valet-parking attendants** $2 per vehicle.

As for other service personnel, tip **cab drivers** 15 percent of the fare; tip **skycaps** at airports at least $1 per bag ($2–$3 if you have a lot of luggage); and tip

hairdressers and **barbers** 15 to 20 percent.

Toilets You won't find public toilets or "restrooms" on the streets in most Puerto Rico cities but they can be found in hotel lobbies, bars, restaurants, museums, department stores, railway and bus stations, and service stations. Large hotels and fast-food restaurants are often the best bet for clean facilities. Public beaches, called *balnearios,* run by the commonwealth's National Parks Company or by municipal governments, have restrooms, showers, and changing facilities. Restaurants and bars in resorts or heavily visited areas may reserve their restrooms for patrons.

VAT See "Taxes" earlier in this section.

Visas The U.S. State Department has a **Visa Waiver Program (VWP)** allowing citizens of the following countries to enter the United States without a visa for stays of up to 90 days: Andorra, Australia, Austria, Belgium, Brunei, Czech Republic, Denmark, Estonia, Finland, France, Germany, Greece, Hungary, Iceland, Ireland, Italy, Japan, Latvia, Liechtenstein, Lithuania, Luxembourg, Malta, Monaco, the Netherlands, New Zealand, Norway, Portugal, San Marino, Singapore, Slovakia, Slovenia, South Korea, Spain, Sweden, Switzerland, and the United Kingdom. (**Note:** This list was accurate at press time; for the most up-to-date list of countries in the VWP, consult http://

travel.state.gov/visa.) Even though a visa isn't necessary, in an effort to help U.S. officials check travelers against terror watch lists before they arrive at U.S. borders, visitors from VWP countries must register online through the Electronic System for Travel Authorization (ESTA) before boarding a plane or a boat to the U.S. Travelers must complete an electronic application providing basic personal and travel eligibility information. The Department of Homeland Security recommends filling out the form at least 3 days before traveling. Authorizations will be valid for up to 2 years or until the traveler's passport expires, whichever comes first. Currently, there is a US$14 fee for the online application. Existing ESTA registrations remain valid through their expiration dates. **Note:** Any passport issued on or after October 26, 2006, by a VWP country must be an **e-Passport** for VWP travelers to be eligible to enter the U.S. without a visa. Citizens of these nations also need to present a round-trip air or cruise ticket upon arrival. E-Passports contain computer chips capable of storing biometric information, such as the required digital photograph of the holder. If your passport doesn't have this feature, you can still travel without a visa if the valid passport was issued before October 26, 2005, and includes a machine-readable zone; or if the valid passport was issued between October 26, 2005, and October 25, 2006, and includes a digital photograph. For more information, go to **http://travel.state.gov/visa**. Canadian citizens may enter the United States without visas, but will need to show passports and proof of residence.

Citizens of all other countries must have (1) a valid passport that expires at least 6 months later than the scheduled end of their visit to the U.S.; and (2) a tourist visa.

For information about U.S. visas, go to **http://travel.state.gov** and click on "Visas." Or go to one of the following websites:

Australian citizens can obtain up-to-date visa information from the **U.S. Embassy Canberra,** Moonah Place, Yarralumla, ACT 2600 (© **02/6214-5600**), or by checking the U.S. Diplomatic Mission's website at **http://canberra.usembassy.gov/visas.html**.

British subjects can obtain up-to-date visa information by calling the **U.S. Embassy Visa Information Line** (© **09042-450-100** from within the U.K. at £1.20 per minute; or © **866/382-3589** from within the U.S. at a flat rate of $16, payable by credit card only) or by visiting the "Visas to the U.S." section of the American Embassy London's website at http://london.usembassy.gov/visas.html.

Irish citizens can obtain up-to-date visa information

through the **U.S. Embassy Dublin,** 42 Elgin Rd., Ballsbridge, Dublin 4 (© **1580-47-VISA** [8472] from within the Republic of Ireland at €2.40 per minute; http://dublin.usembassy.gov).

Citizens of **New Zealand** can obtain up-to-date visa information by contacting the **U.S. Embassy New Zealand,** 29 Fitzherbert Terrace, Thorndon, Wellington (© **644/462-6000;** http://newzealand.usembassy.gov).

Visitor Information

For information before you leave home, visit **www.seepuertorico.com** or contact the **Puerto Rico Tourism Company** offices at La Princesa Building, Paseo La Princesa 2, Old San Juan (© **800/866-7827** or 787/721-2400).

Other Tourism Company offices are located at Luís Muñoz Marín Airport (© **787/791-1014** or 787/721-2400, exts. 5216, 5223), open December to April daily from 9am to 7pm; and La Casita, at Plaza de la Darsena, Old San Juan, near pier 1, where the cruise ships come in (© **787/722-1709**). This office is open daily 9:30am to 5:30pm.

There are several tourism-related websites on Puerto Rico. Some of the best are dedicated to specific areas: the **Tourism Association of Rincón** (www.rincon.org), **Enchanted Isles** (www.enchanted-isle.com), and **Discover Culebra**

(www.culebra-island.com). **Puerto Rico Travel Maps** (www.travelmaps.com) offers useful interactive and downloadable travel maps, while **Eye Tour Puerto Rico** (http://places.eyetour.com) offers travel videos of sites, attractions, hotels, and restaurants. Ask for a copy of "Qué Pasa," the official visitors' guide, which is distributed free at many hotels and restaurants. "Bienvenidos," a publication of the Puerto Rico Hotel & Tourism Association, is also chockfull of up-to-date visitor information and is also distributed free at island hotels.

A good travel agent can be a source of information. Make sure your agent is a member of the **American Society of Travel Agents (ASTA).** If you get poor service from an ASTA member agent, you can write to them at 1101 King St., Alexandria, VA 22314 (© **703/739-2782;** www.astanet.com).

Water Although tap water is safe to drink, some visitors may experience diarrhea, even if they follow the usual precautions. It's best to stick to bottled water. The illness usually passes quickly without medication if you eat simply prepared food and drink only mineral water until you recover. If symptoms persist, consult a doctor.

Wi-Fi See "Internet & Wi-Fi," earlier in this section.

Index

See also Accommodations and
Restaurant indexes, below.

General Index

A

Accommodations, 5, 226–228
Aguadilla, 26, 183–189
Aguadilla Ice Skating Rink, 187
Aibonito, 141, 144
Air travel, 223–224
Alcaldía (City Hall; San Juan), 93
Amadeus Bistro Bar (San Juan),
   119
Amador Island Tours (San Juan),
   97–98
Anam Spa Cocktail Lounge
   (San Juan), 95
Apartment rentals, 77, 228
Arecibo, 26, 39
Arecibo Lighthouse & Historic
   Park, 138–139
Arecibo Observatory, 125,
   137–138
Art-Furniture-Art (San Juan), 113
Art galleries, 98, 109–110
   Vieques, 217
Atocha Pedestrian Mall (Ponce),
   154
Auto Cine Santana (Arecibo), 139

B

Bahía Sucia, 159
Bahía Urbana (San Juan), 96
Ballena Beach, 157, 159
Bared & Sons (San Juan), 115
Bar Plaza (Vieques), 217
Barrachina (San Juan), 113
Beaches, 4–5. See also specific
   beaches
   Culebra, 221–222
   Dorado, 134
   Mayagüez, 171–172
   Palmas del Mar, 199
   Rincón, 176
   San Juan, 100–101
   southwestern, 159
   Vieques, 205–215
Berwind Country Club (Loiza), 103
Beta Book Café (San Juan), 110
Big Kahuna Burger Bar & Grill
   (Rincón), 183
Biking
   Culebra, 219
   San Juan, 50, 102
   Vieques, 215–216
Bird-watching, Guánica State
   Forest, 156
Blue Beach, 214
Boating and sailing, 228–229. See
   also Kayaking
   Fajardo, 195
   Rincón, 177–178

C

Cabo Rojo, 28–29
Caficultura (San Juan), 54
Caja de Muertos (Coffin Island),
   153
Calendar of events, 20–22
Calypso's Tropical Bar (Rincón),
   183
Camarero Racetrack (Canovanas),
   103
Camping, 229–230
Caña Gorda, 159
Capilla de Cristo (San Juan), 88
Caribe Hilton (San Juan), 105
Carite Forest Reserve (Guavate),
   143
Carite State Forest, 142
Carnival masks, 110–111
Car travel and rentals, 44,
   224–225
Casa Acosta y Fores
   (San Germán), 165
Casa Bacardi Visitor Center
   (Cataño), 100
Casa Blanca (San Juan), 93
Casa Cortés Chocobar (San Juan),
   112–113
Casa Juán Perichi (San Germán),
   165
Casals Festival (San Juan), 20
Casa Morales (San Germán), 164
Casa Museo Canales (Jayuya), 167
Casa Salazar (Museum of the
   History of Ponce), 151
Casinos, San Juan, 124
Castillo de San Felipe del Morro
   (San Juan), 86, 88
Castillo Sightseeing Tours &
   Travel Services (San Juan), 97
Catedral de San Juan, 88–89
Cathedral of Our Lady of
   Guadalupe (Ponce), 150
Cayey, 141
Cayo Santiago, 31
Ceiba, 197–198
Cellphones, 241
Cemi Museum (Jayuya), 167
Central Mountains, 140–141
Centro de Bellas Artes (San Juan),
   117
Cerro de Punta, 166
Cerro Gordo, 134
Children's Museum (San Juan), 99
The Cigar House & Lounge (San
   Juan), 111
Cigars, 111
Circo Bar (San Juan), 123
City Hall (Alcaldía; San Juan), 93
Climate, 17

Bohio Beach Bar (Rincón), 183
Boquerón, 28, 159, 161–163
Bóveda (San Juan), 113
The Brick Haus (San Juan), 119
Business hours, 235
Bus travel, 225–226
Butterfly People (San Juan), 109

Club Brava and Ultra Lounge
   (San Juan), 117–118
Coach (San Juan), 116
Coamo, 30
Coffin Island (Caja de Muertos),
   153
Condado (San Juan), 46, 107
   accommodations, 78–80
   restaurants, 60–64
Condado Beach (San Juan), 101
Consulates, 237–238
Córcega, 176
Cordillera Central, 140–141
Corné Port-Royal Chocolatier
   (San Juan), 113
Costazul (San Juan), 111–112
Crash Boat beach (Aguadilla),
   184–185
Cruises, San Juan Bay, 102
Cuatro Estaciones (San Juan), 54
Cuatro Sombras (San Juan), 54
Cueva Trail, 156
Culebra, 31, 37, 204, 205,
   218–222
Culebra Wildlife Refuge, 218
Culebrita, 218
Customs regulations, 235–236

D

Delavida Restobar (San Juan), 119
Desecheo Island, 31, 177, 233
Disabled travelers, 236–237
Diving, 232–233
   Aguadilla, 186
   Boquerón, 161–162
   Culebra, 222
   Fajardo, 195
   Guánica, 156–157
   La Parguera, 160
   Palmas del Mar, 200
   Rincón, 177
   San Juan, 103–104
   southwest coast, 155
Domes, 176
Don Collin's Cigars (San Juan),
   111
Dooney & Bourke Factory Store
   (San Juan), 116
Dorado, 27, 133–137
Drinking laws, 237
Drugstores, 237

E

Eastern Puerto Rico, 191–203
Eating and drinking, 15–17
   Flavors of San Juan, 99
Ecléctica (San Juan), 113–114
Eight Noodle Bar Chinese
   (San Juan), 120
El Alcazar (San Juan), 109
El Arsenal (San Juan), 93–94
El Batey (San Juan), 120
El Candil (Ponce), 155
El Cañuelo, 134
El Casino (Mayagüez), 174
El Convento Beach, 194

Restaurants